P9-BXW-277

Microsoft® Official Academic Course

Microsoft® Project 2013

WILEY

Credits

EDITOR	Bryan Gambrel
DIRECTOR OF SALES	Mitchell Beaton
EXECUTIVE MARKETING MANAGER	Chris Ruel
MICROSOFT STRATEGIC RELATIONSHIPS MANAGER	Gene Longo of Microsoft Learning eXperience
EDITORIAL PROGRAM ASSISTANT	Allison Winkle
SENIOR PRODUCTION AND MANUFACTURING MANAGER	Janis Soo
ASSOCIATE PRODUCTION MANAGER	Joel Balbin
CREATIVE DIRECTOR	Harry Nolan
COVER DESIGNER	Tom Nery
PHOTO EDITOR	Felicia Ruocco
TECHNOLOGY AND MEDIA	Wendy Ashenberg

Cover Photo Credit: Getty Images, Inc.

This book was set in Garamond by Aptara, Inc. and printed and bound by Bind Rite Robbinsville. The covers were printed by Bind Rite Robbinsville.

Copyright © 2013 by John Wiley & Sons, Inc. All rights reserved.

No part of this publication may be reproduced, stored in a retrieval system or transmitted in any form or by any means, electronic, mechanical, photocopying, recording, scanning or otherwise, except as permitted under Sections 107 or 108 of the 1976 United States Copyright Act, without either the prior written permission of the Publisher, or authorization through payment of the appropriate per-copy fee to the Copyright Clearance Center, Inc. 222 Rosewood Drive, Danvers, MA 01923, (978) 750-8400, fax (978) 646-8600. Requests to the Publisher for permission should be addressed to the Permissions Department, John Wiley & Sons, Inc., 111 River Street, Hoboken, NJ 07030-5774, (201) 748-6011, fax (201) 748-6008. To order books or for customer service, please call 1-800-CALL WILEY (225-5945).

Microsoft, ActiveX, Excel, InfoPath, Microsoft Press, MSDN, OneNote, Outlook, PivotChart, PivotTable, PowerPoint, SharePoint, SQL Server, Visio, Windows, Windows Mobile, and Windows Server are either registered trademarks or trademarks of Microsoft Corporation in the United States and/or other countries. Other product and company names mentioned herein may be the trademarks of their respective owners.

The example companies, organizations, products, domain names, e-mail addresses, logos, people, places, and events depicted herein are fictitious. No association with any real company, organization, product, domain name, e-mail address, logo, person, place, or event is intended or should be inferred.

The book expresses the author's views and opinions. The information contained in this book is provided without any express, statutory, or implied warranties. Neither the authors, John Wiley & Sons, Inc., Microsoft Corporation, nor their resellers or distributors will be held liable for any damages caused or alleged to be caused either directly or indirectly by this book.

Founded in 1807, John Wiley & Sons, Inc. has been a valued source of knowledge and understanding for more than 200 years, helping people around the world meet their needs and fulfill their aspirations. Our company is built on a foundation of principles that include responsibility to the communities we serve and where we live and work. In 2008, we launched a Corporate Citizenship Initiative, a global effort to address the environmental, social, economic, and ethical challenges we face in our business. Among the issues we are addressing are carbon impact, paper specifications and procurement, ethical conduct within our business and among our vendors, and community and charitable support. For more information, please visit our website: www.wiley.com/go/citizenship.

ISBN 978-047-0-13312-5

Printed in the United States of America

10 9 8 7 6 5 4 3 2

www.wiley.com/college/microsoft or call the MOAC
Toll-Free Number: 1+(888) 764-7001 (U.S. & Canada only)

Foreword from the Publisher

Wiley's publishing vision for the Microsoft Official Academic Course series is to provide students and instructors with the skills and knowledge they need to use Microsoft technology effectively in all aspects of their personal and professional lives. Quality instruction is required to help both educators and students get the most from Microsoft's software tools and to become more productive. Thus our mission is to make our instructional programs trusted educational companions for life.

To accomplish this mission, Wiley and Microsoft have partnered to develop the highest quality educational programs for Information Workers, IT Professionals, and Developers. Materials created by this partnership carry the brand name "Microsoft Official Academic Course," assuring instructors and students alike that the content of these textbooks is fully endorsed by Microsoft, and that they provide the highest quality information and instruction on Microsoft products. The Microsoft Official Academic Course textbooks are "Official" in still one more way – they are the officially sanctioned courseware for Microsoft IT Academy members.

The Microsoft Official Academic Course series focuses on *workforce development*. These programs are aimed at those students seeking to enter the workforce, change jobs, or embark on new careers as information workers, IT professionals, and developers. Microsoft Official Academic Course programs address their needs by emphasizing authentic workplace scenarios with an abundance of projects, exercises, cases, and assessments.

The Microsoft Official Academic Courses focus on real skills for real jobs. As students work through the projects and exercises in the textbooks, they enhance their level of knowledge and their ability to apply the latest Microsoft technology to everyday tasks. These students also gain resume-building credentials that can assist them in finding a job, keeping their current job, or in furthering their education.

The concept of lifelong learning is today an utmost necessity. Job roles, and even whole job categories, are changing so quickly that none of us can stay competitive and productive without continuously updating our skills and capabilities. The Microsoft Official Academic Course offerings, and their focus on Microsoft certification exam preparation, provide a means for people to acquire and effectively update their skills and knowledge. Wiley supports students in this endeavor through the development and distribution of these courses as Microsoft's official academic publisher.

Joe Heider
General Manager and Senior Vice President

Preface

Welcome to the Microsoft Official Academic Course (MOAC) program for Microsoft Project 2013. MOAC represents the collaboration between Microsoft Learning and John Wiley & Sons, Inc. publishing company. Microsoft and Wiley teamed up to produce a series of textbooks that deliver compelling and innovative teaching solutions to instructors and superior learning experiences for students. Infused and informed by in-depth knowledge from the creators of Microsoft Project and Windows, and crafted by a publisher known worldwide for the pedagogical quality of its products, these textbooks maximize skills transfer in minimum time. Students are challenged to reach their potential by using their new technical skills as highly productive members of the workforce.

Because this knowledgebase comes directly from Microsoft, creator of Microsoft Project 2013, you are sure to receive the topical coverage that is most relevant to students' personal and professional success. Microsoft's direct participation not only assures you that MOAC textbook content is accurate and current; it also means that students will receive the best instruction possible to enable their success in the workplace.

■ The Microsoft Official Academic Course Program

The *Microsoft Official Academic Course* series is a complete program for instructors and institutions to prepare and deliver great courses on Microsoft software technologies. With MOAC, we recognize that, because of the rapid pace of change in the technology and curriculum developed by Microsoft, there is an ongoing set of needs beyond classroom instruction tools for an instructor to be ready to teach the course. The MOAC program endeavors to provide solutions for all these needs in a systematic manner in order to ensure a successful and rewarding course experience for both instructor and student – technical and curriculum training for instructor readiness with new software releases; the software itself for student use at home for building hands-on skills, assessment, and validation of skill development; and a great set of tools for delivering instruction in the classroom and lab. All are important to the smooth delivery of an interesting course on Microsoft software, and all are provided with the MOAC program. We think about the model that follows as a gauge for ensuring that we completely support you in your goal of teaching a great course. As you evaluate your instructional materials options, you may wish to use the model for comparison purposes with available products.

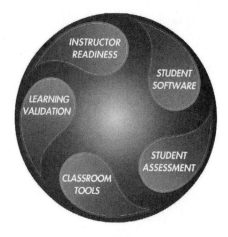

www.wiley.com/college/microsoft or call the MOAC
Toll-Free Number: 1+(888) 764-7001 (U.S. & Canada only)

■ Pedagogical Features

Many pedagogical features have been developed specifically for *Microsoft Official Academic Course* programs. Unique features of our task-based approach include a Lesson Skill Matrix Workplace Ready, and Step by Step exercises; and three levels of increasingly rigorous lesson-ending activities: Competency, Proficiency, and Mastery Assessment.

Presenting the extensive procedural information and technical concepts woven throughout the textbook raises challenges for the student and instructor alike. The Illustrated Book Tour that follows provides a guide to the rich features contributing to *Microsoft Official Academic Course* program's pedagogical plan. Following is a list of key features in the lessons, which are designed to prepare students for success on the certification exams and in the workplace:

- **Lesson Skill Matrix:** Each lesson begins with a **lesson skill matrix**. This feature outlines all the topics covered in the lesson.

- **Business Cases:** Each lesson features a real-world **business case** scenario that places the software skills and knowledge to be acquired in a real-world setting.

- **Software Orientation:** Every lesson includes a **software orientation**. This feature provides an overview of the software features students will be working with in the lesson. The orientation will detail the general properties of the software or specific features, such as a ribbon or dialog box, and it includes a large, labeled screen image.

- **Step-by-Step Instructions:** Concise and frequent **step-by-step** instructions teach students new features and provide an opportunity for hands-on practice. Numbered steps give detailed instructions to help students learn software skills. The steps also show results and screen images to match what students should see on their computer screens.

- **Illustrations:** Screen images provide visual feedback as students work through the exercises. The images reinforce key concepts, provide visual clues about the steps, and allow students to check their progress.

- **Button Images:** When the text instructs a student to click a particular button, an image of that button is shown in the margin or in the text.

- **Key Terms:** Important technical vocabulary is listed at the beginning of the lesson. When these terms are used later in the lesson, they appear in bold italic type and are defined. The Glossary contains all of the key terms and their definitions.

- **Reader Aids:** Engaging point-of-use **reader aids**, located throughout the lessons, tell students why this topic is relevant (*The Bottom Line*), provide students with helpful hints (*Take Note*), show alternate ways to accomplish tasks (*Another Way*), or point out things to watch out for or avoid (*Troubleshooting*). Reader aids also provide additional relevant or background information that adds value to the lesson.

- **Skill Summary:** Each lesson ends with a recapping of the skills covered in the lesson.

- **Knowledge Assessment:** Provides a total of 20 questions from a mix of True/False, Fill-in-the-Blank, Matching, or Multiple Choice, testing students on concepts learned in the lesson.

- **Competency, Proficiency, and Mastery Assessment:** Provide three progressively more challenging lesson-ending activities.

- **Circling Back:** These integrated projects provide students with an opportunity to renew and practice skills learned in previous lessons.

- **Online Files:** The student companion website contains the data files needed for each lesson. These files are indicated by the icon in the margin of the textbook.

www.wiley.com/college/microsoft or call the MOAC
Toll-Free Number: 1+(888) 764-7001 (U.S. & Canada only)

■ Lesson Features

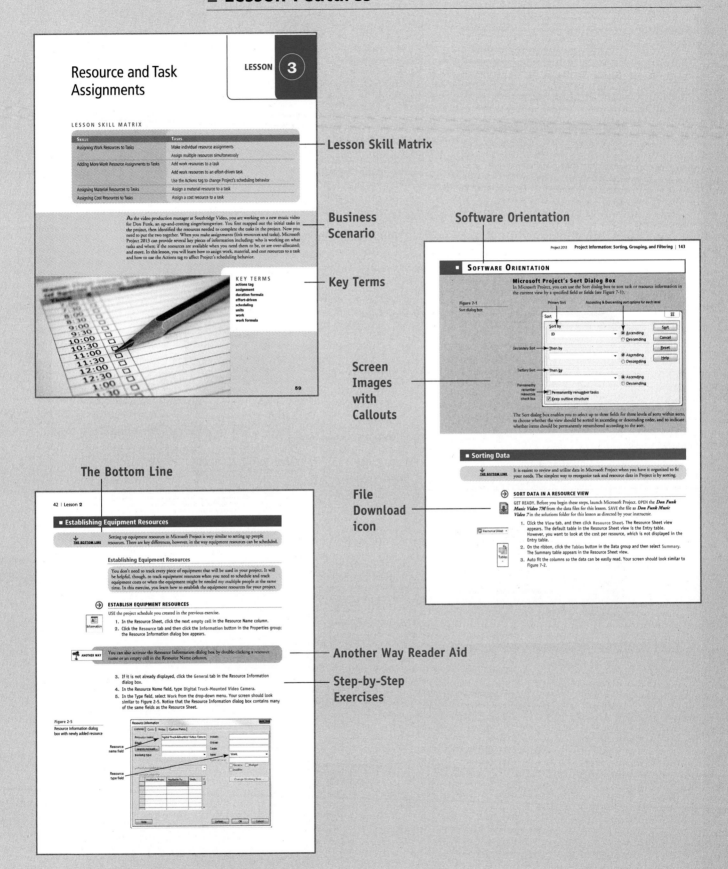

Lesson Skill Matrix

Business Scenario

Key Terms

Software Orientation

Screen Images with Callouts

The Bottom Line

File Download icon

Another Way Reader Aid

Step-by-Step Exercises

20 | Lesson 1

lunch each day. Microsoft Project differentiates between working and nonworking time, so the duration of a task doesn't always correspond to elapsed time. If you estimate that a task will take 24 hours of working time, you would enter its duration as 3d to schedule the task over three 8-hour workdays. If this task were to start at 8:00 A.M. on Thursday, it would not be completed until 5:00 P.M. on Monday. No work is scheduled on evenings or weekends because these have been defined as nonworking times.

You can also schedule tasks to occur over working and nonworking time by assigning an elapsed duration to a task. *Elapsed duration* is the total length of working and nonworking time you expect it will take to complete a task. Suppose you own an automobile body shop. In the process of repainting a car, you have the tasks "Apply rustproof undercoat" and "Apply first color overcoat." You also need a task called "Wait for undercoat to dry" because you cannot apply the color paint until the undercoat is dry. The task "Wait for undercoat to dry" will have an elapsed duration because the undercoat will dry over a contiguous range of hours, whether they are working or nonworking. If the undercoat takes 24 hours to cure, you would enter the duration for this task as 1ed (or 1 elapsed day). If you scheduled it to start at 11 A.M. on Wednesday, it would be complete at 11 A.M. on Thursday.

Table 1-1 shows abbreviations and meanings for actual and elapsed times in Microsoft Project.

Table 1-2
Abbreviations and meanings for actual and elapsed times

If You Enter This Abbreviation	It Appears Like This	And Means
m	min	minute
h	hr	hour
d	dy	day
w	wk	week
mo	mon	month
em	emin	elapsed minute
eh	ehr	elapsed hour
ed	eday	elapsed day
ew	ewk	elapsed week
emo	emon	elapsed month

Easy-to-Read Tables

TROUBLE SHOOTING   For most projects, you will use task durations of hours, days, and weeks. When estimating task durations, think carefully about the level of detail you want to apply to your project's tasks. If you have a multiyear project, it is probably not practical or even possible to track tasks that are measured in minutes or hours. You should measure task durations at the lowest level of detail or control necessary, but no lower.

Troubleshooting Reader Aid

Although the task durations are supplied for you for the exercises in this book, you and the project team will have to estimate task durations for most real-world projects. There are a number of sources of task duration estimates:

- Information from previous, similar projects
- Estimates from the people who will actually complete the tasks
- Recommendations from people who have managed similar projects
- Professional or industry organizations that deal with the project subject matter

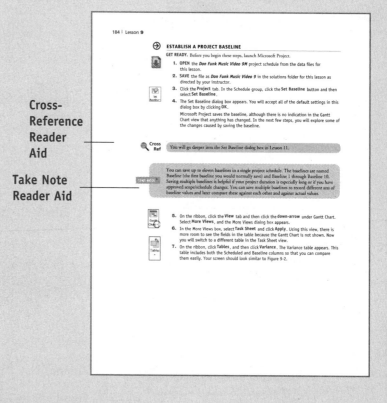

184 | Lesson 9

ESTABLISH A PROJECT BASELINE

GET READY. Before you begin these steps, launch Microsoft Project.

1. **OPEN** the *Don Funk Music Video 9M* project schedule from the data files for this lesson.
2. **SAVE** the file as *Don Funk Music Video 9* in the solutions folder for this lesson as directed by your instructor.
3. Click the **Project** tab. In the Schedule group, click the **Set Baseline** button and then select **Set Baseline**.
4. The Set Baseline dialog box appears. You will accept all of the default settings in this dialog box by clicking OK.
   Microsoft Project saves the baseline, although there is no indication in the Gantt Chart view that anything has changed. In the next few steps, you will explore some of the changes caused by saving the baseline.

Cross-Reference Reader Aid

Cross Ref   You will go deeper into the Set Baseline dialog box in Lesson 11.

Take Note Reader Aid

TAKE NOTE   You can save up to eleven baselines in a single project schedule. The baselines are named Baseline (the first baseline you would normally save) and Baseline 1 through Baseline 10. Saving multiple baselines is helpful if your project duration is especially long or if you have approved scope/schedule changes. You can save multiple baselines to record different sets of baseline values and later compare these against each other and against actual values.

5. On the ribbon, click the **View** tab and then click the **down-arrow** under Gantt Chart. Select **More Views**, and the More Views dialog box appears.
6. In the More Views box, select **Task Sheet** and click **Apply**. Using this view, there is more room to see the fields in the table because the Gantt Chart is not shown. Now you will switch to a different table in the Task Sheet view.
7. On the ribbon, click **Tables**, and then click **Variance**. The Variance table appears. This table includes both the Scheduled and Baseline columns so that you can compare them easily. Your screen should look similar to Figure 9-2.

Summary Skill Matrix

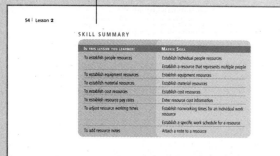

54 | Lesson 2

SKILL SUMMARY

In This Lesson You Learned:	Matrix Skill
To establish people resources	Establish individual people resources
	Establish a resource that represents multiple people
To establish equipment resources	Establish equipment resources
To establish material resources	Establish material resources
To establish cost resources	Establish cost resources
To establish resource pay rates	Enter resource cost information
To adjust resource working times	Establish nonworking times for an individual work resource
	Establish a specific work schedule for a resource
To add resource notes	Attach a note to a resource

Knowledge Assessment

Matching

Match the term in column 1 to its description in column 2.

Column 1	Column 2
1. resource calendar	a. the maximum capacity of a resource to accomplish tasks
2. Max. Units	b. specifies default working and nonworking times for a resource, a project, or a task
3. material resource	c. when and how much of a resource's time can be assigned to work on tasks
4. project calendar	d. the people and equipment that do work to accomplish the tasks of the project
5. cost resource	e. the people, equipment, money, and materials used to complete the tasks in a project
6. work resource	f. a way of documenting information about resources, tasks, and assignments
7. base calendar	g. consumable items used up as the tasks in a project are accomplished
8. availability	h. a resource that doesn't depend on the amount of work on a task or the duration of a task
9. resources	i. the base calendar that provides default working times for an entire project
10. note	j. defines the working and nonworking time for an individual resource

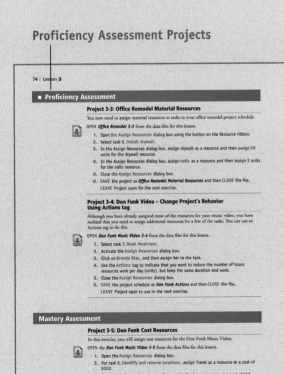

Knowledge Assessment Questions

216 | Lesson **10**

■ Knowledge Assessment

Fill in the Blank

Complete the following sentences by writing the correct word or words in the blanks provided.

1. _____ enables you to see on your screen what will print on paper before you print it.
2. People or organizations that might be affected by project activities are called _____.
3. If you have two views displayed in a combination view and want to print the view, only the view in the _____ pane will print.
4. When previewing a view in print preview, you can change the number of pages visible by selecting either the _____ or _____ pages button.
5. A common activity for project managers is to _____ information from the project schedule to share with stakeholders.
6. To add your company name so that it prints at the top of every page, use the _____ dialog box to add the company name to the header.
7. A _____ is a predefined format intended for printing Microsoft Project data.
8. A _____ report is used to represent high-level information usually on one page.
9. If subtasks are hidden in a view, reports that contain task lists will include only _____ tasks.
10. In a report, you can only _____ information.

Multiple Choice

Select the best response for the following statements.

1. In a view, you can _____ information.
   a. enter
   b. edit
   c. print
   d. All of the above are correct.
2. If assignments are hidden under tasks or resources in a usage view, what will the usage report show?
   a. tasks or resources with corresponding assignment details
   b. only the tasks or resources
   c. only overallocated assignment details
   d. it depends on how you set up the report
3. In the Print Preview window, the status bar shows "4 rows by 3 columns." How many pages will be printed?
   a. 7
   b. 4
   c. 12
   d. 3

Competency Assessment Projects

158 | Lesson **7**

■ Competency Assessment

Project 7-1: Sorting by Multiple Criteria

You have some additional setup work that needs to be completed before the shooting of one of the Don Funk Music Video scenes can begin. Because you will need to pay overtime (time and one-half) for this additional work, you would like to get a volunteer who has a low standard rate. Sort your resources according to Standard Rate and Max Units so that you can make your request from the least-cost group of employees.

GET READY. Launch Microsoft Project if it is not already running.

OPEN *Don Funk Music Video 7-1* from the data files for this lesson.

1. Click the View ribbon, then in the Resource Views group, click Resource Sheet.
2. On the ribbon, click Sort, and then click Sort by.
3. In the Sort by section select Type from the dropdown menu. Next to that, click Descending.
4. In the first Then by section, select Standard Rate from the dropdown menu. Next to that, click Descending.
5. In the last Then by section, select Max Units from the dropdown menu. Next to that, click on Descending. Make sure the Permanently renumber resources box is not checked.
6. Click the Sort button.
7. SAVE the project schedule as *Don Funk Standard Rate Sort* and then CLOSE the file. LEAVE Project open for the next exercise.

Project 7-2: Apply HR Filter

You are reviewing your project schedule for hiring a new employee. You want to specifically review the staff members from the Human Resources (HR) department who are involved with this project. You need to apply a filter that will screen out any staff except HR. OPEN *Hiring New Employee 7-2* from the data files for this lesson.

1. Click the View ribbon and then click Resource Sheet.
2. Click the down-arrow in the Group column heading, point to Filters and then click [Custom . . .].
3. In the Group section, select contains from the dropdown list in the first box if it is not already visible. In the adjacent box, type HR.
4. Click the OK button.
5. SAVE the project schedule as *Hiring New Employee HR Filter* and then CLOSE the project schedule. PAUSE. LEAVE Project open to use in the next exercise.

■ Proficiency Assessment

Project 7-3: Resource Groups by Standard Rate for Don Funk Music Video

You are working on employee reviews and pay increases for your staff for the upcoming year. You have decided it would be beneficial to be able to look at the standard rate variation within resource groups working on this project. You need to set up a custom group that will enable you to do this. OPEN *Don Funk Music Video 7-3* from the data files for this lesson.

Proficiency Assessment Projects

74 | Lesson **3**

■ Proficiency Assessment

Project 3-3: Office Remodel Material Resources

You now need to assign material resources to tasks in your office remodel project schedule.

OPEN *Office Remodel 3-3* from the data files for this lesson.

1. Open the Assign Resources dialog box using the button on the Resource ribbon.
2. Select task 9, Install drywall.
3. In the Assign Resources dialog box, assign drywall as a resource and then assign 50 units for the drywall resource.
4. In the Assign Resources dialog box, assign nails as a resource and then assign 5 units for the nails resource.
5. Close the Assign Resources dialog box.
6. SAVE the project as *Office Remodel Material Resources* and then CLOSE the file. LEAVE Project open for the next exercise.

Project 3-4: Don Funk Video – Change Project's Behavior Using Actions tag

Although you have already assigned most of the resources for your music video, you have realized that you need to assign additional resources for a few of the tasks. You can use an Actions tag to do this.

OPEN *Don Funk Music Video 3-4* from the data files for this lesson.

1. Select task 7, Book Musicians.
2. Activate the Assign Resources dialog box.
3. Click on Brenda Diaz, and then assign her to the task.
4. Use the Actions tag to indicate that you want to reduce the number of hours resources work per day (units), but keep the same duration and work.
5. Close the Assign Resources dialog box.
6. SAVE the project schedule as *Don Funk Actions* and then CLOSE the file. LEAVE Project open to use in the next exercise.

■ Mastery Assessment

Project 3-5: Don Funk Cost Resources

In this exercise, you will assign cost resources for the Don Funk Music Video.

OPEN the *Don Funk Music Video 3-5* from the data files for this lesson.

1. Open the Assign Resources dialog box.
2. For task 6, Identify and reserve locations, assign Travel as a resource at a cost of 5000.
3. For task 18, Scene 1 vocal recording, assign Food as a resource at a cost of 250.
4. Close the Assign Resources dialog box.
5. SAVE the project schedule as *Don Funk Cost Resources* and then CLOSE the file. LEAVE Project open for the next exercise.

Mastery Assessment Projects

---

198 | Lesson 9

OPEN *Don Funk Music Video 9-4* from the data files for this lesson.

1. Activate the Project Statistics box to view the costs for the project.
2. Display the Cost table.
3. Filter the tasks to show only the tasks that are over budget.
4. Collapse all Production Scene summary tasks (hide subtasks) except for the Scene summary task with the greatest cost variance.
5. SAVE the project schedule as *Don Funk Overbudget*, and then CLOSE the file.
   LEAVE Project open to use in the next exercise.

■ **Mastery Assessment**

Project 9-5: Office Remodel Task Delay

You have just been informed that while the plumber was re-running the pipes for the office lunchroom remodel, a pipe burst and the floor was flooded with several inches of water. It will take a week to clean and dry the water damage. You need to reschedule the remaining work on incomplete tasks to restart when the cleanup is complete.

OPEN the *Office Remodel 9-5* project schedule from the data files for this lesson.

1. Activate the Update Project dialog box.
2. Reschedule uncompleted work to start after Thursday, October 22, 2016.
3. SAVE the project schedule as *Office Remodel Reschedule*, and then CLOSE the file.
   LEAVE Project open to use in the next exercise.

Project 9-6: Tracking the Don Funk Music Video as Scheduled

The last phase of the Don Funk Music Video, Post-Production, is going well. Tasks are being completed on schedule. You want to update the project to show that the tasks are complete through a specified current date.

OPEN the *Don Funk Music Video 9-6* project schedule from the data files for this lesson.

1. Activate the Update Project dialog box.
2. Update the project as complete through July 15, 2016.
3. Scroll the Gantt Chart bars so that the task and progress bars on the week of July 10, 2016 are visible.
4. SAVE the project schedule as *Don Funk On Schedule*, and then CLOSE the file.
   CLOSE Project.

Circling Back Exercises

Project 2013   **Circling Back** | 117

■ **Circling Back**

Mete Goktepe is a project management specialist at Woodgrove Bank. The management at Woodgrove has recently decided that the eight-year old commercial lending software currently in use is outdated and needs to be replaced. Mete has been assigned as the project manager for the Request For Proposal (RFP) process to evaluate and select new software. This process entails determining needs, identifying vendors, requesting proposals, reviewing proposals, and selecting the software.

Project 1: Entering Tasks

Acting as Mete, you first need to enter project information and then enter and organize the tasks for this project.

GET READY. Launch Project if it is not already running.

1. In the New section of the Backstage area, double-click Blank Project.
2. On the Tasks tab, in the Tasks command group, click the Mode button. From the list, click Auto Schedule.
3. Click the Project tab, then click Project Information. Set the start date to May 2, 2016.
4. SAVE the project plan as *RFP Bank Software Tasks*.
5. In the Properties group on the ribbon, click the Change Working Time button.
6. Add the following exception dates:
   - Memorial Day to begin on May 30, 2016 and to occur yearly on the last Monday of May for 2 occurrences.
   - Independence Day to begin on July 4, 2016 and to occur yearly on July 4 for 2 occurrences.
   - Labor Day to begin on September 5, 2016 and to occur the first Monday of September for 2 occurrences
   - Thanksgiving Day to begin on November 24, 2016 and to occur on the fourth Thursday of November for 2 occurrences
7. Click OK to close the Change Working Time dialog box.
8. In the Gantt Chart view, enter the following task names and durations (enter all tasks, even if no duration is listed). [This is a partial list of tasks in the project plan. Additional data will be available in future exercises.]

Conventions and Features Used in This Book

This book uses particular fonts, symbols, and heading conventions to highlight important information or to call your attention to special steps. For more information about the features in each lesson, refer to the Illustrated Book Tour section.

CONVENTION	MEANING
CLOSE	Words in all capital letters indicate instructions for opening, saving, or closing files or programs. They also point out items you should check or actions you should take.
TAKE NOTE*	Reader aids appear in shaded boxes found in your text. *Take Note* provides helpful hints related to particular tasks or topics.
ANOTHER WAY	*Another Way* provides an alternative procedure for accomplishing a particular task.
Cross Ref	These notes provide pointers to information discussed elsewhere in the textbook or describe interesting features that are not directly addressed in the current topic or exercise.
Alt + Tab	A plus sign (+) between two key names means that you must press both keys at the same time. Keys that you are instructed to press in an exercise will appear in the font shown here.
A *shared printer* can be used by many individuals on a network.	Key terms appear in bold italic.
Key My Name is.	Any text you are asked to key appears in blue.
Click OK.	Any button on the screen you are supposed to click on or select will also appear in color.
OPEN *BudgetWorksheet1*	The names of data files will appear in bold, italic font for easy identification.
	This icon notifies you that a file is available for download in the accompanying student data files.

Instructor Support Program

The *Microsoft Official Academic Course* programs are accompanied by a rich array of resources that incorporate the extensive textbook visuals to form a pedagogically cohesive package. These resources provide all the materials instructors need to deploy and deliver their courses. Resources available online for download include:

- The **Instructor's Guide** contains solutions to all the textbook exercises as well as chapter summaries and lecture notes. The Instructor's Guide and Syllabi for various term lengths are available from the Instructor's Book Companion site (www.wiley.com/college/microsoft).

- The **Solution Files** for all the projects in the book are available online from our Instructor's Book Companion site (www.wiley.com/college/microsoft).

- The **Test Bank** contains hundreds of questions organized by lesson in multiple-choice, true-false, short answer, and essay formats and is available to download from the Instructor's Book Companion site (www.wiley.com/college/microsoft). A complete answer key is provided.

  This title's test bank is available for use in Respondus' easy-to-use software. You can download the test bank for free using your Respondus, Respondus LE, or StudyMate Author software.

  Respondus is a powerful tool for creating and managing exams that can be printed to paper or published directly to Blackboard, WebCT, Desire2Learn, eCollege, ANGEL, and other eLearning systems.

- A complete set of **PowerPoint Presentations and Images** is available on the Instructor's Book Companion site (www.wiley.com/college/microsoft) to enhance classroom presentations. Tailored to the text's topical coverage and Skills Matrix, these presentations are designed to convey key Microsoft Project concepts addressed in the text.

  All figures from the text are on the Instructor's Book Companion site (www.wiley.com/college/microsoft). You can incorporate them into your PowerPoint presentations, or create your own overhead transparencies and handouts.

  By using these visuals in class discussions, you can help focus students' attention on key elements of Microsoft Project and help them understand how to use it effectively in the workplace.

- The **Student Data Files** are available online on both the Instructor's Book Companion Site and for students on the Student Book Companion Site.

WFN

- When it comes to improving the classroom experience, there is no better source of ideas and inspiration than your fellow colleagues. The Wiley Faculty Network connects teachers with technology, facilitates the exchange of best practices, and helps to enhance instructional efficiency and effectiveness. Faculty Network activities include technology training and tutorials, virtual seminars, peer-to-peer exchanges of experiences and ideas, personal consulting, and sharing of resources. For details visit www.WhereFacultyConnect.com.

DREAMSPARK PREMIUM—FREE 3-YEAR MEMBERSHIP AVAILABLE TO QUALIFIED ADOPTERS!

DreamSpark Premium is designed to provide the easiest and most inexpensive way for schools to make the latest Microsoft developer tools, products, and technologies available in labs, classrooms, and on student PCs. DreamSpark Premium is an annual membership program for departments teaching Science, Technology, Engineering, and Mathematics (STEM) courses. The membership provides a complete solution to keep academic labs, faculty, and students on the leading edge of technology.

Software available through the DreamSpark Premium program is provided at no charge to adopting departments through the Wiley and Microsoft publishing partnership.

Note: Microsoft Project 2013 Professional can be downloaded from DreamSpark Premium for use by students in this course.

Contact your Wiley rep for details.

For more information about the DreamSpark Premium program, go to Microsoft's DreamSpark website

Important Web Addresses and Phone Numbers

To locate the Wiley Higher Education Representative in your area, go to the following Web address and click on the *"Contact Us"* link at the top of the page:

www.wiley.com/college

Or call the MOAC toll-free number: 1 + (888) 764-7001 (U.S. & Canada only).

Student Support Program

Book Companion Web Site (www.wiley.com/college/microsoft)

The students' book companion site for the MOAC series includes any resources, exercise files, and Web links that will be used in conjunction with this course.

Wiley Desktop Editions

Wiley MOAC Desktop Editions are innovative, electronic versions of printed textbooks. Students buy the desktop version for 50% off the U.S. price of the printed text, and get the added value of permanence and portability. Wiley Desktop Editions provide students with numerous additional benefits that are not available with other e-text solutions.

Students also have access to fully integrated resources within their Wiley Desktop Edition. From highlighting their e-text to taking and sharing notes, students can easily personalize their Wiley Desktop Edition as they are reading or following along in class.

Wiley E-Text: Powered by Vitalsource

When you choose a Wiley E-Text you not only save money; you benefit from being able to access course materials and content anytime, anywhere through a user experience that makes learning rewarding.

With the Wiley E-Text you will be able to easily:

- Search
- Take notes
- Highlight key materials
- Have all your work in one place for more efficient studying

In addition, the Wiley E-Text is fully portable. Students can access it online and download to their computer for off line access and access read and study on their device of preference—computer, tablet, or smartphone.

**www.wiley.com/college/microsoft or call the MOAC
Toll-Free Number: 1+(888) 764-7001 (U.S. & Canada only)**

Student Data Files

All of the practice files that you will use as you perform the exercises in the book are available for download on our student companion site. By using the practice files, you will not waste time creating the samples used in the lessons, and you can concentrate on learning how to use Microsoft Project 2013. With the files and the step-by-step instructions in the lessons, you will learn by doing, which is an easy and effective way to acquire and remember new skills.

Copying the Practice Files

Your instructor might already have copied the practice files before you arrive in class. However, your instructor might ask you to copy the practice files on your own at the start of class. Also, if you want to work through any of the exercises in this book on your own at home or at your place of business after class, you may want to copy the practice files.

OPEN Internet Explorer.

1. In Internet Explorer, go to the student companion site: www.wiley.com.
2. Search for your book title in the upper-right corner.
3. On the Search Results page, locate your book and click the **Visit the Companion Sites** link.
4. Select **Student Companion Site** from the pop-up box.
5. In the left-hand column, under "Browse by Resource" select **Student Data Files**.
6. Now select **Student Data Files** from the center of the screen.
7. In the File Download dialog box, select **Save** to save the data files to your external drive (often called a ZIP drive, a USB drive, or a thumb drive) or a local drive.
8. In the Save As dialog box, select from the left-hand panel a local drive that you'd like to save your files to; again, this should be an external drive or a local drive. Remember the drive name that you saved your files to.

Acknowledgments

We would like to thank the many instructors and reviewers who pored over the Microsoft Official Academic Course series design, outlines and manuscript, providing invaluable feedback in the service of quality instructional materials.

Erik Amerikaner, *Oak Park Unified*

Connie Aragon, *Seattle Central Community College*

Sue Bajt, *Harper College*

Gregory Ballinger, *Miami—Dade College*

Catherine Bradfield, *DeVry University*

DeAnnia Clements, *Wiregrass Georgia Technical College*

Mary Corcoran, *Bellevue College*

Andrea Cluff, *Freemont High School*

Caroline de Gruchy, *Conestoga College*

Janis DeHaven, *Central Community College*

Rob Durrance, *East Lee County High School*

Janet Flusche, *Frenship High School*

Greg Gardiner, *SIAST*

Debi Griggs, *Bellevue College*

Phil Hanney, *Orem Junior High School*

Portia Hatfield, *Tennessee Technology Center—Jacksboro*

Dee Hobson, *Richland College*

Terri Holly, *Indian River State College*

Kim Hopkins, *Weatherford College*

Sandra Jolley, *Tarrant County College*

Keith Hoell, *Briarcliffe College*

Joe LaMontagne, *Davenport University*

Tanya MacNeil, *American InterContinental University*

Donna Madsen, *Kirkwood Community College*

Lynn Mancini, *Delaware Technical Community College*

Edward Martin, *Kingsborough Community College—City University of New York*

Lisa Mears, *Palm Beach State College*

Denise Merrell, *Jefferson Community and Technical College*

Diane Mickey, *Northern Virginia Community College*

Robert Mike, *Alaska Career College*

Cynthia Miller, *Harper College*

Sandra Miller, *Wenatchee Valley College*

Mustafa Muflehi, *The Sheffield College*

www.wiley.com/college/microsoft or call the MOAC
Toll-Free Number: 1+(888) 764-7001 (U.S. & Canada only)

Aditi Mukherjee, *University of Florida—Gainesville*
Linda Nutter, *Peninsula College*
Diana Pack, *Big Sandy Community & Technical College*
Bettye Parham, *Daytona State College*
Tatyana Pashnyak, *Bainbridge State College*
Kari Phillips, *Davis Applied Technical College*
Michelle Poertner, *Northwestern Michigan College*
Barbara Purvis, *Centura College*
Dave Rotherham, *Sheffield Hallam University*
Theresa Savarese, *San Diego City College*
Janet Sebesy, *Cuyahoga Community College—Western*
Lourdes Sevilla, *Southwestern College*
Elizabeth Snow, *Southwest Florida College*
Denise Spence, *Dunbar High School*
Amy Stolte, *Lincoln Land Community College*
Linda Silva, *El Paso Community College*
Dorothy Weiner, *Manchester Community College*

We would also like to thank the team at Microsoft Learning Xperiences (LeX), including Alison Cunard, Tim Sneath, Zubair Murtaza, Keith Loeber, Rob Linsky, Anne Hamilton, Wendy Johnson, Gene Longo, Julia Stasio, and Josh Barnhill for their encouragement and support in making the Microsoft Official Academic Course programs the finest academic materials for mastering the newest Microsoft technologies for both students and instructors. Finally we would like to thank Jeff Riley and his team at Box Twelve Communications, Laura Town and her team at WilliamsTown Communications, Debbie Collins and Sandy DuBose for their editorial and technical assistance.

We would like to thank the following instructors for their contributions to particular titles in the series as well:

Access 2013

Catherine Bradfield, DeVry University
Mary Corcoran, Bellevue College
Cynthia Miller, Harper College
Elizabeth Snow, Southwest Florida College
Aditi Mukherjee, University of Florida—Gainesville

Excel 2013

Catherine Bradfield, DeVry University
DeAnnia Clements, Wiregrass Technical College
Sandy Jolley, Tarrant County College
Dee Hobson, Richland College
Joe Lamontagne, Davenport University
Edward Martin, Kingsborough Community College-City University of New York
Aditi Mukherjee, University of Florida—Gainesville
Linda Nutter, Peninsula College
Dave Rotherham, Sheffield Hallam University

Outlook 2013

Erik Amerikaner, Oak Park Unified
Sue VanLanen, Gwinnett Technical College
Robert Mike, Alaska Career College
Lourdes Sevilla, Southwestern College—Chula Vista
Kari Phillips, Davis Applied Technical College

PowerPoint 2013

Mary Corcoran, Bellevue College
Rob Durrance, East Lee County High School
Phil Hanney, Orem Junior High School
Terri Holly, Indian River State College
Michelle Poertner, Northwestern Michigan College
Kim Hopkins, Weatherford College
Tatyana Pashnyak, Bainbridge State College
Theresa Savarese, San Diego City College

Project 2013

Sandy Jolley, Tarrant County College
Debi Griggs, Bellevue College
Elizabeth Snow, Southwest Florida College

Word 2013

Erik Amerikaner, Oak Park Unified
Sue Bajt, Harper College
Gregory Ballinger, Miami-Dade College
Barb Purvis, Centura College
Janet Sebesy, Cuyahoga Community College
Andrea Cluff, Freemont High School
Caroline de Gruchy, Conestoga College
Donna Madsen, Kirkwood Community College
Lynn Mancini, Delaware Technical Community College
Denise Merrell, Jefferson Community and Technical College
Diane Mickey, Northern Virginia Community College
Robert Mike, Alaska Career College
Bettye Parham, Daytona State College
Dorothy Weiner, Manchester Community College

Author Credits

Gregg D. Richie

Gregg D. Richie, PMP, MCTS is the founding member and managing partner of P8, LLC, which is a consulting firm that provides consulting and training in project management techniques, including advanced usage and application of Microsoft Project. He is an adjunct faculty member teaching project planning and risk management for the University of Washington's Project Management Certificate Program. With more than 30 years of experience in the field of project management, working on projects on almost every continent, he travels all over the world as an international project management consultant and speaker. He joined the US Navy in 1979 and is a 20-year veteran of the SEABEES, which is the self-sustained, combat-trained construction force for the US Navy. It was here that his love for both teaching and project management was discovered and developed. He began instructing in 1983, has taught thousands people in classroom environments, and publicly spoken to thousands at a time. His education includes two technical degrees; one in computer programming and the other in civil engineering and architectural drafting; he also holds a Bachelor of Science from Southern Illinois University in Workforce Education and Development, and a Master's Certificate from Villanova University in Applied Project Management.

Brief Contents

Lesson 1: Project Basics   1

Lesson 2: Establishing Resources   37

Lesson 3: Resource and Task Assignments   59

Lesson 4: Refining Your Project Schedule   76

Lesson 5: Fine-Tuning Tasks   101

Circling Back 1   117

Lesson 6: Fine-Tuning Resources   121

Lesson 7: Project Information: Sorting, Grouping, and Filtering   142

Lesson 8: Project Schedule Formatting Fundamentals   161

Lesson 9: Project Schedule Tracking Fundamentals   182

Lesson 10: Project Reporting   199

Circling Back 2   221

Lesson 11: Advanced Project Schedule Tracking   224

Lesson 12: Integrating Microsoft Project with Other Programs   240

Lesson 13: Project Schedule Optimization   255

Lesson 14: Advanced Project Schedule Formatting   277

Lesson 15: Managing Multiple Projects   294

Lesson 16: Working with Resource Pools   307

Lesson 17: Customizing Microsoft Project   328

Circling Back 3   341

**www.wiley.com/college/microsoft or call the MOAC
Toll-Free Number: 1+(888) 764-7001 (U.S. & Canada only)**

Contents

UNIT 1

Lesson 1: Project Basics   1

Navigating in Microsoft Project 2013   3
   Starting Microsoft Project 2013 and Opening a Template   3
Creating a Project Schedule   11
   Opening a New Blank Project Schedule   11
   Specifying the Project's Start Date   12
   Saving the Newly Created Project Schedule   13
Defining Project Calendars   14
   Defining Project Calendars   14
Entering Tasks and Task Details   16
   Entering Tasks   16
   Entering Task Durations   18
   Switching from Manual to Automatic Scheduling   21
   Creating a Milestone   22
Organizing Tasks into Phases   23
   Create Summary Tasks   23
Linking Tasks   26
   Linking Two Tasks   26
   Linking Several Tasks   27
   Linking Milestones   28
Documenting Tasks   29
   Entering Task Notes   30
Reviewing the Project Schedule's Duration   31
   Checking Project Duration   31
Knowledge Assessment   33
Competency Assessment   34
Proficiency Assessment   35
Mastery Assessment   36

Lesson 2: Establishing Resources   37

Establishing People Resources   38
   Establishing Individual People Resources   38
   Establishing a Group Resource   40
Establishing Equipment Resources   42
   Establishing Equipment Resources   42
Establishing Material Resources   44
   Establishing Material Resources   44
Establishing Cost Resources   45
   Establishing Cost Resources   45

Establishing Resource Pay Rates   46
   Entering Resource Cost Information   46
Adjusting Resource Working Times   49
   Establishing Nonworking Times   49
   Establishing Specific Work Schedules   50
Adding Resource Notes   53
   Attaching a Note to a Resource   53
Knowledge Assessment   54
Competency Assessment   56
Proficiency Assessment   57
Mastery Assessment   58

Lesson 3: Resource and Task Assignments   59

Assigning Work Resources to Tasks   61
   Making Individual Resource Assignments   61
   Assigning Multiple Resources Simultaneously   62
Adding More Work Resource Assignments to Tasks   64
   Adding Work Resources to a Task   64
   Using the Actions Tag to Change Project's Scheduling Behavior   66
Assigning Material Resources to Tasks   69
Assigning Cost Resources to Tasks   70
   Assigning a Cost Resource to a Task   70
Knowledge Assessment   71
Competency Assessment   73
Proficiency Assessment   74
Mastery Assessment   74

Lesson 4: Refining Your Project Schedule   75

Applying a Task Calendar to an Individual Task   78
   Assigning a Task Calendar to an Individual Task   78
Changing Task Types   80
   Task Types and the Effect of the Work Formula   81
   Using the Task Information Dialog Box to Change a Task Type   83

Splitting a Task 84
Splitting a Task 84
Establishing Recurring Tasks 86
Setting Up a Recurring Task 86
Assigning Resources to a Recurring Task 88
Applying Task Constraints 89
Applying a Constraint to a Task 90
Reviewing the Project's Critical Path 92
Reviewing the Project's Critical Path 92
Viewing Resource Allocations Over Time 93
Reviewing Resource Allocations 93
Knowledge Assessment 97
Competency Assessment 98
Proficiency Assessment 99
Mastery Assessment 99

Lesson 5: Fine-Tuning Tasks 101

Managing Task Constraints and
Relationships 102
Exploring Effects of Constraints and Relationships 102
Setting Deadline Dates 105
Setting Task Deadline Dates 106
Establishing Task Priorities 107
Establish Manually Scheduled Tasks 108
Manually Scheduling Tasks 108
Knowledge Assessment 112
Competency Assessment 113
Proficiency Assessment 114
Mastery Assessment 115

Circling Back 117

UNIT 2

Lesson 6: Fine-Tuning Resources 121

Entering Material Resource Consumption
Rates 122
Entering Costs Per Use for Resources 123
Assigning Multiple Pay Rates for a Resource 124
Applying Different Cost Rates to
Assignments 126
Specifying Resource Availability at Different
Times 127
Resolving Resource Over Allocations
Manually 129

Leveling Over Allocated Resources 134
Knowledge Assessment 138
Competency Assessment 139
Proficiency Assessment 139
Mastery Assessment 140

Lesson 7: Project Information: Sorting, Grouping, and Filtering 142

Sorting Data 143
Grouping Data 148
Filtering Data 151
Creating and Applying a Filter 151
Creating a Custom Filter 154
Knowledge Assessment 156
Competency Assessment 158
Proficiency Assessment 158
Mastery Assessment 159

Lesson 8: Project Schedule Formatting Fundamentals 161

Gantt Chart Formatting 163
Modifying the Gantt Chart Using the Bar Styles
Dialog Box 163
Modifying the Gantt Chart Using Gantt Chart Styles 165
Modifying Text Appearance In a View 168
Modifying the Appearance of a Single Piece of Text 170
Creating Custom Fields 171
Creating and Editing Tables 173
Creating Custom Views 176
Knowledge Assessment 178
Competency Assessment 179
Proficiency Assessment 180
Mastery Assessment 181

Lesson 9: Project Schedule Tracking Fundamentals 182

Establishing a Project Baseline 183
Tracking a Project as Scheduled 187
Entering the Completion Percentage for a Task 188
Identifying Over Budget Tasks and Resources 190

Identifying Time and Schedule Problems   193
Knowledge Assessment   196
Competency Assessment   197
Proficiency Assessment   197
Mastery Assessment   198

Lesson 10: Project Reporting   199

Activate and Print a Dashboard Report   201
Customize and Print a Report   203
Reporting Project Status   205
Using Visual Reports   207
Customizing and Printing a View   211
Knowledge Assessment   216
Competency Assessment   218
Proficiency Assessment   219
Mastery Assessment   219

Circling Back   221

UNIT 3

Lesson 11: Advanced Project Schedule Tracking   224

Recording Actual Start, Finish, and Duration
   Values of Tasks   226
Adjusting Remaining Work of Tasks   228
Evaluating Performance with Earned Value
   Analysis   232
Knowledge Assessment   235
Competency Assessment   237
Proficiency Assessment   238
Mastery Assessment   239

Lesson 12: Integrating Microsoft Project with Other Programs   240

Using a GIF Image to Display Project
   Information   241
Using the Timeline View to Display Project
   Information   244
Saving Project Information In Other File
   Formats   247

Knowledge Assessment   250
Competency Assessment   251
Proficiency Assessment   253
Mastery Assessment   254

Lesson 13: Project Schedule Optimization   255

Making Time and Date Adjustments   256
Viewing the Project's Critical Path   258
Delaying the Start of Assignments   261
Applying Contours to Assignments   263
   Applying a Contour to a Resource Assignment   263
   Manually Editing a Task Assignment   265
Optimizing the Project Schedule   266
   Identifying the Project Finish Date and
      Total Cost   266
   Compressing the Project Schedule   267
Knowledge Assessment   273
Competency Assessment   274
Proficiency Assessment   275
Mastery Assessment   276

Lesson 14: Advanced Project Schedule Formatting   277

Customizing the Calendar View   278
Using Task IDs and WBs Codes   281
Formatting the Network Diagram   287
Knowledge Assessment   290
Competency Assessment   291
Proficiency Assessment   292
Mastery Assessment   293

Lesson 15: Managing Multiple Projects   294

Managing Consolidated Projects   295
Creating Task Relationships Between
   Projects   298
Knowledge Assessment   302
Competency Assessment   303
Proficiency Assessment   304
Mastery Assessment   305

www.wiley.com/college/microsoft or call the MOAC
Toll-Free Number: 1+(888) 764-7001 (U.S. & Canada only)

Lesson 16: Working with Resource Pools 307

Developing a Resource Pool   308

Viewing Assignment Details in a Resource Pool   312

Revising Assignments in a Sharer File   314

Updating Resource Information in a Resource Pool   315

Updating Working Time for All Projects in a Resource Pool   317

Adding New Project Schedules to a Resource Pool   319

Revising a Sharer File and Updating a Resource Pool   321

Knowledge Assessment   323

Competency Assessment   324

Proficiency Assessment   325

Mastery Assessment   326

Lesson 17: Customizing Microsoft Project 328

Defining General Preferences   329

Working with Templates   330

Working with the Organizer   332

Knowledge Assessment   337

Competency Assessment   338

Proficiency Assessment   339

Mastery Assessment   340

Circling Back   341

Glossary   344

Index   347

Project Basics

LESSON SKILL MATRIX

SKILLS	TASKS
Navigating in Microsoft Project 2013	Start Microsoft Project Open a template The ribbon and its dynamic view The Backstage area How Microsoft Project handles project data Default views
Creating a Project Schedule	Open a new blank project schedule Specify a start date Save the project schedule
Defining Project Calendars	Define the project calendar
Entering Tasks and Task Details	Enter tasks Enter task durations Switch from Manual to Automatic Scheduling Create a milestone
Organizing Tasks into Phases	Create summary tasks
Linking Tasks	Link two tasks Link several tasks at once Link the milestone tasks
Documenting Tasks	Enter a task note
Reviewing the Project Schedule's Duration	Check the project's duration

Southridge Video is a video production and editing agency that works primarily with clients in the music industry to produce promotional videos for tours and full-length music videos for television play. Video production managers must identify the production tasks, plan and manage the schedule, and communicate project information to all the members of the production team. Microsoft Project 2013 is the perfect tool for managing a project such as this. In this lesson, you will learn how to navigate in Microsoft Project 2013, how the software handles data, how to create a new project schedule, enter tasks, durations, and milestones into the schedule, and organize the tasks in the schedule.

© jerges/iStockphoto

KEY TERMS

base calendar	project schedule
bottom–up planning	resource calendar
calendar	ribbon
deliverable	risk
dependency	sequence
duration	successor
elapsed duration	summary task
Gantt Chart view	task
link	task calendar
milestone	Task ID
note	template
phase	top–down planning
predecessor	work breakdown
project calendar	structure

■ SOFTWARE ORIENTATION

Microsoft Project's Start Screen

When you first launch Microsoft Project, you will see a screen similar to that shown in Figure 1-1. Your screen may be different if default settings have been changed or if other preferences have been set. Later, you will set the option directing the software to go directly to the Gantt Chart view.

Figure 1-1

Microsoft Project 2013 Start screen

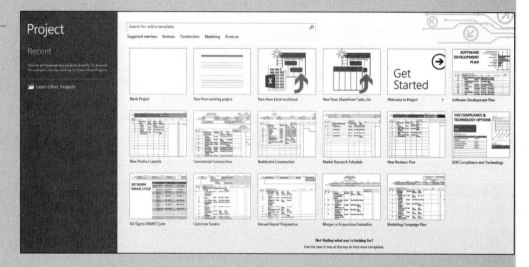

Before you begin using Microsoft Project 2013, you will need to become familiar with the user interface, also known as the *Ribbon.* This is similar to other Office applications in that the commands are in tabs, such as File, Task, Resource, Report, Project, and View. Selecting a tab activates the ribbon. Within each ribbon, commands are organized into groups; each command has its own button, which you activate by clicking with the mouse. Project's user interface makes it easy to find the commands you need more quickly.

Figure 1-2

Gantt Chart view

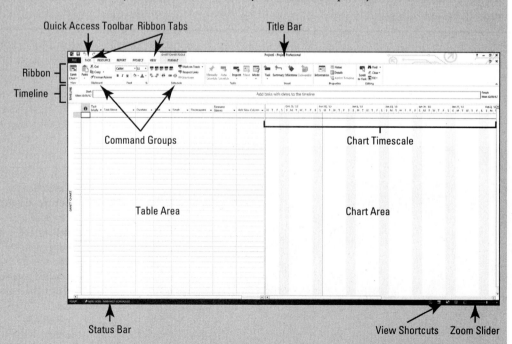

The most widely used view is the Gantt Chart view as shown in Figure 1-2. This view displays various task data as well as a graphical display of how the project is currently scheduled.

The *Gantt Chart view* is the primary way of viewing the data in a project schedule. It became the standard for visualizing project schedules in the early twentieth century when American engineer and management consultant Henry L. Gantt developed a bar chart with two main principles; 1) to measure activities by the amount of time needed to complete them; and 2) to represent the amount of the activity that should have been done in a given time.

In Microsoft Project, the Gantt Chart view is the default view. A view is a window through which you can see various elements of your project schedule. You will learn more about the Gantt Chart view in Lesson 8.

■ Navigating in Microsoft Project 2013

↓
THE BOTTOM LINE

Microsoft Project is the tool used by project managers to manage project schedules – it is not the process of project management. A *project schedule* is a model of a real project – what you want to happen or what you think will happen throughout the project. The schedule contains all of the tasks, resources, time frames, and costs that might be associated with such a project. You can modify this schedule (or any other project template) to fit your specific project needs. Later in this lesson you will learn how to create a project schedule from a blank template. A *template* is a predefined file that can be blank with the default characteristics set, or it could already contain project task and resource information. Knowing how to navigate in Microsoft Project and how Microsoft Project handles data will increase your efficiency in locating needed information.

Starting Microsoft Project 2013 and Opening a Template

When you launch Project, the Start screen appears. In this exercise, you learn how to start Microsoft Project and open a template.

 START MICROSOFT PROJECT

GET READY. Before you begin these steps, be sure to turn on or log on to your computer.

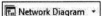

1. On the Windows taskbar, click the Start button. The Start screen appears.
2. On the Start menu, point to All Programs, point to Microsoft Office 2013, and then click Microsoft Project 2013. Microsoft Project opens.
3. Your screen should look similar to Figure 1-1. This is the start screen. From this screen you can choose to open a blank project, import information from Microsoft Excel or a SharePoint task list, open an existing project file, or open a template.

   PAUSE. LEAVE Microsoft Project open for the next exercise.

TAKE NOTE*

This manual is based on the Windows 7 operating system. If you are using Windows 8, some of the commands (such as "Start button") do not exist. Additionally there are some slight visual variations between the two operating systems. You are encouraged to use this manual with either operating system and understand that the differences are cosmetic only and in no way affect the functionality of Microsoft Project 2013.

TAKE NOTE*

You must be connected to the Internet to gain access to online templates.

Figure 1-3

Preview of the Annual Report Preparation template

OPEN A TEMPLATE

GET READY. Microsoft Project should be open.

1. On the Start screen (Figure 1-1), click the **Search for online templates** box located at the top of the screen. Type **annual report preparation**, then press **Enter.** The template is displayed and a preview of it is on the left of the screen as in Figure 1-3.

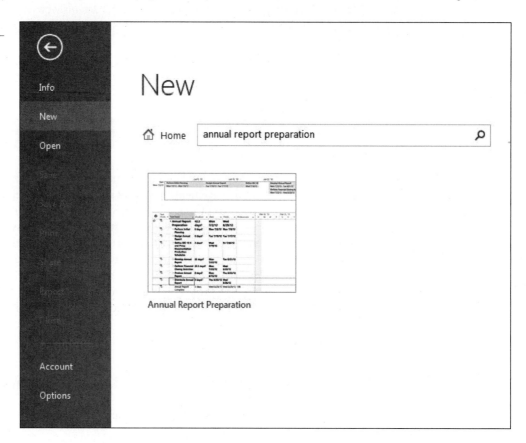

Figure 1-4

Project created from the Annual Report Preparation template

2. Double-click the **Annual Report Preparation template** graphic. The template is downloaded to your system, then opens a new project based on the template in the Gantt Chart view and closes the New Project screen. Your screen should look similar to Figure 1-4.

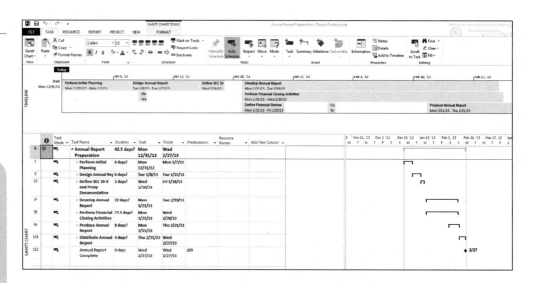

TAKE NOTE*

As you create your own templates, you can store them wherever you wish. However, it is recommended that they are stored in the default Microsoft templates folder.

PAUSE. LEAVE Microsoft Project open for the next exercise.

You have just opened a project schedule from a template in Microsoft Project. A project schedule is a model of a real project – what you want to happen or what you think will happen. The schedule contains tasks, resources, time frames, and costs that might be associated with such a project. You can modify this schedule (or any other project template) to fit your specific project needs. Later in this lesson, you will learn how to create a project schedule from a blank template.

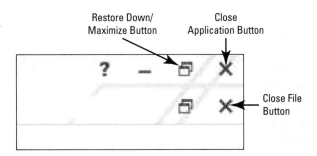

THE RIBBON AND ITS DYNAMIC VIEW

USE the project schedule you created from a template in the previous exercise.

1. To demonstrate the dynamic nature of the ribbon, click the **Restore Down/Maximize** button. This is located in the upper right corner of the screen, just to the left of the close application button. See Figure 1-5.

Figure 1-5

The Restore Down/Maximize button

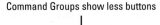

2. Using the resizing feature, change the width of the reduced window and watch how the ribbon changes with the changing width. Figure 1-6 shows an example of the ribbon at a reduced level of resolution.

Figure 1-6

The Ribbon at a reduced level of resolution

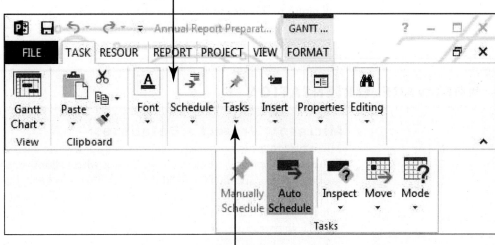

3. Click the **Restore Down/Maximize** button again. This will set the window back to full screen. Note the automatic change in the ribbon as shown in Figure 1-7.

Figure 1-7

The Ribbon at full resolution

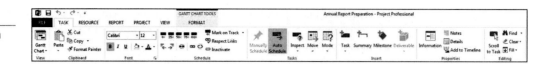

PAUSE. LEAVE Microsoft Project open for the next exercise.

In this exercise, you changed the resolution of the Project window and the software automatically changed the resolution of the ribbon command groups.

➔ THE BACKSTAGE AREA

The Backstage Area is the name given to the File tab. This is where the user will change options, save, print, import and export, set file properties, and much more.

USE the project schedule you created in the previous exercise.

1. Click the **File** tab. On the left navigation bar click **New**.
2. This screen is similar to the Start screen that appeared when you first started the software. From this screen you can open an existing schedule, start a new project from a blank template, or import from Excel or SharePoint.
3. Click **Print** in the left navigation bar. This section provides a print preview, allows the user to change printers and the print settings, as well as setting the page options such as headers, footers, and margins.
4. Click **Share** in the left navigation bar. Here the user can send the project file as an email attachment or sync it with SharePoint.
5. Click **Export** in the left navigation bar. This section allows the user to create a PDF/XPS Document or to save the project file in different formats such as Excel, XML, or legacy versions of Microsoft Project.

PAUSE. LEAVE Microsoft Project open for the next exercise.

TAKE NOTE*

You must have Microsoft Project Professional 2013 to sync or import tasks from a SharePoint task list.

In this exercise, you reviewed some sections of the Backstage Area. Throughout this text, you will return to this area to check and change options.

■ SOFTWARE ORIENTATION

Microsoft Project's Databases

Microsoft Project is a database. More correctly, it is three databases in one, as shown in Figure 1-8. The first is a task database. This is where all task-related information such as the task name, start, finish, cost, duration, and work is kept. The second is the resource database. All resource-related information is stored in the resource database, such as resource name, type of resource, standard rate (pay rate), resource group they belong to, the base calendar they are assigned, and the maximum number of units for the resource.

The third database is called the assignment database. When a resource is assigned to a task, all of the assignment-related information for each specific resource on each specific task is stored here. Items stored in the assignment database include a resource's start and finish date and the amount of work and the total cost for that resource on a specific task.

Figure 1-8

Microsoft Project's three databases

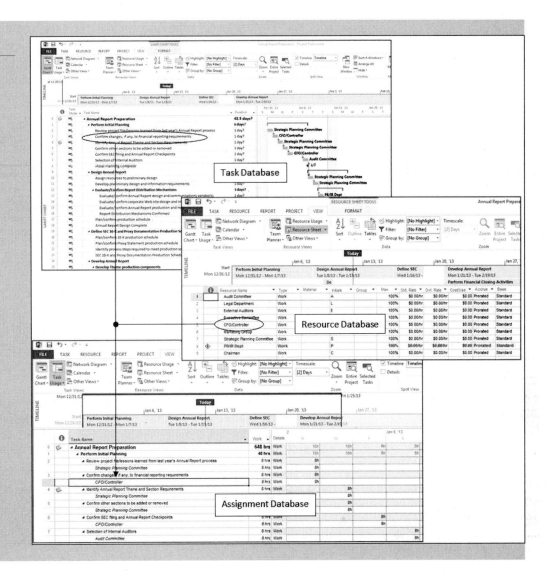

HOW MICROSOFT PROJECT HANDLES PROJECT DATA

In this exercise, you will learn how the software displays data from each of its three databases.

USE the project schedule you created in the previous exercise.

1. Your screen should be on the Gantt Chart view. Place your mouse cursor on the **Task Name** column heading, but do not click it. You will notice that a ScreenTip appears, displaying the title of the column (Task Name) and its actual name (Name). See Figure 1-9.

Figure 1-9

ScreenTip for Task Name column

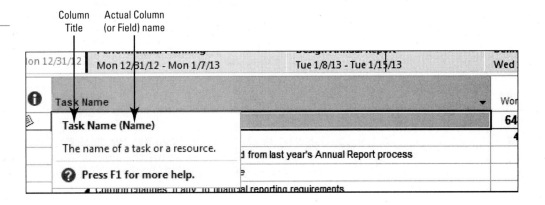

8 | Lesson 1

2. Click the **View** tab then, in the Resource Views command group, select the **Resource Sheet** view.

3. Place the mouse cursor on the **Resource Name** column heading and observe the ScreenTip that appears as in Figure 1-10. You will notice that this field has the same name as the one in Figure 1-9. You have just witnessed two of the databases.

Figure 1-10

ScreenTip for Resource Name column

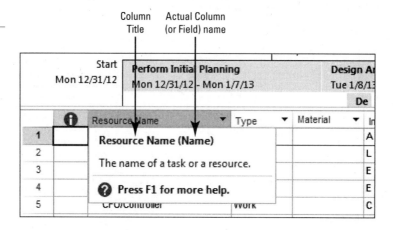

4. On the ribbon, click the **Task Usage** button, located in the Task Views command group. This is one of two views that displays information from the assignment database. Note the Task Usage button is a two-part button, with a submenu on the bottom half.

5. Select the **name cell** of task 1, Perform Initial Planning.

6. Press the key stroke combination of **Ctrl+Shift+F5**. This is the Scroll to Task feature which will be discussed later. Your screen should look similar to Figure 1-11.

Figure 1-11

Task Usage View

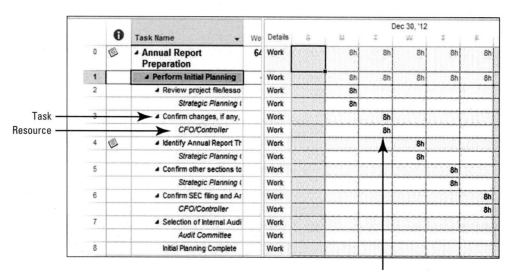

Table 1-1 shows the default view and the databases from which they collect information. Knowing which database has the information will help later in knowing not only which view to activate but will also assist in developing custom reports.

Table 1-1

Default Views and their respective databases

DEFAULT VIEW	DATABASE
Calendar	Task
Gantt Chart	Task
Network Diagram	Task
Task Usage	Assignment
Timeline	Task
Tracking Gantt	Task
Resource Form	Resource
Resource Graph	Assignment
Resource Sheet	Resource
Resource Usage	Assignment
Team Planner	Assignment

PAUSE. LEAVE Microsoft Project open for the next exercise.

In this exercise, you viewed some of basic views in the software and the database that held the information. In the next exercise, you will become familiar with more views.

 DEFAULT VIEWS

In the previous exercise you learned that Microsoft Project consists of three databases. When you want to look at data from any one of the databases, you must activate a view. In this exercise, you will learn about some of the common, default views and how to activate them.

USE the project schedule you created in the previous exercise.

You have already seen three of the default views in Microsoft Project, including the Gantt Chart view, Resource Sheet view, and the Task Usage view.

1. On the View tab, select the **Calendar** view from the Task View command group. Your screen should look similar to Figure 1-12.

Figure 1-12

Calendar View

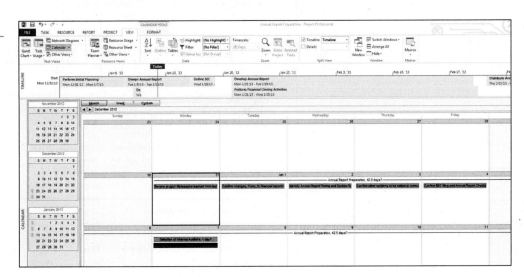

2. The Calendar view provides task data in a calendar format. It is helpful when you need to get project information to those project team members who may not have, or know how to operate, Microsoft Project.

3. On the View tab, select the **Network Diagram** view. Your screen should look similar to Figure 1-13.

Figure 1-13

Network Diagram view

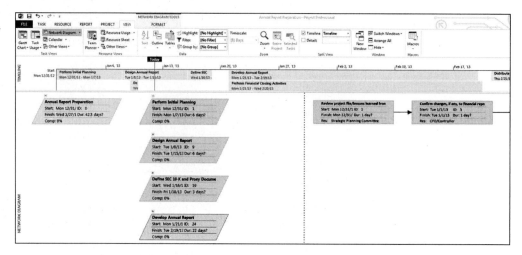

The network diagram view displays the logical sequencing of the tasks and the relationship these tasks have with other tasks in the project. It is helpful during planning and execution and can show the complexity of a project.

4. On the View tab, select the **Resource Usage** view. Click the **Resource Name** column once to highlight the entire column.

5. On the ribbon, in the Data command group, click the **Outline** button then select **Hide Subtasks**.

6. Auto fit the **Resource Name** column. You do this by placing your cursor on the right side of the column name and double-clicking.

7. Click the **Expand** button at the left of resource 1, Audit Committee. Your screen should look like Figure 1-14.

Figure 1-14

Resource Usage view

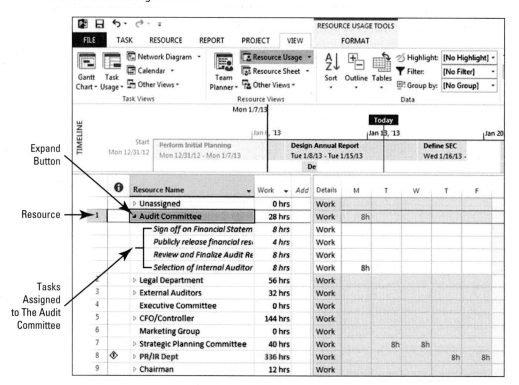

The Resource Usage view shows assignments, categorized by resource. In other words, it is helpful to see the assignments each resource has been assigned. This is opposite from the Task Usage view you selected earlier, which categorized assignments by task.

8. **CLOSE** the file. When asked to save the file, click **No**.

   LEAVE Microsoft Project open for the next exercise.

In this exercise, you viewed three additional, commonly used views in the software. Now that you are familiar with how to navigate in the program, you will now create your own project schedule.

■ Creating a Project Schedule

THE BOTTOM LINE

Microsoft Project is an active scheduling tool. You should perform all the planning processes associated with the project management methodology of your organization before entering any information into Microsoft Project 2013. When you create a new project schedule, the first task is to set a start date for your project.

Opening a New Blank Project Schedule

Rather than use a project schedule template, you can create a new, blank project schedule that you can fine-tune to your specific project. In this exercise, you open a new project schedule.

⊕ **OPEN A NEW BLANK PROJECT SCHEDULE**

GET READY. Microsoft Project should be open.

1. On the Start screen, click **New**.

2. On the screen, double-click the **Blank Project** option. A new blank project schedule appears and you are briefly notified that new tasks will be created in the new Manually Scheduled Mode, which is discussed in lesson 2. Your screen will look like Figure 1-15.

Figure 1-15

Manual scheduling notification

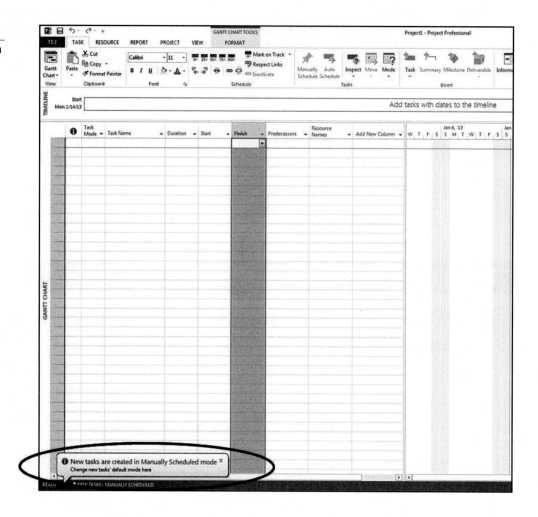

PAUSE. LEAVE the project schedule open to use in the next exercise.

In this exercise, you created a new, blank project schedule. Now you will begin to add details to the project schedule, such as start date, tasks, durations, and calendars. This information should be entered in the sequence presented. When using Microsoft Project the user must perform data entry steps in a specific order. Entering information out of sequence could result in inaccurate information or re-entry of the data. For example, if you enter duration information before setting the calendar options, the durations entered will be altered when calendar options are set.

Specifying the Project's Start Date

The first step of creating a new project schedule is to specify the start date for the project. In this exercise, you create a start date for the new project you have created.

 SPECIFY A START DATE

TAKE NOTE*

By default, Microsoft Project uses the current date as the project start date.

USE the project schedule you opened in the previous exercise.

1. Click the **Project** tab. In the Properties group click the **Project Information** button. The Project Information dialog box appears.

2. Single-click the **drop-down arrow** next to the Start Date text box once. For this exercise, you will change the project start date to January 4, 2016.

3. Click the calendar's **Left** or **Right Arrow** key until January 2016 is displayed, as shown in Figure 1-16.

4. In the January calendar, click **January 4th**.

Figure 1-16

Setting the Start Date in the project information dialog box

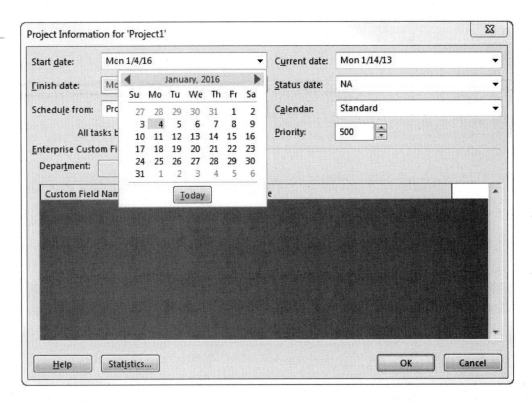

5. Click **OK** at the bottom of the dialog box.

PAUSE. LEAVE the project schedule open to use in the next exercise.

You can also quickly set the start date in the Project Information dialog box by highlighting the current date in the Start Date box and typing the start date in month/day/year format.

In this exercise, you specified a start date for your project. You can schedule a project from either the start date or the end date, but not both. Most projects should be scheduled from a start date. Scheduling from a start date causes all tasks to start as soon as possible, and it gives you the greatest scheduling flexibility. Scheduling from a finish date can be helpful in determining when a project must start if the finish date is fixed.

Saving the Newly Created Project Schedule

Once you have created a new project schedule and specified the start date, you need to save the file.

 SAVE THE PROJECT SCHEDULE

USE the project schedule you created in the previous exercise.

1. On the ribbon, click the **File** tab and then click the **Save** option. Because you have not previously saved the project schedule, the Save-As section is activated.

2. In the Save As section, click **Computer** then select **Browse**.

Browse

3. Locate and select the solutions folder for this lesson as directed by your instructor.

4. In the File Name box, type **Don Funk Music Video 1**.

5. Click **Save**. The Save As dialog box closes and the project schedule is saved as **Don Funk Music Video 1**.

PAUSE. **Leave** the project schedule open to use in the next exercise.

In this exercise, you named and saved your project file. It is important to get into the habit of saving your file frequently so that minimal information is lost should you experience a software or hardware malfunction.

TAKE NOTE *

You can also have Microsoft Project save your project schedule at specified intervals. Under the File tab, click **Options** in the navigation bar, then select **Save**. In the Save Options dialog box, under Save Projects, select the **Auto Save Every** check box and then specify the time interval at which you want Microsoft Project to automatically save your file.

■ Defining Project Calendars

THE BOTTOM LINE

In Microsoft Project, calendars determine how tasks and resources assigned to these tasks are scheduled. You can set your project calendar to reflect the working days and hours of your project, as well as nonworking times such as evenings, weekends, and holidays.

Defining Project Calendars

In this exercise, you define the calendar for your project and set up two exception days (holidays).

➡ **DEFINE THE PROJECT CALENDAR**

USE the project schedule you created in the previous exercise.

1. On the ribbon, in the Properties command group, select the **Change Working Time** button. The Change Working Time dialog box is displayed.

2. Click the **For Calendar** drop-down arrow. In the dropdown menu, select **Standard**, if it is not already selected.

3. Using the scroll control at the right of the calendar, navigate until the calendar displays January, 2016. Click the date box for **January 18**.

4. In the Exceptions tab, click in the first **Name** field and type **Martin Luther King Jr. Day** and press **Enter**. Your screen should look similar to Figure 1-17.

Figure 1-17

Change Working Time
dialog box

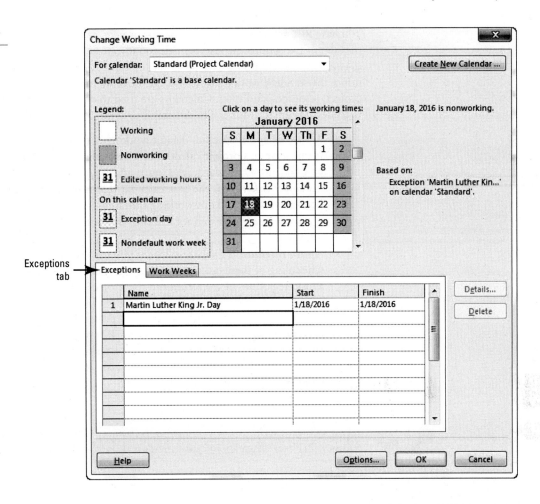

Exceptions
tab

Details...

5. Single-click the name of the exception you just entered. Then click the **Details** button. The Details dialog box appears. Under Recurrence Pattern, click **Yearly**.

6. Click the **The:** button, and use the arrows next to each selection box to select **Third**, **Monday**, and **January**.

7. In the Range of Recurrence section, select the option for *End after:* then type **3**, then press **Enter**.

8. Note the new finish date of the exception is now 1/15/2018.

9. Scroll until calendar in the Change Working Time dialog box displays May, 2016. Click once on **May 30, 2016**.

10. In the next blank exception name cell, type **Memorial Day** and press **Enter**.

11. Single-click the name of the exception you just entered. Then click the **Details** button. The Details dialog box reappears. Under Recurrence Pattern, click **Yearly**.

12. Click the **The:** button, and use the arrows next to each selection box to select **Last**, **Monday**, and **May**.

13. In the Range of Recurrence section, select the option for *End after:* then type **3**.

14. Note the new finish date of the exception is now 5/28/2018.

15. Click **OK** to close the Details dialog box, and then click **OK** to close the Change Working Time dialog box.

16. **SAVE** the project schedule.

    PAUSE. LEAVE the project schedule open to use in the next exercise.

You have just defined the calendar for this project, as well as set up two exception days (holidays). Exceptions can also be used to indicate additional time away from the project, such as company-wide training days or morale events. A *calendar* is a scheduling tool that determines the standard working time and nonworking time (such as evening or holidays) for the project, resources, and tasks. Calendars are used to determine how tasks and resources assigned to these tasks are scheduled. Project uses four types of calendars:

- A *base calendar* specifies default working and nonworking times for a set of resources. It can serve as a project calendar or a task calendar. Microsoft Project provides three base calendars: Standard, 24-Hours, and Night Shift.
- A *project calendar* is the base calendar that is used for an entire project. It defines the normal working and nonworking times.
- A *resource calendar* defines working and nonworking times for an individual work resource.
- A *task calendar* is the base calendar you can use for individual tasks to manage the scheduling of these tasks. A task calendar defines working and nonworking times for a task, regardless of the settings in the project calendar.

Base calendars can be created and assigned to a project, a resource, or a task. Project, resource, and task calendars are used in scheduling tasks. If resources are assigned to tasks, the task is scheduled based upon the resource calendar. If a task calendar is used to schedule a task and the resources assigned do not work during the task calendar's working hours, you will receive a warning about an assignment mismatch.

Cross Ref

You will learn more about base calendars, project calendars, and resource calendars in Lesson 2. You'll learn about task calendars in Lesson 4.

■ Entering Tasks and Task Details

THE BOTTOM LINE

Tasks represent the actual individual work activities that must be completed to accomplish a project's final goal, or *deliverable*. In Microsoft Project, the tasks you define contain the details about each activity or event that must occur in order for your project to be completed. These details include the order and duration of tasks, critical tasks, and resource requirements.

Entering Tasks

Once you have created and saved a new project schedule and defined the project's working times, you can begin to enter tasks. Tasks are the most basic building blocks of any project schedule. In this exercise, you will enter a single task in each row of the Entry table.

→ **ENTER TASKS**

USE the project schedule you created in the previous exercise.

1. Click the **first blank cell** directly below the Task Name column heading.
2. Type **Review screenplay** and press **Enter**. Your screen should look similar to Figure 1-18.

Figure 1-18

First task for Don Funk Music
Video 1

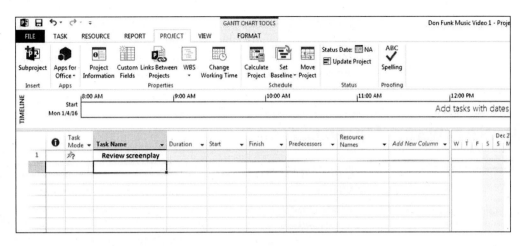

3. Enter the following task names below the Review screenplay task name. Press **Enter** after each task name.

   Develop scene blocking and schedule

   Develop production layouts

   Identify and reserve locations

   Book musicians

   Book dancers

   Reserve audio recording equipment

   Reserve video recording equipment

4. As you enter new tasks, you will note that each cell automatically wraps the text. Your screen should look similar to Figure 1-19.

Figure 1-19

Task List for Don Funk Music
Video 1

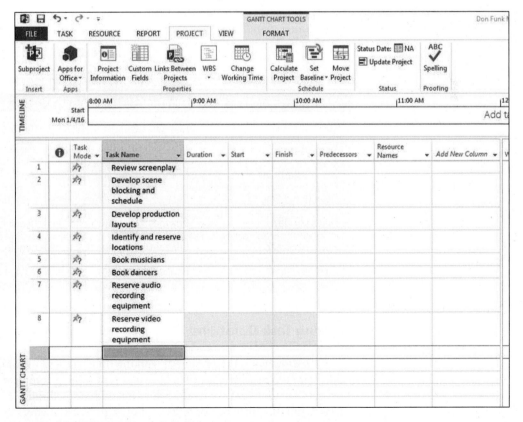

5. **SAVE** the project schedule.

   PAUSE. LEAVE the project schedule open to use in the next exercise.

You have just added eight tasks to your project schedule. Note that as you entered a task on each row of the Entry table, Microsoft Project assigned a Task ID (see Figure 1-19). The *Task ID* (sometimes simply referred to as ID) is a unique number that is assigned to each task in the project. It appears on the left side of the task's row.

■ SOFTWARE ORIENTATION

Calendar Options

Microsoft Project uses standard values of minutes and hours for durations: one minute equals 60 seconds, and one hour equals 60 minutes. However, you can define the duration of days, weeks, and months for your project. Click the **File** tab, select **Options**, then click the **Schedule** option, and look under **Calendar options for this project:** See Figure 1-20.

Figure 1-20

Calendar options

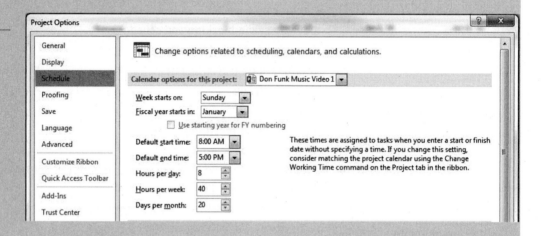

CALENDAR OPTION	FUNCTION
Week starts on	Changes the day on which the project week starts
Fiscal year starts in	Changes the month in which the project fiscal year begins
Default start time	Changes the default start time for scheduled tasks
Default end time	Changes the default end time for scheduled tasks
Hours per day	Changes how many hours are scheduled for one day
Hours per week	Changes how many hours are scheduled for one week
Days per month	Changes how many days are scheduled for one month

Entering Task Durations

A task's *duration* is the amount of working time required to complete a task. Because different tasks usually take different amounts of time to complete, each task is assigned a separate duration. Do not confuse duration with elapsed time or work effort. For example, a task's duration may be two weeks but only 20 hours of effort to complete. By contrast, a task can have four work resources assigned and equate to 24 hours of effort in a single, eight hour work day.

ENTER TASK DURATIONS

In Manual Scheduling mode, the user can enter either a specified duration or an approximate duration. An approximate duration is something like "about two days". This applies to start dates and finish dates as well.

USE the project schedule you created in the previous exercise.

1. Click the first **cell** in the Duration column next to the task 1, **Review screenplay**. The Duration field for task 1 is selected.

2. Type **3w** and then press **Enter**. The value 3 wks appears in the Duration field.

3. Enter the following durations for the remaining tasks.

TASK ID	TASK NAME	DURATION
2	Develop scene blocking and schedule	1w
3	Develop production layouts	About 1 month
4	Identify and reserve locations	5w
5	Book musicians	2w
6	Book dancers	2w
7	Reserve audio recording equipment	1w
8	Reserve video recording equipment	3-5 days

Your screen should look similar to Figure 1-21.

Figure 1-21

Gantt Chart showing task durations entered.

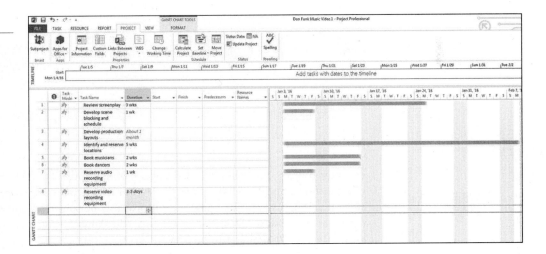

4. **SAVE** the project schedule.

   PAUSE. LEAVE the project schedule open to use in the next exercise.

You may notice that for those tasks where you entered approximate durations, the software did not draw a corresponding Gantt Chart bar. This is the result of Manual Scheduling. Later in this lesson you will change the scheduling mode to Automatic Scheduling.

Recall that when you set up your project calendar in the previous exercise, the working times for your project were Monday through Friday from 8:00 A.M.–5:00 P.M. with an hour off for lunch each day. Microsoft Project differentiates between working and nonworking time, so the duration of a task doesn't always correspond to elapsed time. If you estimate that a task will take 24 hours of working time, you would enter its duration as 3d to schedule the task over three 8-hour workdays. If this task were to start at 8:00 A.M. on Thursday, it would not be completed until 5:00 P.M. on Monday. No work is scheduled on evenings or weekends because these have been defined as nonworking times.

You can also schedule tasks to occur over working and nonworking time by assigning an elapsed duration to a task. *Elapsed duration* is the total length of working and nonworking time you expect it will take to complete a task. Suppose you own an automobile body shop. In the process of repainting a car, you have the tasks "Apply rustproof undercoat" and "Apply first color overcoat." You also need a task called "Wait for undercoat to dry" because you cannot apply the color paint until the undercoat is dry. The task "Wait for undercoat to dry" will have an elapsed duration because the undercoat will dry over a contiguous range of hours, whether they are working or nonworking. If the undercoat takes 24 hours to cure, you would enter the duration for this task as **1ed** (or 1 elapsed day). If you scheduled it to start at 11 A.M. on Wednesday, it would be complete at 11 A.M. on Thursday.

Table 1-1 shows abbreviations and meanings for actual and elapsed times in Microsoft Project.

Table 1-2

Abbreviations and meanings for actual and elapsed times

IF YOU ENTER THIS ABBREVIATION	IT APPEARS LIKE THIS	AND MEANS
m	min	minute
h	hr	hour
d	day	day
w	wk	week
mo	mon	month
em	emin	elapsed minute
eh	ehr	elapsed hour
ed	eday	elapsed day
ew	ewk	elapsed week
emo	emon	elapsed month

TROUBLE**SHOOTING**

For most projects, you will use task durations of hours, days, and weeks. When estimating task durations, think carefully about the level of detail you want to apply to your project's tasks. If you have a multiyear project, it is probably not practical or even possible to track tasks that are measured in minutes or hours. You should measure task durations at the lowest level of detail or control necessary, but no lower.

Although the task durations are supplied for you for the exercises in this book, you and the project team will have to estimate task durations for most real-world projects. There are a number of sources of task duration estimates:

- Information from previous, similar projects
- Estimates from the people who will actually complete the tasks
- Recommendations from people who have managed similar projects
- Professional or industry organizations that deal with the project subject matter

For any project, a major source of risk is inaccurate task duration estimates. *Risk* is an uncertain event or condition that, if it occurs, will have an impact on your project, either positively or negatively. Inaccurate task duration estimates (negative risk) decreases the likelihood of completing the project on time, within budget and to specification. Developing good estimates is worth the time and effort.

➔ MANUAL SCHEDULING VS. AUTOMATIC SCHEDULING

Microsoft Project 2013 has two scheduling modes, Manual and Automatic. In the Manual mode (which is the default), Project allows the user some flexibility in entering information. However, this mode does not allow the software to schedule tasks in a dynamic manner, meaning it requires more attention to maintain the schedule. Automatic scheduling mode reduces the flexibility of entering approximate durations and dates. This mode does allow the user to create a dynamic schedule which requires less maintenance.

Switching from Manual to Automatic Scheduling

> When you entered durations earlier, you noticed how the software dealt with approximate duration information – it did not draw a Gantt bar. In this exercise you will learn how to change the scheduling mode. You can do this for an entire project or you can do it on a task-by-task basis, depending on your needs. By default, all new tasks are set to manual scheduling.

➔ SWITCH FROM MANUAL TO AUTOMATIC SCHEDULING

USE the project schedule you created in the previous exercise.

1. Select the Task Name for task 1, Review screenplay.

2. Click the Task tab. Then, in the Tasks command group, click the Auto Schedule button. Notice the change in the Gantt Chart bar for task 1. Your screen should look similar to Figure 1-22.

Figure 1-22

Default appearance of Manual and Automatic Gantt bars

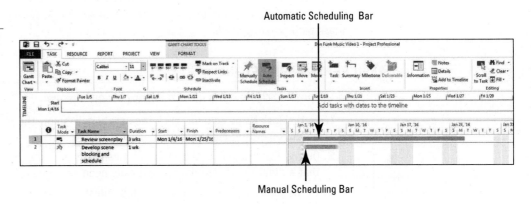

Automatic Scheduling Bar

Manual Scheduling Bar

3. Select the duration cell of task 3, Develop production layouts. Type **1mo** and press Enter. This sets the duration for that task.

4. Note the duration of task 8 is currently "3-5 days". Single-click task name column heading to select all tasks. On the ribbon, select the Auto Schedule button. Note the duration of task 8 now displays 1 day with a question mark behind it.

5. Select the duration cell of task 8, Reserve audio recording equipment. Key **5d** and press Enter. Your screen should look similar to Figure 1-23.

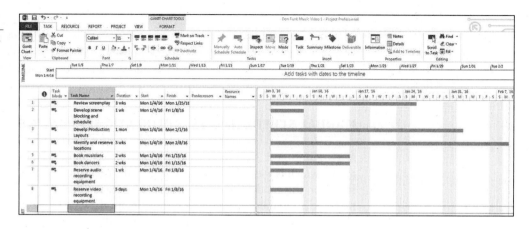

6. Click the **File** tab then select Options.

7. In the Project Options dialog box, in the navigation bar on the left side of the dialog box, click **Schedule**.

8. Look in the *Scheduling options for this project:* section. Change the first option, *New tasks created:* from Manually Scheduled to **Auto Scheduled**. Note that you have only changed the options for this file, not the behavior of the software.

9. Click **OK** to close the options dialog box. Notice that at the bottom of the screen, on the status bar, that all new tasks are auto scheduled.

10. **SAVE** the project schedule.

PAUSE. LEAVE the project schedule open to use in the next exercise.

In this exercise you changed the scheduling mode for a single task then changed it for all entered tasks. You then changed the scheduling mode for all new tasks to be entered into the file.

Creating a Milestone

A **milestone** represents a major event or a significant point in a project. Milestones can be either imposed upon the project by the project sponsor or they can be set by the project team to monitor the project's progress. In Microsoft Project, milestones are represented as a task with zero duration.

 CREATE A MILESTONE

USE the project schedule you created in the previous exercise.

1. In the Task Name column, click the **empty cell** below the name of task 8, **Reserve Video Recording Equipment**.

2. On the Task ribbon, in the Insert command group, click the **Milestone** button. Notice that a duration of zero days has already been entered.

3. In the **Name** cell of the newly created milestone, type **Pre-Production complete** and press **Enter**.

4. In the Task Name column, click the name of task 1, **Review screenplay**.

5. On the Task ribbon, in the Insert command group, click the **Milestone** button. Microsoft Project inserts and numbers the new milestone as ID 1. Notice that the other tasks after this new task insertion point have been renumbered.

6. Type **Pre-Production** begins and press **Enter**. Your screen should look similar to Figure 1-24.

Figure 1-24

Gantt Chart showing
milestones entered

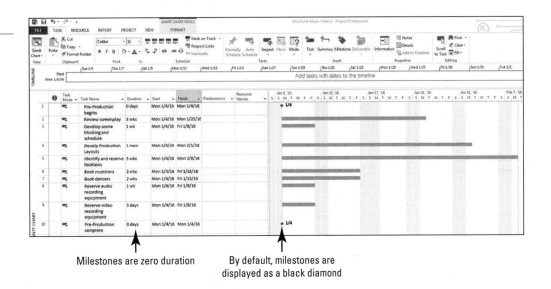

Milestones are zero duration

By default, milestones are
displayed as a black diamond

 ANOTHER WAY   You can also press **Insert** to add a new task above the selected task. To insert multiple new tasks, select multiple tasks and then press **Insert**. The same number of new tasks will be inserted as the number you selected.

7. **SAVE** the project schedule.

    PAUSE. LEAVE the project schedule open to use in the next exercise.

■ Organizing Tasks into Phases

THE BOTTOM LINE   During the planning portion of a project, teams often create a Work Breakdown Structure (WBS) to ensure no work is missed. A sample WBS for this project is shown in Figure 1-25.

Create Summary Tasks

After you enter tasks in your project, it can be helpful to organize your project by grouping related tasks into *phases*, or groups of closely related tasks that encompass a major section of your project. The phases, represented by summary tasks, identify the major phases and sub-phases in your project. A *summary task* is made up of and summarizes all of the tasks within its hierarchical structure, which could also include other summary tasks, detail tasks, or subtasks that fall below it. You cannot directly edit a summary task's duration, start date, or other calculated values. In this exercise, you organize your project's tasks into summary tasks to identify the task's phases.

A *work breakdown structure* (WBS) is the hierarchical decomposition of the work to complete the project. Figure 1-25 depicts a box-type, or graphical, WBS for the case study project you are working on in this book. Microsoft Project, however, displays the WBS in a format called a tabular WBS. There are other WBS formats that can be used but these are the two most common.

Figure 1-25

Work Breakdown Structure
(WBS) for Don Funk Music
Video

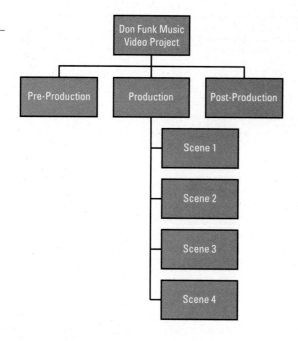

CREATE SUMMARY TASKS

USE the project schedule you created in the previous exercise.

1. Select tasks 1 through 10.

2. On the **Task** ribbon, in the Insert command group, click the **Summary** button. A new summary task row is inserted above the selected tasks, all selected tasks are shifted down and renumbered, and they are all now part of this new summary task.

3. In the Task Name field for the new summary task, type **Pre-Production** and press **Enter**.

4. Type the following task names below task 11, Pre-Production complete. Press **Enter** after each task name.

   Production

   Post-Production

Note that each of these became part of the previous section. You want each of these to become a summary task.

5. Select tasks **12** and **13**. On the ribbon, in the Schedule command group, select the **Outdent** button.

6. Click the **name** of task 13, **Post-Production**, and press **Insert** twice. Two blank tasks are inserted above the Post-Production task.

7. Type the following task names and durations below task 12, Production.

Task Name	Duration
Production begins	0d
Production complete	0d

8. Type the following tasks names and durations below task 15, Post-Production.

Task Name	Duration
Post-Production begins	0d
Post-Production complete	0d

9. Select tasks **13** and **14**. On the **Task** ribbon, in the Schedule group, click the **Indent** button. Tasks 13 and 14 are indented and task 12 becomes a summary task.

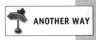

To quickly set a summary task for a range of selected tasks, highlight the range of tasks to be indented under a summary task, then on the Task ribbon, click the **Summary** button. All of the selected tasks will be indented and a new summary task line will appear.

10. Select tasks **16** and **17**. Hold down **Alt+Shift+Right Arrow**. Tasks 16 and 17 are indented and task 15 becomes a summary task. Your screen should look similar to Figure 1-26.

Figure 1-26

Gantt Chart showing summary and indented tasks.

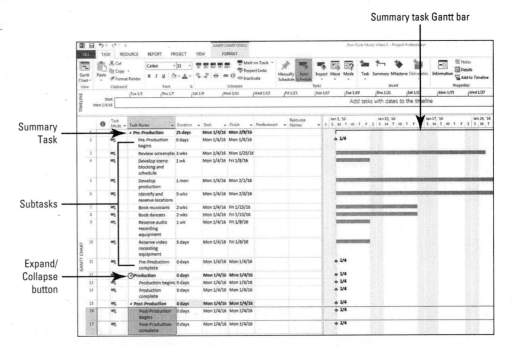

The Production and Post-Production summary tasks appear as milestones because they have no subtasks with a positive duration below them (only milestones with zero duration). The appearance of the Production and Post-production summary tasks will change once additional tasks are added in later lessons.

11. SAVE the project schedule.

PAUSE. LEAVE the project schedule open to use in the next exercise.

You have just organized your tasks into phases. Working with phases and tasks in Microsoft Project is similar to working with an outline in Microsoft Word. You can create phases by indenting and outdenting tasks, and you can collapse an entire task list into its phase components.

Most complex projects require a combination of both top-down and bottom-up planning in order to create accurate tasks and phases:

- *Top–down planning* develops a project schedule by identifying the highest level phases or summary tasks before breaking them into lower level components or subtasks. This approach works from general to specific.
- *Bottom–up planning* develops a project schedule by starting with the lowest level tasks before organizing them into higher level phases or summary tasks. This approach works from specific to general.

■ Linking Tasks

↓
THE BOTTOM LINE
You can create task relationships by creating links between tasks. In the Auto Scheduling mode, the links create a sequential dependency in which one task depends on the start or completion of another task in order to begin or end.

Linking Two Tasks

When you created your project, all of the tasks in the project schedule were scheduled to start on the same date – the project start date. You must create a dependency, or *link*, between tasks to correctly reflect the order in which work must be completed. In this exercise, you will link two tasks to reflect the actual order in which they will occur.

 LINK TWO TASKS

USE the project schedule you created in the previous exercise.

1. Select tasks **2 and 3**.

2. On the Task ribbon, under the Schedule group, click the **Link the Selected Tasks** button.
3. Tasks 2 and 3 are now linked with a finish-to-start relationship.
4. Select the **name cells** of tasks 3 and 4.
5. Press **Ctrl+F2**. Microsoft Project changed the start date of task 4 to the next working day following the completion of task 3. Note that because January 18 was a nonworking day (the Martin Luther King holiday you set up), task 3 does not finish until January 25 and task 4 does not start until January 26. If necessary, scroll the Gantt Chart to January 24 so that the link you just created is visible.
6. SAVE the project schedule.

   PAUSE. LEAVE the project schedule open to use in the next exercise.

When you started the exercise in this section, all of the tasks in the project schedule were scheduled to start on the same date – the project start date. You have just linked two tasks to reflect the actual order in which they will occur. A link is a logical connection between tasks that controls sequence and defines the relationship between two or more tasks. These two tasks have a finish-to-start relationship.

The first task is called the *predecessor*, a task whose start or end date determines the start or finish of another task or tasks. Any task can be a predecessor for one or more tasks. The second task is called the *successor*, a task whose start or finish is driven by another task or tasks. Again, any task can be a successor to one or more predecessor tasks. The second task occurs after the first task. This is called a *sequence*, or the chronological order in which tasks must occur. Tasks can have only one of four types of task relationships, as shown in Table 1-3.

Do not get task relationships in Microsoft Project confused with task dependencies in project management. A *dependency* is a need or a condition that exists between two elements. Knowing the dependency is an important factor in defining the task relationships. Dependencies come in three types:

- **Mandatory:** Also known as a hard logic dependency. The first task MUST be done before the second task, i.e. you must construct the walls of a house before you install the sheetrock. Dependencies of this type usually have relationships of FS, but can be SS with a Lag applied. Lags will be discussed in detail in Lesson 13.

Table 1-3

The four types of task relationships

THIS TASK RELATIONSHIP	MEANS	LOOKS LIKE THIS IN THE GANTT CHART	EXAMPLE
Finish-to-start (FS)	The finish date of the predecessor task determines the start date of the successor task.		A music track must be recorded before it can be edited.
Start-to-start (SS)	The start date of the predecessor task determines the start date of the successor task.		Booking musicians and Booking dancers are related tasks and can occur simultaneously.
Finish-to-finish (FF)	The finish date of the predecessor task determines the finish date of the successor task.		Tasks that require the use of specific equipment must end when the equipment rental ends.
Start-to-finish (SF) (This relationship type is rarely used.)	The start date of the predecessor task determines the finish date of the successor task.		The time when the production sound studio becomes available determines when rehearsals must end.

- **Discretionary:** Also known as a soft logic or preferred dependency. The first task does not necessarily have to be done in order to complete the second task, i.e., you do not have to paint the walls before you install the carpet. It is preferred, but not absolutely necessary. Dependencies of this type can have any one of the relationships.
- **External:** Something from outside the project is driving the task, i.e., I cannot paint the walls until the vendor delivers the paint. Dependencies of this type can have any one of the relationships. External dependencies are usually outside of the control of the project team.

Linking Several Tasks

In this exercise, you use Microsoft Project to link several tasks at once.

 LINK SEVERAL TASKS AT ONCE

USE the project schedule you created in the previous exercise.

1. Select the **names** of tasks 4 through 11. Note the new feature in Project 2013 where the row height indicators extend out into the Gantt Chart area. This makes locating the task's Gantt bar much easier.

2. On the Task ribbon, under the Schedule group, click the **Link the Selected Tasks** button. Tasks 4 through 11 are now linked with a finish-to-start relationship.

Entire
Project

3. Select the View tab. In the Zoom group, click the **Entire Project** button. Your screen should look similar to Figure 1-27.

Figure 1-27

Gantt Chart showing tasks 4 through 11 linked with a finish-to-start relationship

When you select a task, the new row height feature extends the row lines into the Gantt Chart area

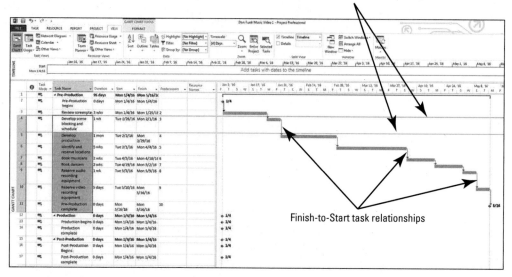

Finish-to-Start task relationships

 **ANOTHER WAY**

You can also set finish-to-start links using the Task Information dialog box. Click the name of the task that you wish to set as the successor. Then on the Task ribbon, click the Information button, and then click the **Predecessors** tab. Click the **first cell** in the Task Name column, and then click the **arrow** to select the task you wish to set as the predecessor.

4. SAVE the project schedule.

PAUSE. LEAVE the project schedule open to use in the next exercise.

Linking Milestones

Now that you have linked some of the tasks in the project schedule, you will link milestones across summary tasks. Linking milestones to each other reflects the sequential nature of the overall phases.

⊙ **LINK THE MILESTONE TASKS**

USE the project schedule you created in the previous exercise.

1. Select the name of task 11, **Pre-Production complete**, and, while holding down the Ctrl key, select the name of task 13, **Production begins**. This is how you select nonadjacent tasks in a table in Microsoft Project.

2. Click the Task tab. In the Schedule group click the **Link the Selected Tasks** button. Tasks 11 and 13 are linked with a finish-to-start relationship.

3. Select the **predecessor cell** of task 16, Production complete. Type **14** and press **Enter**. Tasks 14 and 16 are linked with a finish-to-start relationship. Your screen should look similar to Figure 1-28.

 TAKE NOTE

It is considered a poor practice to link summary tasks, therefore it should not be done.

Figure 1-28

Gantt Chart showing
milestones linked with
finish-to-start relationships

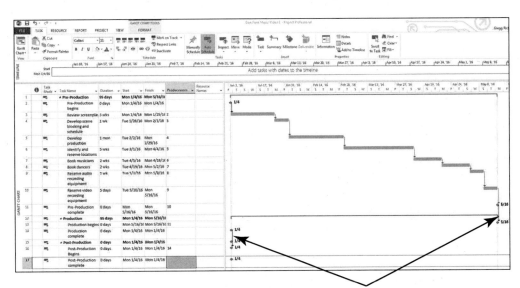

Link milestones between phases rather than summary tasks

Because you have not yet entered and linked actual tasks under the Production and Post-Production summary tasks, the last three milestones for these phases (tasks 14, 16, and 17) remain at the beginning (left end) of the Gantt bar chart. They will move to the right side of the Gantt bar chart once you add and link more subtasks in a future lesson.

6. SAVE the project schedule.

You can also create finish-to-start relationships between tasks directly in the Gantt Chart. Point to the predecessor task until the pointer changes to a four-arrow star. Drag the pointer up or down to the task bar of the successor task. Microsoft Project will link the two tasks. Notice that while you are dragging, the pointer image changes to a chain link. Be aware, however, that this method requires very precise and accurate mouse control and is not recommended.

PAUSE. LEAVE the project schedule open to use in the next exercise.

In this exercise, you linked milestones across summary tasks. When you link milestones, you set up the natural flow of the project – when one phase finishes, the next phase begins. In this particular project, you have not yet entered all of the subtasks for the Production and Post-Production phases, so the graphical representation of the milestones and links on the Gantt Chart may have looked a bit strange. Once you begin to enter and link these tasks, the project will begin to look more like the Pre-Production section of the Gantt Chart.

■ Documenting Tasks

THE BOTTOM LINE

You should keep the tasks in a project schedule simple and specific. Additional task information that is important to the project can be recorded in a note. You can also provide more information about a task by linking it to another file, an intranet page, or an Internet page through a hyperlink.

Entering Task Notes

A *note* is supplemental text that you can attach to a task, resource, or assignment. Attaching a note to a task in a project schedule allows you to document important information while keeping your project schedule succinct. In this exercise, you enter a task note.

⊕ ENTER A TASK NOTE

USE the project schedule you created in the previous exercise.

1. Select task 7, **Book musicians**, by clicking on the task number (7).

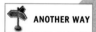

2. On the Task ribbon, in the Properties group, click the Task Notes icon. The Task Information dialog box appears with the Notes tab displayed.

3. In the Notes box, type **Call Andy Teal for the mandolin** and click OK. A note icon appears in the Indicators column for task 7. The Indicators column is the first column to the right of the task ID column.

🚩 **ANOTHER WAY**   You can also add a note by clicking the **Task Notes** button on the Task ribbon or by right-clicking on the task name and selecting **Notes** from the shortcut menu.

4. Point to the note icon. The note appears in a ScreenTip. For longer notes, or to see other task information, you can double-click the **note** icon and the Task Information box will display the full text of the note. The note icon and ScreenTip are shown in Figure 1-29.

Figure 1-29

Notes icon in the Indicators column with a ScreenTip view of the note

Task note icon

		production			2/29/16
6	➥	Identify and reserve locations	5 wks	Tue 3/1/16	Mon 4/4/16 5
7	📝	Book musicians	2 wks	Tue 4/5/16	Mon 4/18/16 6
8		Notes: 'Call Andy Teal for the mandolin'	2 wks	Tue 4/19/16	Mon 5/2/16 7
9	➥	Reserve audio recording equipment	1 wk	Tue 5/3/16	Mon 5/9/16 8
10	➥	Reserve video recording equipment	5 days	Tue 5/10/16	Mon 5/16/16 9
11	➥	Pre-Production complete	0 days	Mon 5/16/16	Mon 5/16/16 10

Note displayed as a ScreenTip

5. SAVE the project schedule.

PAUSE. LEAVE the project schedule open to use in the next exercise.

TAKE NOTE*

If you add photos or videos to you Project file, the file size can become quite large.

As you saw in this exercise, you enter and review task notes on the Notes tab in the Task Information dialog box. You can enter a wide variety of additional information to help clarify or enhance your project schedule. You can also attach a file, paste text and graphics from other Microsoft programs, insert sound or video files, add photos (to link faces with resource names), company logos, PowerPoint slides or presentations, and organizational charts. Do not worry about filling this field up – it can hold 64,000 characters.

■ Reviewing the Project Schedule's Duration

THE BOTTOM LINE Microsoft Project calculates both the current project duration and the scheduled finish date based on the task durations and relationships you entered. You can view both the project statistics and the Gantt Chart for the entire project.

Checking Project Duration

In this exercise, you practice using the Project Information dialog box to view and check the project's duration.

➔ **CHECK THE PROJECT'S DURATION**

USE the project schedule you created in the last exercise.

1. Click the **Project** tab, and then click **Project Information** in the Properties group. The Project Information dialog box appears, as shown in Figure 1-30.

Figure 1-30

Project Information dialog box

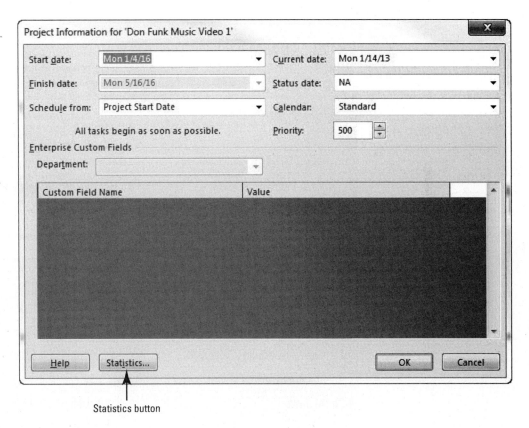

Statistics button

2. Click the **Statistics** button. The Project Statistics dialog box appears and displays information such as the project start and finish dates and duration. The statistics dialog box is shown in Figure 1-31.

3. Note that, based on the current information entered, this project is slated for **95 days** of duration, starting on January 4 and ending on May 16, 2016. Click the **Close** button to close the Project Statistics dialog box.

Figure 1-31

Project Statistics dialog box

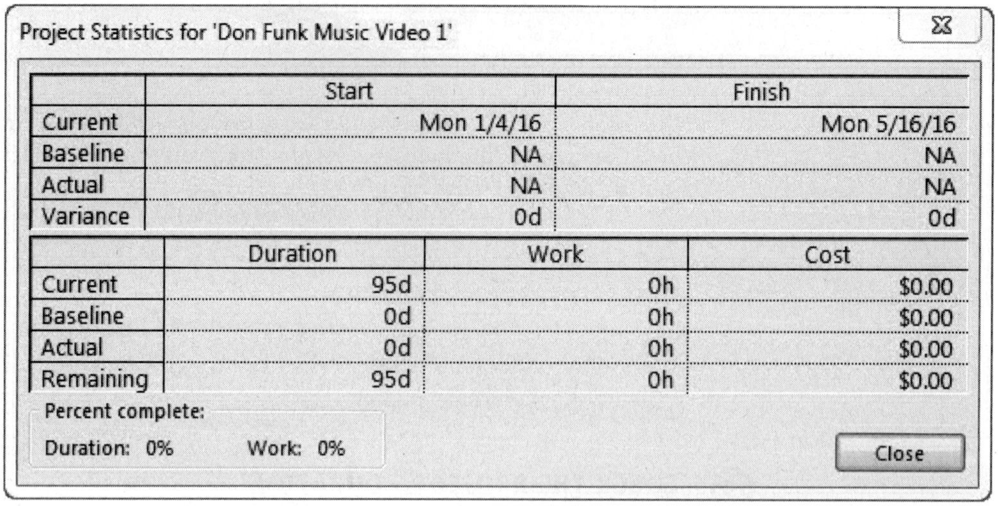

	Start	Finish
Current	Mon 1/4/16	Mon 5/16/16
Baseline	NA	NA
Actual	NA	NA
Variance	0d	0d

	Duration	Work	Cost
Current	95d	0h	$0.00
Baseline	0d	0h	$0.00
Actual	0d	0h	$0.00
Remaining	95d	0h	$0.00

Percent complete:

Duration: 0%   Work: 0%

4. **SAVE** and **CLOSE** the *Don Funk Music Video 1 file*.

   PAUSE. If you are continuing to the next lesson, keep Project open. If you are not continuing to additional lessons, **Close** Project.

SKILL SUMMARY

IN THIS LESSON YOU LEARNED:	MATRIX SKILL
To navigate in Microsoft Project	Navigate in Microsoft Project
	Start Microsoft Project
To open a template	Open a template
To create a project schedule	Open a new blank project schedule
	Specify a start date
	Save the project schedule
To define project calendars	Define the project calendar
To enter tasks and task details	Enter tasks
	Enter task durations
To switch from manual to auto scheduling	Switch from manual to auto scheduling
To create a milestone	Create a milestone
To organize tasks into phases	Create summary tasks
To link tasks	Link two tasks
	Link several tasks at once
	Link the milestone tasks
To document tasks	Enter a task note
To review project schedule duration	Check the project's duration

■ Knowledge Assessment

Fill in the Blank

Complete the following sentences by writing the correct word or words in the blanks provided.

1. A(n) _____ is a model of a real project—what you want to happen or what you think will happen.

2. A(n) _____ is a logical connection between tasks that controls sequence and dependency.

3. A group of closely related tasks that encompass a major section of your project is a(n) _____.

4. A(n) _____ is a scheduling tool that determines the standard working time and nonworking time for the project, resources, and tasks.

5. A(n) _____ is a pre-defined file that can be used as a starting point to create a project schedule.

6. A(n) _____ is supplemental text that you can attach to a task, resource, or assignment.

7. A(n) _____ is added to the project calendar to denote something different from the standard working times.

8. A task whose start or end date determines the start or finish of another task or tasks is a(n) _____.

9. A(n) _____ represents a significant event reached within the project or imposed upon the project.

10. A(n) _____ represents the actual individual work activities that must be done to accomplish the final goal.

True/False

Circle T if the statement is true or F if the statement is false.

T F **1.** Manual scheduling is not the default mode and creates a dynamic schedule.

T F **2.** When you initially enter tasks into Project, they are linked in a finish-to-start relationship that can be changed later.

T F **3.** The task note field can only contain words and not pictures.

T F **4.** A milestone can be imposed on the project or developed and used by the project team to track project progress.

T F **5.** An estimated duration of 3 weeks for a task would be shown as 3ew.

T F **6.** A task calendar defines working and nonworking times for an individual work resource.

T F **7.** A summary task is derived from all of the detail tasks that fall below it.

T F **8.** Once you have entered all of the tasks and durations for a project, the project duration does not change.

T F **9.** Tasks that are indented below a summary task are called successors.

T F **10.** For tasks that are linked in a finish-to-start relationship, the finish date of the predecessor task determines the start date of the successor task.

■ Competency Assessment

Project 1-1: Don Funk Scene 1 Production Tasks

Using the project schedule you previously created in this lesson, you will add several tasks and their durations under a summary task.

GET READY. Launch Microsoft Project if it is not already running.

OPEN *Don Funk Music Video 1-1* from the data files for this lesson.

1. Click the name of task 14, Production complete. Drag your cursor downward so that 5 rows are highlighted, including the row for task 14.
2. On the ribbon, in the Insert group, click Task.
3. Click the blank Task Name field for task 14. Starting in this field, enter the following tasks and durations:

Task	Duration
Scene 1 setup	2d
Scene 1 rehearsal	6h
Scene 1 vocal recording	1d
Scene 1 video shoot	2d
Scene 1 teardown	1d

4. SAVE the project as *Don Funk Scene 1* in the solutions folder for this lesson and then CLOSE the file.

   LEAVE Project open for the next exercise.

Project 1-2: New Employee Orientation

Add a note and hyperlink to a project schedule as reminders of information to be given to new employees.

GET READY. Launch Microsoft Project if it is not already running.

OPEN *New Employee 1-2* from the data files for this lesson.

1. Double-click the name of task 9, Take picture for employee ID.
2. In the Task Information dialog box, on the Notes tab, key Remember to use blue backdrop for digital pics.
3. Click OK.
4. Double-click the name of task 22, Complete health insurance paperwork.
5. In the Task Information dialog box, key the note, Verify all insurance needs and any other insurance carriers.
6. Click OK.
7. SAVE the project schedule as *New Employee Orientation* in the solutions folder for this lesson and then CLOSE the file.

   LEAVE Project open for the next exercise.

■ Proficiency Assessment

Project 1-3: Hiring a New Employee

You need to create a project schedule for the process of hiring a new employee for your department.

OPEN a new blank project schedule.

1. Set the project start date to be October 19, 2015.
2. Enter the following tasks and durations:

Task	Duration
Write job description	2d
Notify departmental recruiter	1d
Post job internally	5d
Post job externally	5d
Collect resumes	10d
Review resumes	5d
Set up interviews	3d
Conduct interviews	8d
Select candidate	1d
Make offer	milestone

3. Assign a finish-to-start relationship to all the tasks.
4. Change the dependency between tasks 3 and 4 to a start-to-start relationship.
5. Change all tasks to the Auto Schedule mode.
5. Use the Statistics button on the Project Information dialog box to determine the current project duration.
6. SAVE the project schedule in the solutions folder for this lesson as *Hiring Employee xxd* where the xx in the file name is the duration (in days) of the project. (For example, if the project is 13 days long, save the file as *Hiring Employee 13d*.) CLOSE the file.

   LEAVE Project open for the next exercise.

Project 1-4: Don Funk Video: New Task Dependencies

After reviewing your project schedule, you have determined that some of the tasks could be linked in a different way to make your project more efficient.

 OPEN *Don Funk Music Video 1-4* from the data files for this lesson.

1. Change tasks 9 and 10 so that they have a start-to-start relationship.
2. Change tasks 7 and 8 so that they have a start-to-start relationship.
3. Adjust the chart area of your screen so that the Gantt bars for these new relationships are visible.
4. SAVE the project schedule as *Don Funk Revised Links* in the solutions folder for this lesson and then CLOSE the file.

   LEAVE Project open to use in the next exercise.

■ Mastery Assessment

Project 1-5: Setting Up a Home Office

You are ordering equipment and setting up a home office and need to create a schedule to minimize the amount of time it takes to do this.

OPEN *Home Office 1-5* from the data files for this lesson.

1. Convert all tasks to Auto Schedule.
2. Set tasks 6, 9, 10, and 14 as milestones.
3. Assign a start-to-start relationship for tasks 1, 2, and 3.
4. Assign a finish-to-start relationship for tasks 1 and 6, 3 and 9, and 2 and 10.
5. Assign a finish-to-start relationship for tasks 4, 5, 7, and 8.
6. Assign a finish-to-start relationship for tasks 10 through 14.
7. SAVE the project schedule as *Home Office* in the solutions folder for this lesson and then CLOSE the file.

   LEAVE Project open for the next exercise.

Project 1-6: Don Funk All Scenes Production

You need to enter and organize the tasks for producing three scenes in the Don Funk music video.

OPEN *Don Funk Music Video 1-6* from the data files for this lesson.

1. Insert a new row after task 13. Name this new task Scene 1.
2. Add a milestone to begin the scene (Scene 1 begin) and a milestone to end the scene (Scene 1 complete).
3. Indent tasks 15 through 21 under the Scene 1 summary task you just created.
4. Add two more sets of summary and subtasks (including durations) for Scenes 2 and 3 under the Production summary task. They will be identical to the Scene 1 tasks and durations except for the scene number.
5. Assign the subtasks for Scenes 1, 2 and 3 finish-to-start relationships.
6. Assign a finish-to-start relationship between the Scene 1 complete milestone and the Scene 2 begin milestone. Assign a finish-to-start relationship between the Scene 2 complete milestone and the Scene 3 begin milestone.
7. Link the Scene 3 complete milestone and the Production complete milestone with a finish-to-start dependency.
8. Link the Production complete milestone and the Post-Production begins milestone with a finish-to-start dependency.
9. SAVE the project schedule as *Don Funk 3 Scenes* in the solutions folder for this lesson and then CLOSE the file.

   CLOSE Project.

Establishing Resources

LESSON SKILL MATRIX

Skills	Tasks
Establishing People Resources	Establish individual people resources
	Establish a resource that represents multiple people
Establishing Equipment Resources	Establish equipment resources
Establishing Material Resources	Establish material resources
Establishing Cost Resources	Establish cost resources
Establishing Resource Pay Rates	Enter resource cost information
Adjusting Resource Working Times	Establish nonworking times for an individual work resource
	Establish a specific work schedule for a resource
Adding Resource Notes	Attach a note to a resource

Now that Southridge Video has laid out the initial project schedule for Don Funk's latest music video, the next step for the video production manager is to identify the people, equipment, and materials needed to complete the tasks in this project. He must also determine when these resources are available, how much work they can do, and their cost. One of the most powerful tools in Microsoft Project 2013 is the ability to manage resources effectively. In this lesson, you will learn how to set up basic resource information for people, equipment, and materials; how to set up cost information for a resource; and how to change a resource's availability for work.

KEY TERMS

availability
base calendar
cost
cost resource
material resource
maximum units
resource calendar
resources
work resource

© joebrandt/iStockphoto

■ Software Orientation

Microsoft Project's Resource Sheet View

You have several views available when working in Microsoft Project. One view you will use in this lesson is the Resource Sheet view, as shown in Figure 2-1.

Figure 2-1

Resource sheet view

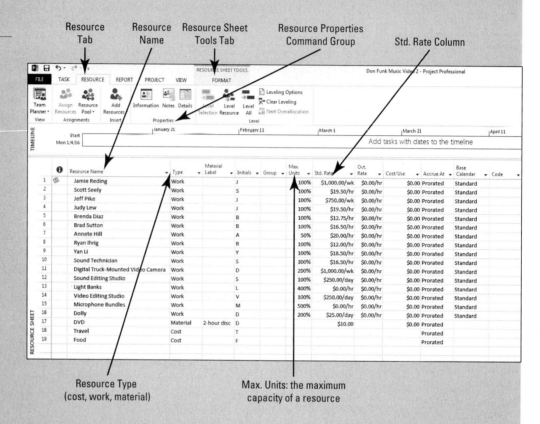

Resource Tab · Resource Name · Resource Sheet Tools Tab · Resource Properties Command Group · Std. Rate Column

Resource Type (cost, work, material) · Max. Units: the maximum capacity of a resource

In this lesson, you will be working on establishing your project ***resources*** – which are the people, equipment, materials, and money used to complete the tasks in a project. Some of the features you will use in this lesson are shown on this screen. Your screen may be different if default settings have been changed or if other preferences have been set. Use this figure as a reference for this lesson.

■ Establishing People Resources

THE BOTTOM LINE

When you set up people resources in Microsoft Project, you are able to track who is available to work, the type of work they can do, and when they are available to do it. In this section, you learn how to establish and enter people resources in Project 2013.

Establishing Individual People Resources

People resources can be in the form of individuals, individuals identified by their job function or title, or groups of individuals with a common skill. In this exercise, you practice setting up resource information for the individual people who will perform the tasks on the project.

ESTABLISH INDIVIDUAL PEOPLE RESOURCES

GET READY. Before you begin these steps, launch Microsoft Project, and **OPEN** *Don Funk Music Video 2M* from the data files for this lesson.

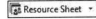

1. Click the **View** tab, then in the Resource Views group, select **Resource Sheet** to open the Resource Sheet view.

ANOTHER WAY — If your resource information for your own project exists on your network, such as in a Microsoft Outlook address book, you can quickly import the resource information into Microsoft Project. This saves the time and effort of retyping the information and reduces the possibility of data entry errors.

2. In the Resource Sheet view, click the **empty cell** directly below the Resource Name column heading.
3. Type **Jamie Reding** and press **Enter**. Microsoft Project adds Jamie Reding as a work resource and automatically enters additional, default information. Your screen should look similar to Figure 2-2.

Figure 2-2

Resource Sheet with newly entered resource

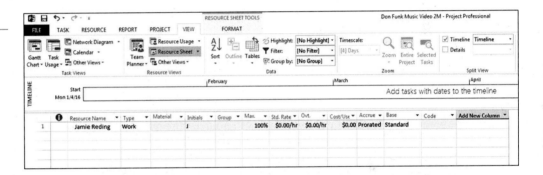

4. Enter the remaining resource names into the Simple Resource Sheet. Enter the first column of names (Scott Seely, Jeff Pike, etc.), then the second column.

Scott Seely	Brad Sutton
Jeff Pike	Annette Hill
Judy Lew	Ryan Ihrig
Brenda Diaz	Yan Li

Your screen should look similar to Figure 2-3.

Figure 2-3

Resource Sheet with resources added

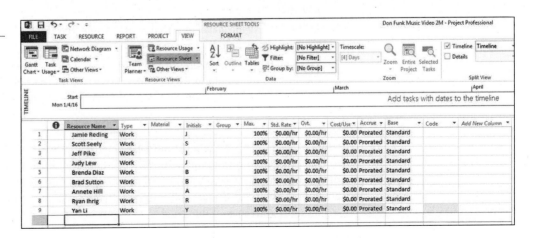

5. SAVE the file as *Don Funk Music Video 2.*

   PAUSE. LEAVE the project schedule open to use in the next exercise.

You are beginning to set up some of the basic resource information for the people who will work on this project. As you are entering this information, keep in mind two important aspects of resources: availability and cost. *Availability* determines when and how much of a resource's time can be assigned to work on tasks. *Cost* refers to how much money will be needed to pay for the resources on a project. Although setting up resource information in Microsoft Project may take a little extra time and effort, entering this information will provide you with more control over your project.

You will work with three types of resources in Microsoft Project: work resources, material resources, and cost resources. *Work resources* are the people and equipment that do work to accomplish the tasks of the project. Work resources use time to accomplish tasks. You will learn about material resources and cost resources later in this lesson. Work resources can be in many different forms:

WORK RESOURCE	EXAMPLE
Individual people	Yan Li; Jeff Pike
Individual people identified by job title or function	editor; camera person
Groups of people with a common skill	sound technician; dancer
Equipment	keyboard; digital recorder

When establishing your resources, use resource names that will make sense to you and anyone else using the project schedule.

Establishing a Group Resource

In the previous exercise, you set up resources that were individuals. Now, you will set up a single resource that represents multiple people, sometimes called a Generic Resource.

ESTABLISH A RESOURCE THAT REPRESENTS MULTIPLE PEOPLE

USE the project schedule you saved in the previous exercise.

1. Click the blank Resource Name field below the last resource, type Sound Technician and then press Tab.

2. In the Type field, make sure that Work is selected. Press Tab four times to move to the Max. Units field.

   You may only see a portion of the field name. To see the entire field name, expand the row just as you would in Excel. Place the cursor on the bottom of the header row in the ID column (just above resource 1). Click and drag the row down.

TAKE NOTE*

Maximum Units refers to the maximum capacity of a resource to accomplish tasks. The default value for maximum units is 100%. For example, specifying that a resource has 75% maximum units means that 75 percent of the resource's time is available to work on tasks assigned to it. Microsoft Project will warn you if you assign a resource to more tasks than it can accomplish at its maximum units.

3. In the Max. Units field for the sound technician, type or select 300%, to indicate that you will have three sound technicians devoting 100% of their working time to this project, and then press Enter.

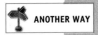

ANOTHER WAY When you tab into or click a numeric field, up and down arrows appear in the field. You can simply click these arrows to scroll to the number you want displayed.

4. Click the Max. Units field for Annette Hill, type or select 50% and then press Enter. This represents that she is only available part time on this project. Your screen should look similar to Figure 2-4.

Figure 2-4

Resource Sheet with a part-time resource and a group resource

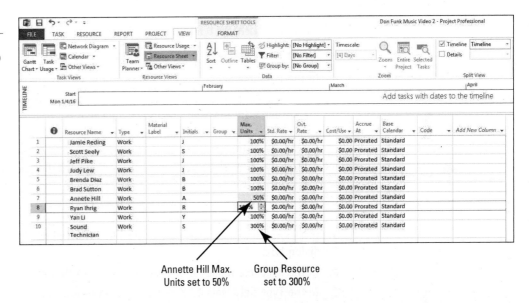

Annette Hill Max. Units set to 50%

Group Resource set to 300%

ANOTHER WAY You can also enter maximum units as a decimal rather than a percentage. To change to this format, click **File** on the ribbon, then **Options**, and then click the **Schedule** option. In the *Show assignment units as a* box, select **Decimal**.

5. SAVE the project schedule.

PAUSE. LEAVE the project schedule open to use in the next exercise.

In this exercise, you established a group resource. The resource named Sound Technician does not represent a single person. It actually represents a group of people called sound technicians. By setting the Max. Units for this resource at 300%, you are indicating that three sound technicians will be available to work full time on every workday. You might not know specifically who the sound technicians will be at this point, but you can still proceed with more planning. Keep in mind if you use a group resource, a single resource calendar will be assigned to that resource name. Therefore, it is beneficial to have all of the people represented by the resource name work the same hours.

■ Establishing Equipment Resources

THE BOTTOM LINE	Setting up equipment resources in Microsoft Project is very similar to setting up people resources. There are key differences, however, in the way equipment resources can be scheduled.

Establishing Equipment Resources

You don't need to track every piece of equipment that will be used in your project. It will be helpful, though, to track equipment resources when you need to schedule and track equipment costs or when the equipment might be needed my multiple people at the same time. In this exercise, you learn how to establish the equipment resources for your project.

⊕ ESTABLISH EQUIPMENT RESOURCES

USE the project schedule you created in the previous exercise.

Information

1. In the Resource Sheet, click the next **empty cell** in the Resource Name column.
2. Click the **Resource** tab and then click the **Information** button in the Properties group; the Resource Information dialog box appears.

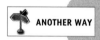

ANOTHER WAY	You can also activate the Resource Information dialog box by double-clicking a resource name or an empty cell in the Resource Name column.

3. If it is not already displayed, click the **General** tab in the Resource Information dialog box.
4. In the Resource Name field, type **Digital Truck-Mounted Video Camera**.
5. In the Type field, select **Work** from the drop-down menu. Your screen should look similar to Figure 2-5. Notice that the Resource Information dialog box contains many of the same fields as the Resource Sheet.

Figure 2-5

Resource Information dialog box with newly added resource

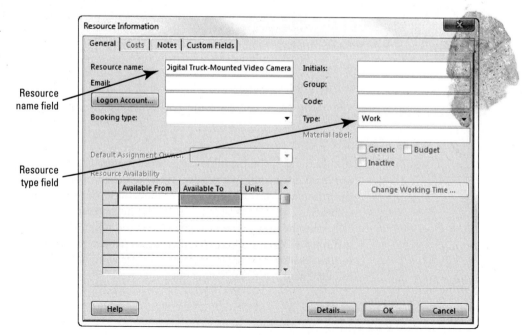

6. Click **OK**. The Resource Information dialog box closes and the resource has been added. Notice that Microsoft Project has automatically wrapped the text in the Resource Name field. Note that the Max. Units field is set to the default of 100%.

7. In the Max. Units field for the Digital Truck-Mounted Video Camera, type **200** or press the arrows until the value shown is 200%, and then press **Enter**. This indicates that you will have two truck cameras available every workday.

8. Add the following additional equipment resources to the project schedule. You can use the Resource Information dialog box to enter your information, but entering it directly in Resource Sheet view is faster. Make sure that **Work** is selected in the Type field for each resource.

Resource Name	Max. Units
Sound Editing Studio	100%
Light Banks	400%
Video Editing Studio	100%
Microphone Bundles	500%
Dolly	200%

Your screen should look similar to Figure 2-6.

Figure 2-6

Resource Sheet showing equipment resources added

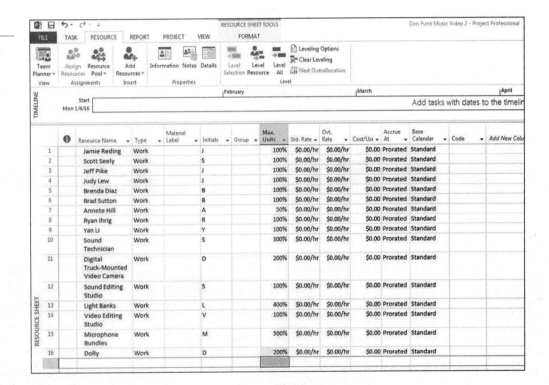

9. **SAVE** the project schedule.

PAUSE. LEAVE the project schedule open to use in the next exercise.

There's an important difference between scheduling equipment resources and scheduling people resources. Equipment resources tend to be more specialized than people resources. For example, a microphone can't be used as a video recorder, but an audio technician might be able to fill in as an "extra" in a video shoot. Also, some equipment resources might work 24 hours a day, but most people resources don't work more than 8 or 12 hours a day.

■ Establishing Material Resources

THE BOTTOM LINE

Just as you established people and equipment resources in your project schedule, you can also set up material resources in Microsoft Project to track the rate of use of the particular resource and its related cost. Depending on the depth of your planning, Microsoft Project can provide an accurate Bill of Material (BOM) for your project's material resources.

Establishing Material Resources

Material resources are consumable items used up as the tasks in a project are completed. Unlike work resources (including human resources and equipment resources), material resources have no effect on the total amount of work scheduled to be performed on a task. For your music video project, DVDs are the consumable that interests you most. In this exercise, you practice entering material resources for your project.

⊕ ESTABLISH MATERIAL RESOURCES

USE the project schedule you created in the previous exercise.

1. In the Resource Sheet, click the next **empty cell** in the Resource Name column.
2. Type **DVD** and press **Tab**.
3. In the Type field, click the **arrow** and select **Material**, then press **Tab**. Notice that some of the fields (columns), such as Max. Units, Ovt. Rate and Calendar, are not available when you change to a material type resource.
4. In the Material Label field, type **2-hour disc** and press **Enter**. This means you will use 2-hour discs as the unit of measure to track consumption during the project. Your screen should look similar to Figure 2-7.

Figure 2-7

Material resource added to resource sheet

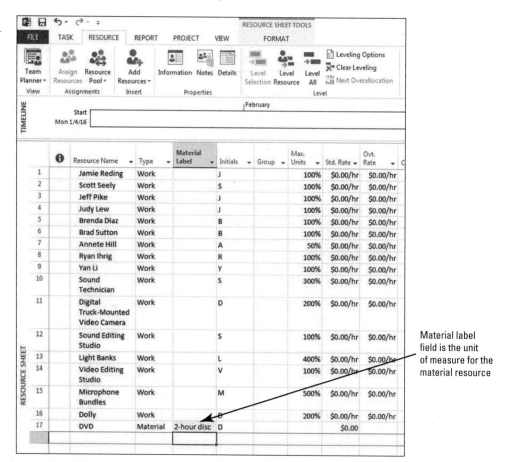

5. SAVE the project schedule.

   PAUSE. LEAVE the project schedule open to use in the next exercise.

In this exercise you entered a material resource. Depending on the project management approach of your organization, you may or may not be required to track project material resources. Bear in mind that if the project requires material and these are not entered into the software, the final cost, as calculated by the software, will not be a true reflection of the project estimate.

■ Establishing Cost Resources

THE BOTTOM LINE

Cost resources are financial obligations to your project. A cost resource enables you to apply a cost to a task by assigning a cost item (such as travel) to that task. The cost resource has no relationship to the work assigned to the task, but assigning cost resources gives you more control when applying various types of costs to tasks within your project.

Establishing Cost Resources

A *cost resource* is a resource that doesn't depend on the amount of work on a task or the duration of a task. Unlike fixed costs, you can apply as many cost resources to a task as necessary. In this exercise, you add cost resources to the resource sheet for your project.

⊘ ESTABLISH COST RESOURCES

USE the project schedule you created in the previous exercise.

1. In the Resource Sheet, click the next empty cell in the Resource Name column.
2. Type Travel and then press Tab.
3. In the Type field, click the arrow and select Cost. The travel resource has now been established as a cost resource. Just as with a material resource, some fields are not available with a cost resource.
4. In the blank Resource Name field below Travel, type Food and press Tab.
5. In the Type field, select Cost and press Enter. Your screen should look like Figure 2-8.

Figure 2-8

Resource Sheet view with cost resources added

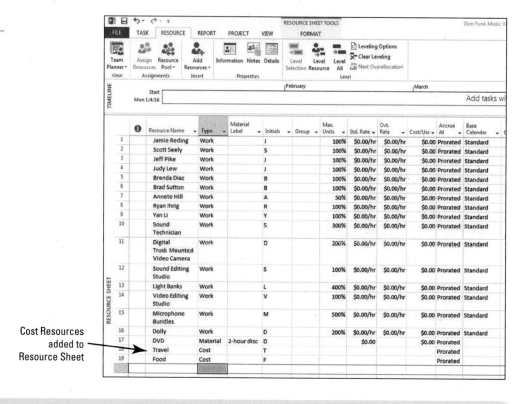

Cost Resources added to Resource Sheet ⟶

> **TAKE NOTE** *
>
> Cost resources differ from fixed costs in that cost resources are created as a type of resource and then assigned to a task. Also, unlike work resources, cost resources cannot have a calendar applied to them and therefore do not affect the scheduling of the task. The dollar value of cost resources doesn't depend on the amount of work done on the task to which they are assigned.

6. **SAVE** the project schedule.

  PAUSE. LEAVE the project schedule open to use in the next exercise.

■ Establishing Resource Pay Rates

> **↓ THE BOTTOM LINE**
>
> Although you might not track costs on small or personal projects, managing cost information is a key part of most project managers' job descriptions. When you enter the cost information for resources, tracking the finances of a project becomes a more manageable task.

Entering Resource Cost Information

> Knowing resource cost information will help you take full advantage of the cost management features of Microsoft Project. In this exercise, you practice entering cost information for both work and material resources.

⊙ **ENTER RESOURCE COST INFORMATION**

USE the project schedule you created in the previous exercise.

1. In the Resource Sheet, click the **Std.** (Standard) **Rate** field for resource 1, Jamie Reding.

2. Type **1000/w** and press **Enter**. Jamie's standard weekly rate of $1,000 per week appears in the Std. rate column.

3. In the Std. Rate column for resource 2, Scott Seely, type **19.50/h** and press **Enter**. Scott's standard hourly rate of $19.50 appears in the Std. Rate column.

4. Widen the **Std. Rate** column by moving the mouse pointer to the vertical divider line between the Std. Rate column and Ovt. Rate column. Double-click the **divider line**. This is called "auto-fitting". Your screen should look similar to Figure 2-9.

Figure 2-9

Resource Sheet with the standard rate for first two resources entered.

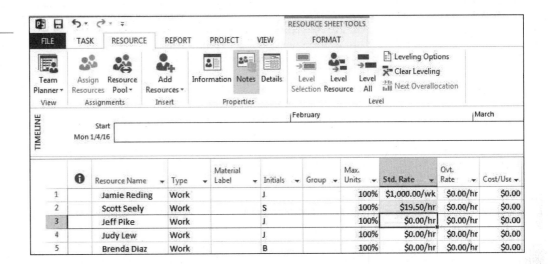

5. Enter the following standard pay rates for the remaining resources:

Resource Name	Standard Rate
Jeff Pike	750/w
Judy Lew	19.50/h
Brenda Diaz	12.75/h
Brad Sutton	16.50/h
Annette Hill	20.00/h
Ryan Ihrig	12.00/h
Yan Li	18.50/h
Sound Technician	16.50/h
Digital Truck-Mounted Video Camera	1000/w
Sound Editing Studio	250/d
Light Banks	0/h
Video Editing Studio	250/d
Microphone Bundles	0/h
Dolly	25/d
DVD	10

6. Your screen should look similar to Figure 2-10.

Figure 2-10

Standard rates for all resources added to the Resource Sheet

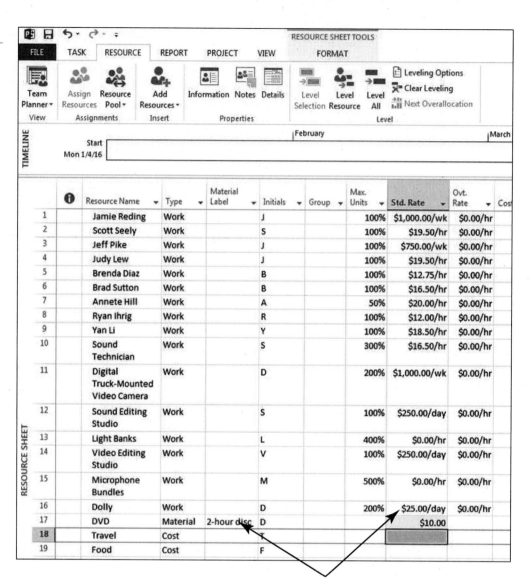

Material resource cost
will be the per unit cost listed
in the material label field

TAKE NOTE * Notice that you didn't enter a rate (weekly, hourly, or daily) for the cost of the DVD. For a material resource, the standard rate is per unit of consumption. For this exercise, that is a 2-hour DVD. Also note that you did not assign a cost to the cost resources; this is done when the cost resources are assigned to a task (covered in Lesson 3).

7. **SAVE** the project schedule.

PAUSE. LEAVE the project schedule open to use in the next exercise.

In the real world, it is often difficult to get cost information for people resources because this information is usually considered confidential. As a project manager, it is important that you are aware of the limitations of your project schedule because of the information available to you, and that you communicate these limitations to your project team and management. Some suggested methods of inserting rates costs without using actual pay rates:

- Use publicly available salary data such as from the Federal Bureau of Labor and Statistics.
- Ask for an average salary rate from the accounting department for various skill sets (e.g., electrician and administrative).

As a project manager, tracking and managing cost information may be a significant part of your project responsibilities. Understanding the cost details of your project will allow you to stay on top of such key information as

- The expected total cost of the project
- Resource costs over the life of the project
- Possible cost savings from using one resource versus another
- The rate of spending in relation to the length of the project

These and other cost limits often drive the scope of your project and may become critical to project decisions that you will make.

■ Adjusting Resource Working Times

THE BOTTOM LINE

Microsoft Project 2013 uses resource working and nonworking times to schedule the tasks. You should define these times prior to assigning them to tasks. Resource working times apply only to people and equipment (work) resources – not to material resources. Now that you have entered resources and their associated pay rates in your project schedule, you can specify the working and nonworking times for some of these resources.

Establishing Nonworking Times

When you establish work resources in your project schedule, a *resource calendar* is automatically created for each resource to define the resource's working and nonworking time. The resource calendar provides default working times for an entire project. Typically, you will need to make changes to the individual resource calendars to reflect vacation, flex-time work schedules, or conference attendance. In this exercise, you establish nonworking times for your individual work resources.

 ESTABLISH NONWORKING TIMES FOR AN INDIVIDUAL WORK RESOURCE

USE the project schedule you created in the previous exercise.

1. Click the **Project** tab, then click **Change Working Time**. The Change Working Time dialog box appears.
2. In the For Calendar box, select **Jamie Reding**. Jamie Reding's resource calendar appears in the Change Working Time dialog box.
3. Slide the button next to the calendar until the calendar is on January, 2016.
4. Select the dates January **28** and **29**.
5. In the first Name field under the Exceptions tab, type **Vacation Days**.
6. Press **Enter**. The Start field displays 1/28/2016 and the Finish field displays 1/29/2016. Microsoft Project will not schedule Jamie Reding to work on these two days. Your screen should look similar to Figure 2-11.

Figure 2-11

Change Working Time dialog
box showing the exception
days for Jamie Reding

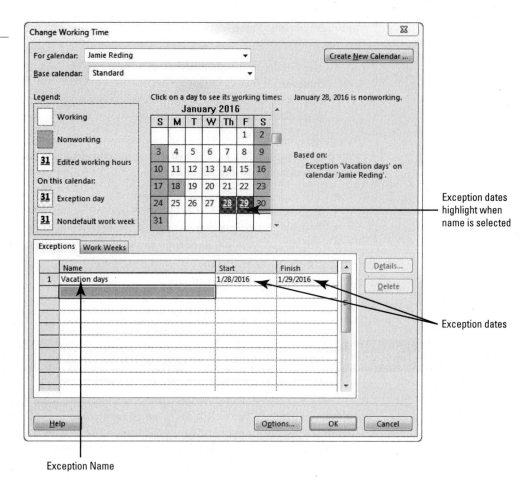

Exception dates
highlight when
name is selected

Exception dates

Exception Name

7. Click **OK** to close the Change Working Time dialog box.
8. **SAVE** the project schedule.

    PAUSE. LEAVE the project schedule open to use in the next exercise.

**Cross
Ref**

Refer back to Lesson 1 for a quick refresher on the types of calendars used by
Microsoft Project.

TAKE NOTE*

Keep in mind that when you make changes to the project calendar, the changes are reflected
in all resource calendars which are based on the project calendar. However, changes you make
to the working times of an individual resource are not reflected in the project calendar.

Establishing Specific Work Schedules

In addition to specifying exception times for resources, you can also set up a specific work
schedule for any given resource. To practice establishing working times for your project's
work resources, in this exercise you make a change to the resource calendar for an individual resource.

ESTABLISH A SPECIFIC WORK SCHEDULE FOR A RESOURCE

USE the project schedule you created in the previous exercise.

Change
Working Time

1. Click the **Project** ribbon and then click **Change Working Time** to open the Change
   Working Time dialog box.

2. In the For Calendar box, select **Scott Seely**. Scott works a scheduled commonly called 4-10's, which means he works 4 days a week, 10 hours per day.

3. Click the **Work Weeks** tab, and then click the **Details** button. The Details dialog box appears.

4. In the Select day(s) box, click and drag to select **Monday** through **Thursday**.

5. Select the **radio button** next to *Set day(s) to these specific working times*.

6. On line 1 of the Working Times box, click the **8:00 AM** box and type **7:00 AM**.

7. On line 2 of the Working Times box, click the **5:00 PM** box and type **6:00 PM**.

8. Press **Enter** to set your changes. Your screen should look similar to Figure 2-12.

Figure 2-12

Details dialog box showing modified working times for Scott Seely

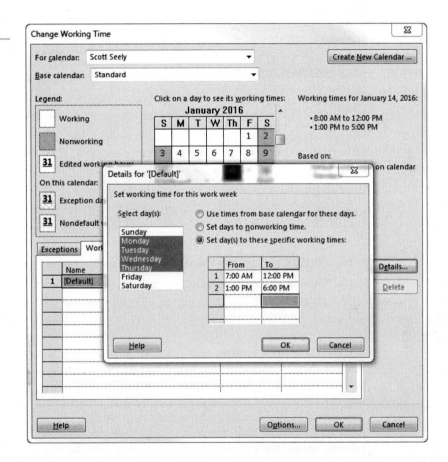

9. In the Select day(s) box, click **Friday**.

10. Select the **radio button** next to *Select Set days to nonworking time*.

11. Click **OK** to close the Details dialog box. Microsoft Project can now schedule Scott Seely to work as early as 7:00 AM and as late as 6:00 PM on Monday through Thursday, but it will not schedule him to work on Friday.

12. Click any **Friday** in the Change Working Time dialog box. Note that these days are set to nonworking time.

13. Click any one **day of the week**, Monday – Thursday. Note the working times for these days. Your screen should look similar to Figure 2-13.

Figure 2-13

Change Working Time dialog
box showing the modified
resource calendar for Scott
Seely.

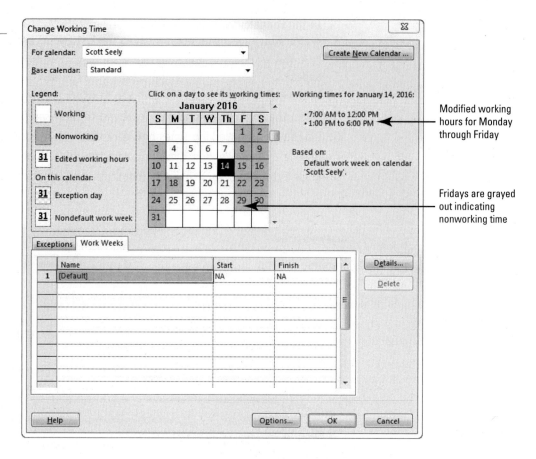

Figure 2-13

Change Working Time dialog
box showing the modified
resource calendar for Scott
Seely.

14. Click **OK** to close the Change Working Time dialog box.

15. SAVE the project schedule.

   PAUSE. LEAVE the project schedule open to use in the next exercise.

If you need to edit several resource calendars in the same way (to handle a flex-time schedule
or night shift, for example), you might find it easier to assign a different base calendar to this
group of resources. A *base calendar* can be used as a task calendar, a project calendar, or
resource calendar and specifies default working and nonworking times. Assigning a different
base calendar is quicker than editing each individual's resource calendar, and it allows you to
make future project-wide changes to a single base calendar (rather than editing each resource
calendar again). You can change a resource's base calendar by opening the Change Working
Time dialog box from the Tools menu. In the For Calendar box, select the desired resource
and then in the Base Calendar box, select the desired base calendar. For a group of resources
that will be using the same calendar, you can change the calendar directly in the Base Calendar
column of the Entry table in the Resource Sheet view. Microsoft Project includes three base
calendars: Standard, 24 Hours, and Night Shift. You can customize these or use them as a
basis for your own base calendar.

 Cross Ref   You will create a new base calendar in lesson 4.

 ANOTHER WAY   You can also change a resource's base calendar in the Resource Sheet View by clicking the
arrow in the Base Calendar field of that resource.

■ Adding Resource Notes

THE BOTTOM LINE

At times, you may want to provide the details regarding how (and why) a resource is scheduled a certain way. You can add this additional information about a resource by attaching a note.

Attaching a Note to a Resource

In this exercise, you learn how to attach a scheduling note to a resource in Project 2013.

ATTACH A NOTE TO A RESOURCE

USE the project schedule you created in the previous exercise. Make sure you are still in the Resource Sheet view of the ***Don Funk Music Video 2*** file.

Notes

1. In the Resource Name column, select the name of the resource 1, Jamie Reding.
2. On the ribbon, click the Resource tab, then click the Resource Notes button in the Properties command group on the ribbon. The Resource Information dialog box is displayed with the Notes tab visible.
3. In the Notes box, type Jamie on vacation Jan 28 and 29; available for consult at home if necessary and click OK. A note icon appears in the indicator column.
4. Point to the note icon in the Resource sheet. The note appears in a ScreenTip (double-click the icon to display the full text of longer notes). Your screen should look similar to Figure 2-14.

Figure 2-14

Resource note displayed as a ScreenTip.

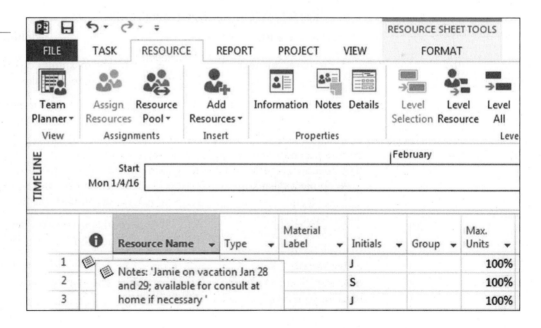

5. SAVE the project schedule.
6. CLOSE the ***Don Funk Music Video 2*** file.

   PAUSE. If you are continuing to the next lesson, keep Project open. If not continuing to additional lessons, CLOSE Project.

SKILL SUMMARY

In this lesson you learned:	Matrix Skill
To establish people resources	Establish individual people resources
	Establish a resource that represents multiple people
To establish equipment resources	Establish equipment resources
To establish material resources	Establish material resources
To establish cost resources	Establish cost resources
To establish resource pay rates	Enter resource cost information
To adjust resource working times	Establish nonworking times for an individual work resource
	Establish a specific work schedule for a resource
To add resource notes	Attach a note to a resource

■ Knowledge Assessment

Matching

Match the term in column 1 to its description in column 2.

Column 1	Column 2
1. resource calendar	a. the maximum capacity of a resource to accomplish tasks
2. Max. Units	b. specifies default working and nonworking times for a resource, a project, or a task
3. material resource	c. when and how much of a resource's time can be assigned to work on tasks
4. project calendar	d. the people and equipment that do work to accomplish the tasks of the project
5. cost resource	e. the people, equipment, money, and materials used to complete the tasks in a project
6. work resource	f. a way of documenting information about resources, tasks, and assignments
7. base calendar	g. consumable items used up as the tasks in a project are accomplished
8. availability	h. a resource that doesn't depend on the amount of work on a task or the duration of a task
9. resources	i. the base calendar that provides default working times for an entire project
10. note	j. defines the working and nonworking time for an individual resource

Multiple Choice

Select the best response for the following statements.

1. Which of the following is NOT an example of a work resource?

    a. Yan Li

    b. keyboard

    c. DVD Disc

    d. electrician

2. It is helpful to assign a base calendar to a group of resources when they all

    a. have the same pay rate.

    b. work night shift.

    c. have the same Max. units.

    d. do the same job function.

3. A resource calendar does not apply to

    a. material resources.

    b. people resources.

    c. equipment resources.

    d. work resources.

4. You can view information for the individual people who will perform the tasks on the project in the

    a. Calendar view.

    b. Gantt Chart view.

    c. Task Usage view.

    d. Resource Sheet view.

5. You can provide additional information about how a resource is scheduled by

    a. changing the Max. Units.

    b. establishing a project calendar.

    c. adding a resource note.

    d. setting constraints.

6. For which resource is the standard rate listed per tracking unit of consumption?

    a. material

    b. equipment

    c. people

    d. all of the above

7. If you have four electricians who can each work part-time (4 hours rather than 8), what value should you assign to Max. Units for the resource "electrician"?

    a. 50%

    b. 25%

    c. 100%

    d. 200%

8. If you assign a resource to more tasks than it can accomplish at its maximum units, the resource is

    a. maxed out.

    b. over-allocated.

    c. constrained.

    d. in default.

3. In the Task Name column of the Gantt Chart view, click the name of task 3, Review screenplay.

4. In the Resource Name column of the Assign Resources dialog box, scroll down and click Scott Seely and then click the Assign button. In the Assign Resource dialog box, a check appears next to Scott Seely's name, indicating that you have assigned him to the task of reviewing the screenplay. Your screen should look similar to Figure 3-4.

Figure 3-4

Gantt Chart showing Scott Seely assigned

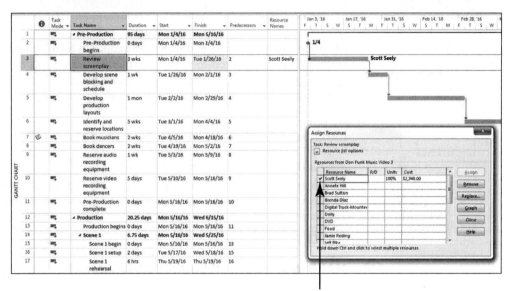

Checkmark indicates resources assigned to this task

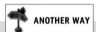

ANOTHER WAY

You can also assign resources via the Resources tab on the Task Information dialog box. To access this dialog box, double click on the task you want to assign resources.

5. In the Task Name column, click the name of task 5, Develop production layouts.

6. In the Assign Resources dialog box, click Jeff Pike and then click the Assign button. A check appears next to Jeff's name to show that you have assigned him to task 5.

7. SAVE the project schedule.

PAUSE. LEAVE the project schedule open to use in the next exercise.

Assigning Multiple Resources Simultaneously

You have just assigned one resource to a task. In this exercise, you will practice assigning multiple resources simultaneously to a task.

⊕ ASSIGN MULTIPLE RESOURCES SIMULTANEOUSLY

USE the project schedule you created in the previous exercise.

1. In the Task Name column, click the name of task 4, Develop scene blocking and schedule.

2. In the Assign Resources dialog box, scroll down and click the name cell for Scott Seely. Scroll up or down in the list until the name Judy Lew is visible. Hold down Ctrl, then click the name cell for Judy Lew.

3. Release the Ctrl key and then click the Assign button. Check marks appear next to the names of Scott Seely and Judy Lew, indicating you have assigned them both to task 4.

4. Close the Assign Resources dialog box.

TAKE NOTE*

Resources are sorted alphabetically in the Assign Resources dialog box. Once the resource has been assigned, it is moved to the top of the list.

Multiple Choice

Select the best response for the following statements.

1. Which of the following is NOT an example of a work resource?

    a. Yan Li

    b. keyboard

    c. DVD Disc

    d. electrician

2. It is helpful to assign a base calendar to a group of resources when they all

    a. have the same pay rate.

    b. work night shift.

    c. have the same Max. units.

    d. do the same job function.

3. A resource calendar does not apply to

    a. material resources.

    b. people resources.

    c. equipment resources.

    d. work resources.

4. You can view information for the individual people who will perform the tasks on the project in the

    a. Calendar view.

    b. Gantt Chart view.

    c. Task Usage view.

    d. Resource Sheet view.

5. You can provide additional information about how a resource is scheduled by

    a. changing the Max. Units.

    b. establishing a project calendar.

    c. adding a resource note.

    d. setting constraints.

6. For which resource is the standard rate listed per tracking unit of consumption?

    a. material

    b. equipment

    c. people

    d. all of the above

7. If you have four electricians who can each work part-time (4 hours rather than 8), what value should you assign to Max. Units for the resource "electrician"?

    a. 50%

    b. 25%

    c. 100%

    d. 200%

8. If you assign a resource to more tasks than it can accomplish at its maximum units, the resource is

    a. maxed out.

    b. over-allocated.

    c. constrained.

    d. in default.

9. To add vacation days to the calendar for an individual work resource, which dialog box would you use?

   a. Resource Information

   b. Resource Notes

   c. Change Working Time

   d. none of the above

10. It is often difficult to get cost information for people resources because

    a. the information is often confidential.

    b. the information is too complex to calculate.

    c. the information changes too frequently.

    d. the costs are large in comparison with other resource costs.

■ Competency Assessment

Project 2-1: Hiring a New Employee

In the previous lesson, you entered the tasks of a project schedule for hiring a new employee. Now you need to add some of the people resources that will be responsible for performing those tasks.

GET READY. Launch Microsoft Project if it is not already running.

OPEN *Hiring New Employee 2-1* from the data files for this lesson.

1. Click the View tab, then in the Resource Views group, select Resource Sheet.

2. In the Resource Sheet view, click the empty cell directly below the Resource Name column heading.

3. Enter the following resource names into the Simple Resource Sheet.

   Gabe Mares

   Barry Potter

   Amy Rusko

   Jeff Smith

4. SAVE the project as *Hire New Employee* and then CLOSE the file.

   LEAVE Project open for the next exercise.

Project 2-2: Office Remodel

You are in charge of the remodeling project for the kitchen and lunchroom for your office. Your facilities manager has just provided you with the resource pay rates for this project. You need to enter the pay rates in the project schedule.

OPEN *Office Remodel 2-2* from the data files for this lesson.

1. Select the Resource Sheet view.

2. For the drywall resource, click the Type field drop-down arrow and select Material, then press Tab. For the nails resource, click the Type field drop-down arrow and select Material, then press Tab.

3. In the Resource Sheet, click the Std. Rate field for resource 1, Toby Nixon.

4. Type 500/w and press Enter.

5. Enter the following standard pay rates for the remaining resources.

Resource Name	Standard Rate
Lori Kane	500/w
Run Liu	20/h
electrician	30/h
plumber	30/h
drywall	11
nails	5
John Emory	450/w
scaffolding	50/d
table saw	35/d

6. SAVE the project as *Remodel-2* and then CLOSE the file.

   LEAVE Project open for the next exercise.

■ Proficiency Assessment

Project 2-3: Resource Note for Hiring New Employee

You have created a project schedule for hiring a new employee. Now you need to add a note to one of the resources on the project.

 OPEN *Hiring Empl–Note 2-3* from the data files for this lesson.

1. Select the name of resource 3, Amy Rusko.
2. On the Resource ribbon, click the Resource Notes button in the Properties command group.
3. Add the following note: Amy will be at the SHRM conference on November 24-26. Not available for any interviews.
4. Close the Resource Information box.
5. Select the name of resource 4, Jeff Smith.
6. Click the Resource Notes button.
7. Add the following note: Jeff will be at the SHRM conference on November 25-26. Available for interviews on November 27.
8. Close the Resource Information box.
9. SAVE the project schedule as *Hiring Employee Note* and then CLOSE the file.

   LEAVE Project open for the next exercise.

Project 2-4: Equipment Resources for New Employee Orientation

You have already developed a project schedule for a New Employee Orientation in your department. Now you need to add several equipment resources to make sure that your schedule flows smoothly.

 OPEN *Employee Orientation 2-4* from the data files for this lesson.

1. Change the view to Resource Sheet.

    2. Add the following equipment resources to the project schedule.

Resource Name	Max. Units
DVD/TV Combo	100%
Digital Camera	50%
Laminating Machine	50%
Laptop Computer	600%
Large Conference Room	100%

    3. SAVE the project schedule as *Employee Orientation Resources* and then CLOSE the file.

       LEAVE Project open for the next exercise.

■ Mastery Assessment

Project 2-5: Change Work Times for a Resource on Office Remodel

You have just been told that one of your resources on your office remodel project is planning to take a week of vacation. You need to add this information to your project schedule.

 OPEN *Office Remodel 2-5* from the data files for this lesson.

    1. Open the Change Working Time dialog box.

    2. Change Lori Kane's resource calendar to reflect her vacation from October 19-23, 2015.

    3. SAVE the project schedule as *Office Remodel Vacation* and then CLOSE the file.

       LEAVE Project open to use in the next exercise.

Project 2-6: Don Funk Music Video Problems

A student who is interning with your company made some updates to the music video project schedule. Unfortunately, he is still learning about Microsoft Project and has entered some information incorrectly. You need to correct the problems with the project schedule before distributing it to your team.

 OPEN *Don Funk Incorrect 2-6* from the data files for this lesson.

    1. Review the Resource Sheet for this project schedule.

    2. Based on what you have learned in this lesson about Resource Types, Maximum Units, and Standard Rates, find the resource errors in this project schedule and make corrections to them. (*Hint:* There are three resource errors in the project schedule.)

    3. Study the last three resources on the sheet. If dry ice is a work resource and bottled water is a cost resource, make corrections to the information given for these resources (estimate the rate if necessary).

    4. SAVE the project schedule as *Don Funk Corrected* and then CLOSE the file.

       CLOSE Project.

Resource and Task Assignments

LESSON SKILL MATRIX

SKILLS	TASKS
Assigning Work Resources to Tasks	Make individual resource assignments
	Assign multiple resources simultaneously
Adding More Work Resource Assignments to Tasks	Add work resources to a task
	Add work resources to an effort-driven task
	Use the Actions tag to change Project's scheduling behavior
Assigning Material Resources to Tasks	Assign a material resource to a task
Assigning Cost Resources to Tasks	Assign a cost resource to a task

As the video production manager at Southridge Video, you are working on a new music video for Don Funk, an up-and-coming singer/songwriter. You first mapped out the initial tasks in the project, then identified the resources needed to complete the tasks in the project. Now you need to put the two together. When you make assignments (link resources and tasks), Microsoft Project 2013 can provide several key pieces of information including: who is working on what tasks and when; if the resources are available when you need them to be, or are over-allocated; and more. In this lesson, you will learn how to assign work, material, and cost resources to a task and how to use the Actions tag to affect Project's scheduling behavior.

KEY TERMS

actions tag
assignment
duration formula
effort-driven
scheduling
units
work
work formula

© alexskopje/iStockphoto

■ SOFTWARE ORIENTATION

Microsoft Project's Assign Resources Dialog Box

In Microsoft Project, when you assign resources to a task, you can use the Assign Resources dialog box. You activate the Assign Resources dialog box via the Assign Resources button located in the Assignments group on the Resource ribbon. Your Assign Resources dialog box should look similar to Figure 3-1 or 3-2, depending upon whether the Resource List options are collapsed or expanded.

Figure 3-1

Assign Resources dialog box with Resource list options collapsed

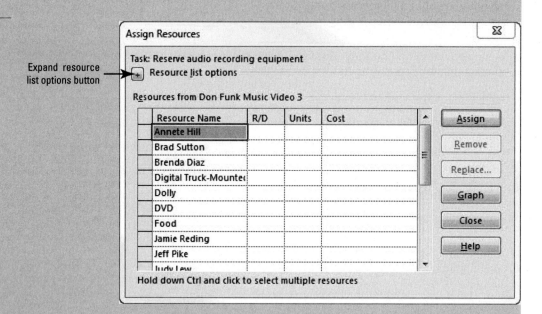

Figure 3-2

Assign Resources dialog box with Resource list options expanded

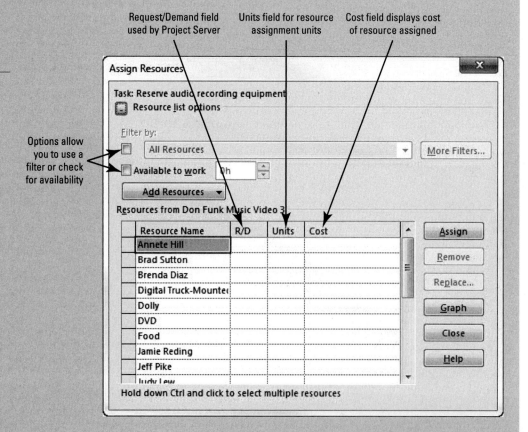

You can expand the Resource list options by clicking on the button marked with a plus sign next to Resource list options heading. You can collapse the expanded list by clicking the button, now marked with a minus sign, once again.

In this lesson you will use the Assign Resources dialog box and other methods to assign resources.

■ Assigning Work Resources to Tasks

THE BOTTOM LINE

Microsoft Project provides you with various options for assigning resources to tasks. You can assign individual resources to a task or multiple resources to a task at one time. Once assigned, you can track the resource working on the task. Microsoft Project also enables you to see whether or not resource assignments affect task duration.

Making Individual Resource Assignments

An *assignment* is the matching of a specific resource to a particular task, to either perform work or as a material or cost. Depending on your perspective, you might call it a resource assignment or you might call it a task assignment. In the previous lessons, you mapped out tasks and resources for your project schedule. In this exercise, you learn how to assign work resources to the tasks they will perform.

 MAKE INDIVIDUAL RESOURCE ASSIGNMENTS

GET READY. Before you begin these steps, launch Microsoft Project. OPEN *Don Funk Music Video 3M* from the data files for this lesson. SAVE the file as *Don Funk Music Video 3*.

1. Click the Resource tab and then click the Assign Resources button in the Assignments group. The Assign Resources dialog box appears.

2. If the Assign Resources dialog box is covering the task name column, drag the dialog box into the middle of the screen. Your screen should look similar to Figure 3-3.

Figure 3-3

Gantt Chart view with Assign Resources dialog box open

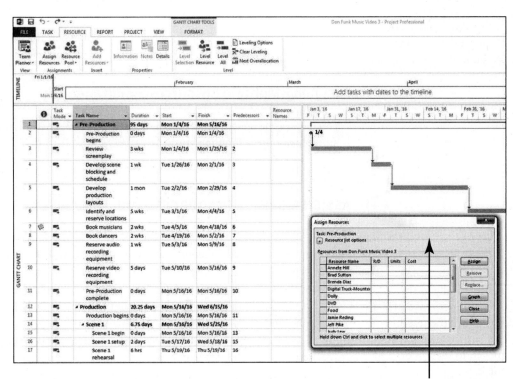

Assign Resources dialog Box

3. In the Task Name column of the Gantt Chart view, click the name of task 3, **Review screenplay**.

4. In the Resource Name column of the Assign Resources dialog box, scroll down and click **Scott Seely** and then click the **Assign** button. In the Assign Resource dialog box, a check appears next to Scott Seely's name, indicating that you have assigned him to the task of reviewing the screenplay. Your screen should look similar to Figure 3-4.

Figure 3-4

Gantt Chart showing Scott Seely assigned

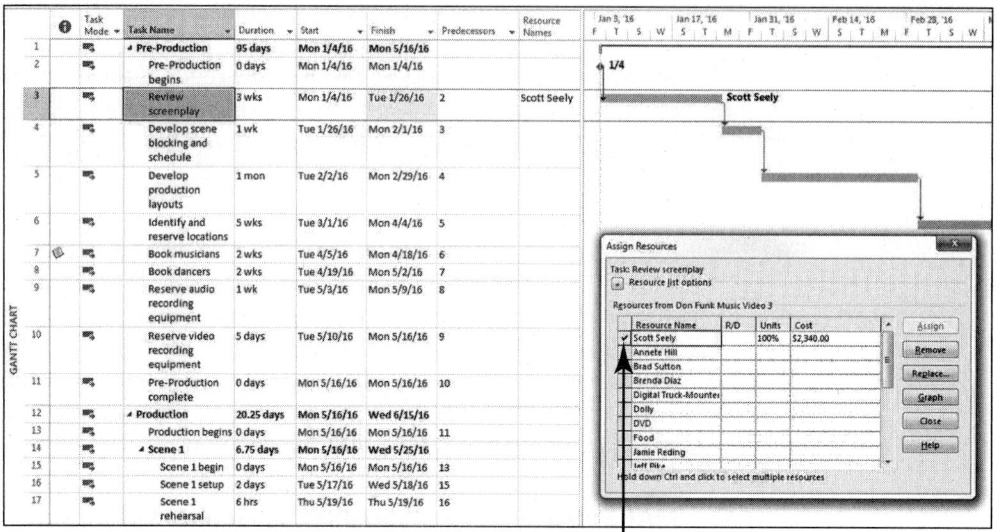

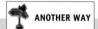

Checkmark indicates resources assigned to this task

ANOTHER WAY

You can also assign resources via the Resources tab on the Task Information dialog box. To access this dialog box, double click on the task you want to assign resources.

5. In the Task Name column, click the name of task 5, **Develop production layouts**.

6. In the Assign Resources dialog box, click **Jeff Pike** and then click the **Assign** button. A check appears next to Jeff's name to show that you have assigned him to task 5.

7. SAVE the project schedule.

PAUSE. LEAVE the project schedule open to use in the next exercise.

Assigning Multiple Resources Simultaneously

You have just assigned one resource to a task. In this exercise, you will practice assigning multiple resources simultaneously to a task.

ASSIGN MULTIPLE RESOURCES SIMULTANEOUSLY

USE the project schedule you created in the previous exercise.

1. In the Task Name column, click the name of task 4, **Develop scene blocking and schedule**.

2. In the Assign Resources dialog box, scroll down and click the name cell for **Scott Seely**. Scroll up or down in the list until the name Judy Lew is visible. Hold down **Ctrl**, then click the name cell for **Judy Lew**.

3. Release the **Ctrl** key and then click the **Assign** button. Check marks appear next to the names of Scott Seely and Judy Lew, indicating you have assigned them both to task 4.

4. Close the Assign Resources dialog box.

TAKE NOTE*

Resources are sorted alphabetically in the Assign Resources dialog box. Once the resource has been assigned, it is moved to the top of the list.

TAKE NOTE*

If you want to remove or un-assign a resource from a task in the Assign Resources dialog box, click the resource you want removed and then click the **Remove** button.

5. Move the center divider to the right to allow the Resource Names column to be visible.
6. Click once on the **Resource Name cell** for task 6, Identify and reserve locations. Then click the **sub-menu arrow** at the right of the cell.
7. In the drop-down list, select the checkboxes for **Jeff Pike** and **Yan Li**. Your screen should look similar to Figure 3-5.
8. Press **Enter**.

Figure 3-5

Assigning resources using the drop-down list in the *Resource Names* column

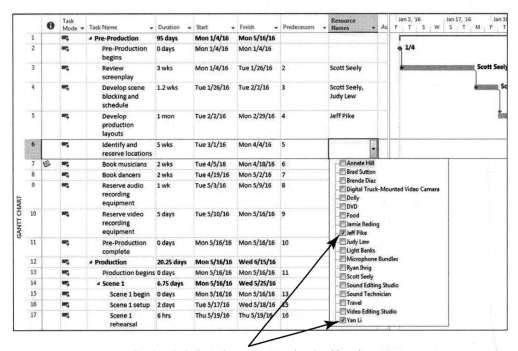

Checkmarks indicate the resources assigned to this task

9. SAVE the project schedule.

PAUSE. LEAVE the project schedule open to use in the next exercise.

 Cross Ref

Recall that in Lesson 2 you learned that Max. Units referred to the maximum capacity of a resource to accomplish tasks.

You may have noticed that the duration of task number 4 changed from 1 week to 1.2 weeks when you assigned Scott and Judy to the task. Bear in mind that Microsoft Project is using the resource calendars to schedule the tasks. The duration is extended by .2 weeks (1 day) due to the fact that Scott works Monday thru Thursday. The last 8 hours of his portion of the work will not be completed until the following week.

The capacity of a resource to work when you assign that resource to a task is measured in *units*. Units are recorded in the Max. Units field on the Resource Sheet view. One full-time resource has 100% (or 1.0) resource units. As you are assigning resources, you need to be careful that you do not over-allocate a resource, by assigning it more work than can be done within the normal work capacity of the resource. This may happen if you assign a resource to a task with more units than the resource has available. Another possibility is that you assign the resource to multiple tasks with schedules that overlap and with combined units that exceed those of the resource. Keep in mind that Microsoft Project assumes that all of a resource's work time can be allotted to an assigned task unless you specify otherwise. If the resource has less than 100 percent maximum units, Microsoft Project assigns the value of the resource's maximum units.

■ Adding More Work Resource Assignments to Tasks

THE BOTTOM LINE

Microsoft Project's default method of scheduling is considered non-effort driven. This means that as you assign resources to a task, the duration remains constant and the work value is calculated. The most obvious effect of this scheduling method is that, as you add or remove resources, the work value changes and therefore the costs change.

Adding Work Resources to a Task

You have started to define resource assignments for several tasks in your project schedule. Now you will assign additional resources to those tasks. To view work information in each task, you will use a split view. Pay close attention to the results in relation to task duration and work in the split view.

→ ADD WORK RESOURCES TO A TASK

USE the project schedule you created in the previous exercise.

1. Click the **View** tab. In the Split View group on the ribbon, select the **Details** checkbox. The Task Form view appears in the bottom part of your screen.

2. Click the name of task 3, **Review screenplay**. In the Task Form pane at the bottom of your screen, note the Work value of this task – 120 hours.

3. In the Task Form view single-click the **first cell** below Scott Seely's name. Click the sub-menu arrow at the right of this cell, then select **Jeff Pike**.

4. At the top of the Task Form portion of the screen, click the **OK** button. Microsoft Project assigns Jeff Pike to task 3. Your screen should look similar to Figure 3-6.

Figure 3-6

Split window view with Gantt Chart (top) and Task Form (bottom) views

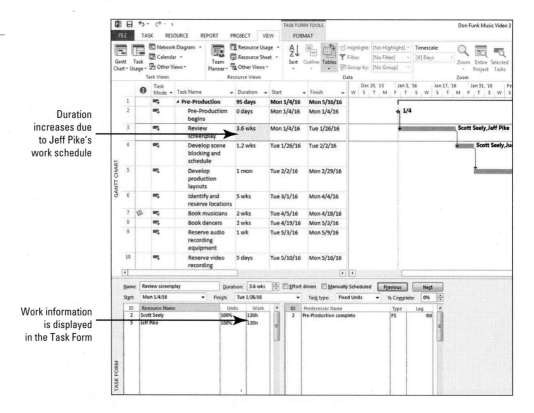

5. SAVE the project schedule.

   PAUSE. LEAVE the project schedule open to use in the next exercise.

Wowk is the total amount of effort expended to complete a task. Microsoft Project calculates work using a *work formula*: Work = Duration × Units. While you have the option of entering and displaying work in different units, by default, work is expressed in hours.

Notice that when you added Jeff to task 3, Microsoft Project calculated his work using the formula above. Jeff's schedule is 5 days/week, 8 hours/day and the task was three weeks in duration (or 15 days @ 8 hours each day). Therefore, Work = **120** hours of duration * **1** full time resource = **120** hours of work. The total work of the task doubled with the addition of this one resource. Notice also that Project automatically highlighted the duration, which changed as a result of adding Jeff, based on his work schedule.

⊙ ADD WORK RESOURCES TO AN EFFORT-DRIVEN TASK

USE the project schedule you created in the previous exercise.

1. Click the name of task 5, **Develop production layouts**. Jeff Pike is the only resource currently assigned to this task, work is calculated at 160 hours and the duration is 1 month. You'd like to assign an additional resource and reduce the task's duration.

2. In the Task Form screen click the check box for Effort driven.

TAKE NOTE* Although effort-driven scheduling is not the default for tasks you create in Microsoft Project, you can change this setting for all new tasks in a project schedule. On the Ribbon bar, click **File**, then select **Options**. On the Project Option dialog box, select **Schedule**. Navigate down to Scheduling options for this project and clear or select the New tasks are **Effort driven** check box. To change effort-driven scheduling for a single task or group of tasks, select the desired task(s). Click the **Task** ribbon and then in the Properties group, select the **Information** button. Select the **Advanced** tab of the Multiple Task Information dialog box. Clear or select the **Effort driven** check box.

3. Click once in the blank cell below Jeff Pike. From the drop-down menu, select Brenda Diaz. Then click the OK button at the upper portion of the Task Form screen. Your screen should look similar to Figure 3-7.

4. Notice that the duration has been changed to .5 months and the total work (160 hours) has now been evenly distributed between Jeff Pike and Brenda Diaz. In this instance you applied effort-driven scheduling, which tells Microsoft Project to hold the work value constant and change the duration when resources are added or removed.

5. SAVE the project schedule.

6. PAUSE. LEAVE the project schedule open to use in the next exercise.

Similar to the work formula but in the context of duration, the *duration formula* is used in effort-driven scheduling. The formula is Duration = Work / Units. In an effort-driven task, the work value is held steady and the variable is units. In the example you used in the previous exercise, 160 hours was the work value with one resource assigned. When you assigned Brenda Diaz to the task (a second full-time resource) the duration formula was applied as: Duration = 160 / 2 (units @ full time). So, Duration = 80 hours or .5 months.

Figure 3-7

Addition of a resource to task 5 resulting in less duration

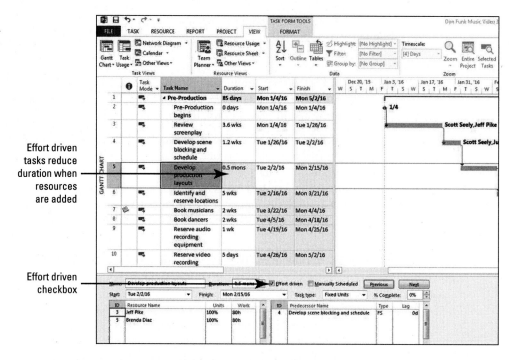

Effort driven tasks reduce duration when resources are added

Effort driven checkbox

Using the Actions Tag to Change Project's Scheduling Behavior

Now that you have assigned resources to tasks that are both effort driven and non-effort driven, in this exercise you will learn how to use the Actions tag to change how Project behaves. An *Actions tag* is an indicator that signals the user of a change, additional information, formatting options, etc. In Project 2013, the Actions tag appears mainly when changes to units, duration, or work occurs. The Actions tag will appear only when certain methods are used to apply changes, such as adding resources with the Assign Resources dialog box. The Actions tag only remains available until you perform your next action.

➔ USE THE ACTIONS TAG TO CHANGE PROJECT'S SCHEDULING BEHAVIOR

USE the project schedule you created in the previous exercise.

1. In the Gantt Chart portion of the view, click on the name of task 5, **Develop production layouts**. You'd like to assign an additional resource and reduce the task's duration.

2. Click the **Resource** tab and then click the **Assign Resources** button in the Assignments group. The Assign Resources dialog box appears.

3. In the Resource Name column of the Assign Resources dialog box, locate and click **Annete Hill**. Hold down **Ctrl** then locate and click **Brad Sutton**. Release the **Ctrl** key.

4. Click the **Assign** button. These two resources are added to the task. In addition, an Actions tag appears to the left of the task name column.

5. Click the **Actions tag** button. A list of options regarding how you want to handle this additional resource is displayed. Your screen should look similar to Figure 3-8.

Figure 3-8

Actions tag options list

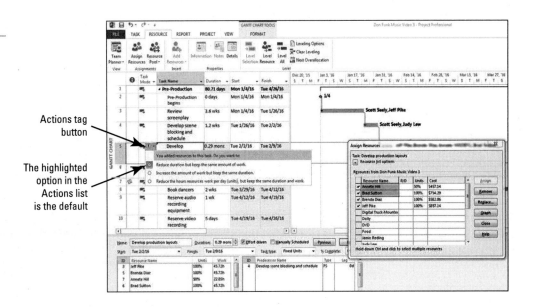

Actions tag button

The highlighted option in the Actions list is the default

TROUBLESHOOTING Microsoft Project will only display the Actions tag under certain circumstances. For example, if you assigned resources in the Task Form on an effort-driven task, the Actions tag would not appear in the Gantt Chart portion of the view.

6. Select **Increase the amount of work but keep the same duration**.

7. Click the name of task 6, **Identify and reserve locations**. Notice in the Task Form screen that the **Effort driven** check box is NOT checked for this task. Take note of the work data in the Task Form pane (400 hours total).

8. In the Resource Name column of the Assign Resources dialog box, click **Annete Hill**.

9. Scroll down until Ryan Ihrig's name is visible. Hold down **Ctrl**, click **Ryan Ihrig**. Release the **Ctrl** key then click the **Assign** button.

   Microsoft Project assigns Annete and Ryan to the task. Because this task is using the default settings, Microsoft Project increases the total work value and keeps the task duration constant. However, you do not want the additional resources to change the task's work. You have determined that this task does not require a full-time effort because these two additional resources will take over some of the administrative functions.

10. Click the **Actions tag** button. Select: **Reduce the hours resources work per day (units), but keep the same duration and work.** Your screen should look similar to Figure 3-9.

    Microsoft Project calculates the work values for each resource, keeps the task's duration at 5 weeks and adjusts the units for each resource.

Figure 3-9

Split view showing details of task information after a resource addition

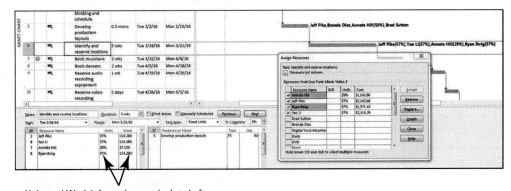

Units and Work information recalculated after selecting the Actions option to reduce hours per day

11. Click the **Close** button in the Assign Resources dialog box.

12. SAVE the project schedule.

13. PAUSE. LEAVE the project schedule open to use in the next exercise.

Using *effort-driven scheduling,* Microsoft Project will maintain that work amount as the total effort required to perform that task until you tell it otherwise. In this mode, Microsoft Project performs the work calculation at the **FIRST** work resource assignment, regardless of the number of work resources assigned (i.e., a single resource or multiple resources). Here is an example using the same task duration and different approaches of assigning the same total number of resources:

Table 3-1

Varying approaches to assigning the same total number of resources

ASSIGNING A SINGLE RESOURCE THEN ADDING TWO RESOURCES	ASSIGNING TWO TESOURCES THEN ADDING A SINGLE SESOURCE
Task Duration: 6 days (8 hour days)	Task Duration: 6 days (8 hour days)
Task Work: 0 hrs (no resources have been assigned yet)	Task Work: 0 hrs (no resources have been assigned yet)
At the first single resource assignment (100% Max Units):	At the first assignment of two resources (100% Max Units):
Task Duration: 6 days	Task Duration: 6 days
Task Work: 48 Hours	Task Work: 96 Hours
If you assign two additional resources (100% Max. Units):	If you assign an additional resource (100% Max. Units):
Task Duration: 2 Days	Task Duration: 4 Days
Task Work: 48 Hours	Task Work: 96 Hours

Cross Ref

You can find more information on the work formula in Lesson 4.

In general, if you have one resource working full-time on a task, the amount of work (effort) will match the duration. If your resource is not working full-time, or if you assign more than one resource to a task, then work and duration will not be equal. You can now see the benefit of creating task relationships rather than setting start or finish dates. Because effort-driven scheduling results in decreased task durations, Microsoft Project adjusts the start dates of successor tasks that did not have a constraint such as a start or finish date.

It is important to remember that effort-driven scheduling adjusts task duration only if you add or delete resources from a task. Whether or not to use effort-driven scheduling is a topic for discussion with your organization. It has both benefits and risks.

TROUBLESHOOTING

Exercise caution when determining the extent to which effort-driven scheduling should apply to the tasks in your project. Although applying more resources to your tasks may reduce their duration on paper, this may not be possible in a real-world situation. For example, if one resource could complete a task in 20 hours, could 20 resources complete the task in one hour? What about 40 resources in 30 minutes? In reality, the resources would probably get in each other's way, and productivity may even decrease. Additional coordination might be needed. For complex tasks, a resource might need specialized training before it could be productive. There is no exact rule about when you should or should not apply effort-driven scheduling. As a project manager, you need to review the requirements of your project tasks and use your best reasoning.

■ Assigning Material Resources to Tasks

THE BOTTOM LINE

In this exercise, you will assign material resources to tasks. Most projects use at least some material resources. When you assign material resources to tasks, Microsoft Project can track their consumption and cost.

➔ ASSIGN A MATERIAL RESOURCE TO A TASK

USE the project schedule you created in the previous exercise.

Assign
Resources

1. In the Task Name column, click the name of task 6, **Identify and reserve locations**.

2. Click the **Resource** tab and then click the Assign Resources button in the Assignments group. The **Assign Resources** dialog box appears.

3. In the Assign Resources dialog box, click once in the **Units** field for the DVD resource. Type **8**, and then click the **Assign** button.

4. If the Assign Resources dialog box is covering the scroll bars for the Gantt bar portion of your screen, drag the dialog box into the middle of the screen.

5. Scroll the Gantt bar portion of your screen so that the right end of the bar for task 6 is visible. You will use eight DVDs while identifying locations for this video. Remember that a DVD is a material resource and cannot do work, so assigning it to a task does not affect the task's duration. Your screen should look similar to Figure 3-10.

Figure 3-10

DVD resource added to Task 6

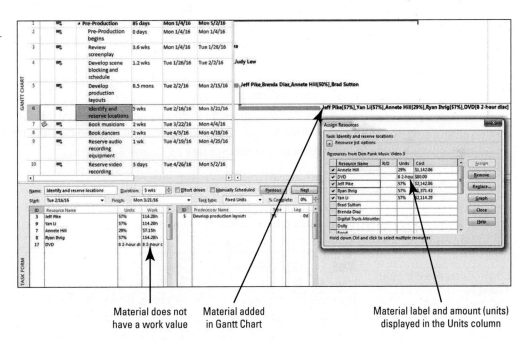

Material does not have a work value

Material added in Gantt Chart

Material label and amount (units) displayed in the Units column

6. In the Assign Resources dialog box, click **Close**.

7. SAVE the project schedule.

PAUSE. LEAVE the project schedule open to use in the next exercise.

When you assign a material resource to a task, there are two ways in which you can handle their consumption and cost:

- Assign a fixed unit quantity of the material resource. This is what you did in the preceding exercise. Microsoft Project then multiplied the unit cost of the resource by the number of units to calculate the total cost.
- Assign a variable rate quantity of the material resource. For example, if two DVDs will be used per day, you would enter 2/day as the assignment unit. Microsoft Project will

adjust the quantity and cost of the resource as the duration of the task changes. You will assign a material resource using this method in Lesson 6.

Cross Ref

You will learn more about resource consumption rates in Lesson 6.

Assigning Cost Resources to Tasks

THE BOTTOM LINE

A cost resource is another type of resource that you can assign to a task. A cost resource represents a financial obligation to your project. Once you assign the cost resource to the task, you can then assign the cost for the resource.

Assigning a Cost Resource to a Task

In this exercise, you assign cost resources to two different tasks.

 ASSIGN A COST RESOURCE TO A TASK

USE the project schedule you created in the previous exercise.

Assign Resources

1. Click the **Assign Resources** button in the Assignments group. The Assign Resources dialog box appears.
2. Scroll up or down in the Gantt view and in the Task Name column, click the name of task 17, **Scene 1 rehearsal**.
3. In the Resource Name column of the Assign Resources dialog box, click **Food** and then click the **Assign** button.
4. In the Cost column for the Food resource, type **500** and press **Enter**. During the Scene 1 rehearsal, $500 of food will be used to feed the crew and performers working on this task.
5. Click on the name of task 25, **Scene 2 rehearsal**.
6. In the Resource Name column of the Assign Resources dialog box, click **Food** and then click the **Assign** button.
7. In the Cost column for the Food resource, type **500** and press **Enter**. Your screen should look similar to Figure 3-11.

Figure 3-11

Cost resources added to tasks 17 and 25

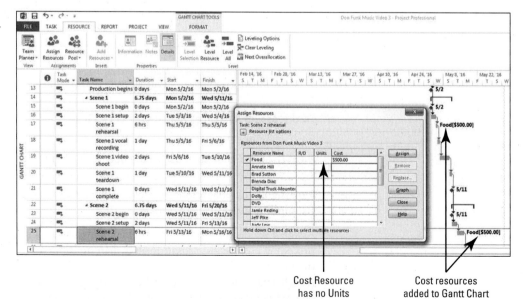

Cost Resource has no Units

Cost resources added to Gantt Chart

8. In the Assign Resources dialog box, click Close.
9. SAVE and then CLOSE the **Don Funk Music Video 3** file.

   PAUSE. If you are continuing to the next lesson, keep Project open. If you are not continuing to additional lessons, CLOSE Project.

SKILL SUMMARY

IN THIS LESSON YOU LEARNED:	MATRIX SKILL
To assign work resources to tasks	Make individual resource assignments
	Assign multiple resources simultaneously
To add more work resource assignments to tasks	Add work resources to a task
	Add work resources to an effort-driven task
	Use the Actions tag to change Project's scheduling behavior
To assign material resources to tasks	Assign a material resource to a task
To assign cost resources to tasks	Assign a cost resource to a task

■ Knowledge Assessment

Fill in the Blank

Complete the following sentences by writing the correct word or words in the blanks provided.

1. A(n) _____ is the matching of a specific resource to a particular task to do work.

2. Assigning a(n) _____ or _____ resource to a task will not affect the duration of the task.

3. In Microsoft Project, when you assign a human or equipment resource to a task, the result is _____.

4. _____ is the amount of work periods you expect the task to take to complete.

5. If a resource is assigned to do more work than can be done within the normal work capacity of the resource, it is _____.

6. The capacity of a resource to work is measured in _____.

7. In Microsoft Project, Duration x Units = Work is known as the _____.

8. Effort-driven scheduling adjusts a task's duration only if you add or remove _____ from a task.

9. When you assign _____ to tasks, you can track their consumption and cost.

10. According to the work formula in Microsoft Project, 20 hours task duration x 200% assignment units = _____ hours work.

Multiple Choice

Select the best response for the following statements.

1. If you assign a resource to a task with more units than the resource has available, then the resource is
   a. maximized.
   b. overutilized.
   c. compromised.
   d. overallocated.

2. The _____ lets you choose the scheduling option you need.
   a. Actions tag list
   b. Work formula
   c. Assign Resources dialog box
   d. Effort Driven scheduler

3. A task plus a resource equals
   a. work.
   b. an assignment.
   c. overallocation.
   d. duration.

4. If, on an effort-driven task, after an initial assignment, you assign more resources to a task, the task's duration
   a. is doubled.
   b. decreases.
   c. is reduced by half.
   d. increases.

5. Where do you normally record the dollar value of the cost resources for your project?
   a. On the resource sheet in the Cost column.
   b. On the resource sheet in the Std. Rate column.
   c. In the Assign Resources dialog box when the cost resource is assigned.
   d. In a separate Excel spreadsheet.

6. If you assign two resources at the same time, each at 100% assignment units, to a task with 24 hours duration, then each resource will work on the task for
   a. 12 hours.
   b. 24 hours.
   c. 36 hours.
   d. 48 hours.

7. To assign more than one resource to a task using the Assign Resources dialog box, click on the first resource name, then hold down the _____ key while clicking the second resource name, and then click Assign.
   a. Alt
   b. Shift
   c. Ctrl
   d. none of the above

8. Which of the following is an advantage of assigning resources to tasks?
   a. You can see if the resource assignment affects task duration.
   b. You can track the progress of the resource in working on the task.
   c. You can track resource and task costs.
   d. All of the above.

9. If you assign a(n) _____ quantity of a material resource to a task, Microsoft Project will adjust the quantity and cost of the resource as the task's duration changes.
   a. variable-rate
   b. open-ended
   c. fixed unit
   d. declining rate

10. You can assign resources to tasks using all the following methods, except:
    a. Assign Resource dialog box.
    b. Resource Names column.
    c. Resource Sheet.
    d. The Resource tab on the Task Information dialog box.

■ Competency Assessment

Project 3-1: Hiring a New Employee–Resource Assignments

You have a project schedule for hiring a new employee that contains tasks and resources. Now you will assign some of the resources to perform specific tasks.

GET READY. Launch Microsoft Project if it is not already running.

OPEN *Hiring Employee 3-1* from the data files for this lesson.

1. Click the Resource tab and then click the Assign Resource button in the Assignments group.
2. In the Task Name column, click name of task 1, Write job description.
3. In the Resources Name column of the Assign Resources dialog box, click Amy Rusko and then click Assign.
4. In the Task Name column, click the name of task 6, Review resumes.
5. In the Resources Name column of the Assign Resources dialog box, click Barry Potter and then click Assign.
6. Click Close in the Assign Resources dialog box.
7. SAVE the project as *Hiring Employee-Resources* and then CLOSE the file.
   LEAVE Project open for the next exercise.

Project 3-2: Office Remodel – Assign Multiple Resources

You are in charge of the remodel for the kitchen and lunchroom of your office. You need to assign resources to tasks. It is necessary to assign several of these resources simultaneously to a task.

OPEN *Office Remodel 3-2* from the data files for this lesson.

1. Click the Assign Resource button in the Assignments group on the Resource ribbon.
2. In the Task Name column, click the name of task 5, Remove drywall from main walls.
3. In the Assign Resources dialog box, select John Emory and Toby Nixon and then click Assign.
4. In the Task Name column, click the name of task 12, Paint walls and woodwork.
5. In the Assign Resources dialog box, select Run Liu and Toby Nixon and then click Assign.
6. Click Close in the Assign Resources dialog box.
7. SAVE the project as *Office Remodel Multiple Resources* and then CLOSE the file.
   LEAVE Project open for the next exercise.

■ Proficiency Assessment

Project 3-3: Office Remodel Material Resources

You now need to assign material resources to tasks in your office remodel project schedule.

 OPEN *Office Remodel 3-3* from the data files for this lesson.

1. Open the Assign Resources dialog box using the button on the Resource ribbon.
2. Select task 9, Install drywall.
3. In the Assign Resources dialog box, assign drywall as a resource and then assign 50 units for the drywall resource.
4. In the Assign Resources dialog box, assign nails as a resource and then assign 5 units for the nails resource.
5. Close the Assign Resources dialog box.
6. SAVE the project as *Office Remodel Material Resources* and then CLOSE the file.

   LEAVE Project open for the next exercise.

Project 3-4: Don Funk Video – Change Project's Behavior Using Actions tag

Although you have already assigned most of the resources for your music video, you have realized that you need to assign additional resources for a few of the tasks. You can use an Actions tag to do this.

 OPEN *Don Funk Music Video 3-4* from the data files for this lesson.

1. Select task 7, Book Musicians.
2. Activate the Assign Resources dialog box.
3. Click on Brenda Diaz, and then assign her to the task.
4. Use the Actions tag to indicate that you want to reduce the number of hours resources work per day (units), but keep the same duration and work.
5. Close the Assign Resources dialog box.
6. SAVE the project schedule as *Don Funk Actions* and then CLOSE the file.

   LEAVE Project open to use in the next exercise.

■ Mastery Assessment

Project 3-5: Don Funk Cost Resources

In this exercise, you will assign cost resources for the Don Funk Music Video.

 OPEN the *Don Funk Music Video 3-5* from the data files for this lesson.

1. Open the Assign Resources dialog box.
2. For task 6, Identify and reserve locations, assign Travel as a resource at a cost of 5000.
3. For task 18, Scene 1 vocal recording, assign Food as a resource at a cost of 250.
4. Close the Assign Resources dialog box.
5. SAVE the project schedule as *Don Funk Cost Resources* and then CLOSE the file.

   LEAVE Project open for the next exercise.

Project 3-6: Hiring a New Employee–Additional Resources

You have just learned of a change in scope for some of the tasks in your project schedule for hiring a new employee. One task will require more work than originally estimated, and for another task, the assigned resources must work fewer hours.

 OPEN *Hiring New Employee 3-6* from the data files for this lesson.

1. For the task Review resumes, assign Gabe Mares and Jeff Smith to assist with this task. Set their assignments so that the total work is increased and the duration is kept constant.

2. For the task Conduct interviews, assign Gabe Mares. Set his assignment so that for this task, the resources work less hours per day, but the work and task duration remain constant.

3. Close the Assign Resources dialog box.

4. SAVE the project schedule as *New Employee Adding Resources* and then CLOSE the file.

   CLOSE Project.

4 LESSON

Refining Your Project Schedule

LESSON SKILL MATRIX

SKILLS	TASKS
Applying a Task Calendar to an Individual Task	Apply a task calendar to an individual task
Changing Task Types	Change values of the work formula
	Change a task type using the Task Information dialog box
Splitting a Task	Split a task
Establishing Recurring Tasks	Set up a recurring task
	Assign resources to a recurring task
Applying Task Constraints	Apply a Start No Earlier Than constraint to a task
Reviewing the Project's Critical Path	Review the project's critical path
Viewing Resource Allocations Over Time	Explore resource allocations

You are Southridge Video's production manager and have been working on a project schedule for a new music video for Don Funk. You have developed the three key building blocks for the project – tasks, resources, and assignments. By setting up tasks and resources, and then assigning one to the other, the schedule is beginning to take shape. Now, you need to fine-tune your schedule to reflect some of the details and exceptions of these building blocks. Some tasks cannot occur during normal working hours, other tasks will have interruptions, and still others will repeat on a regular basis throughout the project. There are also tasks that have limits on when or by whom they can be performed. In this lesson, you will learn how to create task calendars, change task types, split tasks, set up and apply resources to recurring tasks, apply constraints, and identify the critical path of your project.

KEY TERMS

allocation	negative slack
constraint	noncritical tasks
critical path	over allocated
fixed duration	recurring task
fixed units	semi-flexible
fixed work	constraint
flexible constraint	slack
float	split
free slack	task calendar
free float	task type
fully allocated	total float
inflexible constraint	total slack
negative float	under allocated

© webphotographeer/iStockphoto

76

■ SOFTWARE ORIENTATION

Microsoft Project's Change Working Time and Create New Base Calendar Dialog Boxes

In Microsoft Project 2013, there may be times when you want specific tasks to occur at times that are outside the project calendar's working time. To do this, you need to create a new base calendar, a feature that is accessed through the **Change Working Time** dialog box.

Figure 4-1

Change Working Time dialog box, with Create New Base Calendar dialog box open

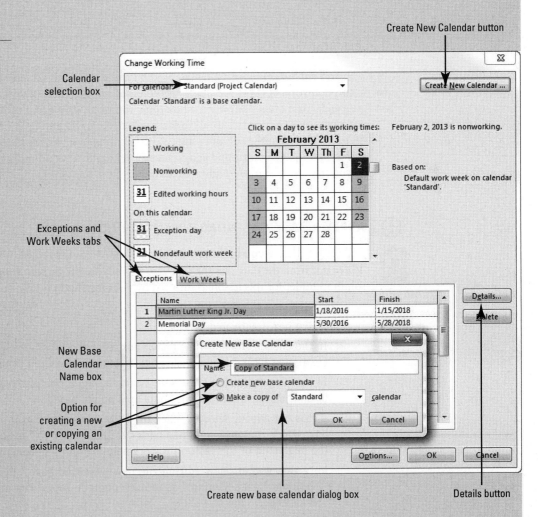

Create New Calendar button

Calendar selection box

Exceptions and Work Weeks tabs

New Base Calendar Name box

Option for creating a new or copying an existing calendar

Create new base calendar dialog box

Details button

This dialog box is accessed by clicking the Create New Calendar button in the Change Working Time dialog box, located on the Project ribbon. The Create new base calendar dialog box enables you to name the new calendar, create a totally new calendar, or make a copy of an existing calendar on which to base your new calendar.

■ Applying a Task Calendar to an Individual Task

THE BOTTOM LINE

When you set up resources in your project schedule, Microsoft Project created a specific calendar for each work resource. Each resource calendar is based on another calendar, usually the project calendar. Sometimes, you need a specific task to occur at a time that is outside the project calendar's working time (such as overnight or on a weekend). To do this, you can assign a task calendar to this task. You can use one of Project's base calendars, or you can create a new base calendar that fits your task requirements.

Assigning a Task Calendar to an Individual Task

A *task calendar* is a base calendar used by a single task for scheduling. It defines working and nonworking times for a task, regardless of settings in the project calendar. Task calendars are often used when a task must run overnight, occur on a specific weekday, or occur over a weekend. Task calendars are beneficial when other base calendars – such as the 24 Hours or Night Shift – are too broad or too specific for the task requirements. In this exercise, you create and assign a task calendar to a task that occurs outside normal working times – an overnight video shoot.

 APPLY A TASK CALENDAR TO AN INDIVIDUAL TASK

 GET READY. Before you begin these steps, launch Microsoft Project. OPEN *Don Funk Music Video 4M* from the data files for this lesson. SAVE the file as *Don Funk Music Video 4* in the solutions folder for this lesson as directed by your instructor.

Change
Working Time

1. Click the Project tab then click Change Working Time. The Change Working Time dialog box is activated.

2. In the Change Working Time dialog box, click the Create New Calendar button. The Create new base calendar dialog box appears as shown in Figure 4-1.

3. In the Name box, type Overnight Beach Filming. One of the scenes for the video will be shot during the overnight hours on a public beach.

4. If it is not already selected, click the Make a copy of button. In the drop-down list box, select Standard, and then click OK. (Refer back to the Software Orientation at the beginning of this lesson for more details on this screen.)

    Note that you are now editing the newly created base calendar called "Overnight Beach Filming," as indicated at the top of the dialog box, in the *"For calendar:"* box.

5. Click Work Weeks tab in the Change Working Time dialog box, and then click the Details button. The Details dialog box appears.

6. In the *Select days* box, drag your pointer to select Tuesday through Friday. Click the Set day(s) to these specific working times button.

7. Click the cell in row 1 of the From column and type 12:00 AM. Click the cell in row 1 of the To column and type 3:00 AM. Click the cell in row 2 of the From column and type 9:00 PM. Click the cell in row 2 of the To column and type 12:00 AM. Press Enter. Your screen should look similar to Figure 4-2.

Figure 4-2

Change Working Time and
Details dialog box showing
evening working times

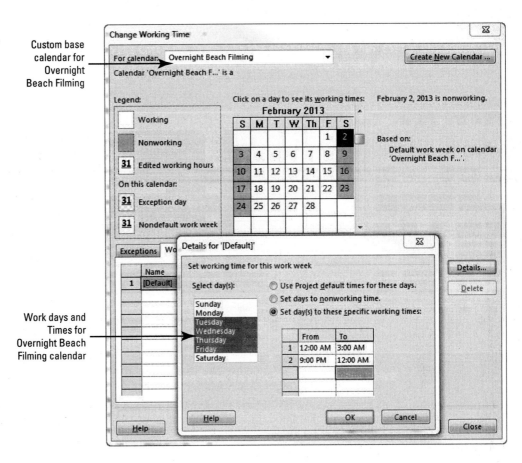

Custom base
calendar for
Overnight
Beach Filming

Work days and
Times for
Overnight Beach
Filming calendar

8. In the Select days box, select **Monday**. Click the **Set day(s) to these specific working times** button. Click the **cell in row 1** of the **From** column and type **9:00 PM**. Click the **cell in row 1** of the **To** column and type **12:00 AM**. Click the **cell in row 2** of the **From** column and press **Delete**.

TROUBLESHOOTING

Microsoft Project will not allow you to set a timeframe that spans two days. For instance, you cannot specify a working time for Monday of 9PM–3AM because 3AM is on Tuesday. You must set the time intervals for each specific day, as you did in this exercise.

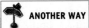 **ANOTHER WAY**

To quickly bring
information into view on
a selected task, press the
keystroke combination
of Ctrl+Shift+F5.

9. Select **Saturday**. Click the **Set day(s) to these specific working times** button. Click the **cell in row 1** of the **From** column and type **12:00 AM**. Click the **cell in row 1** of the **To** column and type **3:00 AM**. Press **Enter**.

10. Click **OK** to close the **Details** dialog box, then click **OK** to close the Change Working Time dialog box.

 You have now created and set the working times for this calendar from 9:00 PM to 3:00 AM from Monday night through Friday night (Saturday morning). Now you must assign the calendar to a task.

11. Select the name of task 35, **Scene 3 video shoot**. If the Gantt bar of this task is not visible, click the **Scroll To Task** button on the Task ribbon.

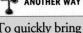

12. Click the **Task** tab then click the **Information** button in the Properties group. The Task Information dialog box appears.

13. Click the **Advanced** tab of the Task Information dialog box.

14. In the Calendar box, select **Overnight Beach Filming** from the drop-down list box. Click the **Scheduling ignores resource calendars** check box. Your screen should look like Figure 4-3.

Figure 4-3

Task Information dialog box on the Advanced tab

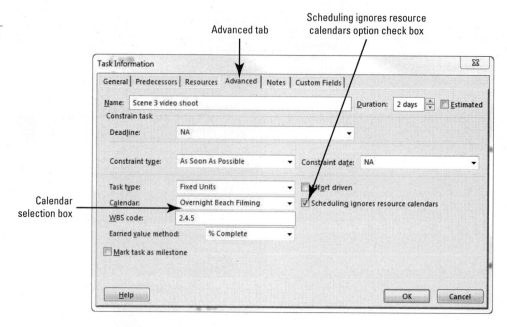

15. Click **OK** to close the Task Information dialog box. Microsoft Project applies the Overnight Beach Filming calendar to task 35, and a calendar icon appears in the Indicators column. Because you chose to ignore resource calendars, the resources for this task will be scheduled at times that would usually be nonworking times for them.

TAKE NOTE*

You will notice that a small, red human icon appears in the Indicators column. This is a feature that notifies the user of a resource over allocation, which will be discussed later in this chapter.

16. **SAVE** the project schedule.

PAUSE. LEAVE the project schedule open to use in the next exercise.

You have just created and assigned a task calendar to a task that occurs outside normal working times – an overnight video shoot. For tasks that have both a task calendar and resource assignments (and therefore a resource calendar), Microsoft Project will schedule work in the working time that is common between the task and resource calendar(s). If there is no common time, Project will alert you when you assign a resource to the task or when you apply the task calendar. As you saw in this exercise, you can specifically choose to ignore resource calendars.

■ Changing Task Types

THE BOTTOM LINE

As you learned in lesson 3, Microsoft Project uses the formula: Duration × Units = Work, called the work formula. The *task type* specifies which value in the formula remains fixed if one of the other two values changes. To determine which task type is the right one to apply to each task in your project schedule, you first need to determine how you want Project to schedule that task.

Task Types and the Effect of the Work Formula

There are three task types: fixed units, fixed duration, and fixed work. The default task type is *fixed units*, which means the units value does not change. With the fixed units task type, if you change a task's duration, Microsoft Project recalculates work. If you change work, duration is recalculated. A *fixed duration* task is one in which the duration value is fixed. If you change the task's work or units value, Project recalculates the other value. A *fixed work* task is one in which the work value is held constant. You can change the duration or units and Project will determine the other value. Project has a bias towards changing duration first. If it cannot change *Duration*, it will change *Work* and then *Units*.

 CHANGE VALUES OF THE WORK FORMULA

In an earlier lesson, you learned that Microsoft Project uses the work formula (Work = Duration × Units) to determine a task's work value. In this exercise, you will examine the relationship between the work formula and task type.

USE the project schedule you created in the previous exercise.

1. Click the **View** tab. Click the **Task Usage** button in the Task Views group on the ribbon. The Task Usage View replaces the Gantt Chart view.

2. Press the **F5** key. In the ID box, type **4**, and then click **OK**. Microsoft Project shifts the project schedule so that task 4, Develop scene blocking and schedule, and its assignments are visible.

3. Auto fit the *Task Name* column and move the center divider to the right until you can see the Start column. To auto fit a column, place the pointer on the right side dividing line of the column name and double-click. Your screen should look similar to Figure 4-4.

Figure 4-4

Task Usage view

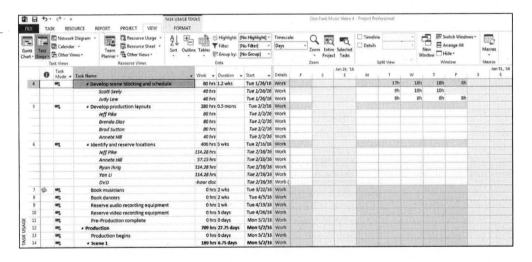

5. Right-click the **Start** column heading. Select **Insert** column. You can search from the drop-down list that appears for the field labeled Assignment Units. You can also start typing the word "assignment" and the list will be reduced in size. Select the **Assignment Units** field when it appears.

Note that task 4 has a total work value of 80 hours, 40 work hours and 100 percent resource units for each of two resources, and a duration of 1.2 weeks. Your team has determined that this task's duration should be two weeks, but the work necessary to complete the task should remain the same.

6. In the Duration field for task 4, select or type **2w**, and press **Enter**. Microsoft Project changes the duration of task 4 to two weeks and increases the work for each resource. You want to increase the duration but keep the work the same.

 TAKE NOTE*

If a task type is fixed, this doesn't mean that its units, work, or duration values are unchangeable. You can change any value for any task type.

7. Point to the **Duration** field for task 4, and then click on the **Actions** button. Your screen should look similar to Figure 4-5. Review the options in the **Smart Tag** list.

Figure 4-5

Actions button options list for Task 4

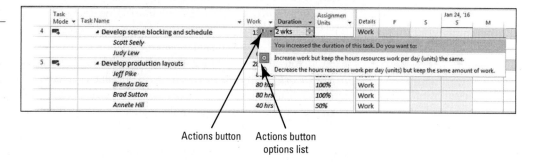

Actions button   Actions button options list

The task type for task 4 is fixed units (the default task type), so the default selection in the Actions options list is to increase work as the duration increases. Based on your team's discussions, you want to keep the work value constant and decrease assignment units for the task's new duration.

8. Select **Decrease the hours resources work per day (units) but keep the same amount of work** in the Actions list. The total work on the task is still 80 hours, but the assignment units value of each resource decreases. Another way to think of this is that the resources will put in the same total effort over a longer period of time. Figure 4-6 shows the adjusted scheduling formula values for task 4.

Figure 4-6

Adjustments made after selecting Action options on Task 4

Adjusted values for assignment units

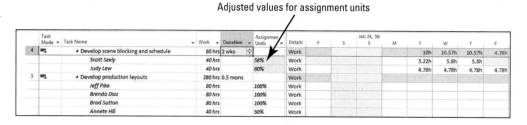

9. SAVE the project schedule.

PAUSE. LEAVE the project schedule open to use in the next exercise.

TROUBLESHOOTING As you fine-tune your project schedule, keep in mind that you cannot turn off effort-driven scheduling for a fixed work task.

The following table highlights the effect of changing any scheduling formula variable for any task type.

Table 4-1

Task types and scheduling formula values

IF THE TASK TYPE IS....	...AND YOU CHANGE THE		
	Duration	*Units*	*Work*
Fixed Duration	Project recalculates work	Project recalculates work	Project recalculates units
Fixed Units	Project recalculates work	Project recalculates duration	Project recalculates duration
Fixed Work	Project recalculates units	Project recalculates duration	Project recalculates duration

TAKE NOTE *

To see the task type of a task you have selected, click the Information button on the **Task** ribbon, and then click the Advanced tab in the **Task Information** dialog box. You can also see the task type when you are in the Gantt Chart view via the Task Form. On View ribbon, click **Details** in the Split View group. The Task form will appear in the lower portion of your screen.

Using the Task Information Dialog Box to Change a Task Type

In the previous exercise, you changed the way Project behaved (from its default action) by using the **Actions** button. In this exercise, you will change the task type using the Task Information dialog box then change one of the values of units, duration, and work and allow the software to perform its normal actions.

⊙ CHANGE A TASK TYPE USING THE TASK INFORMATION DIALOG BOX

USE the project schedule you created in the previous exercise.

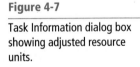

Gantt
Chart ▾

1. Switch back to the Gantt Chart view by clicking on the Gantt Chart button in the View ribbon.

2. Press the F5 key. In the ID box, type 6, and then click OK.

3. Double-click Task 6. The Task Information dialog box appears.

4. Click the Advanced tab if it is not already selected. Note that in the Task type box the task has a Fixed Units task type. You need to adjust this task's resources, but leave its duration fixed at 5 weeks.

5. Select Fixed Duration from the drop-down list box in the Task type box.

6. Click the Resources tab on the Task Information dialog box.

7. In the Units column, set the units value for Jeff Pike to 50% and for Ryan Ihrig to 75%. Your screen should look similar to Figure 4-7.

Figure 4-7

Task Information dialog box showing adjusted resource units.

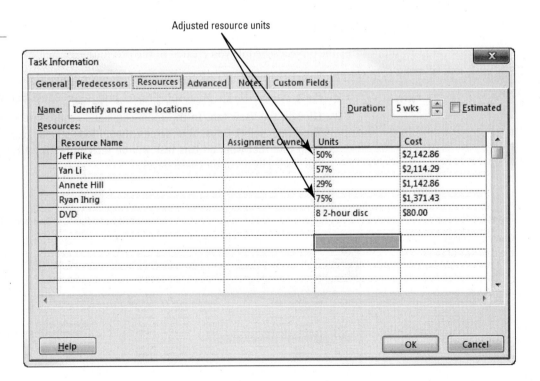

Adjusted resource units

Resource Name	Assignment Owner	Units	Cost
Jeff Pike		50%	$2,142.86
Yan Li		57%	$2,114.29
Annete Hill		29%	$1,142.86
Ryan Ihrig		75%	$1,371.43
DVD		8 2-hour disc	$80.00

Task Information
General | Predecessors | Resources | Advanced | Notes | Custom Fields
Name: Identify and reserve locations   Duration: 5 wks   ☐ Estimated
Resources:

Help   OK   Cancel

8. Click **OK** to close the Task Information dialog box. Note that the duration of the task did not change.

9. **SAVE** the project schedule.

   PAUSE. LEAVE the project schedule open to use in the next exercise.

You cannot change the task type on a summary task – it is always fixed duration. This is because the summary task is based on the earliest start date and the latest finish date of its subtasks.

As you are fine-tuning your project schedule, keep in mind that it is easy to confuse task type and effort-driven scheduling. They are similar in that they both affect work, duration, and units values. The key difference is that effort-driven scheduling affects your schedule only when you add or remove resources from tasks, while task type affects your schedule when you change the value of units, duration, or work.

Splitting a Task

THE BOTTOM LINE

Sometimes, work on certain tasks in a project schedule will stop and then start again, and these interruptions may be planned or unplanned. You split a task to show that work has been interrupted and restarted.

Splitting a Task

A *split* is an interruption in a task, represented in Project's Gantt bar by a dotted line between the two segments of the task. In this exercise, you practice splitting a task to represent some nonworking time in the middle of the task.

⊖ SPLIT A TASK

USE the project schedule you created in the previous exercise.

1. Select the name of task 5, **Develop production layouts**.

2. Press **Ctrl+Shift+F5**. Microsoft Project brings the **Gantt** bar of task 5 into view.

3. Click on the **View** tab. In the Zoom command group, in the selection box below Timescale, select **Days**. Your screen should look similar to Figure 4-8. You have just been told that work on this task will be interrupted from February 9 to February 11 (no work will occur on these days).

Figure 4-8

Gantt Chart view of Task 5 at the day level of zoom

Timescale Zoom Box   Two-tiered time scale   Gantt bar for Task 5

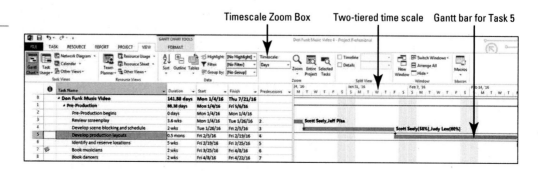

TAKE NOTE* The timescale at the top of the right half of the Gantt Chart (above the graphical bars) determines at what level of time (months, weeks, days, etc.) you can split a task. The calibration of the bottom tier of the timescale is the smallest increment into which you can split a task. In this exercise, you can split a task into one-day increments because days are on the bottom tier. If you wanted to split a task at the hourly level, you would need to adjust the Timescale option on the View ribbon.

4. Right-click the Gantt bar for task 5. From the shortcut menu that appears, click the Split Task button from the upper shortcut menu. A ScreenTip appears and the mouse pointer changes to a double vertical line with an arrow to the right.

5. Move the mouse pointer over the Gantt bar of task 5. Watch the ScreenTip box as you move the pointer – the date changes. The ScreenTip box reflects the date on which you will begin to split the task. Your screen should look similar to Figure 4-9.

Figure 4-9

ScreenTip for splitting a task

Split Task ScreenTip box.
This information changes as you move the mouse

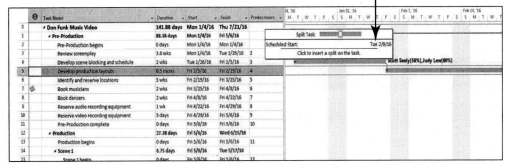

6. Move (but don't click) the mouse pointer over the Gantt bar until the Start date of Tuesday, 2/9/16, appears in the ScreenTip box.

7. Click and hold, then drag the mouse pointer to the right until the Start date of Friday, 2/12/16, appears in the ScreenTip, and then release the mouse button. Microsoft Project inserts a task split between the two parts of the task. The split, or interruption in work, is represented by a dotted line in the Gantt Chart, as shown in Figure 4-10.

Figure 4-10

Gantt Chart view with a split in Task 5

Dotted line indicates a split in the task

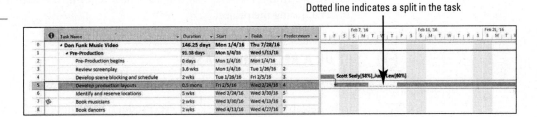

TROUBLESHOOTING Splitting tasks using the mouse pointer takes a little practice. If you split a task on the wrong date, there are two ways you can correct it. First, you can click the **Undo** button on the menu bar to remove the incorrect split. Or, point to the second segment of the task again, and when the mouse pointer changes to a circle with four arrows, drag the segment to the correct start date. You can drag multiple times.

8. SAVE the project schedule.

PAUSE. LEAVE the project schedule open to use in the next exercise.

Keep the following points in mind when splitting a task:

- You can split a task into as many parts as necessary.
- You can drag a segment of a split task either right or left to reschedule the split.
- The time of the actual task split, represented by the dotted line, does not count in the duration of the task unless the task type is fixed duration. Work does not occur during the split.

Cross Ref

Resource leveling or manually contouring assignments can also cause tasks to split. You can find out more about resource leveling in Lesson 6 and about contouring assignments in Lesson 13.

- If the duration of a split task changes, the last segment of the task is lengthened or shortened.
- If a split task is rescheduled, the whole task, including the splits, is rescheduled. The same pattern of segments and splits is preserved.

■ Establishing Recurring Tasks

THE BOTTOM LINE

Many projects require repetitive tasks, such as a status meeting or cleaning a production line. Even though these may seem like negligible tasks, you should account for them in your project schedule because they require time from project resources and therefore have costs associated with them.

Setting Up a Recurring Task

A *recurring task* is a task that is repeated at specified intervals, such as daily, weekly, or monthly. When you create a recurring task, Microsoft Project creates a series of tasks with Start No Earlier Than constraints, no task relationships, and effort-driven scheduling turned off. In this exercise, you will learn how to set up a task that will repeat at a specified interval during the project.

 SET UP A RECURRING TASK

USE the project schedule you created in the previous exercise.

1. Select the name of task 11, **Pre-Production complete**. You want to insert the recurring tasks as the last items in the Pre-Production phase.
2. On the Task ribbon, in the Insert group, click the **down-arrow** under the Task button. Select **Recurring Task**. The Recurring Task Information dialog box appears.
3. In the Task Name box, type **Status Meeting**.
4. In the Duration box, type **1h**.
5. Under Recurrence Pattern, make sure that **Weekly** is selected, and then select the **Monday** check box.
6. In the Start box, type or select **1/4/16**. The first occurrence of your weekly meeting will be on January 4, 2016.

TAKE NOTE*

Microsoft Project schedules a recurring task to start at the Default Start Time value you established at the beginning of your project. To schedule a recurring task to begin at a different time, enter that time along with the start date in the Start box of the Recurring Task Information dialog box. For instance, if you want the status meeting to start at 9 A.M. on January 17, you would enter 1/17/16 9 AM in the Start box.

7. Under **Range of recurrence**, click **End after**, and then type or select **15** occurrences. Your screen should look like Figure 4-11.

Figure 4-11

Recurring Task Information dialog box with all task information

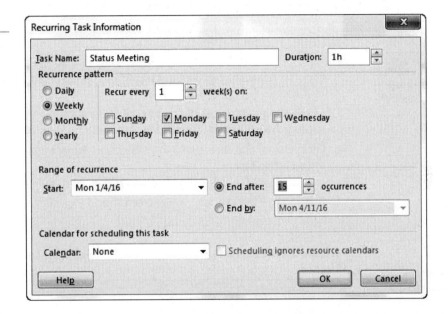

8. Click **OK** to create the recurring task. A Microsoft Project dialog box appears to notify you that one of the instances of the recurring task will occur during nonworking times (the holiday on January 18).

9. Review the options presented in the dialog box. You want to reschedule the status meeting for this particular week. Click **Yes** to reschedule this occurrence of the task. Microsoft Project inserts the recurring tasks within the Pre-Production phase. A recurring task icon appears in the Indicators column, as shown in Figure 4-12.

Figure 4-12

Gantt Chart showing expanded recurring task

Recurring task icon   Each recurrence rolls up to the recurring task summary individually

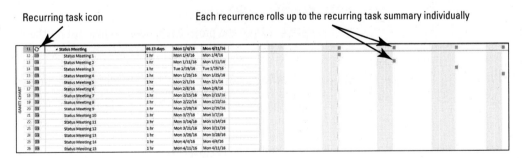

10. Click the name of task 11, **Status Meeting**, and then click the **Scroll to Task** button in the Editing group on the Task ribbon. The Gantt Chart displays the first occurrences of the recurring meeting's Gantt bars. Notice that the Gantt bar at the recurring task level (task 11) task shows only the individual occurrences of the tasks. This is because a recurring task is not a true summary task.

Scroll to Task

11. **SAVE** the project schedule.

PAUSE. LEAVE the project schedule open to use in the next exercise.

Assigning Resources to a Recurring Task

In the previous exercise, you established a recurring task in your project schedule. Now you will assign resources to it.

⊕ ASSIGN RESOURCES TO A RECURRING TASK

USE the project schedule you created in the previous exercise.

Assign Resources

1. If it is not already selected, click the name of task 11, **Status Meeting**.
2. Click the **Resource** tab. In the Assignments group on the ribbon, click **Assign Resources**.
3. In the Assign Resources dialog box, click **Brad Sutton**. Then hold down **Ctrl** while clicking **Chris Preston, Eva Corets, Jamie Reding, Jane Clayton,** and **Judy Lew**.
4. Click **Assign**, and then click **Close**. Microsoft Project assigns the selected resources to the recurring task.
5. If the recurring task is not already expanded, click the **Expand** button next to task 11's title to show the subtasks. Your screen should look similar to Figure 4-13.

Figure 4-13

Gantt Chart displaying resource assignments on recurring tasks

Recurring tasks are sequentially numbered   Resource assignments for each recurrence

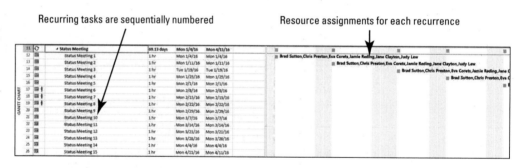

6. Click the **Collapse** button next to task 11's task title to collapse the subtasks under the recurring task.
7. **SAVE** the project schedule.

PAUSE. LEAVE the project schedule open to use in the next exercise.

Keep the following points in mind when establishing a recurring task:

- You can only use the Assign Resources dialog box when assigning resources to all recurring tasks at the same time. If you enter resource names in the Resource Name field of the summary task, the resources will only be assigned to the summary task, not to the individual occurrences.
- If you schedule a recurring task to end on a specific date, Microsoft Project will suggest the current project end date. If you select the project end date, you will need to manually change it later if the project end date changes.
- As you saw in this exercise, Microsoft Project will alert you if an occurrence of a recurring task will take place during nonworking time. You can choose to skip that occurrence or to schedule it for the next working day.

■ Applying Task Constraints

THE BOTTOM LINE

Every task that you enter into your project schedule has some type of limit, or constraint, applied to it. The *constraint* controls the start or finish date or the extent to which the task can be adjusted. There are three categories of constraint, and each has very different effects on the scheduling of tasks. A *flexible constraint* gives Project the ability to change start and finish dates (this is the default type). An *inflexible constraint* forces a task to begin or end on a specific date, and should be used only when necessary. A *semi-flexible constraint* gives Project the ability to change task start and finish dates (but not duration) within one date boundary.

The following table shows the eight types of task constraints within the three constraint categories.

Table 4-2

Constraint categories and constraint types

CONSTRAINT CATEGORY	CONSTRAINT TYPES	PROPERTIES
Flexible	As Soon As Possible (ASAP)	Project will schedule a task to occur as soon as it can happen. The default constraint type applied to new tasks when scheduling from the project start date.
	As Late As Possible (ALAP)	Project will schedule a task to occur as late as it can occur. The default constraint type applied to all new tasks when scheduling from the project finish date.
Semi-Flexible	Start No Earlier Than (SNET)	Project will schedule a task to start on or after the specified constraint date. Use this type to make sure a task will not start before a specific date.
	Start No Later Than (SNLT)	Project will schedule a task to start on or before the specified constraint date. Use this type to make sure a task will not start after a specific date.
	Finish No Earlier Than (FNET)	Project will schedule a task to finish on or after the specified constraint date. Use this type to ensure a task will not finish before a specific date.
	Finish No Later Than (FNLT)	Project will schedule a task to finish on or before the specified constraint date. Use this type to ensure that a task will not finish after a specific date.
Inflexible	Must Start On (MSO)	Project will schedule a task to start on the specified constraint date. Use this type to ensure that a task will start on an exact date.
	Must Finish On (MFO)	Project will schedule a task to finish on the specified constraint date. Use this type to ensure that a task will finish on an exact date.

Applying a Constraint to a Task

In this exercise, you apply a constraint to a task in Microsoft Project.

➔ APPLY A START NO EARLIER THAN CONSTRAINT TO A TASK

USE the project schedule you created in the previous exercise.

1. Press the F5 key. In the ID box, type 39 and press Enter. This scene will be shot at a location that is not available until May 25, 2016.
2. Double-click on Task 39. The Task Information dialog box appears.
3. Click on the Advanced tab. In the Constrain task section, next to Constraint type, select Start No Earlier Than from the drop-down list box.
4. In the Constraint date box, type 5/25/16. Your screen should look similar to Figure 4-14.

Figure 4-14

Task Information dialog box with Start No Earlier Than constraint and constraint date entered

Constraint type box   Constraint date box

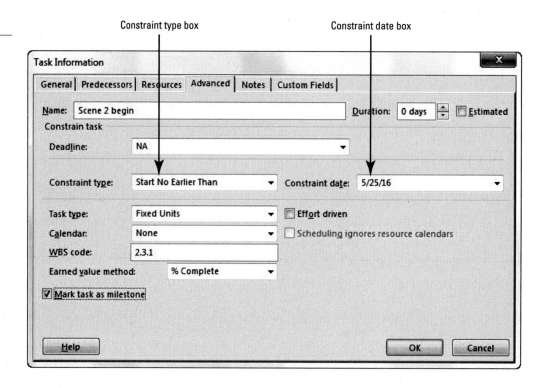

TAKE NOTE*

Unless you specify otherwise, Microsoft Project schedules the start or finish time of a constraint date using the Default Start Time or Default End Time value you established at the beginning of your project (on the ribbon click **File**, then select **Options**, then click the **Schedule** section).

5. Click OK. Note the highlighted cells showing the effect of this change. Widen the table as necessary to view additional data columns.

The constraint is applied and a constraint icon appears in the Indicators column. When you point to the icon, constraint details will be shown in a ScreenTip. The task is rescheduled to start on May 25, and all other tasks that depend on task 38 are also rescheduled.

6. SAVE the project schedule.

   PAUSE. LEAVE the project schedule open to use in the next exercise.

TROUBLESHOOTING Avoid entering task start and finish dates unless absolutely necessary. When you enter start or finish dates, Project applies semi-flexible constraints such as Start No Earlier Than or Finish No Earlier Than, which prevents the project manager from taking advantage of the Microsoft Project scheduling engine.

Keep the following points in mind when setting constraints for tasks:

- To remove a constraint, double-click the task from which you want to remove the constraint. In the Task Information dialog box, click the **Advanced** tab. In the Constraint type box, select **As Soon As Possible** (if scheduling from start date) or **As Late As Possible** (if scheduling from finish date).
- If you try to apply inflexible or semi-flexible constraints to tasks in addition to task links, you might create what is known as *negative float* – or *negative slack* – the amount of time that tasks overlap due to a conflict between task relationships and constraints. For example, a task with a Must Start On (MSO) constraint for April 24 and a finish-to-start relationship to another task will always be scheduled for April 24, no matter when its predecessor finishes. To set Microsoft Project to honor relationships over constraints, select the **File** ribbon, click **Options**, and then click the **Schedule** option. Under Schedule Options for this project, clear the **Tasks will always honor their constraint dates** check box.
- Some constraint behaviors change if you must schedule a project from a finish date rather than a start date. For instance, the ALAP constraint type becomes the default for new tasks, rather than ASAP. Pay close attention to the constraints you apply in this case to make sure the results are what you expected.
- It is considered a best practice to insert a note on a task that has a constraint applied. The reasoning for this is simple – communication. By entering a note, anyone who views the schedule will see why a constraint is applied. In lesson 1 you learned how to insert a note on a task.

Another feature in Microsoft Project 2013 that is helpful in reviewing constraints, assignments, and dependencies is the Task Inspector. The Task Inspector looks at the task drivers show the factors that drive a task's start times and help you backtrack to analyze the constraints. You can use the Task Inspector to determine the factor(s) driving the start date of a task or follow a chain of factors to find the cause of a delay you are tracking. You can access Task Inspector by clicking the **Task** ribbon, then click **Inspect** in the Tasks group. The Task Inspector pane will appear on the left side of your screen. Figure 4-15 shows the Task Inspector pane activated for task 51.

Figure 4-15

Task Inspector activated for
task 51

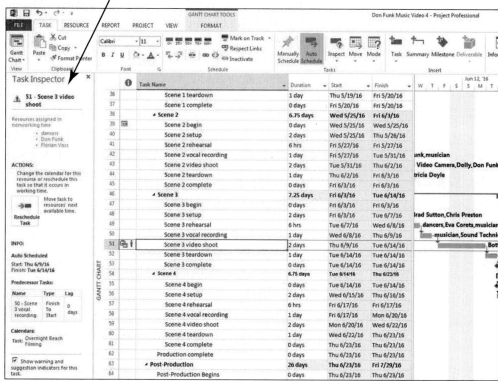

■ Reviewing the Project's Critical Path

THE BOTTOM LINE

In every project, there is a series of tasks, known as the ***critical path***, that directly affect the
finish date of the project. If any one of these tasks is delayed, either in the start or completion
of, the finish date of the project will be delayed.

Reviewing the Project's Critical Path

The term "critical" refers not to the importance of the tasks in the critical path, but rather
to the impact that the scheduling of these tasks have on the finish date of the project. One
of the best ways to shorten the overall duration of a project is to shorten its critical path.
In Project 2013, you can review your project's critical path, including any existing *free
slack* – the amount of time a task can be delayed before it will delay another task. In this
exercise, you review your project's critical path.

→ REVIEW THE PROJECT'S CRITICAL PATH

USE the project schedule you created in the previous exercise.

1. Click the **Task** tab, and then click the **down-arrow** under the **Gantt Chart** button; the
   view list appears. Select **More Views**.

2. In the More Views dialog box, select **Detail Gantt**, and then click the **Apply** button.
   The project schedule is displayed in the Detail Gantt view.

3. Press the **F5** key. The Go To dialog box appears. In the ID box, type **50**, and then click
   OK. The view shifts so that the Gantt bar for task 50 is visible. Scroll down so that

most of the tasks after task 50 are visible, and you can see more of the critical path. Your screen should look similar to Figure 4-16. Almost all of the tasks that fall after task 50, Scene 3 vocal recording, are on the critical path, which is shown in red. Noncritical tasks are displayed in blue and also show free slack. (Total slack is shown as the thin bar that extends to the right of the task bar.)

Figure 4-16

Gantt Chart showing critical path starts at task 52

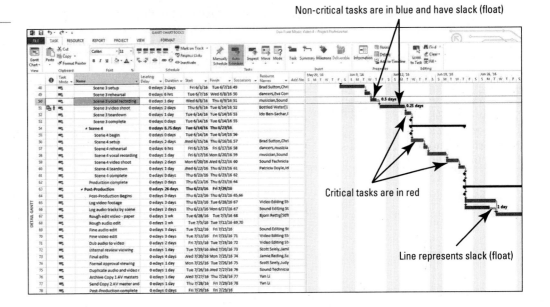

4. **SAVE** the project schedule.

   PAUSE. LEAVE the project schedule open to use in the next exercise.

To fully understand the critical path concept, there are a few other terms with which you need to become familiar. Microsoft Project uses the term *slack* for the term float. *Float* (or slack) is the amount of time a task can be delayed without causing a delay to another task or the overall project. *Free Float* (or Free slack) is the amount of time a task can be delayed before it will delay another task. *Total Float* (or *Total Slack*) is the amount of time a task can be delayed without delaying the project end date. A task is usually considered to be on the critical path if its total float is zero (or occasionally, less than some specified amount). Conversely, *noncritical tasks* have float greater than zero. Their start or finish dates can vary within their slack amounts without affecting the finish date of the project.

■ Viewing Resource Allocations Over Time

THE BOTTOM LINE

As a project manager, you are responsible for distributing work among the people and equipment resources of the project. *Allocation* is the portion of a resource's capacity devoted to work on a specific task. Allocation is how you manage these resources and their assignments over time.

Reviewing Resource Allocations

You need to be able to review each resource's allocation, identify any problems that are evident, and adjust allocations as needed. In this exercise, you will review your resources to identify resource allocation issues.

⊙ EXPLORE RESOURCE ALLOCATIONS

USE the project schedule you created in the previous exercise.

1. On the Task ribbon, in the View group, click the **down-arrow** under the Gantt Chart button. Select **More Views**.

2. In the More Views dialog box, locate and select the **Resource Allocation** view. Click **Apply**. A split view appears: the Resource Usage view is on the top and the **Leveling** Gantt Chart view is at the bottom.

3. Click the **Resource Name** column heading to highlight all cells in that field. Your screen should look similar to Figure 4-17.

Figure 4-17

Split view — the Resource Usage view (top) with Resource Name field selected and the Leveling Gantt view (bottom)

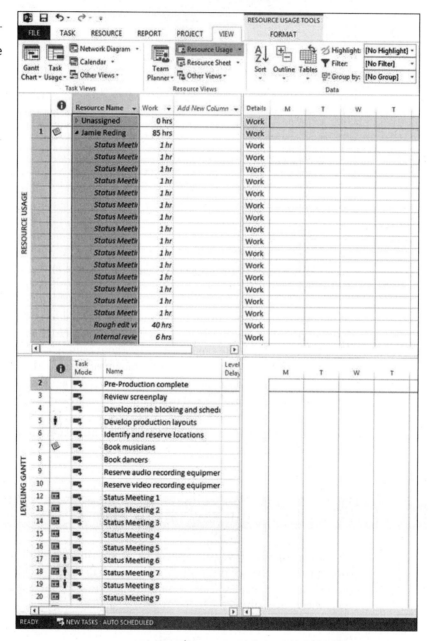

4. Click on the **View** tab. In the Data group, click the **Outline** button, and then select **Hide Subtasks**. Microsoft Project collapses the Resource Usage view.

5. Press **Ctrl+Shift+F5**. The resources' total work values over the project timescale appear in the grid on the right. In the Resource Name column, click the task name cell **Unassigned**. Your screen should look similar to Figure 4-18.

Figure 4-18

Resource Allocation view with assignment collapsed

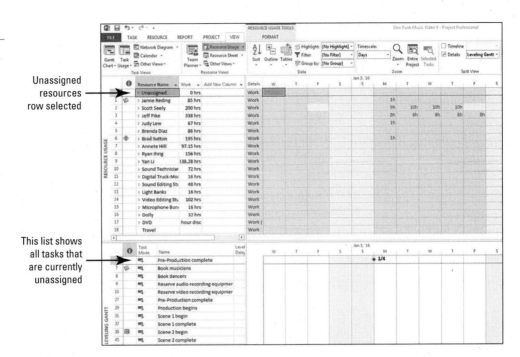

Unassigned resources row selected

This list shows all tasks that are currently unassigned

To the left of the Resource Usage view is the Usage Table, which shows the assignments grouped by resource, the total work assigned to each resource, and the work for each assignment. The outline format can be expanded and collapsed. The right side of the view contains assignment details (default setting is work) displayed on a timescale.

6. Auto fit the **Resource Name** and **Work** columns. Then, in the Resource Name column, click on the **name of resource 3**, Jeff Pike. Note at the bottom of the screen, the Leveling Gantt view shows the actual tasks to which Jeff is assigned.

TAKE NOTE Don't worry if you see a resource group titled Unassigned. Sometimes there are tasks that have no specific resources assigned to them. These tasks are grouped together in this view and listed as a resource named Unassigned.

Timescale:
Days

7. Click the **View** tab. In the Zoom group, click the **down-arrow** below to the **Timescale units** box and select **Months**. The time-scaled grid now shows work values per month. Your screen should look similar to Figure 4-19.

Figure 4-19

Time-scaled grid showing monthly work assignment values

Timescale Zoom Box

Timescale changed to show monthly values

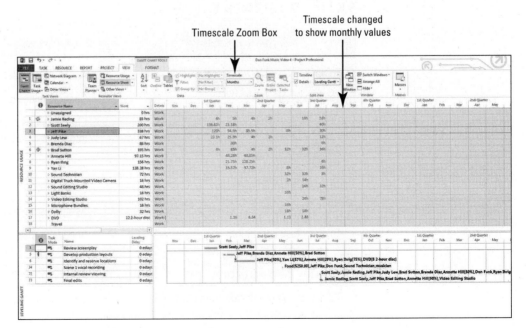

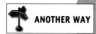 **ANOTHER WAY** Instead of using the Timescale command to change the tiers of the timescale, you can click the **Zoom** slider located at the lower right of your screen. If this method doesn't give you the level of detail you need, then you can use the Timescale command.

8. **SAVE** the project schedule. **CLOSE** the project schedule.

PAUSE. If you are continuing to the next lesson, keep Project open. If you are not continuing to additional lessons, close Project.

As the project manager, the decisions you make regarding task assignments affect the workloads of the resources on the project. Every resource is said to be in one of three states of allocation:

1. *Under allocated* – the work assigned to a resource is less than the resource's maximum capacity. For example, a full-time resource who has only 20 hours of work assigned in a 40-hour work week is under allocated.
2. *Fully allocated* – the condition of a resource when the total work of its task assignments is exactly equal to that resource's work capacity. For example, a full-time resource assigned to work 40 hours per week is fully allocated.
3. *Over allocated* – the work assigned to a resource is more than the resource's maximum capacity. For example, a full-time resource that has 55 hours of work assigned in a 40-hour work week is over allocated.

Allocating resources takes a combination of skill and common sense. It might seem straightforward to say that all resources should be fully allocated all of the time, but this is not always possible, practical, or even desirable. There are situations in which over allocation or under allocation is quite acceptable. As the project manager, you must learn how to identify allocation problems and how to handle them.

You might want to also keep the following points in mind when reviewing resource allocation:

- In the Resource Usage view, the default table is the Usage table. You can display other table views by clicking the View tab, then clicking Usage in the Table command group and selecting the table you want to display.
- Work values are the default in the time-scaled grid of the Resource Usage view. To display other assignment values, such as cost, click the **Format** tab, then click **Details**, and select the value you want to display.

SKILL SUMMARY

IN THIS LESSON YOU LEARNED:	MATRIX SKILL
To apply a task calendar to an individual task	Apply a task calendar to an individual task
To change task types	Change values of the work formula
	Change a task type using the Task Information dialog box
To split a task	Split a task
To establish recurring tasks	Set up a recurring task
	Assign resources to a recurring task
To apply task constraints	Apply a Start No Earlier Than constraint to a task
To review the project's critical path	Review the project's critical path
To view resource allocations over time	Explore resource allocations

■ Knowledge Assessment

Matching

Match the term in column 1 to its description in column 2.

Column 1	Column 2
1. critical path	**a.** the amount of time a task can be delayed before it will delay another task
2. free slack	**b.** a restriction that controls the start or finish date of a task
3. split	**c.** the condition of a resource when the total work of its task assignments is exactly equal to that resource's work capacity
4. under allocated	**d.** the amount of time a task can be delayed without delaying the project completion date
5. recurring task	**e.** the series of tasks whose scheduling directly affects the project's finish date
6. fixed units	**f.** a restriction that forces a task to begin or end on a certain date, preventing the rescheduling of a task
7. constraint	**g.** an interruption in a task
8. fully allocated	**h.** the condition of a resource when the work assigned to a resource is less than the resource's maximum capacity
9. inflexible constraint	**i.** a task that is repeated at specific intervals
10. total slack	**j.** a task type in which the units value does not automatically change

True/False

Circle T if the statement is true or F if the statement is false.

T | F **1.** It is always best to enter a start or finish date for every task.

T | F **2.** By default, critical path tasks are shown in red on the Detail Gantt view.

T | F **3.** It is never acceptable to have an over allocated resource.

T | F **4.** It is not possible to split a task over a weekend.

T | F **5.** Effort-driven scheduling and task types both affect all resources in the same way.

T | F **6.** You cannot change the task type for a summary task.

T | F **7.** You can use a task calendar to schedule a task that will occur during working time that is not available on the project calendar.

T | F **8.** It is acceptable to have a resource group named Unassigned.

T | F **9.** It is not possible to set a specific time of day for a recurring task.

T | F **10.** You can split a task only three times.

■ Competency Assessment

Project 4-1: Adjusting Working Time for Office Remodel

You are in charge of the kitchen and lunchroom remodel for your office. Based on feedback from your associates, you have decided to schedule the drywall installation after working hours due to the noise. You need to set up a task calendar that reflects the different working hours.

GET READY. Launch Microsoft Project if it is not already running. **OPEN** *Office Remodel 4-1* from the data files for this lesson.

1. Click the **Project** tab and then click **Change Working Time**.
2. In the Change Working Time dialog box, click **Create New Calendar**.
3. In the Name box, type **Evening Drywall Install**.
4. If it is not already selected, click the **Make a copy of** button. Select **Standard** from the drop-down list box, and then click **OK**.
5. Click on the **Work Weeks** tab in the Change Working Time dialog box, and then click the **Details** button.
6. In the **Select days** box, drag your pointer to select **Monday** through **Friday**. Click the **Set day(s) to these specific working times** button.
7. Click the **cell in row 1** of the **From** column and type **4:00 PM**. Click the **cell in row 1** of the **To** column and type **12:00 AM**. Click the **cell in row 2** of the **From** column, and press **Delete**. Click **OK**. Click **OK** again to close the **Change Working Time** dialog box.
8. Double-click task 9, **Install drywall**. The Task Information dialog box appears.
9. Click the **Advanced** tab.
10. In the Calendar box, select **Evening Drywall Install** from the drop-down list.
11. Click the **Scheduling ignores resource calendars** check box, and then click **OK**.
12. **SAVE** the project schedule as *Office Remodel Drywall Install*, and then **CLOSE** the file.
    LEAVE Project open for the next exercise.

Project 4-2: Weekly Meeting for Hiring a New Employee

You have developed a project schedule for hiring a new employee. You now need to add a recurring weekly status meeting to your tasks.

OPEN *Hiring New Employee 4-2* from the data files for this lesson.

1. Select the **name cell** of task 5, Collect resumes.
2. Click the **Task** tab. On the **Insert** group, click the **down-arrow** under the **Task** button and then select **Recurring Task**.
3. In the Task Name box, type **Status Meeting**.
4. In the Duration box, type **1h**.
5. Under Recurrence pattern, select **Daily**.
6. In the Every box, type or select 3 and then select **workdays**.
7. In the Start box, type or select **10/22/15**.
8. Under Range of recurrence, select **End after**, and then type or select **10** occurrences.
9. Click **OK**.
10. **SAVE** the project schedule as *Hiring New Employee Recurring* and then **CLOSE** the file.
    LEAVE Project open for the next exercise.

■ Proficiency Assessment

Project 4-3: Splitting a Task for Setting Up a Home Office

You are in the process of setting up a home office, but have just been notified that you will need to be out of town from Wednesday, October 7 through Friday, October 9 for some training. You need to adjust your project schedule to reflect this out-of-town time.

OPEN *Home Office 4-3* from the data files for this lesson.

1. Change to the Gantt Chart view.
2. Select the name cell of task 13. Scroll to the bar chart view for this task.
3. Use the Split Task Button to split the task from Wednesday, October 7 to Monday, October 12 (you will not be in town from Wednesday through Friday.).
4. SAVE the project schedule as *Home Office Split Task*, and then CLOSE the file.

   LEAVE Project open to use in the next exercise.

Project 4-4: Setting a Constraint for the Don Funk Music Video

You have just been informed that Don Funk is not available for the formal approval viewing until July 28, 2016. You need to set a constraint for this task to reflect this.

OPEN *Don Funk Music Video 4-4* from the data files for this lesson.

1. Select the name cell of task 74. Scroll the Gantt bars to this task.
2. Click the Task tab. Press the Information button in the Properties group.
3. Click the Advanced tab and set a Start No Earlier Than constraint with a date of July 28, 2016.
4. SAVE the project schedule as *Don Funk Constraint* and then CLOSE the file.

   LEAVE Project open to use in the next exercise.

■ Mastery Assessment

Project 4-5: Hiring a New Employee – Adding Resources to the Recurring Status Meeting

In Project 4-2, you established a recurring status meeting for the Hiring a New Employee project schedule. Now you will add resources to that task.

OPEN *Hiring New Employee Recurring 4-5* from the data files for this lesson.

1. Assign the resources Amy Rusko, Barry Potter, Gabe Mares, and Jeff Smith to the Status Meeting recurring task.
2. Expand the subtasks for the recurring task to visually confirm that the resources have been assigned.
3. SAVE the project schedule as *Hiring New Employee Recurring Resources* and then CLOSE the file.

   LEAVE Project open to use in the next exercise.

Project 4-6: Don Funk Music Video Over-allocated Resources

Review the resource allocations for the Don Funk Music Video. Pay close attention to over allocated resources.

 OPEN *Don Funk Music Video 4-6* from the data files for this lesson.

1. Use the Resource Usage View to review resource assignments for this project.
2. Locate Yan Li and then review his task assignments for the weeks of April 24 and May 1.
3. In a separate Word document, write a brief paragraph detailing Yan Li's assignments for those weeks. Include any dates/times that he is over allocated, and discuss whether or not you think the over allocation is critical or can be left as is.
4. SAVE the project schedule as *Don Funk-Yan Li* and then CLOSE the file. SAVE the Word document as *Don Funk-Yan Li Discussion* and then CLOSE the file.
   CLOSE Project.

Fine-Tuning Tasks

LESSON SKILL MATRIX

SKILLS	TASKS
Managing Task Constraints and Relationships	Explore the effects of constraints and relationships on task scheduling
Setting Deadline Dates	Set a deadline date for a task
Establishing Task Priorities	Establish task priorities
Establishing Manually Scheduled Tasks	Establish a Manually Scheduled Task

You are a video project manager for Southridge Video, and one of your primary responsibilities recently has been to manage the new Don Funk Music Video project. You have learned most of the basics for building a project schedule, assigning resources, and entering additional tasks such as meetings. In this lesson, you will learn some of the more advanced features of Microsoft Project 2013 that focus on fine-tuning details in a project schedule prior to saving a baseline and commencing project work.

© bjones27/iStockphoto

KEY TERMS
deadline
manually scheduled
resource leveling
task priority

■ SOFTWARE ORIENTATION

Microsoft Project's Task Information Dialog Box—General Tab

The General tab of the Task Information dialog box provides general information about the selected task and allows you to make changes and updates to the task. On the General tab, you can edit the task name, update the duration and the percent complete, change the priority, and modify the start and finish dates (see Figure 5-1).

Figure 5-1

General tab of the Task Information dialog box

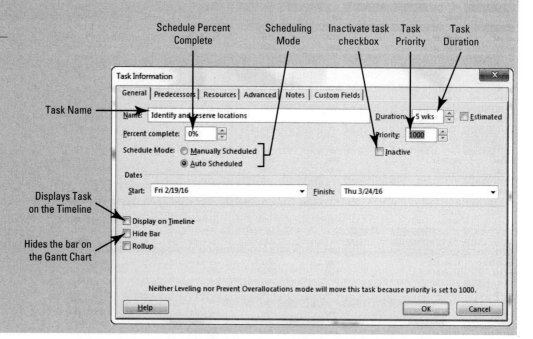

■ Managing Task Constraints and Relationships

THE BOTTOM LINE

As you are building a project schedule, you will usually use both task relationships and constraints within the schedule. You can control how Microsoft Project schedules these elements. Recall that Microsoft Project alerts you to conflicts between relationships and constraints so that you can maintain control over the rules that Microsoft Project follows.It is important to make sure that you understand the effects of the constraints you apply on the overall project schedule–not just on the task to which you have applied the constraint.

Exploring Effects of Constraints and Relationships

In this exercise, you review two of the basic elements of scheduling, constraints and task relationships, and learn how you can control the actions of Microsoft Project when there is a conflict between a constraint and a task relationship. Microsoft Project always honors constraint dates over task relationships by default, even if this causes negative float (slack).

EXPLORE THE EFFECTS OF CONSTRAINTS AND RELATIONSHIPS ON TASK SCHEDULING

GET READY. Before you begin these steps, launch Microsoft Project. OPEN the ***Don Funk Music Video 5M*** project schedule from the data files for this lesson. SAVE the file as ***Don Funk Music Video 5*** in the solutions folder for this lesson as directed by your instructor.

1. In the Gantt Chart view, review the finish-to-start relationship between tasks 3 and 4. Your screen should look similar to Figure 5-2.

Figure 5-2

Gantt Chart view showing finish-to-start relationship between tasks 3 and 4

Finish-to-Start relationship between tasks 3 and 4

Assume you have just been told that task 4, Develop scene blocking and schedule, must begin no later than Wednesday, January 20, 2016.

2. In the Task Name column, select the name of task 4, Develop scene blocking and schedule.

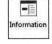

3. On the Task ribbon, in the Properties group, click the Information button. The Task Information dialog box appears.

4. Click the Advanced tab.

5. In the Constraint Type box, select Start No Later Than. In the Constraint Date box, type or select 1/20/16.

6. Click OK to close the dialog box. The Planning Wizard appears, notifying you of a scheduling conflict between the constraint you just applied to task 4, and the existing task relationship between tasks 3 and 4. Your screen should look similar to Figure 5-3.

Figure 5-3

Planning Wizard dialog box

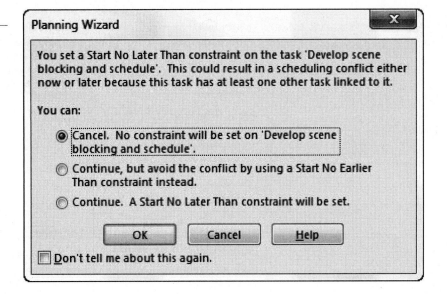

7. In the *You Can* selection list, click **Continue. A Start No Later Than constraint will be set.**

8. Click **OK**.

9. A second alert appears. Click **Continue. Allow the scheduling conflict**, and then click **OK**. Microsoft Project applies the SNLT constraint to task 4 and reschedules it to start on Wednesday, as shown in Figure 5-4.

Figure 5-4

Gantt Chart with SNLT constraint applied

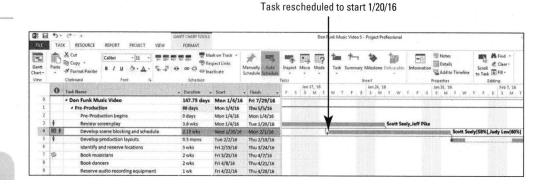

Task rescheduled to start 1/20/16

TAKE NOTE*

Notice also that the red human icon appears in the indicators column, notifying you that this action also causes and resource over allocation on both tasks.

Microsoft Project would reschedule task 4 to avoid the negative slack between tasks 3 and 4, but this SNLT constraint prevents Microsoft Project from doing so.

10. Click the **File** tab and then click **Options**.

11. Select the **Schedule** options then navigate to the **Scheduling options for this project:** section. Your screen should look similar to Figure 5-5.

Figure 5-5

Scheduling Options dialog box

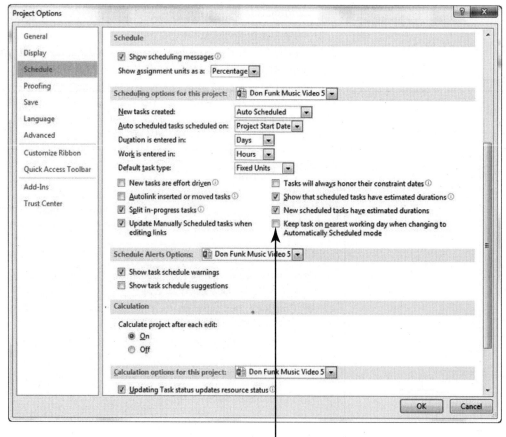

Clear this check box

12. Clear the **Tasks will always honor their constraint dates** check box, and then click **OK**. A calendar alert icon appears in the indicators column for task 4.

13. Rest the mouse pointer on the calendar alert icon in the indicators column. A Screen-Tip appears. Now Microsoft Project honors the task relationship over the constraint. Microsoft Project preserves the constraint information, but does not honor the constraint. If the scheduling conflict is removed (by a change in task duration, for example), Microsoft Project would then honor the constraint. Your screen should look similar to Figure 5-6.

Figure 5-6

Calendar alert and screen tip

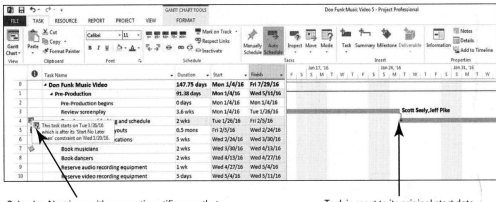

Calendar Alert icon with screen tip notifies you that
Project will honor relationships over the constraint

Task is reset to its original start date

14. Click the **File** tab again and then click **Options**. Select the **Schedule** options then navigate to the **Scheduling options for this project:** section.

15. Click the **Tasks will always honor their constraint dates** check box on the Schedule tab, and then click **OK**. This restores the default behavior to Microsoft Project, and task 4 is rescheduled to honor its constraint date.

16. **SAVE** the project schedule.

    PAUSE. LEAVE Project open to use in the next exercise.

Cross Ref

For a review of task constraints and negative slack, refer back to Lesson 4. The best way to prevent negative float is through the use of leads and lags, which will be discussed in detail in Lesson 13, Project Schedule Optimization.

It is a good idea to develop a consistent strategy for using constraints and relationships in your projects. We recommend using the default behavior of honoring constraint dates. As you learned in previous lessons, you should always set task relationships in your projects, and then apply semi-flexible or inflexible constraints only when truly necessary.

■ Setting Deadline Dates

THE BOTTOM LINE

A **_deadline_** is a date value you enter for a task that indicates the latest date by which you want the task to be completed. The deadline date itself does not constrain the task. When you enter a deadline date, Microsoft Project displays a deadline marker on the Gantt Chart and alerts you if the task's finish date moves beyond the deadline. Assigning a deadline date to a task, rather than a semi-flexible or inflexible constraint, allows the most flexibility in scheduling tasks with commitments.

Setting Task Deadline Dates

Rather than using semi-flexible or inflexible constraints, a better approach to scheduling is to use the default As Soon As Possible (ASAP) constraint and then enter a deadline for the task. In this exercise, you enter a deadline date for a task rather than entering a constraint.

→ SET A DEADLINE DATE FOR A TASK

USE the project schedule you created in the previous exercise.

1. Press the **F5** key; the Go To dialog box appears.

2. In the ID box, type **27** and then click **OK**. Microsoft Project displays task 27. You want to make sure that the pre-production tasks conclude by May 11, 2016, so you will enter a deadline date for this milestone.

3. Double-click the task name of task 27, **Pre-Production Complete**. The Task Information dialog box appears.

4. Click the **Advanced** tab if it is not already selected.

5. In the date box next to Deadline, type or select **5/11/16**, then click **OK**. Microsoft Project inserts a deadline marker in the chart portion of the Gantt Chart view. Your screen should look similar to Figure 5-7.

Figure 5-7

Gantt Chart view with deadline indicator on task 27

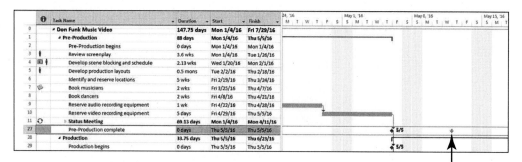

Deadline symbol in the Gantt Chart assigned to task 27

> **TAKE NOTE** *
>
> If the scheduled completion of a task moves past the deadline date, Microsoft Project displays a missed deadline indicator in the Indicators column. To remove a deadline from a task, clear the **Deadline field** on the Advanced tab of the Task Information dialog box.

6. Double-click the name of task 28, **Production**. The Task Information dialog box appears. Click the **Advanced** tab if it is not already selected.

7. In the dropdown date box next to Deadline, type or select **6/28/16**, then click **OK**. Microsoft Project inserts a deadline date marker for the summary task. Scroll the chart portion of the Gantt Chart view to the right to view the marker.

> **TAKE NOTE** *
>
> A deadline date will cause Microsoft Project to notify you if the scheduled completion of a task exceeds its deadline date. Entering a deadline date has no effect on the scheduling of a summary or subtask, except for one situation. The one instance in which the deadline date can affect the scheduling of a summary task (or any task) involves slack. When a task is assigned a deadline date, its slack does not extend beyond the deadline date.

8. SAVE the project schedule.

   PAUSE. LEAVE Project open to use in the next exercise.

■ Establishing Task Priorities

↓
THE BOTTOM LINE

Task priority is a numeric ranking between 0 and 1000 of a task's importance (with 1000 being most important). Microsoft Project uses task priorities to determine which tasks can be delayed in order to resolve periods of resource over allocation. The default task priority Microsoft Project assigns is 500. Task priorities only affect the schedule during resource leveling and have no meaning regarding the urgency or importance of a task beyond resource leveling.

⊙→ **ESTABLISH TASK PRIORITIES**

USE the project schedule you created in the previous exercise.

1. In the Task Name column, select the name of task 6, **Identify and reserve locations**.

2. On the Task ribbon, click the **Information** button, located in the Properties group. The Task Information dialog box appears.

3. Click the **General** tab if it is not already selected.

4. In the Priority box, type or select **1000**. Your screen should look similar to Figure 5-8. A message at the bottom of the Task Information dialog box states the task will not be moved through either Resource Leveling or the Prevent Over allocations mode.

Figure 5-8

Task Information dialog box for task 6 with task Priority set to 1000

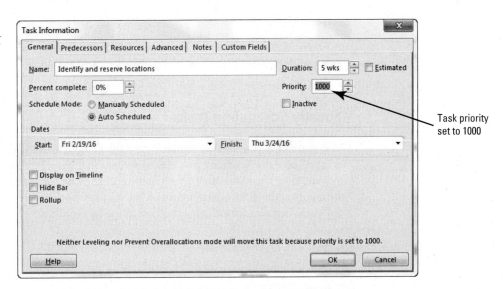

5. Click **OK** to close the dialog box. Microsoft Project adjusts the task's priority. Note that there is no visual indicator for the adjusted priority, and the effect of the new task's priority is only apparent after resource leveling.

ANOTHER WAY

To simultaneously adjust the priority of multiple tasks, select the desired tasks by clicking and holding the **Ctrl** key. Click the **Task Information** button, click the **General** tab, and enter the desired priority in the priority box. Note that because you have selected multiple tasks, this dialog box is now labeled "Multiple Task Information."

6. **SAVE** the project schedule.

   PAUSE. LEAVE Project open to use in the next exercise.

In this exercise, you set the priority for a task, giving it the highest priority possible in Microsoft Project (1000). A task with a priority of 1000 is never delayed by leveling. *Resource leveling* is the process of delaying a resource's work on a task to resolve an over allocation. Depending on the options you choose, resource leveling might delay the start date of an assignment or an entire task, or split up the work on a task. Resource leveling evaluates several factors to determine how to resolve resource over allocation.

One of the factors evaluated during resource leveling is task priorities. Task priority is a numeric ranking between 0 and 1000 of a task's importance and appropriateness for leveling. When you level resources, Microsoft Project will delay a task with a lower priority before delaying a task with a higher priority in order to resolve a resource over allocation:

- Tasks with priority 0 are leveled first, so they are likely to be delayed by leveling.
- Tasks with priority 1000 are never delayed by leveling. Assign this task priority carefully, as it limits Microsoft Project's capabilities to resolve resource over allocations.

 Cross Ref You can find more information about resource leveling in Lesson 6.

■ Establish Manually Scheduled Tasks

 THE BOTTOM LINE Some tasks require the project manager to schedule manually, without regard to predecessors or other project constraints. You will use the new feature, Manual Scheduling, for this action.

Manually Scheduling Tasks

In this exercise, you practice establishing a manually scheduled task. For the purpose of this exercise, note that you have just been informed that your audio team and video team have met and they are unsure about the outcome of the fine editing tasks. The task of dubbing the audio to the video is dependent on one but not both of these tasks. After meeting with the team, you decide to change the scheduling mode of task 70 to manual scheduling.

 ESTABLISH A MANUALLY SCHEDULED TASK

USE the project schedule you created in the previous exercise.

 Manually Schedule

1. Press the F5 key to produce the Go To dialog box. In the ID box, type 70 and click OK.
2. On the Task ribbon, in the Tasks group, click the Manually Schedule button. Note that the Gantt bar has changed to the default formatting of a manually scheduled task. Your screen should look similar to Figure 5-9.

Figure 5-9

Task Gantt Chart view with task 70 set to manually scheduled mode

Button highlighted when task is set to manually scheduled mode

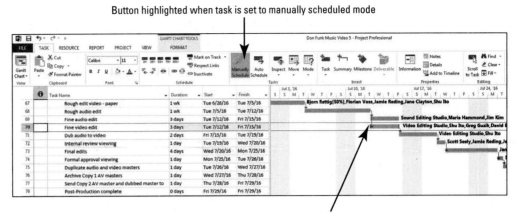

Default formatting for a manually scheduled task

3. Click in the duration cell of task 68, Rough audio edit. You have just been informed that this task will now take 2 weeks instead of one. Type 2w and press Enter. Notice that task 70 did not move from its original start date. Your screen should look like Figure 5-10.

Figure 5-10

Manually scheduled task not honoring its relationship with its predecessor task

Finish-to-Start relationship link is not honored

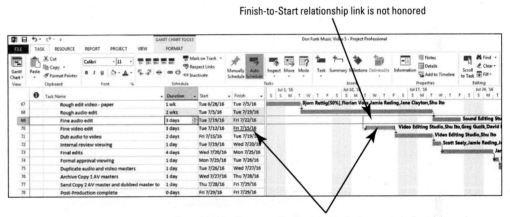

Formatting for the manually scheduled task changes to indicate a warning

Notes

4. Position the mouse pointer over the Gantt bar of the manually scheduled task. Notice that it displays a warning at the top of the ScreenTip. Right-click the Gantt bar of the manually scheduled task and select Fix in Task Inspector. Your screen should look like Figure 5-11.

Figure 5-11

Task Inspector pane visible to make repairs to task 70

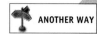 **ANOTHER WAY** You can also activate the task inspector by selecting the Inspect button on the Task ribbon.

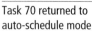

5. Review the various options and information in the Task Inspector pane. After reviewing this information, you have decided that manually scheduling this task is not the best option. In the Task Inspector pane, under the *ACTIONS:* section, click the **Auto Schedule** button. Microsoft Project returns the task to the auto-scheduled mode. Your screen should look like Figure 5-12.

Figure 5-12

Task 70 returned to auto-schedule mode

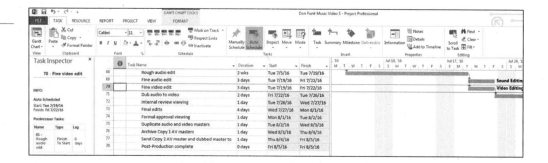

TAKE NOTE * You can change the mode of how new tasks are entered by selecting the Task tab then the Mode button and then Auto Schedule.

6. Single-click the **duration cell** for task 68, Rough audio edit. Type **1w** and press **Enter**.
7. **SAVE** the project schedule, and then close the file.

   PAUSE. If you are continuing to the next lesson, keep Project open. If you are not continuing to additional lessons, **CLOSE** Project.

Manually scheduled tasks are tasks that must be manually scheduled, calculated, and set by the operator. These require much more attention by the project manager and may be needed at certain points of your project. They can allow you more scheduling flexibility, but they should be used sparingly. Microsoft Project treats manually scheduled tasks much differently than auto scheduled tasks. In fact, certain features available with auto scheduled tasks are not available with manually scheduled tasks. For example, Overtime, Actual Overtime, & Remaining Overtime cannot be tracked with manually scheduled tasks. You also cannot use task constraints or work contouring.

When using manually scheduled tasks, Microsoft Project treats non-working times differently. If you use a manually scheduled task during normal working hours, on normal working days, you would not even know the difference. However, start a manually scheduled task on a non-work day, outside of normal, non-work hours, and then you notice the difference. In essence, the system creates an exception on the calendar to close the gap between the manually scheduled task's start and the next working time. It is the author's recommendation that you fully understand all of the pros and cons of using manually scheduled tasks before using them in your schedules. The table below summarizes the difference between auto and manual scheduling.

Table 5-1

Items affected by Manually
Scheduled vs. Automatically
Scheduled

Item	Manually Scheduled	Automatically Scheduled
Duration	Can be number, date, or text information, such as "14d" or "fortnight". Not used by Project to schedule the task.	Only numbers representing time length and units can be used, such as "14d" or "2 months".
Work	Only numbers representing time length and units can be used, such as "14d" or "2 months".	Only numbers representing time length and units can be used, such as "14d" or "2 months".
Resources	Can be assigned to tasks. Not used by Project to schedule the task.	Can be assigned to tasks. Used by Project to help determine best schedule.
Start date	Can be a number, date or text information, such as "Jan 30" or "Sometime soon." Not used by Project to schedule the task.	Only date information can be used.
Finish date	Can be a date or text information, such as "Jan 30" or "Sometime soon." Not used by Project to schedule the task.	Only date information can be used.
Constraints	Ignored by Project.	Observed by Project and entered by the user to fine-tune the schedule.
Task Relationships (links)	Can be used, but won't change the scheduling of the task.	Should be used to affect scheduling of the task.
Project and resource calendars	Ignored by Project.	Used by Project to help determine best schedule.

SKILL SUMMARY

In this lesson you learned:	Matrix Skill
To manage task constraints and relationships	Explore the effects of constraints and relationships on task scheduling
To set deadline dates	Set a deadline date for a task
To establish task priorities	Establish task priorities
To set manually scheduled tasks	Establish a Manually Scheduled Task

■ Knowledge Assessment

Fill in the Blank

Complete the following sentences by writing the correct word or words in the blanks provided.

1. A numeric ranking of a task's importance and appropriateness for leveling is called _____.

2. A better approach to scheduling tasks is to use a deadline date rather than a(n) _____.

3. When you link the tasks in a project schedule, you establish a(n) _____ between the tasks.

4. _____ is the process of delaying a resource's work on a task to resolve an over-allocation.

5. Microsoft Project honors constraint dates over task relationships, even if this causes _____.

6. Tasks with a priority of _____ are leveled first.

7. When you enter a deadline date, Microsoft Project alerts you if the task's _____ moves beyond the deadline.

8. A(n) _____ is a value you enter for a task that indicates the latest date by which you want the task to be completed.

9. The default task priority value for all tasks is _____.

10. Tasks with a priority of _____ are never delayed by leveling.

Multiple Choice

Select the best response for the following statements.

1. Microsoft Project uses_____ to determine which tasks can be delayed in order to resolve periods of resource over allocation.
   a. load balancing
   b. random selection
   c. task priorities
   d. task deadlines

2. The numeric ranking range for task priority is:
   a. 1 to 100.
   b. 0 to 100.
   c. 1 to 500.
   d. 0 to 1000.

3. Entering a deadline date has no effect on the scheduling of a summary or subtask, except when the task involves:
   a. slack.
   b. the critical path.
   c. relationships.
   d. a priority equal to 0.

4. Which of the following is NOT a semi-flexible constraint?

    a. Start No Earlier Than

    b. Must Start On

    c. Finish No Earlier Than

    d. Start No Later Than

5. Depending on options you choose, resource leveling might:

    a. delay the start date of a specific resource's assignment.

    b. delay the start date of an entire task.

    c. split up the work on a task.

    d. all of the above.

6. What must be done to remove a deadline from a task?

    a. Delete the deadline indicator from the bar chart portion of the Gantt Chart.

    b. Slide the deadline indicator off of the active portion of the Gantt Chart.

    c. Clear the Deadline field on the Advanced tab of the Task Information dialog box.

    d. Change the deadline date to 00/00/00.

7. Which of the following is NOT a type of task relationship?

    a. Finish-to-Start

    b. Finish-to-Finish

    c. Start-to-Start

    d. Start-No-Earlier-Than-Finish

8. A deadline date:

    a. is the due date of the project.

    b. does not constrain a task.

    c. is not indicated on the Gantt Chart.

    d. is a semi-flexible constraint.

9. Which of the following allows the most flexibility in scheduling a task?

    a. semi-flexible constraint

    b. deadline date

    c. inflexible constraint

    d. none of the above

10. By default, Microsoft Project honors:

    a. constraint dates over relationships.

    b. deadline dates over relationships.

    c. relationships over constraint dates.

    d. negative slack over relationships.

■ Competency Assessment

Project 5-1: Setting a Constraint for Insurance Claim Processing

You are managing an insurance claim processing process, and have just been informed that the repairer, Chris Gray, will not be available for work after June 10, 2016, for several days. You need to set a constraint on one of his tasks to reflect this information, even if it causes a conflict with existing task relationships.

GET READY. Launch Microsoft Project if it is not already running.

OPEN *Insurance Claim Processing 5-1* from the data files for this lesson.

1. Click the name of task 16, Repairer notifies adjuster.

2. On the Task ribbon, click the Information button, located in the Properties group. Click the Advanced tab.

3. In the Constraint type box, select Start No Later Than. In the Constraint date box, type or select 6/7/16. Click OK.

4. In the Planning Wizard dialog box that appears, select the Continue. A Start No Later Than constraint will be set. option. Click OK.

5. In the next Planning Wizard dialog box that appears, select Continue. Allow the scheduling conflict and then click OK.

6. SAVE the project schedule as *Insurance Claim Processing Constraint*, and then CLOSE the file.

   PAUSE. LEAVE Project open to use in the next exercise.

Project 5-2: Don Funk Music Video Deadlines

You have just received additional information about scheduling on the Don Funk Music Video, and need to add some deadline dates to your project schedule.

 OPEN *Don Funk Music Video 5-2* from the data files for this lesson.

1. Select the name of task 9, Reserve audio recording equipment.

2. On the Task ribbon, click the Scroll to Task button, located in the Editing group.

3. Double-click the task name cell of task 9. Click the Advanced tab if it is not already selected.

4. In the Deadline: box, type or select 5/13/16. Click OK.

5. Select the name of task 62, Production complete. Click the Scroll to Task button.

6. On the Task ribbon, click the Information button, located in the Properties group.

7. Click the Advanced Tab.

8. In the date box, type or select 7/1/16, and then click OK.

9. SAVE the project schedule as *Don Funk Deadlines*, and then CLOSE the file.

   PAUSE. LEAVE Project open to use in the next exercise.

■ Proficiency Assessment

Project 5-3: Task Priorities for HR Interview Schedule

You are making some changes and adjustment to your HR Interview project schedule and have decided to establish task priorities for some tasks in case resource allocation issues arise later. Make the indicated priority assignments.

 OPEN *HR Interview 5-3* from the data files for this lesson.

1. Select the name of task 21.

2. Open the Task Information dialog box.

3. Type or select a priority of 800. Click OK.

4. Select the names of tasks 13 and 14.

5. Open the Task Information dialog box.

6. Type or select a priority of 400 for these two tasks. Click OK.

7. SAVE the project schedule as *HR Interview Priorities*, and then CLOSE the file.

   PAUSE. LEAVE Project open to use in the next exercise.

Project 5-4: Deadline Dates for Office Remodel

You would like to keep a closer eye on some of the tasks for the lunchroom office remodel project you are managing. You decide it is a good idea to add some deadline dates to several tasks. You know that Microsoft Project will alert you if a task's finish date moves beyond the deadline.

OPEN *Office Remodel 5-4* from the data files for this lesson.

1. Select the name of task 7.

2. Open the Task Information dialog box.

3. Set a deadline date of 10/16/15.

4. Select the name of task 14.

5. Open the Task Information dialog box.

6. Set a deadline date of 11/5/15.

7. SAVE the project schedule as *Office Remodel Deadlines*, and then CLOSE the file.

   PAUSE. LEAVE Project open to use in the next exercise.

■ Mastery Assessment

Project 5-5: Changing Default Handling for Task Relationships/ Constraints on Insurance Claim Processing

After a meeting with your project team, a decision has been made to honor task relationships over constraints for the Insurance Claim schedule from Project 5-1. Another repairer has agreed to fill in for Chris Gray if necessary. You need to revise your project schedule to change the default method by which Microsoft Project handles relationships and constraints.

OPEN *Insurance Claim Processing 5-5* from the data files for this lesson.

1. Review the task list.

2. Open the Options dialog box from the File ribbon.

3. Select Schedule.

4. Clear the checkbox so that tasks do not always honor their constraint dates.

5. Close the dialog box.

6. Review the task list and locate the task that has been affected by this change. In a separate Microsoft Word document, state the information that is contained in the calendar alert icon for this task, and briefly explain how your change has affected the task.

7. SAVE the project schedule as *Insurance Claim No Default*. SAVE the Word document as *Insurance Claim No Default*. CLOSE the files.

   PAUSE. LEAVE Project open to use in the next exercise.

Project 5-6: Removing, Adding, and Changing Deadlines

You have just finished reviewing the Don Funk Music Video project schedule and have decided to make some changes and additions to the deadlines on this project.

OPEN *Don Funk Music Video 5-6* from the data files for this lesson.

1. Remove the deadline for task 9.
2. Change the deadline for task 62 to July 8, 2016.
3. Add a deadline of May 27, 2016 for task 37.
4. **SAVE** the project schedule as *Don Funk Revised Deadlines*, and then **CLOSE** the file. **CLOSE** Project.

■ Circling Back

Mete Goktepe is a project management specialist at Woodgrove Bank. The management at Woodgrove has recently decided that the eight-year old commercial lending software currently in use is outdated and needs to be replaced. Mete has been assigned as the project manager for the Request For Proposal (RFP) process to evaluate and select new software. This process entails determining needs, identifying vendors, requesting proposals, reviewing proposals, and selecting the software.

➔ Project 1: Entering Tasks

Acting as Mete, you first need to enter project information and then enter and organize the tasks for this project.

GET READY. Launch Project if it is not already running.

1. In the New section of the Backstage area, double-click Blank Project.
2. On the Tasks tab, in the Tasks command group, click the Mode button. From the list, click Auto Schedule.
3. Click the Project tab, then click Project Information. Set the start date to May 2, 2016.
4. SAVE the project plan as *RFP Bank Software Tasks.*
5. In the Properties group on the ribbon, click the Change Working Time button.
6. Add the following exception dates:
   - Memorial Day to begin on May 30, 2016 and to occur yearly on the last Monday of May for 2 occurrences.
   - Independence Day to begin on July 4, 2016 and to occur yearly on July 4 for 2 occurrences.
   - Labor Day to begin on September 5, 2016 and to occur the first Monday of September for 2 occurrences
   - Thanksgiving Day to begin on November 24, 2016 and to occur on the fourth Thursday of November for 2 occurrences
7. Click OK to close the Change Working Time dialog box.
8. In the Gantt Chart view, enter the following task names and durations (enter all tasks, even if no duration is listed). [This is a partial list of tasks in the project plan. Additional data will be available in future exercises.]

TASK NAME	DURATION
RFP solicitation process begins	0d
RFP Creation	
RFP creation begins	0d
Document software requirements	8d
Define evaluation criteria	2d
Identify evaluation team	1d
Draft RFP	5d
Review RFP with management and commercial lending representatives	1d
Refine RFP	1d
RFP ready to release	0d
RFP Release	
RFP release begins	0d
Identify software suppliers	5d
Determine deadline dates for vendor responses	2h
Finalize RFP with time frames and points of contact	6h
Release RFP to target companies	2d
Conduct RFP briefing	1d
RFP release complete	0d
RFP Solicitation Process Complete	0d

9. SAVE the project plan.
10. Click the Task tab. Using the outline structure in the table above, indent and outdent tasks as necessary to organize the tasks into phases.
11. SAVE the project plan
12. Select tasks 1, 3 through 10, and 12 through 19. Link them with a Finish-to-Start relationship.
13. SAVE the project plan.

    PAUSE. LEAVE Project and the project schedule open to use in the next exercise.

Project 2: Establishing Resources

You now need to establish the resources that will perform the work on the tasks in this project plan. USE the schedule you created in the previous exercise.

1. SAVE the project plan as *RFP Bank Software Resources.*
2. Click the View tab then select Resource Sheet.
3. Enter the following resource information on the Resource Sheet.

Resource Name	Type	Initials	Group	Max Units	Std. Rate
Syed Abbas	Work	SA	CL Mgmt	100	2000/w
Eli Bowen	Work	EB	CL Mgmt	100	1850/w
Nicole Caron	Work	NC	IT Mgmt	100	2200/w
Aaron Con	Work	AC	IT Mgmt	100	2000/w
Andrew Dixon	Work	AD	IT	50	25/h
JoLynn Dobney	Work	JD	IT	100	1400/w
Mete Goktepe	Work	MG	IT	100	1250/w
Nicole Holliday	Work	NH	CL	50	20/h
Marc J. Ingle	Work	MJI	CL	100	1300/w
Kevin Kennedy	Work	KK	CL	100	1200/w
Dan Moyer	Work	DM	SR Mgmt	100	3000/w
Misty Shock	Work	MS	SR Mgmt	100	3500/w
Nate Sun	Work	NS	CL Ops	100	20/h
Tai Yee	Work	TY	CL Ops	100	19.50/h
Frank Miller	Work	FM	CL Ops	100	18/h
Jo Brown	Work	JB	CL Ops Mgmt	100	1850/w
Mike Tiano	Work	MT	CL Ops Mgmt	100	1900/w
CL Usergroup	Work	CLUG	CL	600	100/h
Digital Projector	Work	DP	Equip	200	0
Large Conference Room	Work	LCR	Location	400	0
Small Conference Room	Work	SCR	Location	100	0
Food/Catering	Cost	FOOD	Cost		
Travel	Cost	TRVL	Cost		

4. **SAVE** the project plan.

   PAUSE. LEAVE Project and the project schedule open to use in the next exercise.

Project 3: Assigning Resources to Tasks

Finally, you need to assign the resources to the tasks in your project plan. USE the schedule you created in the previous exercise.

1. **SAVE** the project plan as *RFP Bank Software Assignments.*
2. Switch to the Gantt Chart view.
3. Right-click the Task Mode column heading. From the submenu that appears, select Hide Column.
4. Click the Resource tab and then activate the Assign Resources dialog box.

5. Select the name of task 4, Document software requirements.

6. In the Assign Resources dialog box, select the following resources: JoLynn Dobney, Nicole Holliday, CL Usergroup. Click the Assign button.

7. Select the name of task 5, Define evaluation criteria.

8. In the Assign Resources dialog box, select the following resources: Mete Goktepe, Syed Abbas, Nicole Caron, Mike Tiano. Click the Assign button.

9. Using the same process that you used in steps 4–7, assign the following resources to the corresponding tasks.

Task #	Task Name	Resource Names to Assign
6	Identify evaluation team	Syed Abbas, Nicole Caron, Jo Brown
7	Draft RFP	Mete Goktepe, Kevin Kennedy
8	Review RFP with management . . .	Mete Goktepe, Kevin Kennedy, Eli Bowen, Large Conference Room
9	Refine RFP	Mete Goktepe, Kevin Kennedy
13	Identify software suppliers	Mete Goktepe, Kevin Kennedy
14	Determine deadline dates . . .	Eli Bowen, Mete Goktepe, Aaron Con
15	Finalize RFP with time frames . . .	Kevin Kennedy
16	Release RFP to target companies	Mete Goktepe, Kevin Kennedy
17	Conduct RFP briefing	Mete Goktepe, Kevin Kennedy, Nicole Caron, Small Conference Room

10. Select the name of task 4, Document software requirements.

11. In the Assign Resources dialog box, select the following resources: Marc J. Ingle, Kevin Kennedy, Andrew Dixon. Assign these resources to the task.

12. In the Smart Tag Actions button that appears in the Indicators column, select Reduce the hours resources work per day (units), but keep the same duration and work.

13. Select the name of task 8, Review RFP with management and commercial lending representatives.

14. In the Assign Resources dialog box, select the following resources: Marc J. Ingle, Nicole Holliday, Mike Tiano. Assign these resources to the task.

15. In the Smart Tag Actions button that appears in the Indicators column, select Increase the amount of work but keep the same duration.

16. Select the name of task 17, Conduct RFP briefing.

17. In the Assign Resources dialog box, select the following resources: Eli Bowen, Jo Brown. Assign these resources to the task.

18. In the Smart Tag Actions button that appears in the Indicators column, select Reduce the hours resources work per day (units), but keep the same duration and work.

19. Click Close in the Assign Resources dialog box.

20. SAVE and then CLOSE the project schedule.

CLOSE Microsoft Project.

Fine-Tuning Resources

LESSON 6

LESSON SKILL MATRIX

Skills	Tasks
Entering Material Resource Consumption Rates	Enter a variable consumption rate for a material resource
Entering Costs Per Use for Resources	Enter a cost per use for a resource
Assigning Multiple Pay Rates for a Resource	Assign multiple pay rates for a resource
Applying Different Cost Rates to Assignments	Apply a different cost rate to an assignment
Specifying Resource Availability at Different Times	Specify a resource's availability over time
Resolving Resource Over allocations Manually	Manually resolve a resource over-allocation
Leveling Over allocated Resources	Use resource leveling to resolve an over-allocation

You are a video project manager for Southridge Video, and one of your primary responsibilities recently has been to manage the new Don Funk Music Video project. You have just finished applying some of the more advanced features of Microsoft Project 2013 that focus on fine-tuning task details in a project schedule. Another important part of project management is to understand how to make the best use of resources' time, as people and equipment resources are often the most costly and limited part of a project. In this lesson, you will continue the fine-tuning activities on which you have been working, this time focusing on resources. Work done in this lesson should be completed prior to saving a baseline and commencing project work.

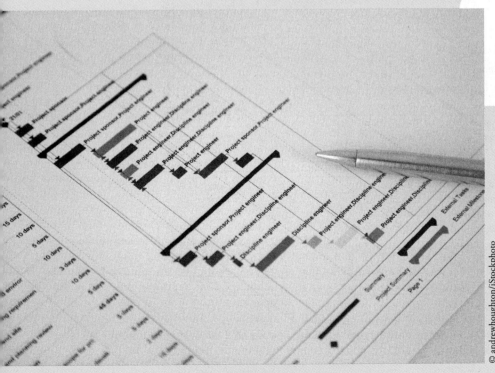

KEY TERMS
cost rate table
fixed consumption rate
variable consumption rate

© andrewhoughton/iStockphoto

121

■ Entering Material Resource Consumption Rates

THE BOTTOM LINE In order to accurately calculate the cost of a material resource, you also need to know its consumption rate, or how quickly it is used up.

 ENTER A VARIABLE CONSUMPTION RATE FOR A MATERIAL RESOURCE

GET READY. Before you begin these steps, launch Microsoft Project. **OPEN** the *Don Funk Music Video 6M* project schedule from the data files for this lesson. **SAVE** the file as *Don Funk Music Video 6* in the solutions folder for this lesson as directed by your instructor.

1. Press the **F5** key. The Go To dialog box appears. Type **35** in the ID box, and then click **OK**. Microsoft Project displays task 35, Scene 1 video shoot.

   This is the first of several scenes that requires DVDs to be recorded. You have determined that the initial estimates for DVD consumption were incorrect. Because for each hour of work you will only be recording for 30 minutes, you have determined that the correct consumption rate for the DVD resource is 0.25 DVD/hour (the DVDs record 2 hours of filming).

2. Click the **Resource** tab and then click the **Assign Resources** button. The Assign Resources dialog box appears.

3. In the Assign Resources dialog box, click the **Units** field for DVD. Type **0.25/h** and then press **Enter**. Microsoft Project changes the consumption rate of DVDs for this task to 0.25 per hour.

4. Double-click the **column divider** between the Units and Cost columns to expand the Units column. The Assign Resources dialog box should look similar to Figure 6-1.

Figure 6-1

Assign Resources dialog box displaying consumption rate for DVD's

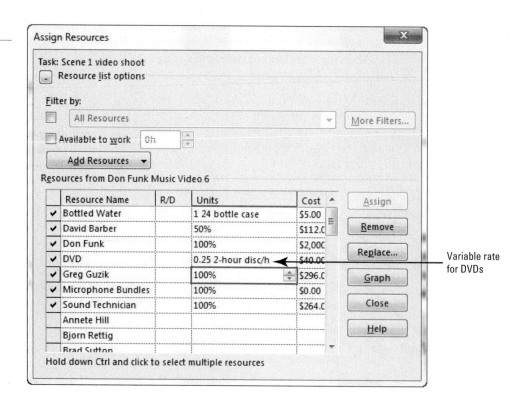

5. Click the **Close** button in the Assign Resources dialog box. You will now verify the cost and work values of the DVD assignment to task 35.

Team
Planner ▾

6. On the ribbon, click the **down-arrow** under the Team Planner button. Click **Task Usage**.

7. Double-click the **DVD resource assignment** under task 35, Scene 1 video shoot. The Assignment Information dialog box appears.

8. Select the **General** tab, if it is not already selected. Note the Work, Units, and Cost fields. The Assignment Information box should look similar to Figure 6-2.

Figure 6-2

Assignment Information dialog box with DVD resource assignment details

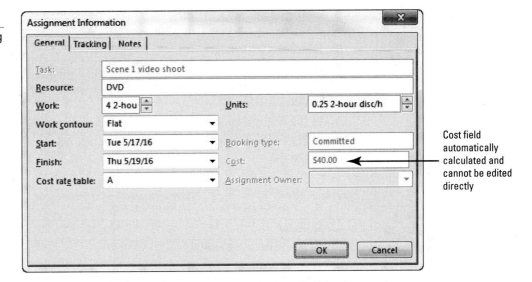

Cost field automatically calculated and cannot be edited directly

9. Click **OK** to close the Assignment Information dialog box.

10. **SAVE** the project schedule.

   PAUSE. LEAVE Project open to use in the next exercise.

In this exercise, you have just assigned a variable consumption rate to a material resource. As you have seen in Microsoft Project, you can assign two types of consumption rates:

- A *fixed consumption rate* means that an absolute quantity of the resources will be used, no matter the duration of the task to which the material is assigned. For example, filling a swimming pool requires a fixed amount of water to be used.

- A *variable consumption rate* means that the amount of the material resource consumed is dependent upon the duration of the task. When shooting DVDs, as in this exercise, you will use more DVDs in six hours than in four. After you enter a variable consumption rate for a material resource's assignment, Microsoft Project calculated the total quantity and cost of the material resource consumed, based on the task's duration. An advantage of using a variable rate of consumption is that as the duration of the task changes, so do the calculated amount and cost of the material resource, since the rate is tied to the task's duration.

■ Entering Costs Per Use for Resources

THE BOTTOM LINE

In addition to its pay or consumption rate, a resource can also have a cost associated with each use.

In this exercise, you enter a per-use cost for a material resource. Any resource can have a cost per use, in place of or in addition to the costs derived from their pay rates (work resources) or consumption rates (material resources). You can also specify whether the per-use cost should accrue at the beginning or end of the task to which it is assigned.

⊕ ENTER A COST PER USE FOR A RESOURCE

USE the project schedule you created in the previous exercise.

1. On the Resource ribbon, click the **down-arrow** under Team Planner button, then select the **Resource Sheet**.

2. On the Resource Sheet, select resource 11, **Digital Truck-Mounted Video Camera**.

3. On the ribbon, click the **Information** button, located in the Properties group. The Resource Information dialog box appears.

4. Select the **Costs** tab.

5. Under Cost rate tables, select the **A (Default)** tab if it is not already selected. The Digital Truck-Mounted Video Camera has a $100 maintenance fee for every time you use it.

6. In the first row under the *Per Use Cost* column, type **100**, and then press **Enter**.

7. Select **End** from the *Cost accrual* dropdown box. Your screen should look similar to Figure 6-3.

Figure 6-3

Resource Information dialog box displaying cost per use for the resource

Cost Rate Table A $100 fee for each use of the resource

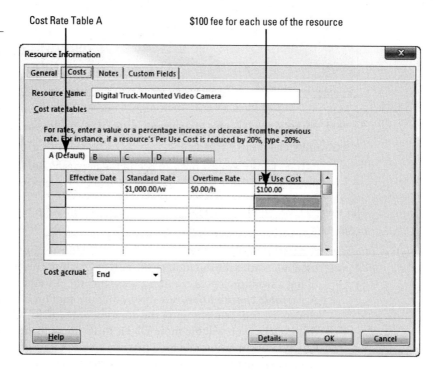

8. Click **OK** to close the Resource Information dialog box.

9. SAVE the project schedule.

PAUSE. LEAVE Project open to use in the next exercise.

■ Assigning Multiple Pay Rates for a Resource

THE BOTTOM LINE

Sometimes, the same work resource may perform different tasks with different pay rates. Microsoft Project enables you to enter multiple pay rates for a single resource.

In this exercise, you enter a second cost rate table for a resource. A ***cost rate table*** is resource pay rates that are stored on the Costs tab of the Resource Information dialog box. For a given resource you can enter up to five cost rate tables. Each table has 25 possible entry lines (125 lines total in the five tables) so you can assign dates at which the new cost rate takes effect. After you assign a resource to a task, you can specify which rate table should apply.

⊕ ASSIGN MULTIPLE PAY RATES FOR A RESOURCE

USE the project schedule you created in the previous exercise. Because Yan Li's rate differs depending on whether he is working on sound production tasks or administrative tasks, you need to enter a second rate for him.

1. In the Resource Sheet view, click the name of resource 9, **Yan Li**.
2. On the ribbon, click the **Information** button. The Resource Information dialog box appears.

 You can also double-click the Resource Name field to activate the Resource Information dialog box.

3. Click the **Costs** tab, if it is not already selected. Each tab of the Cost Rate table corresponds to one of the five pay rates a resource can have.
4. Under Cost rate tables, click the **B** tab.
5. Select the default entry of $0.00/h in the field directly below the Standard Rate column heading, type **15/h**, and then press **Enter**.

TAKE NOTE* When you enter a pay rate, if you do not key in the currency symbol, Microsoft Project will supply it for you.

6. In the Overtime Rate field, type **22.50/h**, and then press **Enter**. Your screen should look similar to Figure 6-4.

Figure 6-4

Resource Information dialog box showing the second rate table for Yan Li

Cost Rate Table B   Overtime rate of 22.50/hr

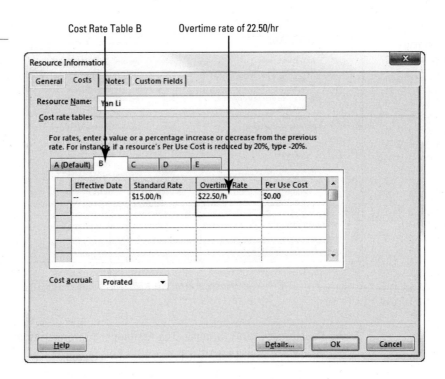

7. Click OK to close the Resource Information dialog box. Note that on the Resource Sheet, Yan Li's standard pay rate is still $18.50 per hour. This was the value in Rate Table A, which is the default rate table. This value will be used for all of Yan Li's task assignments unless you specify a different rate table.

8. SAVE the project schedule.

   PAUSE. LEAVE Project open to use in the next exercise.

■ Applying Different Cost Rates to Assignments

↓
THE BOTTOM LINE   Microsoft Project enables you to enter as many as five different pay rates for a resource. These pay rates may be applied to different assignments as necessary.

 APPLY A DIFFERENT COST RATE TO AN ASSIGNMENT

USE the project schedule you created in the previous exercise.

1. On the Resource ribbon, click the down-arrow under the Team Planner button, and then click Task Usage.

2. Press the F5 key. Type 6 in the ID box, and then click OK.

3. Click the View tab. Verify the Cost table is selected by clicking the Tables button, located in the Data group, and then select Cost.

4. Under task 6, click the row heading directly to the left of Yan Li so that Yan Li's entire assignment is selected.

5. Move the center divider in the table portion (on the left) of the Task Usage view to the right until the Total Cost column is visible. You can see that the total cost of Yan's assignment to this task is $2114.29. Your screen should look similar to Figure 6-5.

Figure 6-5

Task Usage view showing cost for Yan Li's assignment using cost rate table A

	Task Name	Fixed Cost	Fixed Cost Accrual	Total Cost	Details	S	S	M	T	W	T	F
0	⊿ **Don Funk Music Video**	$0.00	Prorated	60,029.64	Work			34h	28h	21.03h	16.85h	16.85h
1	⊿ **Pre-Production**	$0.00	Prorated	$19,399.64	Work			34h	28h	21.03h	16.85h	16.85h
2	Pre-Production begins	$0.00	Prorated	$0.00	Work							
3	⊿ Review screenplay	$0.00	Prorated	$4,590.00	Work							
	Scott Seely			$2,340.00	Work							
	Jeff Pike			$2,250.00	Work							
4	⊿ Develop scene blocking and schedule	$0.00	Prorated	$1,560.00	Work							
	Scott Seely			$780.00	Work							
	Judy Lew			$780.00	Work							
5	⊿ Develop production layouts	$0.00	Prorated	$4,640.00	Work			28h	28h	10.5h		
	Jeff Pike			$1,500.00	Work			8h	8h	3h		
	Brenda Diaz			$1,020.00	Work			8h	8h	3h		
	Brad Sutton			$1,320.00	Work			8h	8h	3h		
	Annete Hill			$800.00	Work			4h	4h	1.5h		
6	⊿ Identify and reserve locations	$0.00	Prorated	$7,012.14	Work					10.53h	16.85h	16.85h
	Jeff Pike			$1,875.00	Work					2.5h	4h	4h
	Annete Hill			$1,142.86	Work					1.43h	2.28h	2.28h
	Ryan Ihrig			$1,800.00	Work					3.75h	6h	6h
	Yan Li			**$2,114.29**	Work					2.85h	4.57h	4.57h
	DVD			$80.00	Work (					0.2	0.32	0.32
7	Book musicians	$0.00	Prorated	$0.00	Work							
8	Book dancers	$0.00	Prorated	$0.00	Work							
9	Reserve audio recording equipment	$0.00	Prorated	$0.00	Work							
10	Reserve video recording equipment	$0.00	Prorated	$0.00	Work							

Yan Li's cost for task 6 is $2114.29 based on Cost Rate Table A

6. Double-click Yan Li's name. The Assignment Information dialog box appears.

7. Click the General tab, if it is not already selected.

8. In the Cost rate table box, type or select **B**, and then click **OK**. Microsoft Project applies Yan Li's Cost Rate Table B to the assignment. The new cost of the assignment, $1,714.29, is reflected in the total cost column. Your screen should look similar to Figure 6-6.

Figure 6-6

Task Usage view showing cost for Yan Li's assignment using cost rate table B

	Task Name	Fixed Cost	Fixed Cost Accrual	Total Cost	Details	S	Feb 21, '16 S	M	T	W	T	F
0	▲ Don Funk Music Video	$0.00	Prorated	59,629.64	Work			34h	28h	21.03h	16.85h	16.85h
1	▲ Pre-Production	$0.00	Prorated	$18,999.64	Work			34h	28h	21.03h	16.85h	16.85h
2	Pre-Production begins	$0.00	Prorated	$0.00	Work							
3	▲ Review screenplay	$0.00	Prorated	$4,590.00	Work							
	Scott Seely			$2,340.00	Work							
	Jeff Pike			$2,250.00	Work							
4	▲ Develop scene blocking and schedule	$0.00	Prorated	$1,560.00	Work							
	Scott Seely			$780.00	Work							
	Judy Lew			$780.00	Work							
5	▲ Develop production layouts	$0.00	Prorated	$4,640.00	Work			28h	28h	10.5h		
	Jeff Pike			$1,500.00	Work			8h	8h	3h		
	Brenda Diaz			$1,020.00	Work			8h	8h	3h		
	Brad Sutton			$1,320.00	Work			8h	8h	3h		
	Annete Hill			$800.00	Work			4h	4h	1.5h		
6	▲ Identify and reserve locations	$0.00	Prorated	$6,612.14	Work					10.53h	16.85h	16.85h
	Jeff Pike			$1,875.00	Work					2.5h	4h	4h
	Annete Hill			$1,142.86	Work					1.43h	2.28h	2.28h
	Ryan Ihrig			$1,800.00	Work					3.75h	6h	6h
	Yan Li			$1,714.29	Work					2.85h	4.57h	4.57h
	DVD			$80.00	Work (					0.2	0.32	0.32
7	Book musicians	$0.00	Prorated	$0.00	Work							
8	Book dancers	$0.00	Prorated	$0.00	Work							
9	Reserve audio recording equipment	$0.00	Prorated	$0.00	Work							
10	Reserve video recording equipment	$0.00	Prorated	$0.00	Work							

Yan Li's cost for task 6 is $1714.29 based on Cost Rate Table B

ANOTHER WAY   If you find that you are changing cost rate tables frequently, it is quicker to display the Cost Rate Table field directly in the Resource Usage or Task Usage view. To add the Cost Rate Table Field, right-click a column heading, then select Insert Column. Select Cost Rate Table from the dropdown list.

9. **SAVE** the project schedule.

PAUSE. LEAVE Project open to use in the next exercise.

In this exercise, you applied an alternate rate table for a resource to reflect a different pay rate for different work. You can set up as many as five pay rates per resource. This enables you to assign different pay rates to different assignments for a resource. By default, Microsoft Project uses cost rate table A, but you can specify any time another rate table should be used.

■ Specifying Resource Availability at Different Times

THE BOTTOM LINE   Sometimes, as you are working on a project schedule, you will find that a resource will have varying availability. To control this availability, Microsoft Project uses Max. Units, or the maximum capacity of a resource, to accomplish tasks.

SPECIFY A RESOURCE'S AVAILABILITY OVER TIME

USE the project schedule you created in the previous exercise.

Change Working Time

1. On the ribbon, click the **Resource Sheet** button.

2. In the Resource Name column, double-click click the name of resource 32, **electrician**. The Resource Information dialog box appears.

3. Click the **General** tab, if it is not already selected.

   You originally planned that there would be three electricians available for the entire video production, but you have just determined that there will only be two electricians available from May 1–May 20, 2016.

4. Under Resource Availability, in the first row of the Available From column, leave **NA** (Microsoft Project's term for a null field, or a field that is blank).

5. In the Available To cell in the first row, key or select **4/30/16**.

6. In the Available From cell in the second row, key or select **5/1/16**.

7. In the Available To cell in the second row, key or select **5/20/16**.

8. In the Units cell in the second row, key or select **200%**.

9. In the Available From cell in the third row, key or select **5/21/16**.

10. Leave the Available To cell in the third row blank. Microsoft Project will fill this with **NA**.

11. In the Units cell in the third row, type or select **300%**, and then press **Enter**. Your screen should look similar to Figure 6-7.

Figure 6-7

Resource Information dialog box with resource availability dates

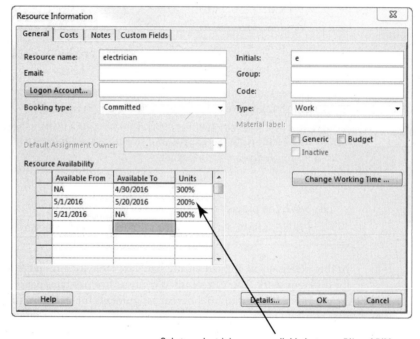

Only two electricians are available between 5/1 and 5/20

12. Click **OK** to close the Resource Information dialog box.

TAKE NOTE*

Microsoft Project will display 200% in the Max. Units field only when the current date (based on your computer's system clock) is within the May 1–May 20 range. At other times it will display 300%.

13. **SAVE** the project schedule.

   PAUSE. LEAVE Project open to use in the next exercise.

In this exercise, you set resource availability over time using the Resource Availability grid on the General tab of the Resource Information dialog box. Recall from Lessons 3 and 4 that a resource's capacity to work is measured in units. The Max. Units value stored in Microsoft Project is the maximum capacity of a resource to accomplish tasks. A resource's calendar determines when a resource is available to work. However, the resource's capacity to work (measured in units and limited by their Max. Units value) determines how much that resource can work within those hours without becoming over allocated.

You can set different Max. Units values to be applied over different time periods for any resource. Setting a resource's availability over time enables you to control exactly what a resource's Max. Units value is at any time.

■ Resolving Resource Over Allocations Manually

THE BOTTOM LINE A resource is over allocated when it is scheduled for work that exceeds its maximum capacity to work. You can manually resolve this situation within the project schedule.

⊕ MANUALLY RESOLVE A RESOURCE OVER ALLOCATION

USE the project schedule you created in the previous exercise.

1. On the View ribbon, click the **down-arrow** to the right of the Resource Sheet button, click **More Views**, select **Resource Allocation**, and then click the **Apply** button. Microsoft Project switches to the Resource Allocation view. This is a split view that displays the Resource Usage view in the top pane and the Leveling Gantt view in the bottom pane.

2. On the ribbon, in the Zoom group, click the **down-arrow** in the Timescale box and select days. Your screen should look similar to Figure 6-8.

Figure 6-8

Resource Allocation view

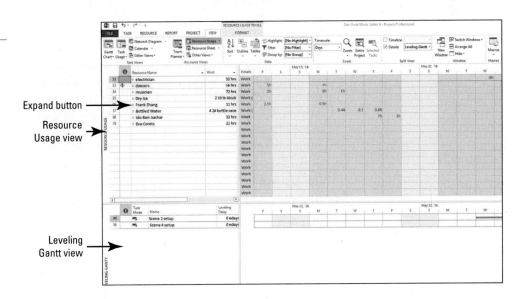

3. In the Resource Usage view, **scroll vertically** through the Resource Name column so that you can see the names. The names you see formatted in red are over allocated resources.

4. In the Resource Name column, navigate (scroll) to and select the name of resource 26, **Greg Guzik**.

5. Click the **expand button** next to Greg Guzik's name to display his assignments. Scroll down to see the assignments, if necessary.

6. Press the **F5** key. Type **7/15/16** in the Date box, and then click **OK**. The Leveling Gantt pane shows the task bars for two of Greg Guzik's assignments. Your screen should look similar to Figure 6-9.

Figure 6-9

Resource Allocation View showing Greg Guzik's over allocated assignments

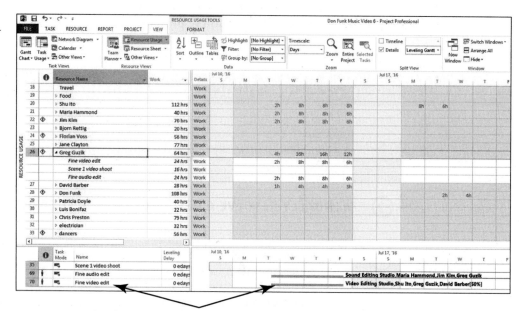

Greg Guzik's assignments and associated Gantt bars

In the upper pane, you see that Greg is assigned full-time to two tasks that both start on Tuesday, July 12. He is over allocated for most of the duration of both tasks. In the lower pane, you can see the Gantt bars for the two tasks that have caused Greg to be over allocated during this time. For tasks 69 and 70, Greg is assigned eight hours of work on both Wednesday and Thursday, and six hours of work on Friday. This results in 16 hours of work on two days, and 12 hours of work on another–beyond Greg's capacity to work. In addition, Greg is assigned four hours of work on Tuesday, performing two tasks at the same time. However, this assignment is NOT shown in red. This is because the default over allocation setting is set to look for over allocations on a "Day-by-Day" basis. Since Greg has 8 hours of availability that day, it does not see this as an over allocation.

7. In the Resource Name column, double-click Greg's first assignment, **Fine video edit**. The Assignment Information dialog box appears.

8. Click the **General** tab, if it is not already selected.

9. In the Units box, select **50%**, and then click **OK** to close the Assignment Information dialog box.

   Note that Greg's daily work assignments on this task are reduced, but the task duration is increased. You want to reduce the work, but not increase the duration of the task. Also note the Actions button that has been activated next to the name of the assignment.

10. Click the **Actions** button. Review the options in the list that appears. Your screen should look similar to Figure 6-10.

Figure 6-10

Resource Allocation view with
Smart Tag action list displayed

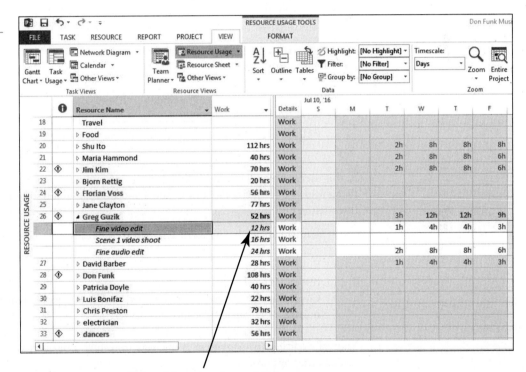

21		▷ Maria Hammond	40 hrs	Work			2h	8h	8h	6h
22	◇	▷ Jim Kim	70 hrs	Work			2h	8h	8h	6h
23		▷ Bjorn Rettig	20 hrs	Work						
24	◇	▷ Florian Voss	56 hrs	Work						
25		▷ Jane Clayton	77 hrs	Work						
26	◇	◢ Greg Guzik	64 hrs	Work			3h	12h	12h	10h
	! ▾	*Fine video edit*	*24 hrs*	Work			1h	4h	4h	4h

You changed the hours resources work per day (units). Do you want to:

◉ Change the duration but keep the amount of work the same.
○ Change the amount of work but keep the duration the same.

Select the second option in the Actions Tag list

11. Click **Change the amount of work but keep the duration the same** in the Actions option list. Microsoft Project reduces Greg's work assignments on the task and restores the task to its original duration. Your screen should look similar to Figure 6-11.

   Notice that Greg is still over allocated, so now you will reduce the assignment units on his second task.

Figure 6-11

Resource Allocation View with
corrected work values

			Work		Details	Jul 10, '16 S	M	T	W	T	F
18		Travel			Work						
19		▷ Food			Work						
20		▷ Shu Ito	112 hrs		Work			2h	8h	8h	8h
21		▷ Maria Hammond	40 hrs		Work			2h	8h	8h	6h
22	◇	▷ Jim Kim	70 hrs		Work			2h	8h	8h	6h
23		▷ Bjorn Rettig	20 hrs		Work						
24	◇	▷ Florian Voss	56 hrs		Work						
25		▷ Jane Clayton	77 hrs		Work						
26	◇	◢ Greg Guzik	52 hrs		Work			3h	12h	12h	9h
		Fine video edit	*12 hrs*		Work			1h	4h	4h	3h
		Scene 1 video shoot	16 hrs		Work						
		Fine audio edit	*24 hrs*		Work			2h	8h	8h	6h
27		▷ David Barber	28 hrs		Work			1h	4h	4h	3h
28	◇	▷ Don Funk	108 hrs		Work						
29		▷ Patricia Doyle	40 hrs		Work						
30		▷ Luis Bonifaz	22 hrs		Work						
31		▷ Chris Preston	79 hrs		Work						
32		▷ electrician	32 hrs		Work						
33	◇	▷ dancers	56 hrs		Work						

Task work hours have been reduced

12. In the Resource Name column, double-click Greg's second assignment, **Fine audio edit**. The Assignment Information dialog box appears.

13. Click the **General** tab if it is not already visible.

14. In the Units box, type or select **50%**, and then click **OK** to close the Assignment Information dialog box.

15. Click the **Actions** button. Click **Change the amount of work but keep the duration the same** in the Actions option list. Greg's assignments on Wednesday and Thursday are now reduced to eight hours each day. You have manually changed Greg's assignments to reduce his work and resolve his over allocation. He is now fully allocated on Wednesday through Friday. Your screen should look similar to Figure 6-12.

Figure 6-12

Resource Allocation view with Greg Guzik's over allocation resolved

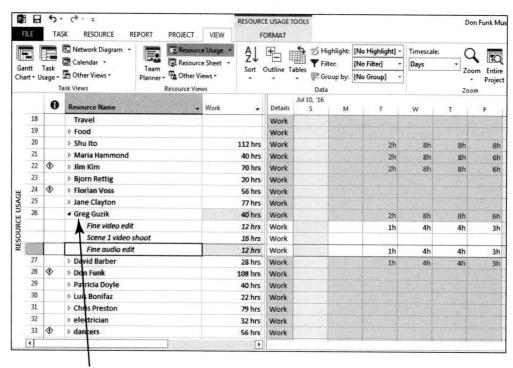

Greg Guzik is no longer over allocated

16. SAVE the project schedule.

PAUSE. LEAVE Project open to use in the next exercise.

In this exercise, you have manually resolved a resource over allocation. Recall from Lesson 4 that a resource's capacity to work is called allocation, and a resource is said to be in one of three states:

- Under allocated: The work assigned to the resource is less than the resource's maximum capacity.
- Fully allocated: The total work of a resource's task assignments is exactly equal to that resource's work capacity.
- Over allocated: A resource is assigned to do more work than can be done within the normal work capacity of the resourceter.

Manually editing an assignment is one way to resolve a resource over allocation, but there are several other options.

- You can replace the over allocated resource with another resource using the Replace button in the Assign Resources dialog box.
- You can reduce the value in the Units field in the Assignment Information or Assign Resources dialog box.
- If the over allocation is not extreme (for instance, 9 hours of work assigned in a normal 8-hour workday), you can just allow the over allocation to remain in the schedule.

In Microsoft Project 2013, over allocations are also noted when you have assigned a work resource to working times outside their normal working hours. Recall from Lesson 4 you assigned a Task Calendar for the overnight beach filming. This resulted in an over allocation for the work resources assigned to that task. They are not truly over allocated by definition. It is simply the software's way of notifying you that you have resources assigned work which is outside their normal working hours.

■ SOFTWARE ORIENTATION

Microsoft Project's Resource Leveling Dialog Box

The Resource Leveling dialog box allows you to specify the rules and options that control how Microsoft Project performs resource leveling (see Figure 6-13).

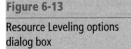

Figure 6-13

Resource Leveling options dialog box

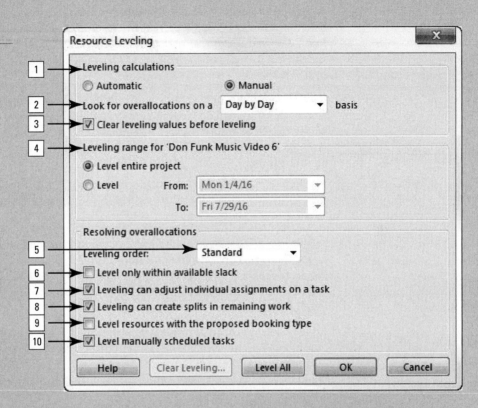

The options in the Resource Leveling Dialog box are as follows:

1. **Leveling calculations** – These selections determine whether Microsoft Project levels resources constantly (Automatic) or only when you tell it to do so (Manual). Automatic leveling occurs as soon as a resource becomes over allocated.

2. **Look for over allocations on a .....basis** – This selection determines the timeframe in which Microsoft Project will look for over allocations. If a resource it is over allocated at the level you choose here, its name will be formatted in red. If a resource is not over allocated at the level you choose, there will be no indication of any over allocation.

3. **Clear leveling values before leveling** – There are times where you may have to level resources repeatedly to get the results you want. (You might first try to level day by day, and then switch to hour by hour, for example.) If the Clear leveling values before leveling check box is selected, Microsoft Project removes any existing delays from all tasks before leveling.

4. **Leveling range for...** – This selection determines whether you level the entire project or only those assignments that fall within a date range you specify. Leveling within a date range is advantageous when you have started tracking actual work and you want to level only the remaining assignments in a project.

5. **Leveling order** – This setting allows you to control the priority Microsoft Project uses to determine which tasks it should delay to resolve a resource conflict. There are three options: ID Only; Standard; and Priority, Standard. The ID Only option

delays tasks according to their ID numbers only. Use this option when your project schedule has no task relationships or constraints. The Standard option delays tasks according to their predecessor relationships, start dates, task constraints, slack, priority, and IDs. The Priority, Standard option looks at the task's priority value before other standard criteria.

6. Level only within available slack – Clearing this setting allows Microsoft Project to extend the project's finish date, if necessary, to resolve resource over allocations. Selecting this setting would prevent Microsoft Project from extending the project's finish date in order to resolve resource over allocations. Instead, Project would only use the free slack of tasks, which may or may not be adequate to fully resolve resource over allocations.

7. Leveling can adjust individual assignments to work on a task – This setting allows Microsoft Project to add leveling delay (or, if Leveling can create splits in remaining work is selected, to split work on assignments) independently of any other resources assigned to the same task. This could cause resources to start and finish work on a task at different times.

8. Leveling can create splits in remaining work – This setting allows Microsoft Project to split work on a task in order to resolve an over allocation.

9. Level resources with the proposed booking type – Use this option only when Microsoft Project 2013 is being used in an enterprise environment, such as Project Server 2013. Using this option allows Microsoft Project to level resources in projects, connected to Project Server 2013, that have a proposed booking type. Deselecting this option will cause the software to ignore all resources that have a proposed booking type.

10. Level manually schedule tasks – If your project contains manually scheduled tasks which have over allocated resources, selecting this option allows the software to split or delay these tasks. Leave this option selected if you want to maintain control and manually resolve over allocations on the manually scheduled tasks.

■ Leveling Over allocated Resources

THE BOTTOM LINE
To avoid an over allocation situation, you can cause a resource's work on a specific task to be delayed through a process known as resource leveling.

⊙ USE RESOURCE LEVELING TO RESOLVE AN OVER ALLOCATION

USE the project schedule you created in the previous exercise.

1. On the ribbon, in the Split View group, deselect the **Details** checkbox.

2. On the ribbon, click **Resource Sheet**, located in the Resource Views group. The Resource Sheet view appears. Take note of the resource names that appear in red and have the over allocated icon in the Indicators column.

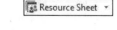

3. Click on the **Resource** tab. In the Level group, select **Leveling Options**. The Resource Leveling dialog box appears.

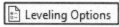

TAKE NOTE*
Depending on previous uses of the Resource Leveling dialog box in Microsoft Project, the options you are selecting in steps 4 through 13 may already be selected for you.

4. In the Resource Leveling dialog box, under Leveling calculations, select **Manual**, if it is not already selected.

TAKE NOTE* All of the settings in the Resource Leveling dialog box apply to all project schedules with which you work in Microsoft Project – NOT just the active project schedule. It might sound easier to use automatic leveling, but it will make frequent adjustments to project schedules whether you want them to occur or not. Because of this, it is recommended that you always have Manual Leveling calculations selected.

5. In the Look for over allocations on a ..... basis box, select **Day by Day**.
6. Select the **Clear leveling values before leveling** box.

TROUBLESHOOTING In most projects, leveling in detail more precise than Day by Day can result in unrealistically precise adjustments to assignments.

7. Under Leveling range for, select **Level entire project**.
8. Under Resolving over allocations, in the Leveling order box, select **Standard**.
9. Clear the **Level only within available slack** check box.
10. Select the **Leveling can adjust individual assignments on a task** check box.
11. Select the **Leveling can create splits in remaining work** check box.
12. Clear the Level resources with the proposed booking type check box.
13. Clear the Level manually scheduled tasks check box. Your screen should look similar to Figure 6-14.

Figure 6-14

Resource Leveling options dialog box

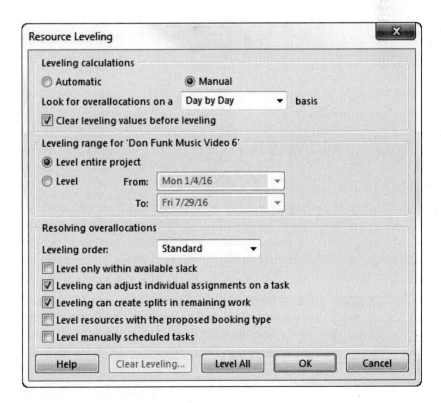

14. Click the **Level All** button.

TAKE NOTE * If you select OK after setting the options, Microsoft Project will not perform leveling, unless you have selected Automatic leveling.

15. Microsoft Project levels the over allocated resources. Notice that resource 6, Brad Sutton and resource 22, Jim Kim no longer are over allocated. Some resources may still be formatted in red, meaning that these resources are still over allocated, probably due to being assigned work during their normal non-working times. Your screen should look similar to Figure 6-15.

Figure 6-15

Resource Sheet view after resource leveling

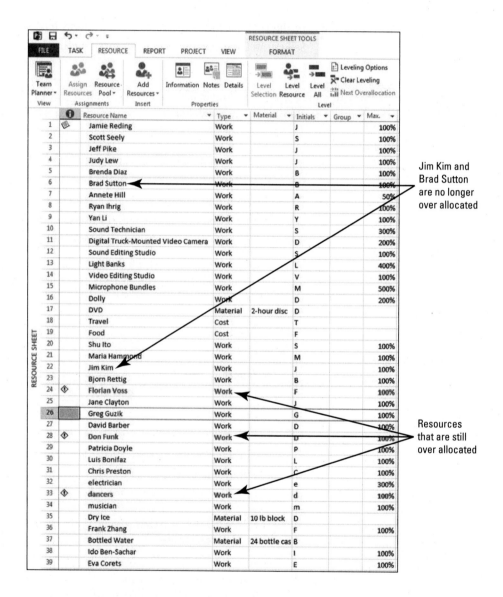

16. On the ribbon, click the **down-arrow** under the Team Planner button. Select **More Views**, select **Leveling Gantt**, and then click **Apply**. Microsoft Project displays the Leveling Gantt view.

17. Press the **F5** key. Type **60** in the ID box. Your screen should look similar to Figure 6-16.

Notice that each task now has two bars. The tan bar on the top represents the pre-leveled task. The light blue bar on the bottom represents the leveled task. For this particular project, the effect leveling had on the project finish date was to extend it by about three days. You can see all of the pre-leveled start, duration, and finish

Figure 6-16

Leveling Gantt view showing
the effects of resource leveling

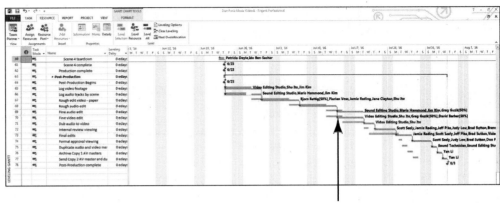

Level Gantt view bars represent values of the
pre-leveled tasks and the values after leveling

values for any task by pointing to the desired tan bar. The solid teal line to the right
of any light blue bar represents the float (slack) for that task.

18. SAVE the project schedule, and then CLOSE the file.

PAUSE. If you are continuing to the next lesson, keep Project open. If not continuing
to additional lessons, CLOSE Project.

TAKE NOTE*

Even though the effects
of resource leveling
might sometimes be
significant, resource
leveling never changes
who is assigned to tasks,
or the total work or
assignment unit values of
those assignments.

In this exercise, you used resource leveling to resolve over-allocations. Recall that resource
leveling is the process of delaying or splitting a resource's work on a task to resolve an over
allocation. The options in the Resource Leveling dialog box enable you to set parameters
about how you want Microsoft Project to resolve resource over allocations. Depending on the
options you choose, Microsoft Project might try to level resources by delaying the start date of
an assignment or task or splitting the work on the task.

Resource leveling is a powerful tool, but it has limits. It can only do a few things: it adds delays
to tasks, it splits tasks, and it adjusts resource assignments. It does this by following a complex
set of rules and options that you specify in the Resource Leveling dialog box. Although
resource leveling is very useful for fine tuning, *it can't replace the judgment of a good project
manager about task durations, relationships, and constraints or resource availability.*
Resource leveling will work with all of this information as it exists in your project schedule,
but it still might not be possible to completely resolve all resource over allocations within the
timeframe you want without changing more basic task and resource information.

SKILL SUMMARY

IN THIS LESSON YOU LEARNED:	MATRIX SKILL
To enter material resource consumption rates	Enter a variable consumption rate for a material resource
To enter costs per use for resources	Enter a cost per use for a resource
To assign multiple pay rates for a resource	Assign multiple pay rates for a resource
To apply different cost rates to assignments	Apply a different cost rate to an assignment
To specify resource availability at different times	Specify a resource's availability over time
To resolve resource over allocations manually	Manually resolve a resource over allocation
To level over-allocated resources	Use resource leveling to resolve an over allocation

■ Knowledge Assessment

Matching

Match the term in column 1 to its description in column 2.

Column 1	Column 2
1. cost rate table	**a.** an absolute quantity of material resources will be used, no matter the duration of the task
2. under allocated	**b.** the total work of a resource's task assignments is exactly equal to that resource's work capacity
3. variable consumption rate	**c.** a resource is assigned to do more work than can be done within the normal capacity of the resource.
4. units	**d.** the amount of the material resource consumed is dependent upon the duration of the task
5. allocation	**e.** the work assigned to a resource is less than the resource's maximum capacity
6. fixed consumption rate	**f.** the process of delaying or splitting a resource's work on a task to resolve an over allocation
7. over allocated	**g.** the maximum capacity of a resource to accomplish work
8. resource leveling	**h.** resource pay rates that are stored on the Costs tab of the Resource Information dialog box
9. fully allocated	**i.** the portion of a resource's capacity devoted to work on a specific task
10. Max. Units	**j.** the measurement of a resource's capacity to work

True / False

Circle T if the statement is true or F if the statement is false.

T | F **1.** Resource leveling cannot always resolve all resource over allocations.

T | F **2.** A resource cannot have both a cost per use and a cost derived from its pay rate.

T | F **3.** Resource leveling never changes who is assigned to tasks, or the total work value of those assignments.

T | F **4.** You can manually resolve a resource over allocation by replacing the over allocated resource with another resource.

T | F **5.** You can assign two types of material consumption rates in Microsoft Project.

T | F **6.** The settings in the Resource Leveling dialog box apply to all of the project schedules you work with in Microsoft Project.

T | F **7.** You can have up to six cost rate tables for a resource.

T | F **8.** It is not acceptable to allow a minor over allocation to remain in a schedule.

T | F **9.** The default rate table in Microsoft Project is Rate Table 1.

T | F **10.** When a variable consumption rate is assigned to a material resource, and the duration of the task to which it is assigned changes, so do the calculated amount and cost of the material resource.

■ Competency Assessment

Project 6-1: Variable Consumption Rate for Water

As you are reviewing your Don Funk Music Video project schedule, you realize you need to make some adjustments to the bottled water material resource. You want to use a variable rate of 0.5 cases of water per hour.

GET READY. Launch Microsoft Project if it is not already running. **OPEN** *Don Funk Music Video 6-1* from the data files for this lesson.

1. Scroll down in the task list to task 35, Scene 1 Video Shoot.
2. Click the Resource ribbon and then click the Assign Resources button.
3. In the Assign Resources dialog box, click the Units field for Bottled Water. Type 0.5/h and then press Enter.
4. Click the Close button in the Assign Resource dialog box.
5. SAVE the project schedule as *Don Funk Bottled Water* and then CLOSE the file.

PAUSE. LEAVE Project open to use in the next exercise.

Project 6-2: Office Remodel Multiple Pay Rates

On the office remodel project you are currently managing, you need to set up different pay rates for one of the resources, Run Lui. He has different pay scales depending upon whether he is moving furniture and appliances or doing painting and material installation work.

OPEN *Office Remodel 6-2* from the data files for this lesson.

1. Click the View tab and then click Resource Sheet in the Resource Views group.
2. In the Resource Sheet view, double-click the name of resource 3, Run Lui. The Resource Information dialog box appears.
3. Click the Costs tab, if it is not already selected
4. Under Cost rate tables, click the B tab.
5. Select the default entry of $0.00/h in the field directly below the Standard Rate column heading, type 12/h, and then press Enter.
6. In the Overtime Rate field, type 18.00/h, and then press Enter.
7. Click OK to close the Resource Information dialog box.
8. SAVE the project schedule as *Office Remodel Multiple Rates* and then CLOSE the file.

PAUSE. LEAVE Project open to use in the next exercise.

■ Proficiency Assessment

Project 6-3: Hiring New Employee Resource Leveling

Several employees on the Hiring New Employee project schedule are over allocated. Use resource leveling to resolve these over allocations.

OPEN *Hiring New Employee 6-3* from the data files for this lesson.

1. Activate the Resource Sheet view.
2. Activate the Resource Leveling dialog box.
3. In the Resource Leveling dialog box, make the selections that correspond to the following options:

- Level manually
- Level day by day
- Clear leveling values before leveling
- Level the entire project
- Use Standard leveling order
- Do not level within available slack
- Allow leveling to adjust individual assignments
- Allow leveling to create splits
- Do not level resources with a proposed booking type
- Do not level manually scheduled tasks

4. Click the **Level All** button.
5. Change the view to the Leveling Gantt.
6. Scroll to **task 4** to view more of the leveled Gantt Chart.
7. **SAVE** the project schedule as *Hiring New Employee Leveled* and then **CLOSE** the file.

   PAUSE. LEAVE Project open to use in the next exercise.

Project 6-4: Employee Orientation – Specifying Conference Room Availability

You have just been told that the Large Conference Room is <u>not</u> available for use from 12/20/14 through 1/2/15 and from 1/12/15 through 1/23/15. Although this does not immediately interfere with your current orientation schedule, you want to update the resource availability information so that you can avoid conflicts if your schedule changes.

 OPEN *Employee Orientation 6-4* from the data files for this lesson.

1. Activate the **Resource Sheet** view.
2. Select the **Large Conference Room** resource.
3. Activate the Resource Information dialog box. Activate the **General** tab, if it is not already selected.
4. Fill in the **Resource Availability** table to reflect that the conference room is available until 12/19/14 and after 1/23/15, but that it is not available on the dates as noted in the instructions above. Close the Resource Information box when you are finished.
5. **SAVE** the project schedule as *Employee Orientation Conf Room Availability* and then **CLOSE** the file.

   PAUSE. LEAVE Project open to use in the next exercise.

■ Mastery Assessment

Project 6-5: Applying a Different Cost Rate

On the office remodel project you are currently managing, you have set up different pay rates for one of the resources, Run Lui. Now you need to apply these pay rates to the appropriate assignments.

 OPEN *Office Remodel 6-5* from the data files for this lesson.

1. For Run Lui's assignment to tasks 2 and 18, change the **cost rate table** to B.
2. **SAVE** the project schedule as *Office Remodel Run Lui B*, and then **CLOSE** the file.

   PAUSE. LEAVE Project open to use in the next exercise.

Project 6-6: Don Funk Music Video – Costs Per Use

You need to update the Don Funk Music Video project schedule to reflect several resources that have a cost associated with each use.

 OPEN *Don Funk Music Video 6-6* from the data files for this lesson.

1. Enter the following cost per use information for the specified resources:

   - the musicians have a $100 travel and set-up/breakdown fee each time they are used
   - the sound editing studio has a $50 cleaning fee per use, payable at the end of the session
   - the video editing studio has a $50 cleaning fee per use, payable at the end of the session

2. SAVE the project schedule as *Don Funk Cost Per Use* and then CLOSE the file. CLOSE Project.

7 LESSON

Project Information: Sorting, Grouping, and Filtering

LESSON SKILL MATRIX

SKILLS	TASKS
Sorting Data	Sort data in a resource view
Grouping Data	Group data in a resource view
Filtering Data	Create and apply a filter in a view
Creating a Custom Filter	Create a custom filter

As a video production manager for Southridge Video and the project manager for the new Don Funk music video, you have invested much time and effort into assembling your project schedule. You have entered and linked tasks, created work and material resources, and assigned these resources to the project tasks. Now that the key elements of the project schedule have been established, you need to be able to view and analyze the project schedule information in different ways. The best project schedule is only as good as the data you are able to get out of it. In this lesson, you will learn to use some of the tools in Microsoft Project 2013, such as views, tables, groups, filters and reports, to modify the way your data is organized. You will also learn about some features that enable you to make custom changes to your data to suit your own specific needs.

KEY TERMS
AutoFilter
filter
group
sort

© egeeksen/iStockphoto

■ SOFTWARE ORIENTATION

Microsoft Project's Sort Dialog Box

In Microsoft Project, you can use the Sort dialog box to sort task or resource information in the current view by a specified field or fields (see Figure 7-1).

Figure 7-1

Sort dialog box

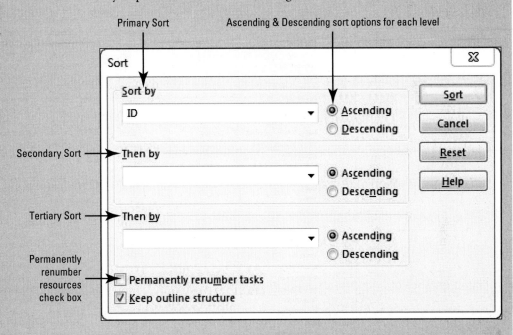

Primary Sort

Ascending & Descending sort options for each level

Secondary Sort

Tertiary Sort

Permanently renumber resources check box

The Sort dialog box enables you to select up to three fields for three levels of sorts within sorts, to choose whether the view should be sorted in ascending or descending order, and to indicate whether items should be permanently renumbered according to the sort.

■ Sorting Data

THE BOTTOM LINE

It is easiest to review and utilize data in Microsoft Project when you have it organized to fit your needs. The simplest way to reorganize task and resource data in Project is by sorting.

➔ SORT DATA IN A RESOURCE VIEW

GET READY. Before you begin these steps, launch Microsoft Project. OPEN the ***Don Funk Music Video 7M*** from the data files for this lesson. SAVE the file as ***Don Funk Music Video 7*** in the solutions folder for this lesson as directed by your instructor.

1. Click the View tab, and then click Resource Sheet. The Resource Sheet view appears. The default table in the Resource Sheet view is the Entry table. However, you want to look at the cost per resource, which is not displayed in the Entry table.

2. On the ribbon, click the Tables button in the Data group and then select Summary. The Summary table appears in the Resource Sheet view.

3. Auto fit the columns so the data can be easily read. Your screen should look similar to Figure 7-2.

Figure 7-2

Resource Sheet with summary table applied

Cost per resource in the summary table

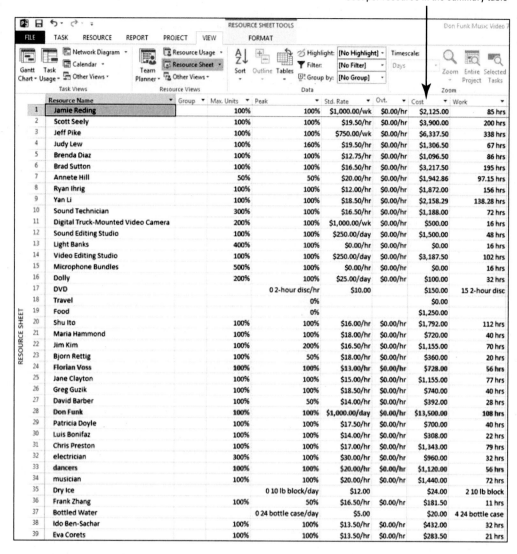

	Resource Name	Group	Max. Units	Peak	Std. Rate	Ovt.	Cost	Work
1	Jamie Reding		100%	100%	$1,000.00/wk	$0.00/hr	$2,125.00	85 hrs
2	Scott Seely		100%	100%	$19.50/hr	$0.00/hr	$3,900.00	200 hrs
3	Jeff Pike		100%	100%	$750.00/wk	$0.00/hr	$6,337.50	338 hrs
4	Judy Lew		100%	160%	$19.50/hr	$0.00/hr	$1,306.50	67 hrs
5	Brenda Diaz		100%	100%	$12.75/hr	$0.00/hr	$1,096.50	86 hrs
6	Brad Sutton		100%	100%	$16.50/hr	$0.00/hr	$3,217.50	195 hrs
7	Annete Hill		50%	50%	$20.00/hr	$0.00/hr	$1,942.86	97.15 hrs
8	Ryan Ihrig		100%	100%	$12.00/hr	$0.00/hr	$1,872.00	156 hrs
9	Yan Li		100%	100%	$18.50/hr	$0.00/hr	$2,158.29	138.28 hrs
10	Sound Technician		300%	100%	$16.50/hr	$0.00/hr	$1,188.00	72 hrs
11	Digital Truck-Mounted Video Camera		200%	100%	$1,000.00/wk	$0.00/hr	$500.00	16 hrs
12	Sound Editing Studio		100%	100%	$250.00/day	$0.00/hr	$1,500.00	48 hrs
13	Light Banks		400%	100%	$0.00/hr	$0.00/hr	$0.00	16 hrs
14	Video Editing Studio		100%	100%	$250.00/day	$0.00/hr	$3,187.50	102 hrs
15	Microphone Bundles		500%	100%	$0.00/hr	$0.00/hr	$0.00	16 hrs
16	Dolly		200%	100%	$25.00/day	$0.00/hr	$100.00	32 hrs
17	DVD			0 2-hour disc/hr	$10.00		$150.00	15 2-hour disc
18	Travel			0%			$0.00	
19	Food			0%			$1,250.00	
20	Shu Ito		100%	100%	$16.00/hr	$0.00/hr	$1,792.00	112 hrs
21	Maria Hammond		100%	100%	$18.00/hr	$0.00/hr	$720.00	40 hrs
22	Jim Kim		100%	200%	$16.50/hr	$0.00/hr	$1,155.00	70 hrs
23	Bjorn Rettig		100%	50%	$18.00/hr	$0.00/hr	$360.00	20 hrs
24	Florian Voss		100%	100%	$13.00/hr	$0.00/hr	$728.00	56 hrs
25	Jane Clayton		100%	100%	$15.00/hr	$0.00/hr	$1,155.00	77 hrs
26	Greg Guzik		100%	100%	$18.50/hr	$0.00/hr	$740.00	40 hrs
27	David Barber		100%	50%	$14.00/hr	$0.00/hr	$392.00	28 hrs
28	Don Funk		100%	100%	$1,000.00/day	$0.00/hr	$13,500.00	108 hrs
29	Patricia Doyle		100%	100%	$17.50/hr	$0.00/hr	$700.00	40 hrs
30	Luis Bonifaz		100%	100%	$14.00/hr	$0.00/hr	$308.00	22 hrs
31	Chris Preston		100%	100%	$17.00/hr	$0.00/hr	$1,343.00	79 hrs
32	electrician		300%	100%	$30.00/hr	$0.00/hr	$960.00	32 hrs
33	dancers		100%	100%	$20.00/hr	$0.00/hr	$1,120.00	56 hrs
34	musician		100%	100%	$20.00/hr	$0.00/hr	$1,440.00	72 hrs
35	Dry Ice			0 10 lb block/day	$12.00		$24.00	2 10 lb block
36	Frank Zhang		100%	50%	$16.50/hr	$0.00/hr	$181.50	11 hrs
37	Bottled Water			0 24 bottle case/day	$5.00		$20.00	4 24 bottle case
38	Ido Ben-Sachar		100%	100%	$13.50/hr	$0.00/hr	$432.00	32 hrs
39	Eva Corets		100%	100%	$13.50/hr	$0.00/hr	$283.50	21 hrs

4. On the ribbon, click the **Sort** button in the Data group and then click **Sort By**. The Sort dialog box appears (as shown in Figure 7-1).

TAKE NOTE Notice that in the Sort box, you can utilize up to three nested levels of sort criteria. Also, you can sort by any field, not just the fields that are visible in the active view.

5. In the **Sort by** section, select **Cost** from the dropdown menu. Next to that, click **Descending**. Make sure that the Permanently renumber resources check box at the bottom of the Sort dialog box is NOT checked.

TROUBLESHOOTING The Permanently renumber resources check box (or when in a task view, Permanently renumber tasks) is a Project-level setting. If you check this box, Project will permanently renumber resources or tasks in ANY Microsoft Project file in which you sort. Since you may not want to permanently renumber tasks or resources every time you sort, it is a good idea to have this option turned off.

6. Click the Sort button. The Summary table is sorted from the highest to lowest value in the Cost column. This sort enables you to look at resource costs across the entire project. Your screen should look similar to Figure 7-3.

Figure 7-3

Resource Sheet sorted with highest cost resource at top

Sorted by cost in descending order

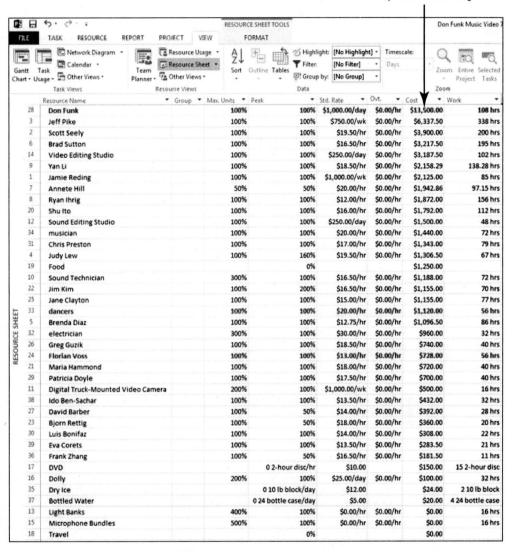

When you sort data in your project, the sort applies to the active view, no matter which table is currently displayed in the view. For example, if you sort the Task Usage view by finish date while the Entry table is visible, and then switch to the Cost table, you will see that the tasks are still sorted by finish date in the Cost column.

TAKE NOTE*

7. On the ribbon, click Sort, and then click Sort by. The Sort dialog box appears.

8. In the Sort by section, select Group from the dropdown menu. Next to that, click Ascending.

9. In the Then by section, select Cost from the dropdown menu. Then click the radio button next to Descending. Make sure the Permanently renumber resources box is not checked. Your screen should look similar to Figure 7-4.

Figure 7-4

Sort dialog box with multiple sort criteria

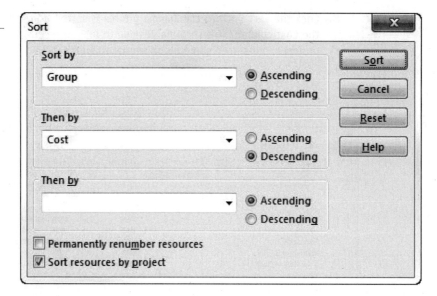

10. Click the **Sort** button. The Resource Sheet view is sorted to display resources sorted first by Group (Equipment, Talent, etc.) and then by Cost within each group. Your screen should look similar to Figure 7-5.

Figure 7-5

Resource Sheet sorted by Group then by Cost

Sorted by Group in ascending order first... ...and then sorted by cost in descending order

	Resource Name	Group	Max. Units	Peak	Std. Rate	Ovt.	Cost	Work
19	Food	Cost		0%			$1,250.00	
18	Travel	Cost		0%			$0.00	
10	Sound Technician	Crew	300%	100%	$16.50/hr	$0.00/hr	$1,188.00	72 hrs
32	electrician	Crew	300%	100%	$30.00/hr	$0.00/hr	$960.00	32 hrs
11	Digital Truck-Mounted Video Camera	Equipment	200%	100%	$1,000.00/wk	$0.00/hr	$500.00	16 hrs
16	Dolly	Equipment	200%	100%	$25.00/day	$0.00/hr	$100.00	32 hrs
13	Light Banks	Equipment	400%	100%	$0.00/hr	$0.00/hr	$0.00	16 hrs
15	Microphone Bundles	Equipment	500%	100%	$0.00/hr	$0.00/hr	$0.00	16 hrs
14	Video Editing Studio	Lab	100%	100%	$250.00/day	$0.00/hr	$3,187.50	102 hrs
12	Sound Editing Studio	Lab	100%	100%	$250.00/day	$0.00/hr	$1,500.00	48 hrs
17	DVD	Materials		0 2-hour disc/hr	$10.00		$150.00	15 2-hour disc
35	Dry Ice	Materials		0 10 lb block/day	$12.00		$24.00	2 10 lb block
37	Bottled Water	Materials		0 24 bottle case/day	$5.00		$20.00	4 24 bottle case
3	Jeff Pike	Production	100%	100%	$750.00/wk	$0.00/hr	$6,337.50	338 hrs
2	Scott Seely	Production	100%	100%	$19.50/hr	$0.00/hr	$3,900.00	200 hrs
6	Brad Sutton	Production	100%	100%	$16.50/hr	$0.00/hr	$3,217.50	195 hrs
9	Yan Li	Production	100%	100%	$18.50/hr	$0.00/hr	$2,158.29	138.28 hrs
1	Jamie Reding	Production	100%	100%	$1,000.00/wk	$0.00/hr	$2,125.00	85 hrs
7	Annete Hill	Production	50%	50%	$20.00/hr	$0.00/hr	$1,942.86	97.15 hrs
8	Ryan Ihrig	Production	100%	100%	$12.00/hr	$0.00/hr	$1,872.00	156 hrs
20	Shu Ito	Production	100%	100%	$16.00/hr	$0.00/hr	$1,792.00	112 hrs
31	Chris Preston	Production	100%	100%	$17.00/hr	$0.00/hr	$1,343.00	79 hrs
4	Judy Lew	Production	100%	160%	$19.50/hr	$0.00/hr	$1,306.50	67 hrs
22	Jim Kim	Production	100%	200%	$16.50/hr	$0.00/hr	$1,155.00	70 hrs
25	Jane Clayton	Production	100%	100%	$15.00/hr	$0.00/hr	$1,155.00	77 hrs
5	Brenda Diaz	Production	100%	100%	$12.75/hr	$0.00/hr	$1,096.50	86 hrs
26	Greg Guzik	Production	100%	100%	$18.50/hr	$0.00/hr	$740.00	40 hrs
24	Florian Voss	Production	100%	100%	$13.00/hr	$0.00/hr	$728.00	56 hrs
21	Maria Hammond	Production	100%	100%	$18.00/hr	$0.00/hr	$720.00	40 hrs
29	Patricia Doyle	Production	100%	100%	$17.50/hr	$0.00/hr	$700.00	40 hrs
38	Ido Ben-Sachar	Production	100%	100%	$13.50/hr	$0.00/hr	$432.00	32 hrs
27	David Barber	Production	100%	50%	$14.00/hr	$0.00/hr	$392.00	28 hrs
23	Bjorn Rettig	Production	100%	50%	$18.00/hr	$0.00/hr	$360.00	20 hrs
30	Luis Bonifaz	Production	100%	100%	$14.00/hr	$0.00/hr	$308.00	22 hrs
39	Eva Corets	Production	100%	100%	$13.50/hr	$0.00/hr	$283.50	21 hrs
36	Frank Zhang	Production	100%	50%	$16.50/hr	$0.00/hr	$181.50	11 hrs
28	Don Funk	Talent	100%	100%	$1,000.00/day	$0.00/hr	$13,500.00	108 hrs
34	musician	Talent	100%	100%	$20.00/hr	$0.00/hr	$1,440.00	72 hrs
33	dancers	Talent	100%	100%	$20.00/hr	$0.00/hr	$1,120.00	56 hrs

When you sort data in this way, it is easy to identify the most and least expensive resources in each group on your project. You can sort your data in any way that is beneficial to the analysis of your project. The sort order you most recently specified will remain in effect until you re-sort the view. Now you will restore the data to its original order.

11. On the Quick Access Toolbar, click the **Undo** button one time. The Undo button reverses the last sort you performed, restoring the data to the original sort order (by Cost only).

12. Now click the **Undo** button again. The data is restored to the original order in the Summary table of the Resource Sheet view (as displayed previously in Figure 7-2). The Multiple Level Undo enables you to undo actions or sets of actions while you are working on your project schedule.

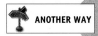 **ANOTHER WAY** You can also "unsort" your data by clicking the Sort button on the View ribbon, and then clicking By ID.

13. SAVE the project schedule.

PAUSE. LEAVE the project schedule open to use in the next exercise.

You have just performed several sorts on your project data to allow you to more closely examine certain aspects of your project. A *sort* is a way of ordering task or resource information in a view by the criteria you specify. You can sort tasks or resources using predefined criteria, or you can create your own sort order with up to three levels (a group within a group within a group). If you need to sort data in a view with more than three criteria, start by sorting your least important factors first and then sort by your three most important factors.

Except for one instance, sorting does not change the actual data of your project schedule, but rather just reorders your data. Sorting allows you to arrange data in an order that answers a question you may have, or in a way that makes more sense or is more user-friendly to your project team. Note that there is no visual indicator that a task or resource view has been sorted other than the order in which the rows of data appear. Furthermore, unlike grouping and filtering, which you will learn about later in this lesson, you cannot save custom sort settings that you have specified.

The one instance in which the actual data of your project is changed by sorting is the option that Project offers to renumber resource or task IDs after sorting. Once resources or tasks are renumbered by sorting, you can't restore their original numeric order. Sometimes, you might want to permanently renumber tasks or resources. For instance, at the beginning of a project, you might enter resource names as they are needed on the project. When you are finished entering resources, you might want to sort them alphabetically and permanently renumber them.

The Multiple Level Undo function you used in this exercise is a very valuable new tool in Microsoft Project. As you saw, this feature allows you to easily undo sets of actions you have performed in Microsoft Project. You can undo changes that you purposely made (as in this exercise), or reverse "mistakes" that you make while working on your project schedule. However, the functionality of Multiple Level Undo doesn't stop there. It enables you to make, undo, and redo changes to views, data, and options – giving you the ability to experiment with different scenarios without causing permanent undesired effects. You can test several approaches to resolving a problem or optimizing a project schedule in order to fully understand the implications of each choice. (You can also use the Visual Change Highlighting as you are making changes to see the effects of your actions.)

A word of caution regarding the Multiple Level Undo feature – it will not undo all actions. For example, if you save a file, the undo feature cache is cleared and you cannot undo the save.

■ Grouping Data

THE BOTTOM LINE

Another way to organize, view, and analyze the data in your project schedule is through grouping. Grouping enables you to organize the task and resource criteria in your schedule according to various criteria that you select. Similar to sorting, grouping only changes the way data is displayed – it does not change the data itself.

→ GROUP DATA IN A RESOURCE VIEW

USE the project schedule you created in the previous exercise.

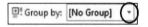

1. On the View ribbon, click the **down-arrow** in the **Group By** box, (currently is has *No Group*) and then click **Resource Group**. Microsoft Project reorganizes the data into resource groups and presents it in an expanded outline form. It also adds summary costs by group. Your screen should look similar to Figure 7-6.

Figure 7-6

Resource Sheet with data summarized and grouped by Resource Group

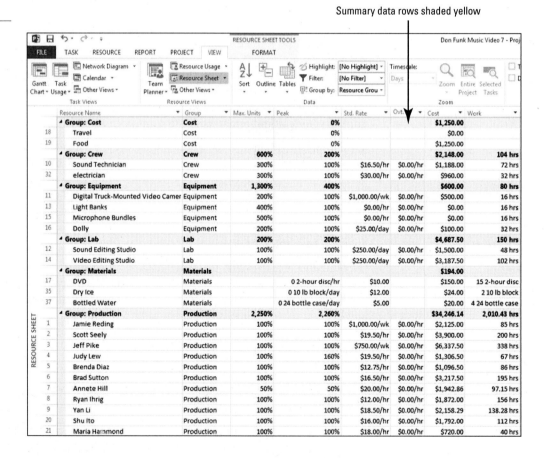

The summary data rows are set off with a colored background (yellow in this case). Because the data in the summary rows is derived from subordinate data, this cannot be changed directly. To have more control over how your data is presented, you can create custom groups.

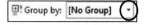

2. On the View ribbon, click the **down-arrow** in the Group By box, (currently it has *Resource Group*) and then click **More Groups**. The More Groups dialog box appears,

displaying all of the predefined groups for tasks and resources available to you. You will create a new group that is similar to the Resource Group.

3. Select Resource Group (if it is not already selected), and then click the Copy button. The Group Definition dialog box appears.

4. In the Names box, key Resource Groups by Cost.

5. In the Field Name column, click the first empty cell below Group.

6. Type or select Cost.

7. In the Order column for the Cost field, click Ascending to select it and then select Descending from the dropdown menu. The resources will be sorted within their groups by descending cost. The Group Definition dialog box should look similar to Figure 7-7.

Figure 7-7

Group Definition dialog box

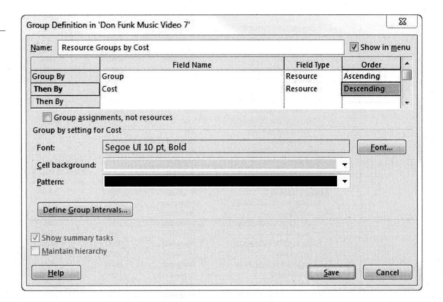

8. In the Group Definition dialog box, click the Define Group Intervals button. The Define Group Intervals dialog box appears.

9. In the Group on box, select Interval from the dropdown menu.

10. Type 500 in the Group interval box, and then click the OK button.

11. Click the Save button in the Group Definition dialog box to close it. Resource Groups by Cost appears as a new group in the More Groups dialog box.

12. Click the Apply button in the More Groups dialog box. Microsoft Project applies the new group to the Resource Sheet view.

13. Right-click the Resource Name column heading then select Field Settings. The Field Settings dialog box appears. You want to widen the Resource Name column.

14. Click the Best Fit button in the Field Settings dialog box. The Resource Name column is widened. If needed, scroll to the top of the view. Your screen should look similar to Figure 7-8.

Figure 7-8

Resource Sheet with multiple level grouping applied

Data grouped by resource group and then by cost

Resource Name	Group	Max. Units	Peak	Std. Rate	Ovt.	Cost	Work
▲ **Group: Cost**	**Cost**			0%		**$1,250.00**	
▲ **Cost: $1,000.00 - <$1,500.00**	**Cost**			0%		**$1,250.00**	
19 Food	Cost			0%		$1,250.00	
▲ **Cost: $0.00 - <$500.00**	**Cost**			0%		**$0.00**	
18 Travel	Cost			0%		$0.00	
▲ **Group: Crew**	**Crew**	600%	200%			**$2,148.00**	**104 hrs**
▲ **Cost: $1,000.00 - <$1,500.00**	**Crew**	300%	100%			**$1,188.00**	**72 hrs**
10 Sound Technician	Crew	300%	100%	$16.50/hr	$0.00/hr	$1,188.00	72 hrs
▲ **Cost: $500.00 - <$1,000.00**	**Crew**	300%	100%			**$960.00**	**32 hrs**
32 electrician	Crew	300%	100%	$30.00/hr	$0.00/hr	$960.00	32 hrs
▲ **Group: Equipment**	**Equipment**	1,300%	400%			**$600.00**	**80 hrs**
▲ **Cost: $500.00 - <$1,000.00**	**Equipment**	200%	100%			**$500.00**	**16 hrs**
11 Digital Truck-Mounted Video Camera	Equipment	200%	100%	$1,000.00/wk	$0.00/hr	$500.00	16 hrs
▲ **Cost: $0.00 - <$500.00**	**Equipment**	1,100%	300%			**$100.00**	**64 hrs**
13 Light Banks	Equipment	400%	100%	$0.00/hr	$0.00/hr	$0.00	16 hrs
15 Microphone Bundles	Equipment	500%	100%	$0.00/hr	$0.00/hr	$0.00	16 hrs
16 Dolly	Equipment	200%	100%	$25.00/day	$0.00/hr	$100.00	32 hrs
▲ **Group: Lab**	**Lab**	200%	200%			**$4,687.50**	**150 hrs**
▲ **Cost: $3,000.00 - <$3,500.00**	**Lab**	100%	100%			**$3,187.50**	**102 hrs**
14 Video Editing Studio	Lab	100%	100%	$250.00/day	$0.00/hr	$3,187.50	102 hrs
▲ **Cost: $1,500.00 - <$2,000.00**	**Lab**	100%	100%			**$1,500.00**	**48 hrs**
12 Sound Editing Studio	Lab	100%	100%	$250.00/day	$0.00/hr	$1,500.00	48 hrs
▲ **Group: Materials**	**Materials**					**$194.00**	
▲ **Cost: $0.00 - <$500.00**	**Materials**					**$194.00**	
17 DVD	Materials		0 2-hour disc/hr	$10.00		$150.00	15 2-hour disc
35 Dry Ice	Materials		0 10 lb block/day	$12.00		$24.00	2 10 lb block
37 Bottled Water	Materials		0 24 bottle case/day	$5.00		$20.00	4 24 bottle case
▲ **Group: Production**	**Production**	2,250%	2,260%			**$34,246.14**	**2,010.43 hrs**
▲ **Cost: $6,000.00 - <$6,500.00**	**Production**	100%	100%			**$6,337.50**	**338 hrs**
3 Jeff Pike	Production	100%	100%	$750.00/wk	$0.00/hr	$6,337.50	338 hrs
▲ **Cost: $3,500.00 - <$4,000.00**	**Production**	100%	100%			**$3,900.00**	**200 hrs**
2 Scott Seely	Production	100%	100%	$19.50/hr	$0.00/hr	$3,900.00	200 hrs
▲ **Cost: $3,000.00 - <$3,500.00**	**Production**	100%	100%			**$3,217.50**	**195 hrs**
6 Brad Sutton	Production	100%	100%	$16.50/hr	$0.00/hr	$3,217.50	195 hrs
▲ **Cost: $2,000.00 - <$2,500.00**	**Production**	200%	200%			**$4,283.29**	**223.28 hrs**
1 Jamie Reding	Production	100%	100%	$1,000.00/wk	$0.00/hr	$2,125.00	85 hrs
9 Yan Li	Production	100%	100%	$18.50/hr	$0.00/hr	$2,158.29	138.28 hrs
▲ **Cost: $1,500.00 - <$2,000.00**	**Production**	250%	250%			**$5,606.86**	**365.15 hrs**
7 Annete Hill	Production	50%	50%	$20.00/hr	$0.00/hr	$1,942.86	97.15 hrs
8 Ryan Ihrig	Production	100%	100%	$12.00/hr	$0.00/hr	$1,872.00	156 hrs
20 Shu Ito	Production	100%	100%	$16.00/hr	$0.00/hr	$1,792.00	112 hrs

The resources are grouped by Resource Group (the yellow shaded cells) and within each group by cost values at $500 increments (the blue shaded cells).

ANOTHER WAY   You can also auto fit any column by placing the cursor on the right side dividing line and double-clicking.

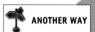

15. After you have reviewed the groupings you created, click the **down-arrow** in the Group By box, (currently it has *Resource Groups by Cost*) in the Data group, and then click **[No Group]**. Microsoft Project removes the groupings, restoring the original data. Displaying or removing a group has no effect on the data in the project.

16. SAVE the project schedule.

PAUSE. LEAVE the project schedule open to use in the next exercise.

In this exercise, you have just reorganized your project data using grouping. A ***group*** is a way to reorder task or resource information in a table and to display summary values for each group according to various criteria you can choose. Grouping goes a step beyond sorting in that grouping your project data will add summary values, called "roll-ups," at customized intervals.

Grouping the data in a project schedule enables you to view your information from a variety of perspectives. It also allows for a more detailed level of data analysis and presentation. In your role as project manager, your project schedule helps you track the work and costs associated with your project. By using grouping, you also have the ability to look at more details – to understand not just what is happening on your project, but also why.

As with sorting, grouping does not change the fundamental structure of your project schedule but rather just reorganizes and summarizes it. Also like sorting, grouping applies to all tables you can display in the view. You can use any of the predefined groups, customize these predefined groups, or create your own.

■ Filtering Data

THE BOTTOM LINE

The feature called filtering allows you to look only at specific task or resource data that meet specific criteria. Filtering hides task or resource data that does not meet the criteria you specify and displays only the data in which you are interested. You can use a predefined filter, AutoFilters, or create a custom filter.

Creating and Applying a Filter

In this exercise, you will create a filter that allows you to focus on tasks related to the video shoot.

 CREATE AND APPLY A FILTER IN A VIEW

USE the project schedule you created in the previous exercise.

Gantt
Chart ▾

1. On the View ribbon, click the Gantt Chart button in the Task Views group. The Gantt Chart view appears.

2. The AutoFilter is on by default in the task and resource views. You can see small, chevron-style arrows on the right side of each column heading. You can use these arrows to select the AutoFilter option you want to use. Adjust the width of the Gantt Chart so that the Task Name, Duration, and Start columns are visible. Your screen should look similar to Figure 7-9.

Figure 7-9

Gantt Chart view displaying
AutoFilter buttons on each
column

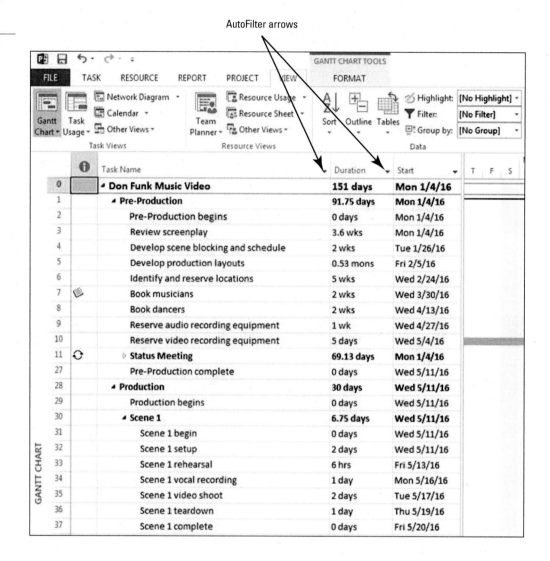

TAKE NOTE* To turn the AutoFilter off or on, click the down-arrow in the (No Filter) box in the Data
Group, then select Display AutoFilter.

3. Click the **AutoFilter** arrow in the Task Name column heading and point to Filters,
   then click **Custom....** The Custom AutoFilter dialog box appears. You want to see
   just the tasks that contain the letter-string of *shoot*, so you need to set up the
   Custom AutoFilter this way.

4. In the Name section, select **contains** from the dropdown list in the first box if it is not
   already visible. In the adjacent box, type **shoot**. The Custom AutoFilter dialog box should
   look similar to Figure 7-10.

Figure 7-10

Custom AutoFilter dialog box with criteria entered

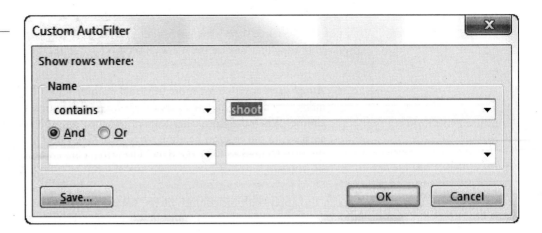

5. Click the **OK** button to apply the filter and close the **Custom AutoFilter** dialog box. Microsoft Project filters the task list to show only the tasks that contain the word shoot, as well as their summary tasks. Your screen should look similar to Figure 7-11.

Figure 7-11

Gantt Chart view with custom AutoFilter applied.

Filtered column indicator

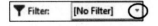

Note on the right side of the Task Name column there is a small "funnel" that appears. This is a visual indicator that an AutoFilter has been applied to this column in this view.

6. On the ribbon, click the **down-arrow** in the **Filter** box in the Data group, (currently has *No Filter*) and then select **Clear Filter**. The AutoFilter is cleared and all the tasks in the project schedule are displayed.

7. **SAVE** the project schedule.

   PAUSE. LEAVE the project schedule open to use in the next exercise.

ANOTHER WAY

You can also use the **F3** key to clear all filters.

In this exercise, you created and applied a filter to the project schedule to enable you to look at only the tasks dealing with scene shoots. A *filter* is a tool that enables you to see or highlight in a table only the task or resource information that meets criteria you choose. Filtering doesn't change the data in your project schedule – it only changes the data's appearance.

There are two ways to apply filters to a view: predefined filters or an AutoFilter.

- Predefined or custom filters allow you to see or highlight only the task or resource information that meets the criteria of the filter. For example, the Milestones filter displays only tasks that are milestones. Some predefined filters, such as the Date Range filter, require you to enter criteria (a date) to set up the filter.

TAKE NOTE If a task or a resource sheet view has a filter applied to it, the name of the filter will be displayed in the Filter box on the View ribbon.

- *AutoFilters* are used for more informal or impromptu filtering. An AutoFilter is a quick way to view only the task or resource information that meets the criteria you choose. When the AutoFilter feature is turned on, small down arrows are visible adjacent to the column heading name. Clicking the arrow activates a list of criteria that can be used to filter the data. The criteria are appropriate for the type of data in the column.

You can also apply multiple column filters. For example, you want to display all tasks that are more than one week in duration, and starts between 2/1/16 and 3/30/16. You would apply an AutoFilter of "1 week or longer" to the duration column and then apply an AutoFilter of "Between" 2/1/16 and 3/30/16 to the start column.

■ Creating a Custom Filter

 THE BOTTOM LINE In the previous exercise, you used AutoFilter to apply a filter to the data of interest. Now, you will create a custom filter that can be used without entering the filtering criteria each time.

⊕ **CREATE A CUSTOM FILTER**

USE the project schedule you created in the previous exercise.

1. On the View ribbon, click the **down-arrow** in the **Filter** box in the Data group, (currently has *No Filter*), then select **More Filters**. The More Filters dialog box appears. This dialog box shows you all of the predefined filters for tasks or resources that are available to you.
2. Click the **New** button. The Filter Definition dialog box appears.

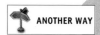 **ANOTHER WAY** You can also click the down-arrow in the (No Filter) box in the Data group and then select New Filter.

3. In the Name box, type **Unfinished Shoots**.
4. In the first row of the Field Name column, type or select **Name**.
5. In the first row of the Test column, type or select **contains**.
6. In the first row of the Value(s) column, type **shoot**. You have now finished entering the first criterion for the filter. Next you will enter the second criterion.
7. In the second row of the And/Or column, select **And**.
8. In the second row of the Field Name column, type or select **Actual Finish**.
9. In the second row of the Actual finish column, type or select **equals**.
10. In the second row of the Value(s) column, type **NA**. "NA" is how Microsoft Project marks fields that do not yet have a value. In other words, any shooting task that does not yet have a value must be uncompleted. Your screen should look similar to Figure 7-12.

Figure 7-12

Filter Definition dialog box with custom criteria entered

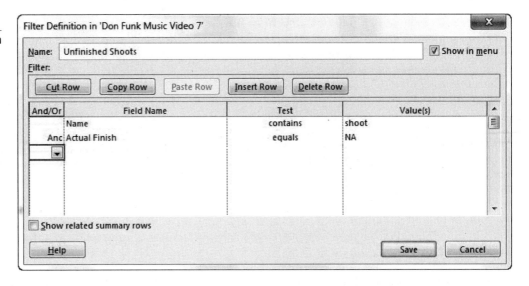

11. Click the Save button to close the Filter Definition dialog box.

12. Locate and select the Unfinished Shoots filter in the list, if necessary. Click the Apply button. Microsoft Project applies the new filter to your project schedule in the Gantt Chart view. Your screen should look similar to Figure 7-13.

Figure 7-13

Gantt Chart view with Unfinished Shoots filter applied

Take note of the gaps in the task IDs. This is one visual way you can tell that a filter has been applied. The tasks are filtered to show uncompleted tasks (and since you haven't started tracking actual work yet, all the shooting tasks are currently uncompleted). Also note that the related summary tasks have not been displayed. This is because we did not tell the filter to display them.

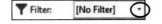

13. On the View ribbon, click the down-arrow in the Filter box in the Data group, (currently has *Unfinished Shoots*) and then select [No Filter]. Microsoft Project removes the filter.

14. SAVE the project schedule. CLOSE the project schedule.

PAUSE. If you are continuing to the next lesson, keep Project open. If you are not continuing to additional lessons, CLOSE Project.

In this exercise, you learned how to create and apply a custom filter. A custom filter works in the same way as a predefined filter, except that you have selected the filtering criterion rather than Microsoft Project. Remember that after filtering, you might see gaps in the task or resource ID numbers. The data has not been deleted – it is only hidden until you remove the filter. Also, as with sorting and grouping, the filtering applies to all the tables you can display in the active view. Some views that do not support tables, such as the Calendar view, do support filtering but not AutoFilters.

SKILL SUMMARY

In this lesson you learned:	Matrix Skill
To sort data	Sort data in a resource view
To group data	Group data in a resource view
To filter data	Create and apply a filter in a view
To create a custom filter	Create a custom filter

■ Knowledge Assessment

Fill in the Blank

Complete the following sentences by writing the correct word or words in the blanks provided.

1. _____ is a quick way to view only the task or resource information you choose.

2. In the Sort dialog box, you can utilize up to ___ nested levels of sort criteria.

3. When you use grouping, the _____ data rows are set off by a colored background.

4. When AutoFilter is turned on, small _____ are visible next to the column headings.

5. A way to reorder task or resource information in a table and to display summary values according to various criteria you can choose is called a(n) _____.

6. The _____ dialog box shows you all of the predefined filters that are available to you for tasks or resources.

7. A(n) _____ is a way of ordering task or resource information in a view by the criteria you specify.

8. When you apply a filter, you may see gaps in the order of the _____.

9. When you sort data in your project, the sort applies to the active _____, no matter which table is displayed.

10. A tool that enables you to see or highlight in a table only the task or resource information that meets criteria you choose is a(n) _____.

Multiple Choice

Select the best response for the following statements.

1. The simplest way to reorganize data in Microsoft Project is by
   a. filtering.
   b. sorting.
   c. grouping.
   d. AutoFiltering.

2. The _____ function lets you reverse actions you have performed in Microsoft Project.
   a. Task Drivers
   b. Reverse Filtering
   c. Multiple Level Undo
   d. Ungrouping

3. The one instance in which the actual data of your project is changed by sorting is when
   a. the Permanently renumber resources check box is selected.
   b. the Multiple Level Undo function is disabled.
   c. the project is saved before the sorting is reversed.
   d. all of the above.

4. When you apply a group to your project schedule, the data in the summary rows cannot be changed directly because
   a. it will cause the grouping to become permanent.
   b. it will alter the data in your project schedule.
   c. it is derived from subordinate data.
   d. it will cause an error in the grouping function.

5. When AutoFilter is on, clicking on the down arrow next to the column heading
   a. sorts the data in descending order.
   b. turns the AutoFilter off.
   c. automatically adjusts the column width.
   d. allows you to select criteria to apply to the filter.

6. Multiple Level Undo can be used
   a. as many times as desired
   b. up to 99 times, or until the original data is restored.
   c. up to 35 consecutive times.
   d. up to 50 consecutive times.

7. If a view has a filter applied to it, the name of the filter will be displayed in the Filter box on the _____ ribbon.
   a. Data
   b. Format
   c. View
   d. Resource Management

8. There is no visual indicator that a task or resource view has been sorted other than
   a. the shaded summary rows.
   b. the small "s" at the top of each data column.
   c. the order in which the rows of data appear.
   d. There is no visual indicator to show a view has been sorted.

9. Grouping might be helpful if you are trying to see
   a. only the tasks that contain the word "Weekly."
   b. the critical path tasks.
   c. the tasks ordered from highest to lowest cost.
   d. the total cost of each resource group.

10. You cannot save custom settings that you have specified for
    a. sorting.
    b. grouping.
    c. filtering.
    d. all of the above.

■ Competency Assessment

Project 7-1: Sorting by Multiple Criteria

You have some additional setup work that needs to be completed before the shooting of one of the Don Funk Music Video scenes can begin. Because you will need to pay overtime (time and one-half) for this additional work, you would like to get a volunteer who has a low standard rate. Sort your resources according to Standard Rate and Max Units so that you can make your request from the least-cost group of employees.

GET READY. Launch Microsoft Project if it is not already running.

 OPEN *Don Funk Music Video 7-1* from the data files for this lesson.

1. Click the View ribbon, then in the **Resource Views** group, click **Resource Sheet**.
2. On the ribbon, click **Sort**, and then click **Sort by**.
3. In the **Sort by** section select **Type** from the dropdown menu. Next to that, click **Descending**.
4. In the first Then by section, select **Standard Rate** from the dropdown menu. Next to that, click **Descending**.
5. In the last Then by section, select **Max Units** from the dropdown menu. Next to that, click on **Descending**. Make sure the Permanently renumber resources box is not checked.
6. Click the **Sort** button.
7. **SAVE** the project schedule as *Don Funk Standard Rate Sort* and then **CLOSE** the file.
   LEAVE Project open for the next exercise.

Project 7-2: Apply HR Filter

 You are reviewing your project schedule for hiring a new employee. You want to specifically review the staff members from the Human Resources (HR) department who are involved with this project. You need to apply a filter that will screen out any staff except HR. **OPEN** *Hiring New Employee 7-2* from the data files for this lesson.

1. Click the View ribbon and then click **Resource Sheet**.
2. Click the down-arrow in the Group column heading, point to Filters and then click [Custom . . .].
3. In the Group section, select **contains** from the dropdown list in the first box if it is not already visible. In the adjacent box, type **HR**.
4. Click the **OK** button.
5. **SAVE** the project schedule as *Hiring New Employee HR Filter* and then **CLOSE** the project schedule.
   PAUSE. LEAVE Project open to use in the next exercise.

■ Proficiency Assessment

Project 7-3: Resource Groups by Standard Rate for Don Funk Music Video

 You are working on employee reviews and pay increases for your staff for the upcoming year. You have decided it would be beneficial to be able to look at the standard rate variation within resource groups working on this project. You need to set up a custom group that will enable you to do this. **OPEN** *Don Funk Music Video 7-3* from the data files for this lesson.

1. Change the view to a resource sheet view.
2. From the ribbon, select Group by: More Groups.
3. Select Resource Group, and then make a copy of this group.
4. In the Group Definition box, name the new group Resource Groups by Standard Rate.
5. On the Group By line, set up the grouping by Standard Rate in descending order.
6. Click Define Group Intervals, then set up this dialog box so that the grouping is done on Intervals of 5.
7. Select the group you have created and apply it to your project schedule.
8. Widen the Resource Name field so that you can see the Standard Rate groupings.
9. SAVE the project schedule as *Don Funk Resource Groupings* and then CLOSE the file.
   PAUSE. LEAVE Project open to use in the next exercise.

Project 7-4: Duration Sort for Office Remodel

 You are responsible for the kitchen and lunchroom remodel for your office. Your manager has asked you which tasks on the project are scheduled to take the longest. You need to do a quick sort on the tasks to respond to his question. OPEN *Office Remodel 7-4* from the data files for this lesson.

1. Change the view to the Gantt Chart view.
2. Change the table view to Summary.
3. From the View ribbon, select Sort, and then Sort by.
4. Set up the dialog box to sort by Duration in descending order. Make sure that the tasks are not permanently renumbered.
5. Perform the sort.
6. SAVE the project schedule as *Office Remodel Duration Sort* and then CLOSE the file.
   PAUSE. LEAVE Project open to use in the next exercise.

■ Mastery Assessment

Project 7-5: Don Funk Filter for Don Funk Music Video

 You are the project manager for the Don Funk Music Video. You need to review all of the Production tasks to which Don Funk, the musical star, is assigned so that you can make sure his dressing room is prepared properly for him on those days. (Hint: Note that all of the Production tasks contain the word "Scene.") You need to apply a filter to show only the Production tasks with Don Funk assigned to them. OPEN *Don Funk Music Video 7-5* from the data files for this lesson.

1. Open the More Filters dialog box.
2. Begin to build a new filter named Don Funk Production Tasks.
3. Build the first level of the filter based on Name, which contains Scene.
4. Using And to link the levels, add a second level of the filter based on Resource Names, which contains Don Funk.
5. Run the filter.
6. SAVE the project schedule as *Don Funk Filter* and then CLOSE the file.
   PAUSE. LEAVE Project open to use in the next exercise.

Project 7-6: Costs and Durations for Hiring a New Employee

 You want to compare the cost of tasks that have the same duration in your project schedule to hire a new employee. You need to set up a custom group in order to group the data by duration and then by cost. OPEN *Hiring New Employee 7-6* from the data files for this lesson.

1. Switch to the Task Usage view.
2. Use the Duration group to set up a new custom group called Duration-Cost.
3. Set up the new group so that it groups by descending Duration and then descending Cost.
4. Apply the Duration-Cost group.
5. SAVE the project schedule as *Hiring Duration Cost Group* and then CLOSE the file. CLOSE Project.

Project Schedule Formatting Fundamentals

LESSON SKILL MATRIX

SKILLS	TASKS
Gantt Chart Formatting	Modify the Gantt Chart using the Bar Styles dialog box
	Modify the Gantt Chart using Gantt Chart Styles
Modifying Text Appearance in a View	Modify the appearance of text in a view
	Modify the appearance of a single piece of text
Creating Custom Fields	Create a custom text field
Creating and Editing Tables	Create a custom table
Creating Custom Views	Create a custom view

As a video production manager for Southridge Video and the project manager for the new Don Funk music video, you have the foundation of your project schedule in place. However, a project manager doesn't usually look at all of the data in a project schedule at once. In this lesson, you will learn to use some of the tools in Microsoft Project 2013, such as views and reports, to look at the element or aspect of the project schedule in which you are currently interested. With these tools, you can significantly impact how your data appears by the way in which you change the data format to meet your needs.

KEY TERMS

Charts view
custom field
diagram view
forms view
sheets view
usage view
view

© andrewhoughton/iStockphoto

- # SOFTWARE ORIENTATION

Microsoft Project's Bar Styles Dialog Box

In Microsoft Project, you can use the Bar Styles dialog box (see Figure 8-1) to customize the appearance of items on the Gantt Chart. This dialog box enables you to change the appearance of items such as task bars, milestones, summary bars, and text that appear on the Gantt Chart. You can change characteristics such as bar types, patterns, colors, splits, and shapes.

Figure 8-1

Bar Styles dialog box

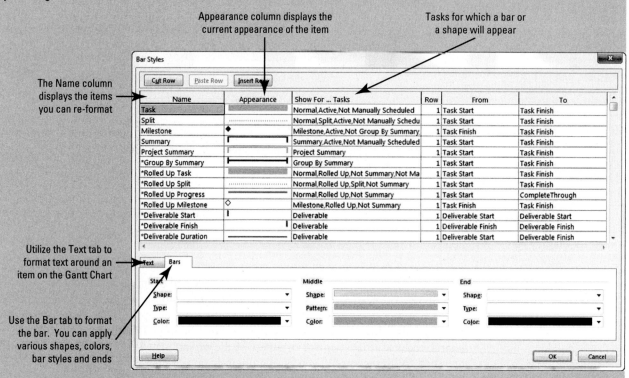

Appearance column displays the current appearance of the item

Tasks for which a bar or a shape will appear

The Name column displays the items you can re-format

Utilize the Text tab to format text around an item on the Gantt Chart

Use the Bar tab to format the bar. You can apply various shapes, colors, bar styles and ends

You will now use one of the features of the ribbon interface in Project 2013, the Format ribbon. With this ribbon you have faster access to formatting options in views. You may have seen in the various views of previous lessons a tab at the very top of the screen, above the ribbon. This is the Format ribbon. This tab provides formatting options available in the view you are in at the time. Figure 8-2 shows the Format ribbon for the Gantt Chart view.

Figure 8-2

Format ribbon for Gantt Chart views

■ Gantt Chart Formatting

↓
THE BOTTOM LINE

The Gantt Chart view consists of two parts: a table on the left and a bar chart on the right. The default formatting of the Gantt Chart view is useful for onscreen project schedule viewing and printing. However, you are able to change the formatting of almost any element on the Gantt Chart to suit your needs. In this exercise, you will learn to format Gantt Chart task bars. You can format whole categories of Gantt Chart task bars via the Bar Styles dialog box, or you can format individual Gantt Chart task bars directly.

Modifying the Gantt Chart Using the Bar Styles Dialog Box

In this exercise, you will modify several items on the Gantt Chart using the Bar Styles dialog box.

 MODIFY THE GANTT CHART USING THE BAR STYLES DIALOG BOX

GET READY. Before you begin these steps, launch Microsoft Project. OPEN the ***Don Funk Music Video 8M*** project schedule from the data files for this lesson. SAVE the file as ***Don Funk Music Video 8*** in the solutions folder for this lesson as directed by your instructor.

1. Click the Format tab, then in the Bar Styles group click the down-arrow under the Format button. Select Bar Styles from the dropdown list. The Bar Styles dialog box appears.

2. In the Name column, select Milestone. You want to change the shape of the milestones on the Gantt Chart.

3. In the bottom half of the dialog box under the Start label, locate the Shape box. Select the star shape from the dropdown list in the Shape box. Note that the star shape now appears in the Appearance column for Milestone. Your screen should look similar to Figure 8-3.

Figure 8-3

Bar Styles dialog box displaying the star as the shape for milestones

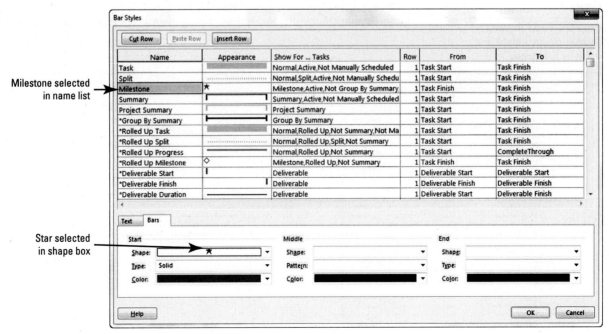

4. In the Name column at the top of the dialog box, select **Task**.

5. In the bottom half of the dialog box, click the **Text** tab. You want to make a change to display the resource groups assigned rather than full names next to the task bars.

6. In the **Text** tab, in the Right box, select **Resource Names**, click the **down-arrow**, and then select **Resource Group**. Your screen should look similar to Figure 8-4.

Figure 8-4

Bar Styles dialog box showing resource group to be listed at the right of all task Gantt chart bars

Resource Group selected to appear at the right of the Gantt bar

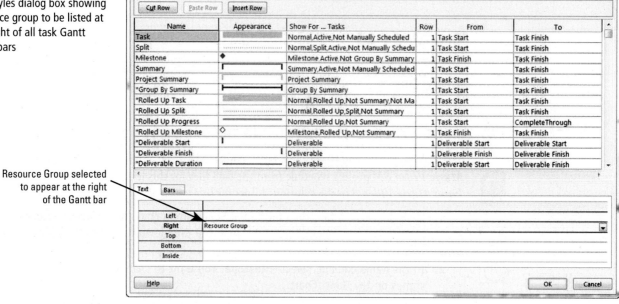

7. Click **OK** to close the Bar Styles dialog box. Microsoft Project applies the formatting changes you made to the Gantt Chart.

8. Select the **name cell** of Task 27, **Pre-Production complete**. Press **Crtl+Shift+F5**. This is the keyboard shortcut for Scroll to Task. Microsoft Project scrolls the Gantt Chart bar view to task 27, where you can see the reformatted milestones and resource groups rather than individual names. Your screen should look similar to Figure 8-5.

Figure 8-5

Gantt Chart view showing resource groups and the new shape for milestones

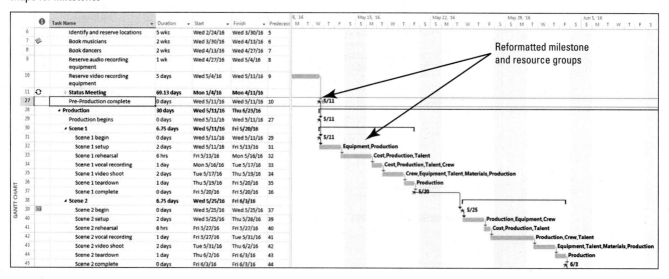

9. SAVE the project schedule.

PAUSE. LEAVE the project schedule open to use in the next exercise.

TAKE NOTE* With the Bar Styles dialog box, the formatting changes you make to a type of item (a milestone, for example) apply to all such items in the Gantt Chart.

You have just used the Bar Styles dialog box to make formatting changes to several items in the Gantt Chart view. As you learned in Lesson 1, the Gantt Chart is the primary way of viewing the data in a project schedule. It became the standard for visualizing project schedules in the early twentieth century when American engineer and management consultant Henry L. Gantt developed a bar chart with two main principles; 1) to measure activities by the amount of time needed to complete them; and 2) to represent the amount of the activity that should have been done in a given time.

In Microsoft Project, the Gantt Chart view is the default view. A *view* is a window through which you can see various elements of your project schedule. The two main view categories are named single view, which you have been using mostly throughout the lessons, and one you will see later in this lesson called a combination view. Views are made up of one or more view elements. The five different view formats and their common use are listed in Table 8-1.

Table 8-1

View elements

FORMAT	PURPOSE OR USE
Charts	Present information graphically, such as the Gantt Chart.
Sheets	Present information in rows and columns, such as the Task Sheet or the Resource Sheet.
Forms	Present detailed information in a structured format about one task or resource at a time, such as the Task Form.
Diagram	Present information in diagram format, such as the Network Diagram.
Usage	Present task or resource information on the left side and time-phased information on the right, such as the Resource Usage or Task Usage views.

Modifying the Gantt Chart Using Gantt Chart Styles

In this exercise, you will create a custom Gantt Chart, format it using predefined Gantt Chart Styles, and save the custom view.

→ MODIFY THE GANTT CHART USING GANTT CHART STYLES

USE the project schedule you created in the previous exercise.

1. Click the Format tab, under Gantt Chart Tools, if necessary.
2. In the Show/Hide group, click the Project Summary Task box.
3. Press the F5 key. In the ID box, type 0 and click OK. Microsoft Project displays the project summary task (task ID 0) at the top of the Gantt Chart view. Now you will make a few adjustments to your screen so that all of the summary task information is visible.
4. Drag the vertical divider bar between the table and chart to the right until at least the Duration and Start columns are visible, if necessary.

☐ Project Summary Task

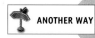

ANOTHER WAY | You can also double-click the divider bar to snap the divider to the nearest column edge.

Figure 8-6

Gantt Chart showing widened Task Name column and project summary task

5. **Double-click** the right edge of the **Task Name** column, in the column heading, to expand the column so that you can see the entire value. Readjust the vertical divider bar, as necessary. Your screen should look similar to Figure 8-6.

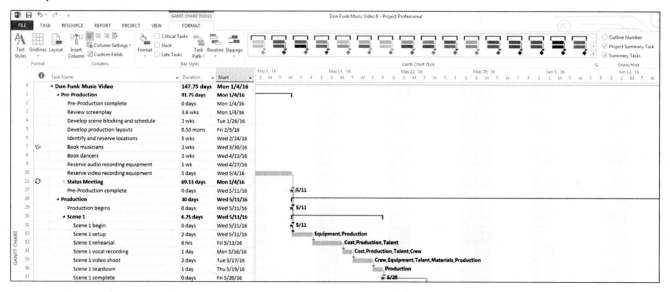

Before you make further formatting changes, you will make a copy of the Gantt Chart view so that you will not affect the original Gantt Chart view.

ANOTHER WAY | Right-clicking anywhere in a column heading will activate the sub-menu for column. Selecting Field Settings will display the Field Settings dialog box. In the dialog box, click the Best Fit button to automatically adjust the column width.

6. Click the **View** tab. In the Task Views group, click the **down-arrow** under the Gantt Chart button then select **Save View**. The Save View dialog box appears with View 1 as the default name as in Figure 8-7.

Figure 8-7

Save View dialog box

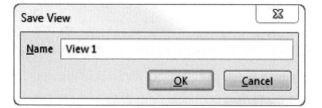

7. In the Name Field, type **My Custom Gantt Chart**, and then click **OK**. The Save View dialog box closes. Note that the name of the new view is listed on the left edge of your screen. Your screen should look similar to Figure 8-8.

Figure 8-8

My Custom Gantt Chart view

Name of view
appears here →

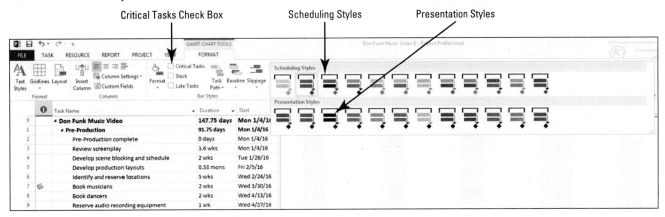

8. Click the **Format** tab. In the Gantt Chart Styles group, click the **More** button located at the lower right of the bar graphics, as shown in Figure 8-9.

Figure 8-9

The More button displays predefined Gantt bar styles

The More button

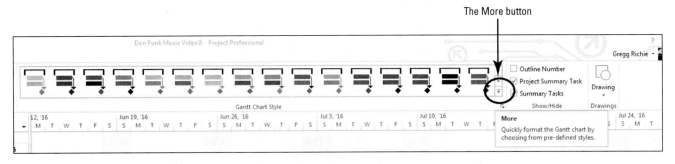

9. The predefined Gantt Chart Style options appear as in Figure 8-10. These are divided into two style categories, one for scheduling and one for presentations. Select the **second style** in the scheduling category.

Figure 8-10

Predefined Gantt Chart styles

Critical Tasks Check Box   Scheduling Styles   Presentation Styles

10. On the Format ribbon, in the Bar Styles group, click the **check box** for **Critical Tasks**.

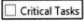

11. Press the **F5** key. In the ID box key **55** and press **Enter**. Notice that most tasks from 52-78 are formatted to display in red. Your screen should look similar to Figure 8-11.

Figure 8-11

My Custom Gantt Chart view with new scheduling style applied and critical tasks

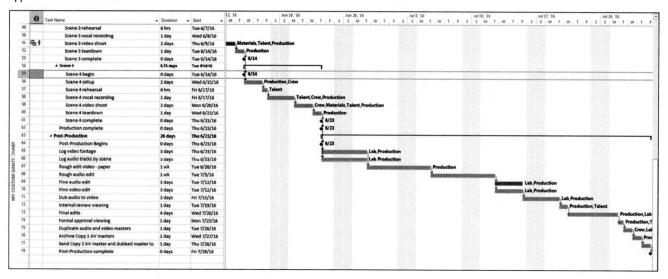

   Notice that the Resource Groups are still displayed to the right of the Gantt bars, but the Milestones have been changed back the default diamond shape.

12. SAVE the project schedule.

PAUSE. LEAVE the project schedule open to use in the next exercise.

In this exercise, you made formatting changes to your project schedule using predefined Gantt Chart Styles. This is similar to making changes using the Bar Styles command; however, the predefined Gantt Chart Styles has fewer choices than the Bar Styles command. As you are reviewing the formatting changes in the My Custom Gantt Chart view, remember that none of the data in the project schedule has changed – just the way it is formatted. These formatting changes affect only the My Custom Gantt Chart view; all other views in Microsoft Project are unaffected.

■ Modifying Text Appearance In a View

THE BOTTOM LINE   Microsoft Project enables you to change the way text appears within a view. You can modify the appearance of an entire category of tasks, such as summary tasks or milestones, or you can change the appearance of an individual cell. This feature allows you to call attention to specific items or to offset a specific type of task with color and font size or type.

 MODIFY THE APPEARANCE OF TEXT IN A VIEW

USE the project schedule you created in the previous exercise.

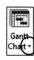

1. Click the Task tab, click the **down-arrow** under the Gantt Chart button and select More Views. The More Views dialog box appears.

2. In the More Views box, select Task Sheet, and then click Apply. The Detail Gantt view appears.

ANOTHER WAY You can also right-click the view name bar at the left edge of the screen and select More Views from the dropdown menu.

3. Press the F5 key. In the ID box, type 0 and then press Enter. This brings you to the top of the Gantt Chart.

4. Click the Format tab under Text Sheet Tools. Then in the Format group click Text Styles. The Text Styles dialog box appears.

5. In the Items to Change: box, click the sub-menu arrow and select Summary Tasks from the list

6. In the Font: box, leave the default font type as it is. In the Font Style: box, select Bold Italic.

7. In the Size: box, select 12 as the font size.

8. In the Color: box, select White.

9. In the Background Color: box select dark blue (ScreenTip will show as Blue, Darker 50%). Your Text Styles dialog box will look similar to Figure 8-12.

Figure 8-12

Text Styles dialog box with summary task formatting changes

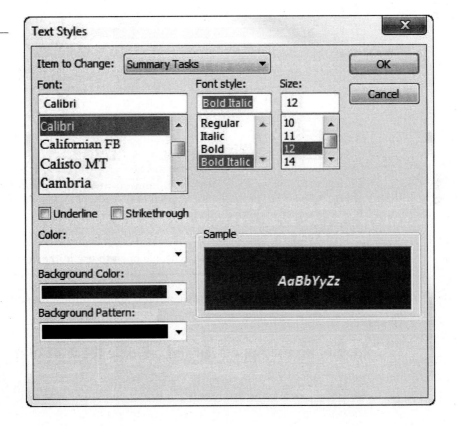

10. Click OK. Microsoft Project changes the formatting of all summary tasks to the attributes you specified. Your screen should look similar to Figure 8-13.

Figure 8-13

Task Sheet view with summary tasks reformatted

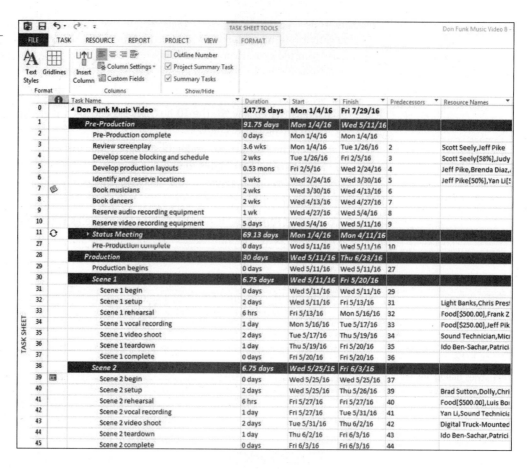

	❶	Task Name	Duration	Start	Finish	Predecessors	Resource Names
0		◢ **Don Funk Music Video**	147.75 days	Mon 1/4/16	Fri 7/29/16		
1		*Pre-Production*	*91.75 days*	*Mon 1/4/16*	*Wed 5/11/16*		
2		Pre-Production complete	0 days	Mon 1/4/16	Mon 1/4/16		
3		Review screenplay	3.6 wks	Mon 1/4/16	Tue 1/26/16	2	Scott Seely,Jeff Pike
4		Develop scene blocking and schedule	2 wks	Tue 1/26/16	Fri 2/5/16	3	Scott Seely[58%],Judy
5		Develop production layouts	0.53 mons	Fri 2/5/16	Wed 2/24/16	4	Jeff Pike,Brenda Diaz,
6		Identify and reserve locations	5 wks	Wed 2/24/16	Wed 3/30/16	5	Jeff Pike[50%],Yan Li[!
7	📎	Book musicians	2 wks	Wed 3/30/16	Wed 4/13/16	6	
8		Book dancers	2 wks	Wed 4/13/16	Wed 4/27/16	7	
9		Reserve audio recording equipment	1 wk	Wed 4/27/16	Wed 5/4/16	8	
10		Reserve video recording equipment	5 days	Wed 5/4/16	Wed 5/11/16	9	
11	🔄	▸ *Status Meeting*	*69.13 days*	*Mon 4/11/16*			
27		Pre-Production complete	0 days	Wed 5/11/16	Wed 5/11/16	10	
28		*Production*	*30 days*	*Wed 5/11/16*	*Thu 6/23/16*		
29		Production begins	0 days	Wed 5/11/16	Wed 5/11/16	27	
30		*Scene 1*	*6.75 days*	*Wed 5/11/16*	*Fri 5/20/16*		
31		Scene 1 begin	0 days	Wed 5/11/16	Wed 5/11/16	29	
32		Scene 1 setup	2 days	Wed 5/11/16	Fri 5/13/16	31	Light Banks,Chris Pres!
33		Scene 1 rehearsal	6 hrs	Fri 5/13/16	Mon 5/16/16	32	Food[$500.00],Frank Z
34		Scene 1 vocal recording	1 day	Mon 5/16/16	Tue 5/17/16	33	Food[$250.00],Jeff Pik
35		Scene 1 video shoot	2 days	Tue 5/17/16	Thu 5/19/16	34	Sound Technician,Mic!
36		Scene 1 teardown	1 day	Thu 5/19/16	Fri 5/20/16	35	Ido Ben-Sachar,Patrici
37		Scene 1 complete	0 days	Fri 5/20/16	Fri 5/20/16	36	
38		*Scene 2*	*6.75 days*	*Wed 5/25/16*	*Fri 6/3/16*		
39	▦	Scene 2 begin	0 days	Wed 5/25/16	Wed 5/25/16	37	
40		Scene 2 setup	2 days	Wed 5/25/16	Thu 5/26/16	39	Brad Sutton,Dolly,Chri
41		Scene 2 rehearsal	6 hrs	Fri 5/27/16	Fri 5/27/16	40	Food[$500.00],Luis Bo!
42		Scene 2 vocal recording	1 day	Fri 5/27/16	Tue 5/31/16	41	Yan Li,Sound Technicia
43		Scene 2 video shoot	2 days	Tue 5/31/16	Thu 6/2/16	42	Digital Truck-Mounted
44		Scene 2 teardown	1 day	Thu 6/2/16	Fri 6/3/16	43	Ido Ben-Sachar,Patrici
45		Scene 2 complete	0 days	Fri 6/3/16	Fri 6/3/16	44	

TAKE NOTE* Notice that the Project summary task was not reformatted. This is because the Project Summary task is a separate category and must be reformatted by itself.

11. **SAVE** the project schedule.

   PAUSE. LEAVE the project schedule open to use in the next exercise.

In this exercise, you modified the way all text appeared for summary tasks. In the exercise you will modify a single piece of text.

Modifying the Appearance of a Single Piece of Text

In this exercise, you will modify a single piece of text in the Task Sheet view using the cost table.

⊙ MODIFY THE APPEARANCE OF A SINGLE PIECE OF TEXT

USE the project schedule you created in the previous exercise.

1. On the ribbon, click the **View** tab. In the Data group click the **Tables** button and then select **Cost**.

2. Auto fit all the columns to see all the data. Select the **Total Cost cell** for task 38, Scene 2.

TROUBLESHOOTING The tables in Microsoft Project may look like Microsoft Excel but there are distinct differences. For example, you can auto-fit all columns in Excel at the same time, but you cannot in do this in Microsoft Project.

3. Select the **Task** tab and then, in the Font group, click the **expand button** at the lower-right corner of that group. The Font dialog box appears.

4. Change the font color to **Automatic** and the background color to **yellow**. Your screen should look similar to Figure 8-14.

Figure 8-14

Task Sheet view with Font dialog box changes made

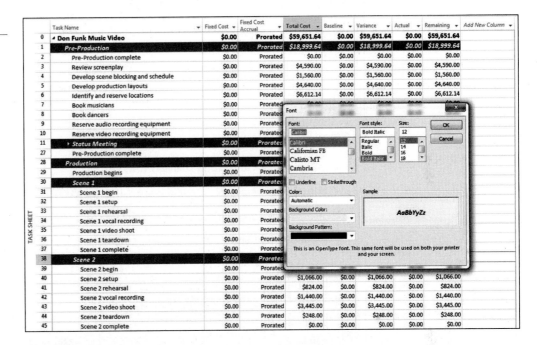

5. Click **OK**. Notice that only that cell has change font color and background color.

6. **SAVE** the project schedule.

    PAUSE. **LEAVE** the project schedule open to use in the next exercise.

In this exercise, you modified a single piece of text. Modified text will remain modified every time it is called up in that view, regardless of the table you are using. For example, if you were to switch to the summary table after you formatted this text, it appears with the new formatting.

■ Creating Custom Fields

THE BOTTOM LINE

As you develop more information about your project tasks, you may want to enter this information into the schedule, but find there is no associated, default field available. With Microsoft Project you have the ability to create custom, user-defined fields to meet your needs. Custom fields are the starting point for you to create customized tables, views and reports.

 CREATE A CUSTOM TEXT FIELD

USE the project schedule you created in the previous exercise.

1. Click the **Format** tab. Then click on **Custom Fields**. The Custom Fields dialog box appears as shown in Figure 8-15.

Figure 8-15

Custom Fields dialog box

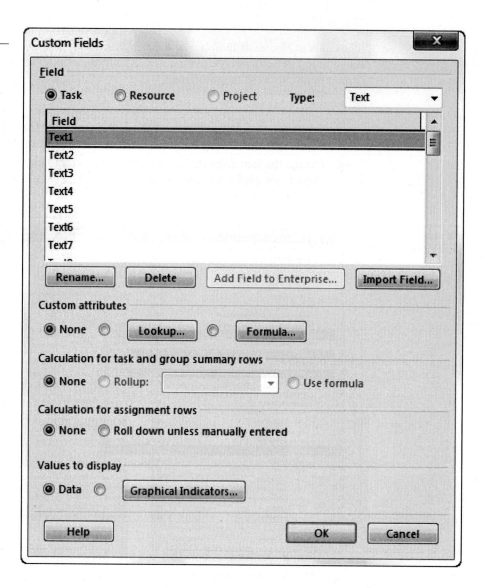

Rename...

2. Click once on the Text1 field and then click the Rename button.
3. In the Rename Field dialog box, type **Cast** and then press **OK**.
4. Click once on the Text2 field and then click the Rename button.
5. In the Rename Field dialog box, type **Location** and then press **OK**.
6. Click **OK** to close the Custom Fields dialog box.

   SAVE and close the project schedule.

   PAUSE. LEAVE Microsoft Project open to use in the next exercise.

In this exercise, you created two custom text fields. A ***custom field*** is a user-definable field. Text fields are available for you to enter any type of text-based information. In this case study, you used them to create a custom field for shooting location and one which you can enter the cast members to be used.

In Microsoft Project's task database there are 130 user-definable fields available for you to use, broken down into nine categories. Some fields lend themselves to be used in calculations while others are for simply storing text-based information. Table 8-2 displays all nine categories, their primary purpose and use, the type of entry, number of fields available in each, and in which database these fields can be used.

Table 8-2

Custom Fields

Category	Purpose or Use	Entry Type	Number Available	Available Database
Cost	Used to display cost-based information and will display in the units selected in the options. Can be used as a variable in calculations.	Calculated or Entered	10	All
Date	Used to display date-based information and will display in the format chosen in the options. Can be used as a variable in calculations.	Calculated or Entered	10	Al
Duration	Used to display duration-based information. Can be used as a variable in calculations.	Calculated or Entered	10	All
Finish	Primarily used in the Interim Plan feature. Used to display date-based information. Can be used as a variable in calculations.	Calculated or Entered	10	All
Flag	Used to set a flag (Yes/No) and will display a Yes or No. Can be used as a conditional variable in calculations.	Calculated or Entered	20	All
Number	Used for numerical information not covered by another field. Can be used as a variable in calculations.	Calculated or Entered	20	All
Start	Primarily used in the Interim Plan feature. Used to display date-based information. Can be used as a variable in calculations.	Calculated or Entered	10	All
Text	Used for any type of text-based information. Certain values of text can display based on a calculation.	Calculated or Entered	30	All
Outline Code	Used to define a structure for tasks or resources only (not used for assignments).	Entered (static)	10	Task/Resource

Custom fields can make the difference between a mediocre Microsoft Project schedule file and a great Microsoft Project schedule file. When planning your project, ensure there is justification to set up custom fields. In other words, collecting and recording data simply because the option is available does not mean it is necessarily a good idea. The data you collect and record should add value.

■ Creating and Editing Tables

THE BOTTOM LINE

Within Microsoft Project are a number of different tables that can be used in various views. These tables contain most of the commonly used data fields. However, you can create new tables that contain exactly the data you want, such as custom fields, or you can modify any predefined table to meet your needs.

CREATE A CUSTOM TABLE

OPEN the ***Don Funk Music Video 8MA*** project schedule from the data files for this lesson.
SAVE the file as ***Don Funk Music Video 8A*** in the solutions folder for this lesson as directed
by your instructor.

1. Click the View tab. Then click Tables and then click More Tables. The More Tables
   dialog box appears and displays all of the predefined tables available to you, depending on the type of view currently displayed (task or resource).

2. Confirm that the Task button is selected as the Tables option. Select Entry, and then
   click the Copy button. The Table Definition dialog box appears.

3. In the Name box, key Music Video Schedule Table. Check the check box to the right
   of the Name box labeled Show in menu. Now you will customize the table.

4. In the Field Name column, select the following field names and then click Delete Row
   after selecting each field name.

   Indicators

   Duration

   Finish

   Predecessors

   Resource Names

   After you have deleted these fields, your screen should look similar to Figure 8-16.

Figure 8-16

Table Definition dialog box

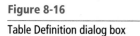

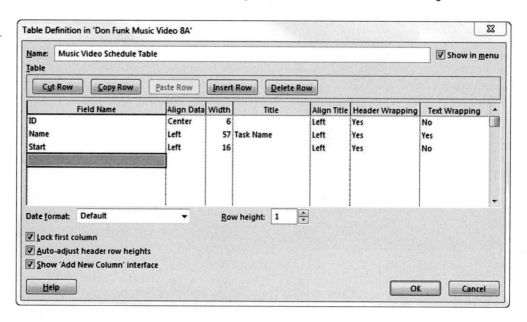

5. In the Field Name column, click the down-arrow in the next empty cell below Start,
   and then type or select Cast (Text1) from the dropdown list.

6. In the Align Data column in the same row, select Left. In the Width column, type or select 50.

7. In the Field Name column in the next empty row below Cast, select Location(Text 2)
   from the dropdown list.

8. In the Align Data column in the same row, select Left. In the Width column, type or select 30.

9. In the Field Name column, select Start, and then click the Cut Row button.

10. In the Field Name column, select Name, and then click the Paste Row button.

11. In the Align Data column in the Start row, select Left. In the Width column, type or select 30.

12. In the Align Data column in the Name row, select Left. In the Width column, type or
    select 60.

13. In the Date Format box, select Wed 1/28/09 12:33 pm. Your screen should look similar to Figure 8-17.

Figure 8-17

Table Definition dialog box with changes

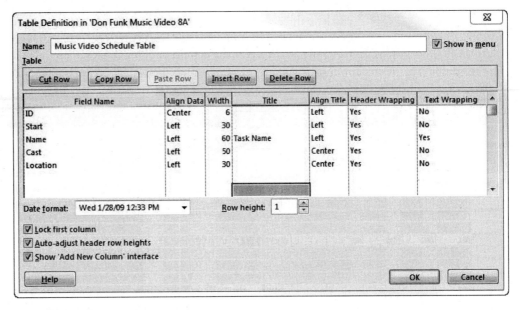

14. Click OK to close the Table Definition dialog box. The new table is highlighted in the More Tables dialog box.

15. Click Apply. Microsoft Project applies the new table to the Task Sheet view. Your screen should look similar to Figure 8-18.

Figure 8-18

Task Sheet with the Music Video Schedule table applied

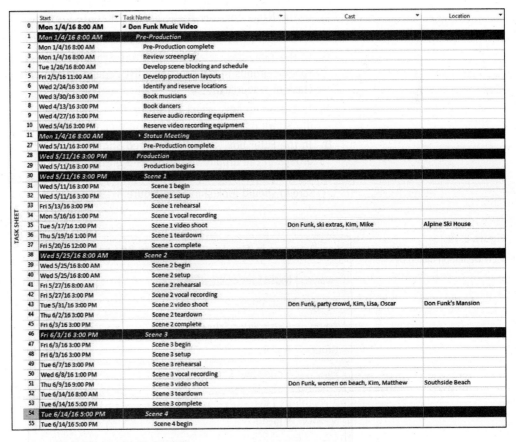

16. SAVE the project schedule.

PAUSE. LEAVE the project schedule open to use in the next exercise.

In this exercise, you created a custom table to display the information typically found on a video shooting schedule. You modified an existing table to include additional data that was important to your project schedule. As you create future project schedules, keep in mind that you have three options when setting up tables: you can create a new table, redefine an existing table, or copy an existing table and modify it as needed. Also note that as you modify any table, you are changing the definition of that table.

■ Creating Custom Views

THE BOTTOM LINE

Almost all of the work you perform in Microsoft Project is done in a view, which allows you to see your project schedule in a useful way. Microsoft Project includes numerous predefined views. You can use these views, edit an existing view, or create your own view. In this exercise, you will create a custom view using the custom filter and custom table you created in earlier lessons.

CREATE A CUSTOM VIEW

USE the project schedule you created in the previous exercise.

1. On the View ribbon, click the **down-arrow** under the Gantt Chart button in the Task Views group, then click **More Views**. The More Views dialog box appears, displaying all of the predefined views available to you.
2. Click the New button. The Define New View dialog box appears. Most views use only a single pane, but a view can consist of two separate panes.
3. Make sure **Single View** is selected, and then click **OK**. The View Definition dialog box appears.
4. In the Name box, key **Music Video Schedule View**.
5. In the Screen box, select **Task Sheet** from the dropdown list.
6. In the Table box, select **Music Video Schedule Table** from the dropdown list. The specific groups in the dropdown list depend on the type of view you selected in step 5 (task or resource).
7. In the Group box, select **No Group** from the dropdown list. The specific groups in the dropdown list again depend on the type of view you selected in step 5.
8. In the Filter box, select **Unfinished Shoots** from the dropdown list. The specific groups in the dropdown list depend on the type of view you selected in step 5. The View Definition dialog box shows all the elements that can make up a view. Your screen should look similar to Figure 8-19.

Figure 8-19

View Definition dialog box

View Definition in 'Don Funk Music Video 8A'

Name:	Musci Video Schedule View
Screen:	Task Sheet
Table:	Music Video Schedule Table
Group:	No Group
Filter:	Unfinished Shoots

☐ Highlight filter
☑ Show in menu

Help   OK   Cancel

9. Select the **Show in Menu** check box, and then click **OK** to close the View Definition dialog box. The new view appears and should be selected in the More Views
   dialog box.

When you select the Show in Menu check box, Microsoft Project adds the new view to the
View bar. This custom view will be saved with this Microsoft Project data file. You have the
option to save all custom items in the Global.MPT (the global template) file, so they are
available each time you use Project.

10. Click **Apply**. Microsoft Project applies the new view. Your screen should look similar to
    Figure 8-20.

Figure 8-20

Custom view with Music Video
Schedule Table and Unfinished
Shoots filter

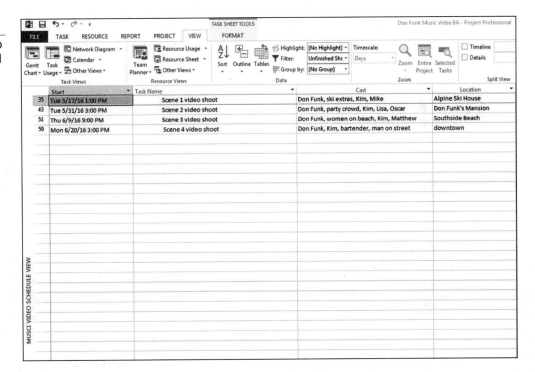

11. **SAVE** the project schedule. **CLOSE** the project schedule.

    PAUSE. If you are continuing to the next lesson, keep Project open. If not continuing
    to additional lessons, **CLOSE** Project.

In this exercise, you created a custom view that enabled you to look specifically at information that was of interest to you. Recall that a view is a window through which you can see
the various elements of a project schedule in a way that is helpful to the viewing audience.
As you saw in this exercise, a view might contain elements such as tables, groups, or filters.
You can combine these with other elements to create almost limitless custom views to suit
any purpose.

SKILL SUMMARY

IN THIS LESSON YOU LEARNED:	MATRIX SKILL
To format the Gantt Chart	Modify the Gantt Chart using the Bar Styles dialog box
	Modify the Gantt Chart using the Gantt Chart Styles
To modify text appearance in a view	Modify the appearance of text in a view
	Modify the appearance of a single piece of text
To create custom fields	Create a custom text field
To create and edit tables	Create a custom table
To create custom views	Create a custom view

■ Knowledge Assessment

Matching

Match the term in column 1 to its description in column 2.

Column 1	Column 2
1. field	a. a spreadsheet-like presentation of project data, organized in vertical columns and horizontal rows
2. custom field	b. the default view in Microsoft Project
3. table	c. the right side of the Gantt Chart view
4. Format	d. the intersection of a row and a column in a table
5. Bar Styles	e. a view that presents information in rows and columns
6. view	f. a ribbon that allows you to add or change the appearance of a view
7. Gantt Chart	g. another name for field
8. cell	h. a feature that allows the user to create columns for specific uses
9. bar chart	i. a window through which you can see the various elements of a project schedule
10. sheet	j. the dialog box that can be used to format the graphical components of the Gantt Chart view

True / False

Circle T if the statement is true or F if the statement is false.

T   F   1. When you make a change to a milestone using the Bar Styles dialog box, the change applies to all milestones in the Gantt Chart.

T   F   2. The custom fields dialog box allows the user to change the name of a custom field.

T   F   3. In Microsoft Project, you can edit predefined tables but you cannot create new custom tables to suit your needs.

T   F   4. The Gantt Chart view can include only the task data without the bar chart.

T   F   5. When you make formatting changes to your project schedule, the data does not change, just the way it appears.

T   F   6. When you add, remove or rearrange columns, or change column widths, you are changing the table's definition.

T   F   7. You can make almost any custom field part of a calculation for another custom field.

T   F   8. If you format data using the Font dialog box, the changes apply to only the data you have specifically selected.

T   F   9. The Gantt Chart Styles has more formatting choices than the Bar Styles dialog box.

T   F   10. Changing the appearance of data in a view can make it easier to read and understand project data.

■ Competency Assessment

Project 8-1: Modifying the Don Funk Music Video Gantt Chart

You are reviewing your project schedule with your team. Several team members make the suggestion that it would be nice to have the summary tasks stand out a little bit more on the project schedule. You decide to format the summary tasks in purple with the task name listed on the right of the bar.

GET READY. Launch Microsoft Project if it is not already running. OPEN *Don Funk Music Video 8-1* from the data files for this lesson.

1. Click the Format tab, and then click the Format button in the Bar Styles group. Select Bar Styles from the dropdown list.

2. In the Name column, select Summary.

3. In the bottom half of the dialog box, make sure the Bars tab is selected. Under the Start, Middle, and End labels, select Purple from the dropdown list in the Color boxes.

4. Click the Text tab.

5. Click the Right box. Click the down-arrow, and select Name from the dropdown list.

6. Click OK.

7. Select the name of Task 27, Pre-Production complete.

8. Click the Task tab, and then click the Scroll to Task button.

9. SAVE the project schedule as *Don Funk Music Video Purple Summary*, and then CLOSE the file.

   LEAVE Project open to use in the next exercise.

Project 8-2: Interviewing Schedule Table

You have created a project schedule for interviewing and hiring a new employee. Now you would like to create a table to display the information found on an internal interview schedule.

OPEN *HR Interview and Hire Schedule 8-2* from the data files for this lesson.

1. Click the View tab. In the Task Views group, click the down-arrow under the Gantt Chart button, and then click More Views.
2. Select Task Sheet from the More Views box, and then click Apply.
3. On the ribbon, in the Data group, click Tables and then click More Tables.
4. Confirm that the Task button is selected as the Tables option. Select Entry, and then click the Copy button.
5. In the Name box, key Interview Schedule Table. Select the Show in Menu check box.
6. In the Field Name column, select each of the following names and then click Delete Row after selecting each field name.

   Indicators

   Finish

   Predecessors

   Resource Names
7. In the Date format box, select 1/28/09 12:33 pm.
8. Click OK.
9. Make sure that Interview Schedule Table is selected in the More Tables dialog box, and then click Apply.
10. SAVE the project schedule as *HR Interview Schedule Table*, and then CLOSE the file.

    LEAVE Project open to use in the next exercise.

■ Proficiency Assessment

Project 8-3: Office Remodel Contractor Tasks

You have developed a project schedule for a kitchen/lunchroom remodel at your business. You are preparing to distribute the schedule to some of the contractors who will work on the project. You would like to call attention to the summary tasks and the specific tasks that these contractors will be undertaking.

OPEN *Office Remodel 8-3* from the data files for this lesson.

1. Change the view to the Task Sheet.
2. Select Text Styles from the Format ribbon.
3. Select Summary Tasks as the item to change.
4. Select font size 12 and color Blue. Click OK.
5. Select tasks 9 through 14.
6. Activate the Font dialog box from the Task ribbon.
7. Select a Background color of Yellow and then click OK.
8. SAVE the project schedule as *Office Remodel Contractor Tasks* and then CLOSE the file.

   LEAVE Project open to use in the next exercise.

Project 8-4: Interviewing Schedule Custom View

You have created an interviewing schedule for hiring a new employee at your company. You want to create a custom view for this project schedule that looks at only the summary tasks in the Interview Schedule format (which you created in Project 8-2).

OPEN *HR Interview Schedule 8-4* from the data files for this lesson.

1. From the More Views dialog box, click New to create a new view.
2. Select Single View.
3. Name the new view Summary Interview Schedule View.
4. Select Task Sheet from the Screen box.
5. Select Interview Schedule Table from the Table box.
6. Select No Group from the Group box.
7. Select Summary Tasks from the Filter box.
8. Select the Show in Menu check box.
9. Apply the new view.
10. SAVE the project schedule as *HR Summary Interview Schedule*, and then CLOSE the file. LEAVE Project open to use in the next exercise.

■ Mastery Assessment

Project 8-5: Don Funk Music Video

You need to make some additional formatting changes to the Don Funk Music Video so that the critical path is more visible for a presentation. You decide to make these changes using the Gantt Chart Tool.

 OPEN *Don Funk Music Video 8-5* from the data files for this lesson.

1. Make a copy of the Gantt Chart view.
2. Name the new view Custom Gantt 8-5.
3. Apply the custom view you have just created.
4. Activate the Gantt Chart Tools – Format ribbon.
5. Select a dark blue Gantt bar style for your presentation.
6. Select Critical Path as the type of information you want to display.
7. SAVE the project schedule as *Don Funk Critical Path*, and then CLOSE the file. LEAVE Project open to use in the next exercise.

Project 8-6: Setting Up a Home Office – Adding a Custom Field

You need to add some information about new phone company billing to your Home Office project schedule. You need to use a custom field in order to capture information about the suppliers on the project.

 OPEN *Home Office Setup 8-6* from the data files for this lesson.

1. Open the Custom Fields dialog box.
2. Create a custom text field named Supplier.
3. Insert the new field between the Task Name column and the Duration column.
4. Type Local Office Supply Store as the supplier for the purchases of all computers, business machines (except phone), office furniture and supplies.
5. Type Phone Company as the supplier for the purchase/ordering of the phone, phone line, and the installation of the phone and the line.
6. Apply your changes.
7. SAVE the project schedule as *Home Office Custom Field Info*, and then CLOSE the file. CLOSE Project.

9 LESSON

Project Schedule Tracking Fundamentals

LESSON SKILL MATRIX

SKILLS	TASKS
Establishing a Project Baseline	Establish a project baseline
Tracking a Project as Scheduled	Track a project as scheduled
Entering the Completion Percentage for a Task	Enter the completion percentage for a task
Identifying Over Budget Tasks and Resources	Identify over budget tasks and resources
Identifying Time and Schedule Problems	Reschedule uncompleted work

You are a video production manager for Southridge Video and the project manager for the new Don Funk music video. Prior to work beginning, you focused on developing and communicating the project details. Your project has been accepted, approved, and work is starting. You are now entering the next phase of project management: tracking progress. In order to properly manage your project, you need to know details such as who did what work, when the work was done, and the cost of the work. In this lesson, you will use Microsoft Project to apply some of the basic project tracking tools such as saving baselines; tracking actual work; entering completion percentages; and troubleshooting budget, time, and scheduling problems.

KEY TERMS

actual cost
actuals
baseline
baseline cost
cost % complete
current cost
physical % complete
planning
progress bar
remaining cost

schedule %
   complete
sponsor
status date
timephased
   fields
tracking
work periods
work % complete
variance

© tonmeistermat/iStockphoto

■ SOFTWARE ORIENTATION

Tracking Table

The Variance Table can be used to review baseline information in table format.

Figure 9-1

The Variance Table in the Task Sheet view

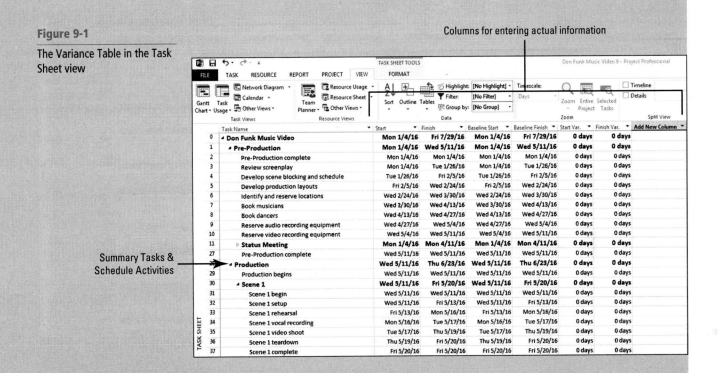

Columns for entering actual information

Summary Tasks & Schedule Activities

On the Variance Table, you can also see the *variance* between the baseline start and the planned or actual start of a task. In other words, this table shows you if the project is ahead of schedule or behind schedule, on a task-by-task basis.

■ Establishing a Project Baseline

THE BOTTOM LINE

In order to evaluate how well a project is progressing, it is important to review how well it was originally planned. The schedule baseline is the project schedule that has been approved by the project sponsor. The baseline is saved and then referred to later to track project progress.

In project management, by definition, a baseline is the approved version of the scope, schedule and budget of a project. In Microsoft Project, a *baseline* is a "snap-shot" of these key values, such as the planned start and finish dates (schedule), planned costs (budget) and the tasks (scope), at a given point in time.

ESTABLISH A PROJECT BASELINE

GET READY. Before you begin these steps, launch Microsoft Project.

1. OPEN the **Don Funk Music Video 9M** project schedule from the data files for this lesson.

2. SAVE the file as **Don Funk Music Video 9** in the solutions folder for this lesson as directed by your instructor.

3. Click the Project tab. In the Schedule group, click the Set Baseline button and then select Set Baseline.

4. The Set Baseline dialog box appears. You will accept all of the default settings in this dialog box by clicking OK.

   Microsoft Project saves the baseline, although there is no indication in the Gantt Chart view that anything has changed. In the next few steps, you will explore some of the changes caused by saving the baseline.

Cross Ref

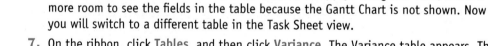
You will go deeper into the Set Baseline dialog box in Lesson 11.

You can save up to eleven baselines in a single project schedule. The baselines are named Baseline (the first baseline you would normally save) and Baseline 1 through Baseline 10. Saving multiple baselines is helpful if your project duration is especially long or if you have approved scope/schedule changes. You can save multiple baselines to record different sets of baseline values and later compare these against each other and against actual values.

5. On the ribbon, click the View tab and then click the down-arrow under Gantt Chart. Select More Views, and the More Views dialog box appears.

6. In the More Views box, select Task Sheet and click Apply. Using this view, there is more room to see the fields in the table because the Gantt Chart is not shown. Now you will switch to a different table in the Task Sheet view.

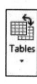

7. On the ribbon, click Tables, and then click Variance. The Variance table appears. This table includes both the Scheduled and Baseline columns so that you can compare them easily. Your screen should look similar to Figure 9-2.

Figure 9-2

Variance Table displaying scheduled and baseline information

Scheduled Start/Finish   Baseline Start/Finish   Start/Finish Variance

	Task Name	Start	Finish	Baseline Start	Baseline Finish	Start Var.	Finish Var.	Add New Column
0	▲ **Don Funk Music Video**	**Mon 1/4/16**	**Fri 7/29/16**	**Mon 1/4/16**	**Fri 7/29/16**	**0 days**	**0 days**	
1	▲ **Pre-Production**	**Mon 1/4/16**	**Wed 5/11/16**	**Mon 1/4/16**	**Wed 5/11/16**	**0 days**	**0 days**	
2	Pre-Production complete	Mon 1/4/16	Mon 1/4/16	Mon 1/4/16	Mon 1/4/16	0 days	0 days	
3	Review screenplay	Mon 1/4/16	Tue 1/26/16	Mon 1/4/16	Tue 1/26/16	0 days	0 days	
4	Develop scene blocking and schedule	Tue 1/26/16	Fri 2/5/16	Tue 1/26/16	Fri 2/5/16	0 days	0 days	
5	Develop production layouts	Fri 2/5/16	Wed 2/24/16	Fri 2/5/16	Wed 2/24/16	0 days	0 days	
6	Identify and reserve locations	Wed 2/24/16	Wed 3/30/16	Wed 2/24/16	Wed 3/30/16	0 days	0 days	
7	Book musicians	Wed 3/30/16	Wed 4/13/16	Wed 3/30/16	Wed 4/13/16	0 days	0 days	
8	Book dancers	Wed 4/13/16	Wed 4/27/16	Wed 4/13/16	Wed 4/27/16	0 days	0 days	
9	Reserve audio recording equipment	Wed 4/27/16	Wed 5/4/16	Wed 4/27/16	Wed 5/4/16	0 days	0 days	
10	Reserve video recording equipment	Wed 5/4/16	Wed 5/11/16	Wed 5/4/16	Wed 5/11/16	0 days	0 days	
11	▷ **Status Meeting**	**Mon 1/4/16**	**Mon 4/11/16**	**Mon 1/4/16**	**Mon 4/11/16**	**0 days**	**0 days**	
27	Pre-Production complete	Wed 5/11/16	Wed 5/11/16	Wed 5/11/16	Wed 5/11/16	0 days	0 days	
28	▲ **Production**	**Wed 5/11/16**	**Thu 6/23/16**	**Wed 5/11/16**	**Thu 6/23/16**	**0 days**	**0 days**	
29	Production begins	Wed 5/11/16	Wed 5/11/16	Wed 5/11/16	Wed 5/11/16	0 days	0 days	
30	▲ **Scene 1**	**Wed 5/11/16**	**Fri 5/20/16**	**Wed 5/11/16**	**Fri 5/20/16**	**0 days**	**0 days**	
31	Scene 1 begin	Wed 5/11/16	Wed 5/11/16	Wed 5/11/16	Wed 5/11/16	0 days	0 days	
32	Scene 1 setup	Wed 5/11/16	Fri 5/13/16	Wed 5/11/16	Fri 5/13/16	0 days	0 days	
33	Scene 1 rehearsal	Fri 5/13/16	Mon 5/16/16	Fri 5/13/16	Mon 5/16/16	0 days	0 days	
34	Scene 1 vocal recording	Mon 5/16/16	Tue 5/17/16	Mon 5/16/16	Tue 5/17/16	0 days	0 days	
35	Scene 1 video shoot	Tue 5/17/16	Thu 5/19/16	Tue 5/17/16	Thu 5/19/16	0 days	0 days	
36	Scene 1 teardown	Thu 5/19/16	Fri 5/20/16	Thu 5/19/16	Fri 5/20/16	0 days	0 days	
37	Scene 1 complete	Fri 5/20/16	Fri 5/20/16	Fri 5/20/16	Fri 5/20/16	0 days	0 days	

TASK SHEET

TROUBLESHOOTING   If any column displays pound signs (####), double-click between the column titles to widen the column.

Note that at this point, the values in the Start and Baseline Start, as well as the values in the Finish and Baseline Finish, are identical. This is because no actual work has occurred and no changes to the scheduled work have been made. Once actual work has been recorded or schedule adjustments have been made, the scheduled values may differ from the baseline values. Any differences would be displayed in the Variance column.

8. **SAVE** the project schedule.

   PAUSE. LEAVE Project open to use in the next exercise.

In this exercise, you learned how to save a baseline for your project schedule. You must save a baseline before you begin tracking project progress. The following table lists the specific values saved in the baseline, which include the task, resource, and assignment fields, as well as the *timephased fields*–task, resource, and assignment values distributed over time.

Table 9-1

Baseline field types saved by Project 2013

Task Fields	Start field
	Finish field
	Duration field
	Work and timephased Work fields
	Cost and timephased Cost fields
Resource Fields	Work and timephased Work fields
	Cost and timephased Cost fields
Assignment Fields	Start field
	Finish field
	Work and timephased Work fields
	Cost and timephased Cost fields

You should save a baseline when:

- You have developed the project schedule as much as possible. (You can still add tasks, resources, or an assignment after the work has begun. This is usually not avoidable.)
- Your project has been approved and accepted by the project sponsor.
- You have not started to enter actual values, such as a percentage of completion for the task.

The first phase of a project focuses on project *planning* – developing and communicating the details of a project before actual work begins. When work begins, so does your next phase of project management: tracking project progress. *Tracking* refers to all of the collecting, entering, and analyzing of actual project performance data, such as actual work values on tasks (usually expressed in hours), actual resource costs, and actual durations. These details, collectively, are often called *actuals* and can be recorded in a Microsoft Project file. Accurately tracking project performance and comparing it against the baseline helps you to answer questions such as:

- Are tasks starting and finishing as planned? If not, what will be the impact on the finish date?
- Are resources completing the proper amount of the scope? Are they doing unapproved work (scope creep)?
- Are resources requiring more or less than the scheduled amount of time to complete tasks?
- Are tasks being completed above or below scheduled cost?

There are several ways to track progress in Microsoft Project, depending on the level of detail or control required by you, the stakeholders, and the project *sponsor* – the individual or organization that provides financial support and supports the project team within the larger organization. Because tracking requires more work from you and possibly from the resources working on the project, you need to determine the level of detail you need. In this lesson, we will examine the following different levels of tracking:

- *Record project work as scheduled.* This works best if everything in the project occurs exactly as it was scheduled.
- *Record each task's percentage of completion.* You can do this at precise values or at increments such as 25%, 50%, 75%, and 100%.
- *Record the actuals.* The actual start, actual finish, actual work, and actual and remaining duration for each task or assignment are recorded.

- *Track assignment-level work by time period.* You record actual work values by day, week, or other time interval that you select. This is the most detailed level of tracking. This is rarely used as a method of tracking project progress as it is too costly and time consuming for the added benefit of detailed information.

You can apply a combination of these approaches within a single project, as different parts of a project may have different tracking needs.

■ Tracking a Project as Scheduled

↓
THE BOTTOM LINE

Once a baseline has been saved for a project schedule, the work done on the project can be tracked against the baseline values. The simplest approach to tracking is to report that the actual work is proceeding as planned. You record project actuals by updating work to the current date.

→ TRACK A PROJECT AS SCHEDULED

USE the project schedule you created in the previous exercise.

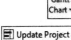

1. On the ribbon, click **Gantt Chart**. The Gantt Chart view appears.
2. Move the vertical divider bar to a point just to the right of the Start column.
3. Click on the **Project** tab, and then click **Update Project** in the Status group. The Update Project dialog box appears.
4. Make sure the **Update work as complete through** option is selected. In the adjacent date box, type or select **February 12, 2016**, and then click **OK**. Microsoft Project records the actual work for the projects that were scheduled to start before February 12. It also draws progress bars in the Gantt bars for those tasks to show this progress visually.

5. Select the name of task 5, **Develop production layouts**. Click the **Task** tab, and then click **Scroll to Task** in the Editing group. Your screen should look similar to Figure 9-3.

Figure 9-3

Progress bars for completed and in-progress tasks in the Gantt Chart view

Checkmarks indicate a completed task   Progress bars indicate the portion of the task that has been completed

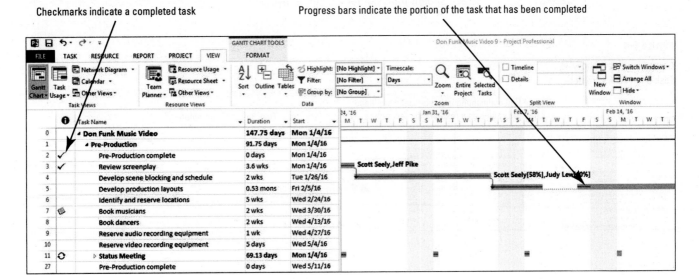

6. **SAVE** the project schedule.

PAUSE. LEAVE the project schedule open to use in the next exercise.

In this exercise, you updated the project to show that work had occurred as scheduled through a certain date. This date is sometimes called the data date or *status date* – the date up to or through which all progress information is collected and entered for a project. The *progress bar* in the Gantt Chart view shows how much of each task has been completed. A check mark appears in the Indicators column for tasks 2 and 3 to indicate these tasks have been completed. In addition, a progress bar is drawn through the entire length of these tasks' Gantt bars. Because only a portion of task 5 has been completed by February 12, the progress bar for this task only extends to February 12 and no check mark appears in the Indicators column.

Also notice that because some of the recurring status meetings have been completed by February 12, progress bars appear in the summary Gantt bars for these tasks.

■ Entering the Completion Percentage for a Task

THE BOTTOM LINE

As you continue to make progress on your project, it is important to record the work that has been done on a task. There are many ways to record this work. One of the quickest ways is to record the completion percentage of the task.

ENTER THE COMPLETION PERCENTAGE FOR A TASK

USE the project schedule you created in the previous exercise.

Tables

1. Click the **View** tab, click the **Tables** button, and then select the **Work** table from the list.
2. Slide the vertical divider bar between the table and the Gantt bar chart so that more of the table columns are visible. You may need to auto fit the columns to see all the data. Notice the Work and % Work Complete columns. You will enter task completion percentages in the % Work Complete column.
3. In the % Work Complete column for Task 5, type or select **100**, and then [press **Enter**]. Microsoft Project extends the progress bar through the length of the Gantt bar for task 5 and records the actual work for the task as scheduled.

Selected Tasks

4. Select **Task 5** again. On the ribbon, click **Selected Tasks** in the Zoom group. Your screen should look similar to Figure 9-4.

Figure 9-4

Gantt Chart view showing Task 5 is 100% complete

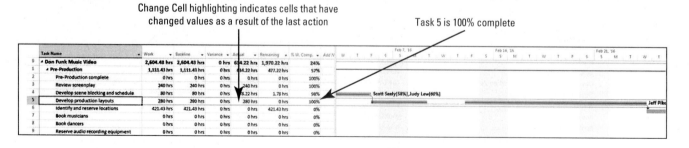

TAKE NOTE*

You can also use the schedule percent complete buttons to quickly update tasks that are 0%, 25%, 50%, 75%, and 100% complete. The schedule percent complete buttons are located in the Schedule group on the Task tab. Select the task you want to update, and then click the appropriate percentage button.

5. In the % Work Complete field for Task 6, type or select **50**, and then [press **Enter**]. Microsoft Project records the actual work for the task as scheduled, calculates the remaining work, and then updates the progress line through 50% of the Gantt bar.

6. Scroll the Gantt Chart to see the Gantt bar for Task 6.

7. **SAVE** the project schedule.

8. **CLOSE** the project schedule. In the next exercise, you will use an updated version of the Don Funk Music Video 9 project schedule to simulate the passage of time.

PAUSE. LEAVE Microsoft Project open to use in the next exercise.

TAKE NOTE*

You can view a task's completion percentage and other tracking information by pointing to a progress bar in a task's Gantt bar. A ScreenTip will appear.

In this exercise, you manually entered the completion percentage for a task. There are several ways you can quickly record task progress as a percentage:

- Use one of the % complete fields in either the Work or Tracking tables.
- Use the preset buttons for recording 0%, 25%, 50%, 75%, and 100% completion on a task.
- Use the Update Tasks dialog box (on the Task ribbon, click the **down-arrow** to the right of the Mark on Track button, and then click **Update Tasks**).
- Use the General tab of the Task Information dialog box (by double-clicking the task you want to update) to update the Percent Complete field.

Using the last two methods, you can also enter any percentage you want.

When you use any of these methods to enter a percentage other than 0% complete, Microsoft Project changes the task's actual start date to match its scheduled start date. It also calculates actual duration, remaining duration, actual costs, and other values, based on the percentage you enter.

In deciding to use "percent complete" as a method of tracking progress, understand that there are four types of percent complete:

Physical % Complete: based on some physical measurement. For example, if you are constructing a two-mile road, and you complete one mile of it, you are physically 50% complete.

Work % Complete: based on the planned amount of work. For example, if you planned to spend 10,000 hours of effort building a two mile road, and you spent 4000 hours to build the first mile, you are only 40% work % complete, even though you are 50% physically complete.

Cost % Complete: based on the approved budget. For example, if the total approved budget for a two-mile road was $468,000, and you have spent $140,000 to build the first mile, you are only about 29.9% cost % complete, even though you have completed half of the total road.

Schedule % Complete: based on planned duration. For example, if a two-mile road project was planned for 120 days, and you built the first mile in 30 days, you are 25% schedule % complete, even though you have completed half the total road.

■ Identifying Over Budget Tasks and Resources

THE BOTTOM LINE

So far, you have focused on a project's schedule as a key part of the overall success of the project. However, another critical piece of information is the cost variance, or how the actual costs compare to the projected costs.

IDENTIFY OVER BUDGET TASKS AND RESOURCES

GET READY. To identify over budget tasks and resources, perform the following steps.

1. OPEN the **Don Funk Music Video 9MA** project schedule from the data files for this lesson.
2. SAVE the file as **Don Funk Music Video 9A** in the solutions folder for this lesson as directed by your instructor.
3. On the ribbon, click the Project tab, and then click Project Information in the Properties group. The Project Information Dialog box appears.
4. Click the Statistics button. The Project Statistics dialog box appears. Your screen should look similar to Figure 9-5.

   The Cost column displays the current, baseline, actual, and remaining cost values for the entire project.

   • The **current cost** is the sum of the actual and remaining cost values.

   • The **baseline cost** is the total planned cost of the project when the baseline was saved.

   • The **actual cost** is the cost that has been incurred so far (after the indicated total work has been completed).

   • The **remaining cost** is the difference between the current cost and actual cost.

Figure 9-5

Project Statistics dialog box

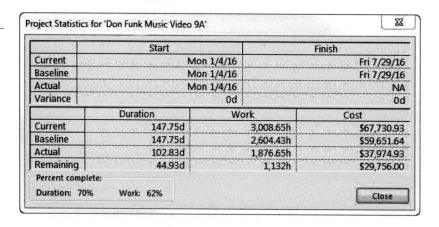

It is obvious that some cost variance has occurred, but it is not possible to tell from the Project Statistics dialog box when or where the variance occurred.

5. Click the Close button. The Project Statistics dialog box closes.

6. On the ribbon, click View. Click the Tables button and then click Cost. The Cost table appears in the Task Sheet view. Move the vertical divider so you can see all the available columns. Take a moment to review the columns in the Cost table. Note that although costs are not scheduled in the same sense that work is scheduled, costs (except fixed costs) are derived from the scheduled work.

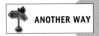 **ANOTHER WAY** To change the table, you can also right-click on the upper left corner of the active table and click Cost in the short-cut menu that appears.

7. Click the **Task Name** column heading. Click the **Outline** button in the Data group, and then select **Level 1**. Microsoft Project collapses the task list to display only the first level of summary tasks (which in this case correspond to the major phases of the project). Your screen should look similar to Figure 9-6.

Figure 9-6

Task sheet view with all subtasks hidden

Production has the greatest variance

	Task Name	Fixed Cost	Fixed Cost Accrual	Total Cost	Baseline	Variance	Actual	Remaining	Actual Cost
0	▲ **Don Funk Music Video**	$0.00	Prorated	$67,730.93	$59,651.64	$8,079.28	37,974.93	$29,756.00	$37,974.93
1	▷ Pre-Production	$0.00	Prorated	$22,223.48	$18,999.64	$3,223.84	$21,264.98	$958.50	$21,264.98
28	▷ **Production**	$0.00	Prorated	$28,354.94	$23,499.50	$4,855.44	$16,709.94	$11,645.00	$16,709.94
63	▷ Post-Production	$0.00	Prorated	$17,152.50	$17,152.50	$0.00	$0.00	$17,152.50	$0.00

8. Click the **expand button** next to Task 28, Production. Using the **collapse button**, hide the subtasks for scenes 1 through 4. Your screen should look similar to Figure 9-7.

Although Scenes 1 and 2 both had some variance, Scene 2 had the greater variance, so you will focus on that scene.

Figure 9-7

Task sheet view with Scenes 1 through 4 subtasks hidden

Scene 2 has the greatest variance

	Task Name	Fixed Cost	Fixed Cost Accrual	Total Cost	Baseline	Variance	Actual	Remaining	Actual Cost
0	▲ **Don Funk Music Video**	$0.00	Prorated	$67,730.93	$59,651.64	$8,079.28	37,974.93	$29,756.00	$37,974.93
1	▷ Pre-Production	$0.00	Prorated	$22,223.48	$18,999.64	$3,223.84	$21,264.98	$958.50	$21,264.98
28	▲ Production	$0.00	Prorated	$28,354.94	$23,499.50	$4,855.44	$16,709.94	$11,645.00	$16,709.94
29	Production begins	$0.00	Prorated	$0.00	$0.00	$0.00	$0.00	$0.00	$0.00
30	▷ Scene 1	$0.00	Prorated	$7,624.94	$6,081.50	$1,543.44	$6,874.94	$750.00	$6,874.94
38	▷ Scene 2	$0.00	Prorated	$10,335.00	$7,023.00	$3,312.00	$9,835.00	$500.00	$9,835.00
46	▷ Scene 3	$0.00	Prorated	$4,952.00	$4,952.00	$0.00	$0.00	$4,952.00	$0.00
54	▷ Scene 4	$0.00	Prorated	$5,443.00	$5,443.00	$0.00	$0.00	$5,443.00	$0.00
62	Production complete	$0.00	Prorated	$0.00	$0.00	$0.00	$0.00	$0.00	$0.00
63	▷ Post-Production	$0.00	Prorated	$17,152.50	$17,152.50	$0.00	$0.00	$17,152.50	$0.00

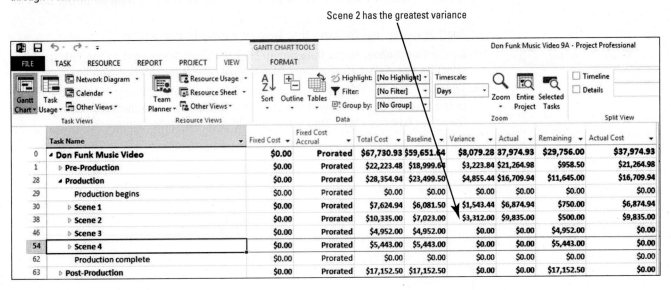

9. Click the **expand button** next to summary Task 38, Scene 2. Microsoft Project expands the Scene 2 summary task to show all of the subtasks. Your screen should look similar to Figure 9-8.

Figure 9-8

Task sheet view with Scene 2 expanded to show subtasks

Scene 2 expanded to reveal all individual subtasks   Task 42 has the greatest variance

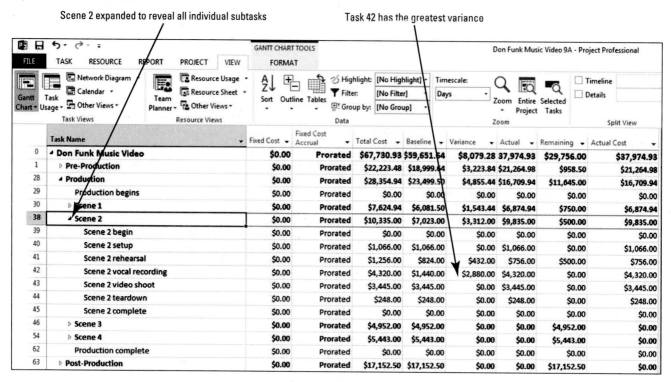

Take note of the variance column. It shows that most of the Scene 2 variance can be tracked to Task 42, Scene 2 vocal recording.

10. Click the **Task Name** column heading.

11. Click the **Outline** button and then select **Show Subtasks** button on the Formatting toolbar. Microsoft Project expands all of the summary tasks to show all of the tasks in the project.

    Another way to look for tasks that are over budget is with a filter.

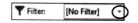

12. On the View ribbon, in the Data group, click the down-arrow next to the **Filter:** selection box. Select **More Filters** from the list. The More Filters dialog box appears.

13. Select the **Cost Overbudget** filter and click **Apply**. Microsoft Project applies the filter to the task list to show only those tasks that had actual and scheduled costs greater than their baseline costs. Your screen should look similar to Figure 9-9.

Figure 9-9

Task sheet view with the Cost
Overbudget filter applied

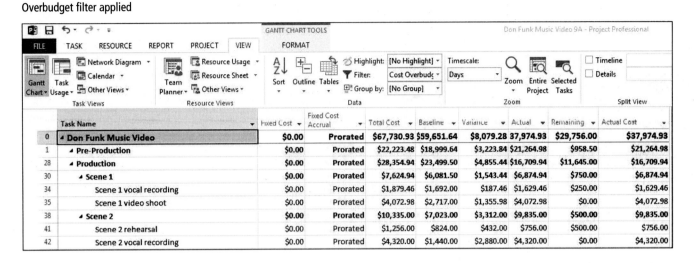

	Task Name	Fixed Cost	Fixed Cost Accrual	Total Cost	Baseline	Variance	Actual	Remaining	Actual Cost
0	◢ **Don Funk Music Video**	$0.00	Prorated	$67,730.93	$59,651.64	$8,079.28	37,974.93	$29,756.00	$37,974.93
1	◢ **Pre-Production**	$0.00	Prorated	$22,223.48	$18,999.64	$3,223.84	$21,264.98	$958.50	$21,264.98
28	◢ **Production**	$0.00	Prorated	$28,354.94	$23,499.50	$4,855.44	$16,709.94	$11,645.00	$16,709.94
30	◢ **Scene 1**	$0.00	Prorated	$7,624.94	$6,081.50	$1,543.44	$6,874.94	$750.00	$6,874.94
34	Scene 1 vocal recording	$0.00	Prorated	$1,879.46	$1,692.00	$187.46	$1,629.46	$250.00	$1,629.46
35	Scene 1 video shoot	$0.00	Prorated	$4,072.98	$2,717.00	$1,355.98	$4,072.98	$0.00	$4,072.98
38	◢ **Scene 2**	$0.00	Prorated	$10,335.00	$7,023.00	$3,312.00	$9,835.00	$500.00	$9,835.00
41	Scene 2 rehearsal	$0.00	Prorated	$1,256.00	$824.00	$432.00	$756.00	$500.00	$756.00
42	Scene 2 vocal recording	$0.00	Prorated	$4,320.00	$1,440.00	$2,880.00	$4,320.00	$0.00	$4,320.00

14. SAVE the project schedule.

15. CLOSE the project schedule. In the next exercise, you will use an updated version of
    the Don Funk Music Video 9 to simulate the passage of time.

    PAUSE. LEAVE Microsoft Project open to use in the next exercise.

In this exercise, you used several different views and tables to identify tasks and resources that
were over budget. Project managers and stakeholders often focus on the project schedule (Did
tasks start and finish on time?). For projects such as this one that include cost information,
cost variance is another critical indicator of overall project health. In Microsoft Project,
evaluating cost variance enables you to make incremental budget adjustments for individual
tasks to avoid exceeding your project's overall budget.

■ Identifying Time and Schedule Problems

THE BOTTOM LINE

In complex projects, it is very likely that there will be some schedule variance. The project
manager must control the project by identifying, understanding, and correcting
the problem.

 RESCHEDULE UNCOMPLETED WORK

GET READY. To reschedule uncompleted work, perform the following tasks:

1. OPEN the **Don Funk Music Video 9MB** project schedule from the data files for
   this lesson.

2. SAVE the file as **Don Funk Music Video 9B** in the solutions folder for this lesson as
   directed by your instructor.

3. [Press the F5 key]. Type 46 in the ID box, and then click OK. The Gantt Chart view
   scrolls to display the Gantt bar for Task 46, Scene 3. At this point in the project, the
   first two scheduled scenes have been completed. This task has one day of actual work
   completed and one day of scheduled work remaining. Your screen should look similar
   to Figure 9-10.

Figure 9-10

Gantt Chart view showing
Task 48 prior to rescheduling
the work

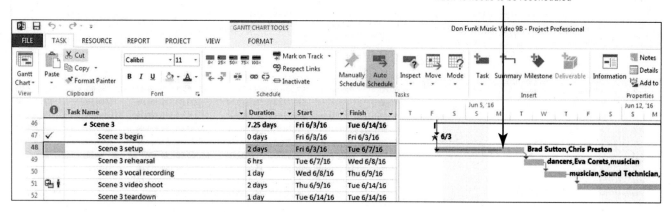

You have just been informed that late on the afternoon of June 6, a lightning strike caused a nearby electrical transformer to short-circuit and repairs will not be completed until Thursday, June 9. You will not be able to resume work in the studio until Friday, June 10.

 Update Project

5. On the ribbon, click the **Project** tab, and then click **Update Project**. The Update Project dialog box appears.

6. Select the **Reschedule uncompleted work to start after:** option, and in the date box type or select **06/09/16**.

7. Click **OK** to close the Update Project dialog box. Microsoft Project splits Task 48 so that the incomplete portion is delayed until Friday, June 10. Your screen should look similar to Figure 9-11.

Figure 9-11

Gantt Chart view after
rescheduling uncompleted
work on Task 48

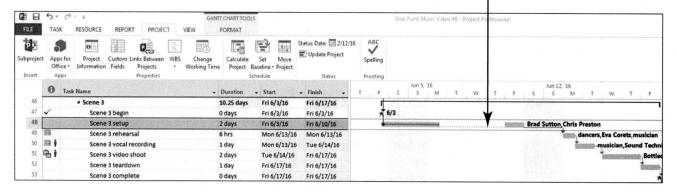

TAKE NOTE*

It is possible to disable the ability of Microsoft Project to reschedule uncompleted work on tasks that are showing any actual work. Click the **File** tab then select **Options.** In the Options dialog box, click the **Schedule** tab. In the section that reads Scheduling options for this project, clear the **Split in-progress tasks** check box.

Note that although the duration of Task 48 remains at two days, its finish and subsequent start dates for successor tasks have been pushed out. Remember that duration is the number of **work periods** required to complete a task, not elapsed time.

8. **SAVE** the project schedule. **CLOSE** the project schedule.

   PAUSE. If you are continuing to the next lesson, keep Project open. If you are not continuing to additional lessons, **CLOSE** Project.

In this exercise, you rescheduled an incomplete task due to an uncontrollable delay. Depending upon the length and complexity of your project, as a project manager you may see one or many of these types of interruptions. When you reschedule incomplete work, you specify the date after which work can resume. Microsoft Project handles tasks in relation to the scheduled restart date in the following ways:

- If the task does not have any actual work recorded for it prior to the rescheduled date and there is no constraint in place, the entire task is rescheduled to begin after that date.
- If the task has some actual work recorded prior to but not after the rescheduled date, the task is split so that all remaining work starts after the rescheduled date. The actual work is not affected.
- If the task has some actual work recorded for it prior to as well as after the rescheduled date, the task is not affected.

Keep in mind that when you address a given problem by rescheduling a task, you may create other issues or problems in the remainder of the project. This is why project management is an iterative process: a change in one part of the schedule – be it a time, cost, or scope change – can, and usually does, affect the schedule elsewhere. Finally, when changing or correcting the schedule due to unforeseen delays, such as the scenario in this exercise, you should also place a note in the notes field of the affected task(s) stating why the task has been changed. These become helpful when looking for explanations regarding why the project is not performing to the baseline.

SKILL SUMMARY

IN THIS LESSON YOU LEARNED:	MATRIX SKILL
To establish a project baseline	Establish a project baseline
To track a project as scheduled	Track a project as scheduled
To enter the completion percentage for a task	Enter the completion percentage for a task
To identify over budget tasks and resources	Identify over budget tasks and resources
To identify time and schedule problems	Reschedule uncompleted work

■ Knowledge Assessment

Match the term in column 1 to its description in column 2.

Column 1

1. actual cost
2. baseline
3. sponsor
4. variance
5. % Work Complete
6. current cost
7. actuals
8. Progress bar
9. tracking
10. baseline cost

Column 2

a. the collecting, entering, and analyzing of actual project performance data

b. the individual or organization that provides financial support and supports the project team

c. the cost that has been incurred so far

d. in the Gantt Chart view, shows how much of the task has been completed

e. the total planned cost of the project when the baseline was saved

f. project work completed and recorded in a Microsoft Project file

g. a collection of key values in the project schedule

h. the amount of work that has been completed in relation to the planned work value

i. the sum of the actual and remaining cost values

j. a deviation from the schedule or budget established

True/False

Circle T if the statement is true or F if the statement is false.

T F **1.** You can save up to 11 different baselines for a single project schedule.

T F **2.** You must provide Microsoft Project a remaining duration value for it to calculate a percentage complete.

T F **3.** A check mark in the Indicators column for a task means that the task is on schedule.

T F **4.** You should save a project baseline when you have developed the project schedule as fully as possible.

T F **5.** Planning refers to the collecting, entering, and analyzing of actual project performance data.

T F **6.** If you reschedule an in-progress task, the delay is shown as a split on the Gantt Chart.

T F **7.** The only true indicator of project health is whether or not the project is on schedule.

T F **8.** The Project Statistics dialog box pinpoints the point of cost variance in a project schedule.

T F **9.** You can only enter completion percentages for a task in multiples of 10.

T F **10.** The remaining cost is the difference between the current cost and the actual cost.

■ Competency Assessment

Project 9-1: Insurance Claim Processing Baseline

You are ready to begin entering actuals on your Insurance Claim Processing schedule. Before you do this, you need to save a baseline for your schedule.

GET READY. Launch Microsoft Project if it is not already running.

OPEN *Insurance Claim Processing 9-1* from the data files for this lesson.

1. On the Project tab, click the Set Baseline button and then select Set Baseline.
2. In the Set Baseline dialog box, click OK.
3. SAVE the project schedule as *Insurance Processing Schedule Baseline*, and then CLOSE the file.

   LEAVE Project open to use in the next exercise.

Project 9-2: Tracking a Project as Scheduled

Now that you have saved a baseline, you are now ready track the project on your Insurance Claim Processing schedule.

OPEN *Insurance Processing Schedule Baseline 9-2* from the data files for this lesson

1. On the Project tab, click the Project Information button.
2. In the Status Date box, enter 6/17/16, and then click OK.
3. Select Tasks 1 through 53.
4. Click the Task tab, and then select the Mark on Track button in the Schedule group.
5. SAVE the project schedule as *Insurance Processing Schedule Tracked*, and then CLOSE the file.

   LEAVE Project open to use in the next exercise.

■ Proficiency Assessment

Project 9-3: Completion Percentages for HR Interview Schedule

Now that portions of your HR Interview project have been completed, you need to record the completion percentages of tasks.

OPEN *HR Interview Schedule 9-3* from the data files for this lesson.

1. Switch to the Work Table and adjust the Gantt Chart so that the Work and % Work Complete columns are visible.
2. Enter percentages to show that the project is 100% complete through Task 10, and that Task 11 is 25% complete. (*Hint:* Remember to make entries for the subtasks, not the summary tasks.)
3. SAVE the project schedule as *HR Interview Schedule Percentages*, and then CLOSE the file.

   LEAVE Project open to use in the next exercise.

Project 9-4: Don Funk Music Video Overbudget Tasks

Even more progress has been made on the Don Funk Music Video, with tasks being complete through the Production phase. You need to analyze the project to determine the over budget tasks.

OPEN *Don Funk Music Video 9-4* from the data files for this lesson.

1. Activate the Project Statistics box to view the costs for the project.
2. Display the Cost table.
3. Filter the tasks to show only the tasks that are over budget.
4. Collapse all Production Scene summary tasks (hide subtasks) except for the Scene summary task with the greatest cost variance
5. SAVE the project schedule as *Don Funk Overbudget*, and then CLOSE the file.
   LEAVE Project open to use in the next exercise.

■ Mastery Assessment

Project 9-5: Office Remodel Task Delay

You have just been informed that while the plumber was re-running the pipes for the office lunchroom remodel, a pipe burst and the floor was flooded with several inches of water. It will take a week to clean and dry the water damage. You need to reschedule the remaining work on incomplete tasks to restart when the cleanup is complete.

OPEN the *Office Remodel 9-5* project schedule from the data files for this lesson.

1. Activate the Update Project dialog box.
2. Reschedule uncompleted work to start after Thursday, October 22, 2016.
3. SAVE the project schedule as *Office Remodel Reschedule*, and then CLOSE the file.
   LEAVE Project open to use in the next exercise.

Project 9-6: Tracking the Don Funk Music Video as Scheduled

The last phase of the Don Funk Music Video, Post-Production, is going well. Tasks are being completed on schedule. You want to update the project to show that the tasks are complete through a specified current date.

OPEN the *Don Funk Music Video 9-6* project schedule from the data files for this lesson.

1. Activate the Update Project dialog box.
2. Update the project as complete through July 15, 2016.
3. Scroll the Gantt Chart bars so that the task and progress bars on the week of July 10, 2016 are visible.
4. SAVE the project schedule as *Don Funk On Schedule*, and then CLOSE the file.
   CLOSE Project.

Project Reporting

LESSON SKILL MATRIX

Skills	Tasks
Activate and Print a Dashboard Report	Select and Print a Dashboard Report
Customizing and Printing Reports	Create, Customize and Print a Report
Reporting Project Status	Report Project Variance with a "Stoplight" View
Using Visual Reports	Create a Visual Report
Printing the Gantt Chart	Customize and Print the Gantt Chart

You are a video production manager for Southridge Video and the project manager for a new Don Funk music video. Your project has been progressing and you now need to keep the stakeholders informed on project status. You know that one of the most important responsibilities for any project manager is communicating project information. It is time for you to begin formally sharing printed information with your project stakeholders. In this lesson, you will learn how to work with some of the many views and reports in Microsoft Project 2013 in order to report project performance.

KEY TERMS
dashboard
report
stakeholder
visual report

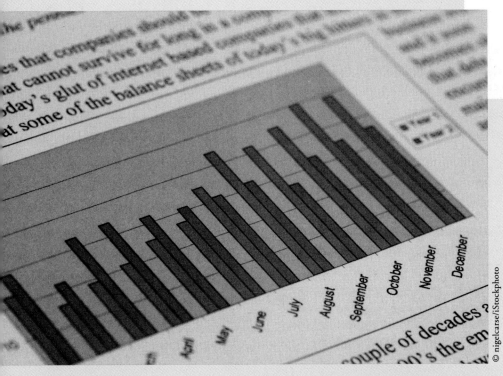

© nigelcarse/iStockphoto

SOFTWARE ORIENTATION

Report Ribbon

The new Report Ribbon makes locating and selecting a report easier than ever before. With predefined dashboard reports, the user can show an overview of the project, project burndown, cost overview, work overview and many more.

Figure 10-1

Project Overview Dashboard report with the Report Tools ribbon

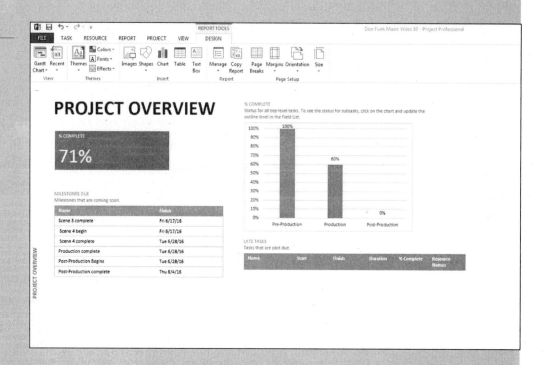

Figure 10-2

Report Ribbon

 The Project Overview Dashboard provides the basic information need to present project performance to date, which tasks are late, which milestones are coming dues and an overall percent complete.

■ Activate and Print a Dashboard Report

↓
THE BOTTOM LINE

Using a Dashboard report you can quickly see all of the major information about your project then print the information on paper.

→ **SELECT AND PRINT A DASHBOARD REPORT**

GET READY. Before you begin these steps, launch Microsoft Project 2013.

1. OPEN the *Don Funk Music Video 10M* project schedule from the data files for this lesson.
2. SAVE the file as *Don Funk Music Video 10* in the solutions folder for this lesson as directed by your instructor.

Status Date: ▦ 2/12/16

3. On the ribbon, click the **Project** tab. In the Status group click the **calendar icon** in the Status Date field. Microsoft Project displays the Status Date dialog box.
4. In the Select Date: field type or select **6/10/16**. Your screen should look like Figure 10-3.

Figure 10-3

Status Date box

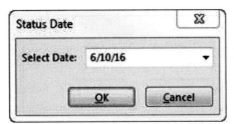

5. Click **OK** or press **Enter** to close the Status Date dialog box. You set the Status Date to tell Microsoft Project you want information as of this date.
6. On the ribbon, click the **Report** tab and then select the **Dashboards** button. From the dropdown menu that appears, select **Project Overview**. Your screen should look similar to Figure 10-4.

Dashboards

Figure 10-4

Project Overview Dashboard

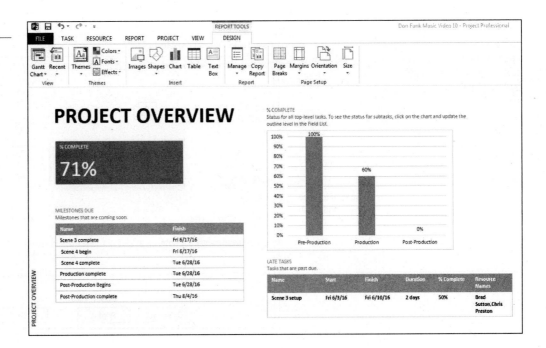

7. On the ribbon, click the **File** tab and then select **Print** from the navigation bar on the left side of the screen. Your screen should look similar to Figure 10-5. You may notice that some of the report is cut off at the right side of the print preview area.

Figure 10-5

Print preview of the Project Overview Dashboard

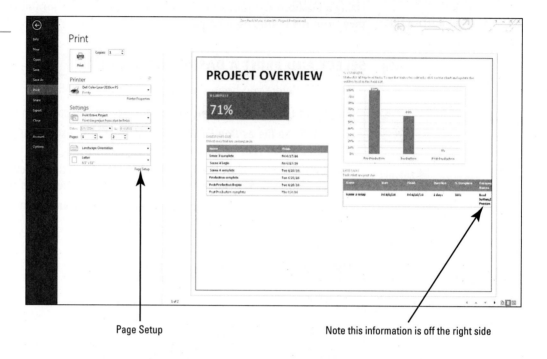

Page Setup   Note this information is off the right side

TAKE NOTE * You may or may not see the Print Preview screens in color, depending upon the printer and print drivers you have installed.

8. At the lower right portion of the Settings section, click the **Page Setup** hyperlink. Microsoft Project displays the Page Setup dialog box.

9. On the Page tab, in the Scaling section, click **Fit to:** and choose **1** against the **pages wide by** and **tall** boxes. Your dialog box should look like Figure 10-6.

Figure 10-6

Page Setup dialog box with scaling set to 1 page wide by 1 page tall

Page Setup Tabs ──▶

Scaling to page height and width

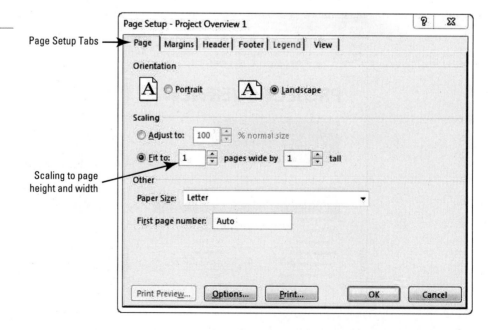

10. Now select the Margins tab. Set all margins to 0.5 inches. Click the OK to close the dialog box. Your screen should now look like Figure 10-7.

Figure 10-7

Print preview of the Project Overview Dashboard with new settings

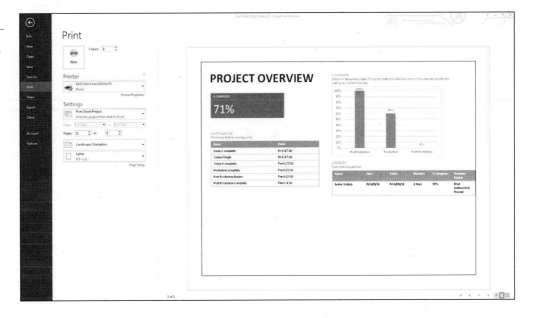

11. SAVE the project schedule.

PAUSE. LEAVE Project open to use in the next exercise.

 In this exercise, you used a dashboard report to view information about your project. A **report** is anything the project manager uses to transmit information about the project. Most all reports are done in writing, using both words and graphics. Some reports are made available through dashboards. A **dashboard** is a generic term used to mean an easy to read, single page interface (usually centrally located – such as a SharePoint web page) that senior management can quickly view to obtain a high-level view of current project status.

■ Customize and Print a Report

 THE BOTTOM LINE Using the new options of the reports feature in Microsoft Project 2013 allows you to fully customize the information you wish to include in the report.

 CREATE, CUSTOMIZE AND PRINT A REPORT

GET READY. USE the project schedule you created in the previous exercise.

1. Click the Report tab. On the ribbon, click the New Report button.
2. On the drop-down menu that appears, click Table.
3. In the Report Name box that appears, name the new report **Remaining Work Report** and then click OK. Your screen should look like Figure 10-8.

Figure 10-8

Newly created Remaining
Work Report

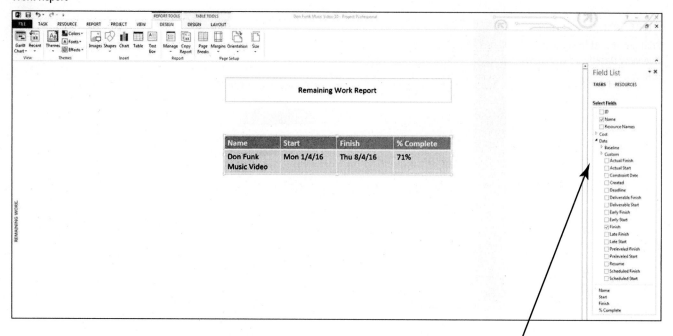

Field List appears when you select the table

4. At the top of the field list at the right of the screen, click Resources.

5. Using the scroll box at the right of the field list box, navigate down until the Work fields are visible and then select the expand button next to Work.

6. Select the check box next to Remaining Work.

7. In the Filter box, select Resources: Work.

8. In the Sort by box, select Name.

9. Auto fit the name and Remaining Work columns (make them wider so all information fits on one line) and then center the entire table on the screen under the report name.

TAKE NOTE*
At this point, you can print the information by clicking the Print button (the print preview is adequate for purposes of this lesson). When printing in Microsoft Project 2013, there are additional options in the Print dialog box (the Print command is accessed from the File tab). For example, you can print specific date or page ranges.

10. Click the File tab and then select Print. You will note that the report may not be centered on the page. This is because the previous report was on Landscape orientation.

11. In the settings section, change the orientation to Portrait.

12. Click the return arrow at the top.

13. Click the minus sign on the zoom slider at the lower right portion of the screen two or three times. Manually move the table and the report name box to the center of the page. You will note page breaks are indicated by the dashed lines. Your screen should look like Figure 10-9.

Figure 10-9

Report View with Remaining Work Report centered on the first page

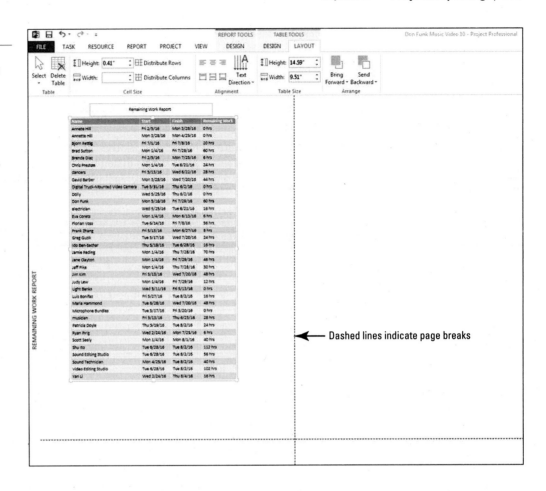

← Dashed lines indicate page breaks

14. Click the **File** tab and then select **Print**. You will note that the report is now centered on the page.
15. **SAVE** the project schedule.

    PAUSE. LEAVE Project open to use in the next exercise.

In this exercise, you created a custom report and added information that you wanted to include. Printing information from a project schedule to share with *stakeholders* is a common activity for project managers. Stakeholders are the people or organizations that might be affected by project activities and can range from resources working on the project to customers receiving the project deliverables.

■ Reporting Project Status

THE BOTTOM LINE

Microsoft Project provides many different ways to report a project's status in terms of budget or variance. A key part of a project manager's job is knowing which stakeholders need to see which details in which format.

REPORT PROJECT VARIANCE WITH A "STOPLIGHT" VIEW

USE the project schedule you created in the previous exercise.

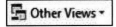

1. Click the **View** tab, then in the Task views group, select **Other Views** then select **More Views**. In the list select **Task Sheet** and then click **Apply**. Microsoft Project displays the Task Sheet view.

Custom
Fields

2. Select the **Tables** button and then click **Cost**.

3. Click on the **Project** tab, and then click the **Custom Fields** button. The Custom Fields dialog box appears.

4. Under the Field label at the top of the dialog box, make sure that **Task** is selected. In the Type box, select **Number** from the dropdown list.

5. In the Field list, select Overbudget (Number3).

6. Under the *Custom attributes* label, click the **Formula** button. The Formula dialog box is displayed. The formula shown in this dialog box has been pre-entered for accuracy and to save time. Your screen should look similar to Figure 10-10.

Figure 10-10

Formula dialog box

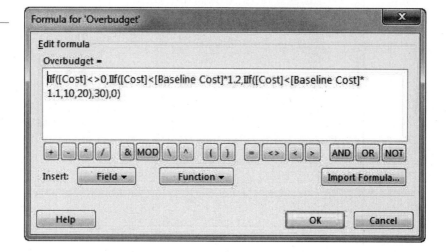

The formula evaluates each task's cost variance. If the task is above 20 percent above baseline, the formula assigns the number 30 to the task; if it is between 20 percent and 10 and percent, a 20; and if below 10 percent, a 10. If the task does not fit within those criteria, such as the case with a milestone task which should have no costs, the formula returns a zero value. *Note:* For the purposes of this project, a variance of 20 percent above baseline has been decided on by the project manager and sponsor as the maximum tolerance level.

7. Click **Cancel** to close the Formula dialog box.

8. In the Custom Fields dialog box, under the Values to display label, click the **Graphical Indicators** button. The Graphical Indicators dialog box appears. This dialog box enables you to specify a unique graphical indicator to display, depending on the value of a field for each task. In this usage, the values returned from the formula in the Figure 10-10 are used to assign the graphical indicator. To save time, the indicators have already been selected.

9. Click the **first cell** under the Image column heading, and then click the **down-arrow**. Here you can see the many graphical indicators you can associate with the values of fields.

10. Click **Cancel** twice to close the Graphical Indicators dialog box, and then click **Cancel** again to close the Custom Fields dialog box.

11. Right-click the **Fixed Cost** column heading. Select **Insert Column** from the list.

12. From the keyboard, start typing the word "**Over**". Notice how Project narrows the list down as you type. You can also navigate using the scroll bar to **Overbudget (Number3)**. Microsoft Project displays the Overbudget column in the Cost table. Your screen should look similar to Figure 10-11.

Figure 10-11

Cost table with the Overbudget
custom field displayed

Overbudget Custom Field   Green indicator says that the variance is inside tolerance limits

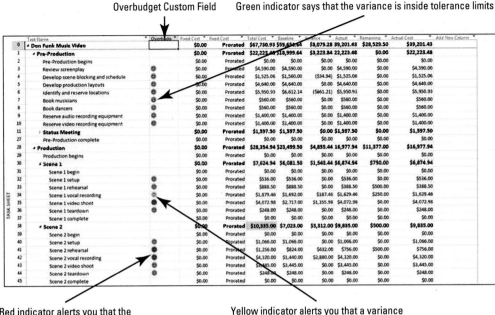

Red indicator alerts you that the
variance is outside the tolerance limits

Yellow indicator alerts you that a variance
is approaching the tolerance limits

The custom field Overbudget (Number3) displays a graphical indicator that represents
one of three different levels of cost variance. The graphical indicators will change,
according to the ranges specified in the formula, as each task's cost variance changes.
This is a useful format for identifying tasks whose cost variance is higher than you
would like (as indicated by the red and yellow indicators). This makes it easy for any
stakeholder to quickly scan the task list and locate tasks that need further attention.

13. SAVE the project schedule.

    PAUSE. LEAVE Project open to use in the next exercise.

In this exercise, you used a custom field with a custom formula to create a custom stoplight report.
As a project manager, you will find many ways to present the current status of your project. Bear
in mind the audience of the report. For example, you will want to present high level information
to upper management. Conversely, you will want to give detailed information to the project team.

 **Cross
Ref**   You will learn more about saving Microsoft Project data in other formats in lesson 12.

■ Using Visual Reports

 THE BOTTOM LINE   The Visual Reports feature of Microsoft Project 2013 combines the power of Microsoft Excel
and Microsoft Visio with the data of your project to create high impact, visually centered
reports. You can use a preformatted report, edit a report or create a new report that includes a
specific set of fields from Microsoft Project.

 CREATE A VISUAL REPORT

 USE the project schedule you created in the previous exercise.

1. On the ribbon, click the **Report** tab, and then select the **Visual Reports** button. The Visual
   Reports – Create Report dialog box appears. Your screen should look like Figure 10-12.

Figure 10-12

Visual Reports – Create Report
dialog box

Report type tabs

Preview area of
report selected

Level of usage data

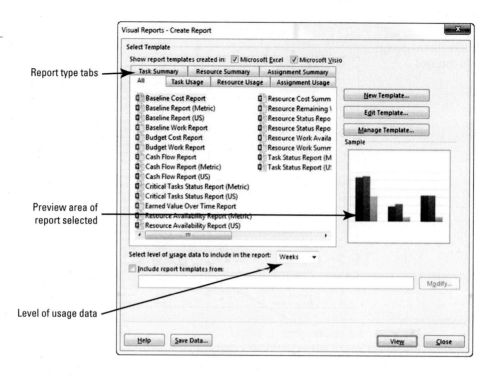

2. Click the Task Usage tab, and then click Cash Flow Report.

3. In the Select level of usage data to include in the report: box, select Months.

4. Click the View button. The Visual Report engine gathers data from your project file and builds an Online Analytical Processing (OLAP) cube. The application Microsoft Excel opens and the report is presented in Chart form from a preformatted report template. Your screen should look similar to Figure 10-13.

Figure 10-13

The Visual Report named
"Cash Flow Report" in
Microsoft Excel

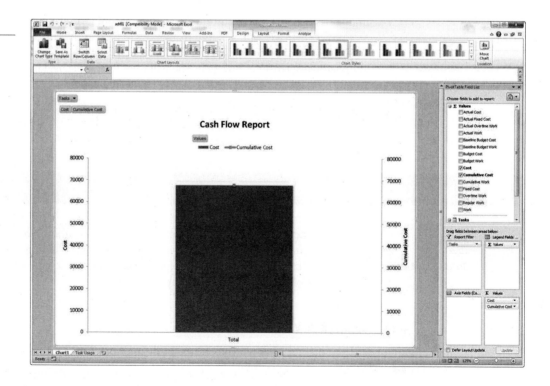

5. At the bottom of the Excel window, select the **Task Usage** sheet tab.

6. In the PivotTable Field List box, navigate to the **Time** field. Place your cursor on **Monthly Calendar** and drag it to the **Rows** box. Your screen should look similar to Figure 10-14.

Figure 10-14

Task Usage sheet tab with Monthly Calendar in the Rows area

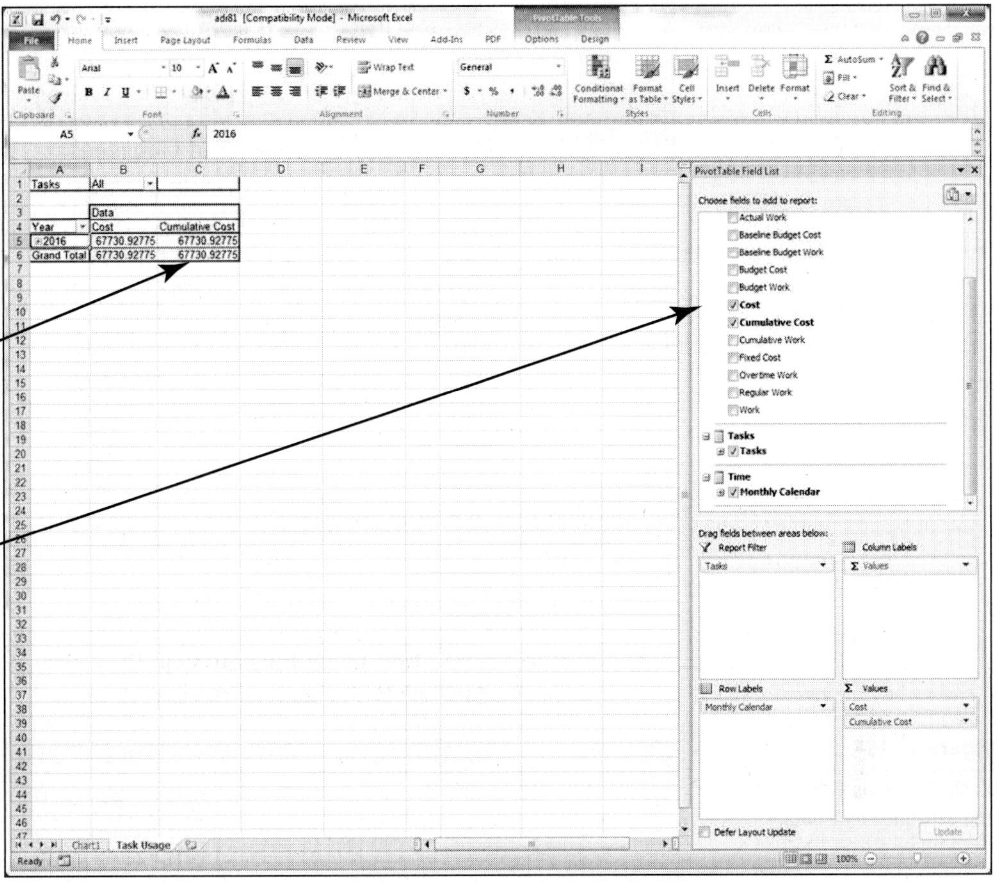

Pivot table created by the Visual Reports feature

Field list to choose fields displayed in the pivot table

7. In the PivotTable area, click the expand button next to the year 2016, to reveal all the available time data. Your screen should look similar to Figure 10-15.

Figure 10-15

Cash Flow Report PivotTable
with all of 2016 time data
showing

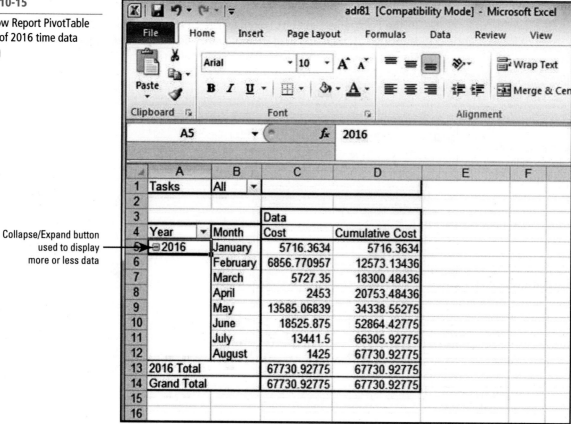

Collapse/Expand button
used to display
more or less data

8. Click the Chart1 sheet tab at the bottom of the screen. Your screen should look
   similar to Figure 10-16.

Figure 10-16

Cash Flow Report chart with
the expanded time data

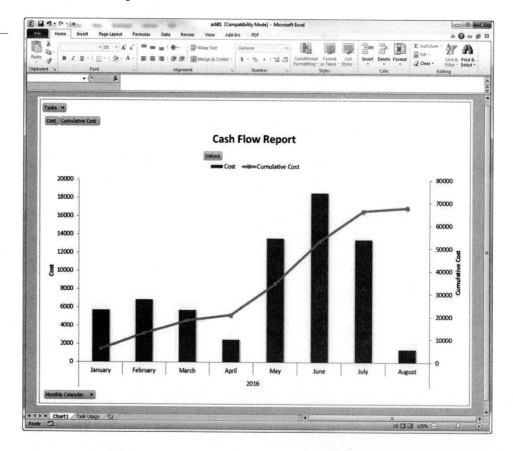

9. Save the Microsoft Excel visual report as ***Don Funk Cash Flow*** in your My Documents folder or another folder directed by your instructor.
10. **CLOSE** Microsoft Excel.
11. **CLOSE** the Visual Reports Dialog box.
12. **SAVE** the project schedule.

   PAUSE. LEAVE Project open to use in the next exercise.

In this exercise, you created a new visual report. A ***visual report*** is a specific type of report that utilizes the combines the power of either Microsoft Excel or Microsoft Visio and the data which you have created in your project file. The data is translated into pivot tables and graphs. You must have Microsoft Excel 2007 or newer to view the Excel reports with the Visual Reports feature. You must have Microsoft Visio 2007 Professional or higher installed on your system to view the Visio reports. If this is not installed, the Visio reports will not be listed in the dialog box.

■ Customizing and Printing a View

THE BOTTOM LINE

Using a view, you can see your project schedule information on screen. You can change what you see by customizing the view. You can also apply these customized views to print the information on paper.

⊙ CUSTOMIZE AND PRINT A GANTT CHART VIEW

USE the project schedule you created in the previous exercise.

1. Click the View tab, then select the Gantt Chart button.
2. Click the File tab and then click Print. Microsoft Project displays print options on the left side and the Gantt Chart view in the right side, which is the Print Preview window. Your screen should look like Figure 10-17.

Figure 10-17

Print section of the File tab

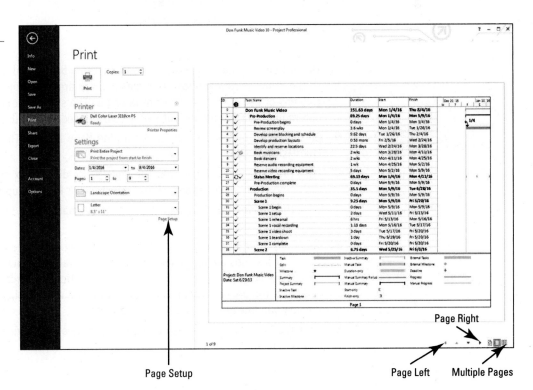

Page Setup

Page Right

Page Left   Multiple Pages

3. On the Print Preview toolbar, click the **Page Right** and/or **Page Down** button to display different pages.

4. On the Print Preview toolbar, click the **Multiple Pages** button. Most of the pages of the Gantt Chart appears in the Print Preview window. When the multiple pages Print Preview is active the printed output is displayed on separate sheets. You navigate using the scroll control at the bottom of the Print Preview pane. The Page Right, Page Left, Page Up, and Page Down buttons are inactive. The paper size displayed is determined by your printer settings. Your screen should look similar to Figure 10-18.

Figure 10-18

Print Preview with multiple pages activated

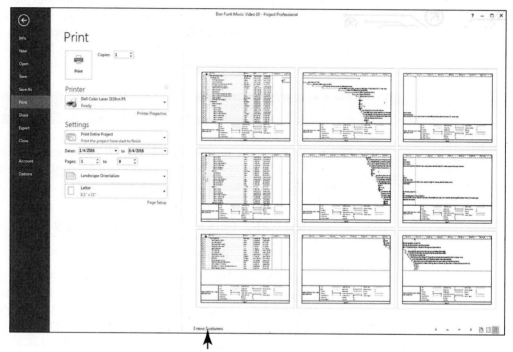

Rows and Columns display

The left side of the Print Preview Toolbar status bar should read "3 rows 3 columns." In the Print Preview window, this means there are three rows of pages by three columns of pages, for a total of nine pages. The status bar can help you quickly determine the total number of pages your printed view will be.

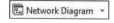

5. On the Print Preview toolbar, click the **One Page** button. The first page of the Gantt Chart is displayed.

6. Click the **Page Setup** hyperlink. The Page Setup dialog box appears. This is the same dialog box that would appear if you selected the Page Setup option on the File tab.

7. Click the **Header** tab. You want to add the company name to the header that prints on each page.

8. There are three Alignment tabs in the center section of the Header tab box. Select **Center** if it is not already selected. In the General box, click **Company Name** and then click the **Add** button next to the General box. Microsoft Project places the following code into the header: &[Company]. The software also displays a preview in the Preview window of the Page Setup dialog box.

9. Click the **Legend** tab. You want to change some of the content of the Gantt Chart view's legend.

10. There are three Alignment tabs in the center of the Legend tab box. Click the **Left** tab. Currently, Microsoft Project is formatted to print the project title and current date on the left side of the legend. You also want to print the start date and duration on the right side of the legend.

12. Click the **Right** Alignment tab. Click the **Right Alignment** box, press **Enter**, and then type **Start:** followed by a space.

13. In the General box, select **Project Start Date** from the dropdown list. Click the **Add** button next to the General box. Microsoft Project adds the label and code for the project start date to the legend.

14. Press **Enter** to add a second line to the legend and then type **Duration:** followed by a space.

15. In the Project Fields box, select **Scheduled Duration** from the dropdown list. Click the **Add** button next to the Project Fields box. Microsoft Project adds the label and code for project duration to the legend.

16. In the Width box, type or use the scroll buttons to enter **3**. This increases the width of the box that appears on the left side of the legend. Your screen should look similar to Figure 10-19.

Figure 10-19

Page Setup dialog box with custom selections for legend

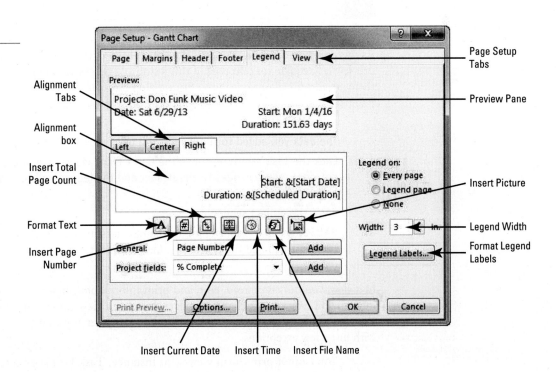

17. Click **OK** to close the Page Setup dialog box. Microsoft Project applies the custom changes to the legend.

18. Move your mouse cursor to the lower left corner of the page preview (your cursor appears as a magnifying glass). Click the **lower left corner** of the page. Microsoft Project zooms in to show the legend. Your screen should look similar to Figure 10-20.

Figure 10-20

Close up view of wider legend area

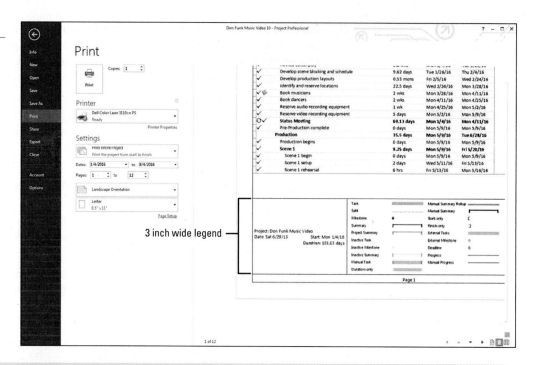

3 inch wide legend

 TAKE NOTE✳ At this point, you can print the project schedule by clicking the Print button (the print preview is adequate for purposes of this lesson). When printing in Microsoft Project 2013, there are additional options in the Print dialog box (the Print command is accessed from the File tab). For example, you can print specific date or page ranges.

The data you added to the legend will print on every page of the printed output.

19. Click the Task tab to return to the Gantt Chart view. Take note that although you did not print, your changes to the header and the legend will be saved when you save the project file.

20. SAVE the project schedule.

PAUSE. If you are continuing to the next lesson, keep Project open. If you are not continuing to additional lessons, CLOSE Project.

In a view, you can enter, read, edit, and print information. In a report, you can only print the information, you cannot change the data. Printing a view allows you to provide, on paper, almost everything you see on your screen. You can print any view you see in Microsoft Project, with just a few exceptions.

- You cannot print form views (for instance, Task Form) or certain diagrams, such as the Relationship Diagram.
- If you have two views displayed in a combination view (one view in the top pane and the other view in the bottom pane), only the view in the active pane will print.

🔍 **Cross Ref** For a review of the types of views, including form views, refer back to Lesson 8.

In this lesson, you applied some custom formulas and graphical indicators to make it simple to review the status of tasks using the Task Sheet view. Communicating the project status to stakeholders is one of the most important functions of a project manager and one that may occupy a significant portion of your working time. It is imperative that the project manager know who needs to know the project status and why, as well as in what format and level of detail these people need the information. The time to find the answers to these questions is in the initial planning stages of the project.

Once work on the project has commenced, your primary communication task will be reporting project status. This can take several forms:

- Status reports describe where the project is in terms of scope, cost, and schedule. These are often referred to as the triple constraint, which is a popular model of project management.
- Progress reports that provide the specific accomplishments of the project team.
- Forecasts that predict future project performance.

Standard report formats may already exist if your organization is highly focused on projects and project management. If your organization does not have standard reports, you may be able to introduce project status formats that are based on clear communication and project management principles. You may be able to report project status using some of the following:

- Printing the Project Overview dashboard report.
- Copying Microsoft Project data to other applications. For example, you could copy the Calendar view to Microsoft Office Word or Microsoft Office PowerPoint.
- Saving Microsoft Project data in other formats, such as Excel, HTML or GIF.

It is important to keep in mind that the part of the project schedule you see on your screen is only a small part of the total project. For example, to print a six-month project with 75 tasks may require more than a dozen letter-sized pages. In general, Gantt Charts and Network Diagrams can use significant amounts of paper on large projects. Some experienced project managers who regularly use Microsoft Project print their projects on poster-sized paper using plotters (a type of printer that draws pictures or graphs using attached pens) or other specialized printing equipment.

Projects with several hundred tasks or long time frames will not print legibly on letter or legal-sized paper. To reduce the number of required pages, you can print just summary tasks or filtered data. If you are interested in a specific timeframe, you can print just that portion of the timescale, which is the band across the top of the Gantt Chart grid that denotes units of time. A filter could be applied to display only the information that is of interest to a specific audience. In any case, it is a good idea to preview the views you want to print. By using the Page Setup dialog box along with the Print Preview window, you can control many features of the view to be printed. For example, you can set the number of pages on which the view will be printed, apply headers and footers, and determine content that appears in the legend of the Gantt Chart and some other views.

TAKE NOTE *

When printing in views that contain a timescale, such as the Gantt Chart view, you can change the number of pages required by adjusting the timescale before printing. To adjust the timescale so that it shows the largest time span in the smallest number of pages, click the **View** tab, then in the Zoom group, click **Entire Project**.

SKILL SUMMARY

In this lesson you learned:	Matrix Skill
To Activate and Print a Dashboard Report	Select and Print a Dashboard Report
To Customize and Print Reports	Create, Customize and Print a Report
To Report Project Status	Report Project Variance with a "Stoplight" View
To Use Visual Reports	Create a Visual Report
To Print the Gantt Chart	Customize and Print the Gantt Chart

■ Knowledge Assessment

Fill in the Blank

Complete the following sentences by writing the correct word or words in the blanks provided.

1. _____ enables you to see on your screen what will print on paper before you print it.

2. People or organizations that might be affected by project activities are called _____.

3. If you have two views displayed in a combination view and want to print the view, only the view in the _____ pane will print.

4. When previewing a view in print preview, you can change the number of pages visible by selecting either the _____ or _____ pages button.

5. A common activity for project managers is to _____ information from the project schedule to share with stakeholders.

6. To add your company name so that it prints at the top of every page, use the _____ dialog box to add the company name to the header.

7. A _____ is a predefined format intended for printing Microsoft Project data.

8. A _____ report is used to represent high-level information usually on one page.

9. If subtasks are hidden in a view, reports that contain task lists will include only _____ tasks.

10. In a report, you can only _____ information.

Multiple Choice

Select the best response for the following statements.

1. In a view, you can _____ information.
   a. enter
   b. edit
   c. print
   d. All of the above are correct.

2. If assignments are hidden under tasks or resources in a usage view, what will the usage report show?
   a. tasks or resources with corresponding assignment details
   b. only the tasks or resources
   c. only overallocated assignment details
   d. it depends on how you set up the report

3. In the Print Preview window, the status bar shows "4 rows by 3 columns." How many pages will be printed?
   a. 7
   b. 4
   c. 12
   d. 3

4. To see all of the pages of a view while using Print Preview, you can click on which one of the following buttons?

    a. Multiple Pages

    b. Page Right

    c. One Page

    d. Page Setup

5. For large projects with several hundred tasks, you can condense the information that will print by _____.

    a. printing just summary data.

    b. printing only the part of the timescale that is of interest.

    c. applying a filter to show only the information of interest.

    d. All of the above are correct.

6. If you wanted to print a list of tasks showing start dates, finish dates, and assigned resources, which view might you use?

    a. Tracking Gantt

    b. Task Sheet

    c. Resource Sheet

    d. Calendar

7. Which one of the following views cannot be printed in Microsoft Project?

    a. Tracking Gantt

    b. Calendar

    c. Task Form

    d. Resource Sheet

8. When printing a view with a legend, you can customize the legend with all the following except:

    a. printing only on one page.

    b. add customized legend items such as custom symbols and logos.

    c. change the size of the legend.

    d. None of the above is correct.

9. In the legend section of a Gantt Chart you can add which of the following information?

    a. Project Start Date

    b. Company Name

    c. Project Duration

    d. All of the above

10. The Reports tab contains

    a. all predefined reports plus any custom report that have been added to Microsoft Project.

    b. all predefined reports in Microsoft Project.

    c. any custom report that has been added to Microsoft Project.

    d. complex reports that have been specifically designed for specific businesses and industries.

■ Competency Assessment

Project 10-1: Creating a Dashboard Report

You are preparing to present the current status of you project to the senior management team. You need to create a report that displays current cost information before the final presentation is complete. **GET READY**. Launch Microsoft Project 2013 if it is not already running. **OPEN** *Don Funk Music Video 10-1* from the data files for this lesson.

1. On the ribbon, click the **Report** tab. Select **Dashboards** and then select **Cost Overview**.
2. Click the **File** tab then select **Print** to view the print preview.
3. Under Settings, click the **Page Setup** hyperlink.
4. Click the **Footer** tab, and then click the **Center** tab in the alignment area.
5. Select the **down-arrow** submenu next to the General box. From the list select **Project Title**. Click the **Add** button.
6. In the alignment area, click the **Right** tab.
7. Click once in the alignment box and type **Date:** (place a space after the colon).
8. In the icon area just below the alignment box, click the **Insert Current Date** button.
9. Click **OK** to close the Page Setup dialog box.
10. At the bottom of the report you should see the current date in the lower right corner with the Don Fun Music Video project name in the center.
11. **SAVE** the project schedule as *Don Funk Dashboard Report* and then **CLOSE** the file.

    LEAVE Project open to use in the next exercise.

Project 10-2: Resources Report in the HR Interview Schedule

For your HR Interview project schedule, you want to print a report that displays the over allocated resources and the work remaining for all resources, for the remaining portion of the project. You will use an existing report to meet your most of your requirements but you will add a table to the report. **OPEN** *HR Interview Schedule 10-2* from the data files for this lesson.

1. Click the **Report** tab.
2. Click the **Resources** button in the View Reports group and then select **Overallocated Resources**.
3. In the Design ribbon click the **Table** button. Grab the inserted table and move it to just below the vertical bar chart on the left side of the screen.
4. In the field list at the right of the screen, click **Resources**.
5. Click the **expand button** next to the Work category to display all the available work fields.
6. Select the **Work** and **Remaining Cumulative Work** check boxes.
7. **SAVE** the project schedule as *HR Interview Resources Work Report* and then **CLOSE** the file.

    LEAVE Project open to use in the next exercise.

■ Proficiency Assessment

Project 10-3: Reducing Insurance Claim Project Schedule Printed Pages

You have a project schedule for processing an insurance claim that you want to print. This schedule has a large number of tasks. Because you are distributing this to a large number of people, you want to reduce the number of pages that will print by changing the way project prints the WBS on the project. OPEN *Insurance Claim 10-3* from the data files for this lesson.

1. From the View ribbon, select Entire Project in the Zoom group.
2. In the Data group, click the Outline button, and then select Level 1.
3. Use Print Preview to view the report.
4. Click Page Setup and then select the Header tab.
5. Key Insurance Claim Processing in the Center alignment section.
6. Add the Time so that it will print under the date in the Left Alignment section of the Legend tab.
7. Close the Page Setup dialog box.
8. SAVE the file as *Insurance Claim Condensed* and then CLOSE the file.

   LEAVE Project open to use in the next exercise.

Project 10-4: Office Remodel Modified Resource View

You have developed a project schedule for a kitchen and lunchroom remodel at your office. You want to distribute a list of tasks by resource so that everyone can see at a glance the tasks for which they are responsible. You will also customize this view to make it easier to read. OPEN *Office Remodel 10-4* from the data files for this lesson.

1. Switch the view to the Resource Usage view. Use the auto fit feature to show the entire width of the Resource Name column.
2. Change the timescale to weeks.
3. Scroll the data in the time-phased grid until the data is at the left.
4. Navigate to the Print Preview.
5. Open the Page Setup dialog box.
6. On the View tab, set up the view so that the first three columns print on all pages.
7. On the Footer tab, on the Left Alignment tab, insert the date. Under the date, insert the time.
8. On the Right Alignment tab, type Start: and then insert the Start Date field.
9. Preview your modified view.
10. SAVE the file as *Office Remodel Resource Usage Report* and then CLOSE the file.

    LEAVE Project open to use in the next exercise.

■ Mastery Assessment

Project 10-5: Don Funk Music Video Calendars

You would like to print a report to show the different calendars that are being used in the production of the Don Funk Music Video. OPEN *Don Funk Music Video 10-5* from the data files for this lesson.

1. Using the Report ribbon, review the various predefined reports that are available for this project. You would like to print a report that shows the actual cost, baseline cost remaining cost, and the cost variance in both chart and table format. Identify the report that meets this need.

2. In a separate Word document, write a short paragraph detailing the steps you took to be able to preview this report.

3. SAVE the Word document as **Don Funk Cost Report**. Save the Project file as **Don Funk Cost Report**. CLOSE both files.

   LEAVE Project open to use in the next exercise.

Project 10-6: HR Interview Custom Network Diagram

 You want to view and print your HR Interview Schedule as a Network Diagram, as well as customize some of the fields for printing. OPEN *HR Interview Schedule 10-6* from the data files for this lesson.

1. Change the view to the Network Diagram.
2. Hide the summary tasks.
3. Collapse the boxes so that only the Task ID displays.
4. Activate the Page Setup dialog box.
5. In the Page Setup dialog box, make the following custom changes:

   - add the time to the left side of the footer
   - type Start: and then insert the Start Date field on the right side of the footer
   - add the title "HR Interview Network Diagram" to the center of the header
   - change the font of the title to Arial Bold 10pt. with color Blue
   - add your name to the second line of the header, under the project title

6. Check your changes to make sure they appear correctly.
7. SAVE the file as **HR Interview Network Diagram** and then CLOSE the file.

   CLOSE Project.

■ Circling Back

Mete Goktepe is a project management specialist at Woodgrove Bank. He has put together the initial components of a project plan for a Request for Proposal (RFP) process to evaluate and select new commercial lending software. This process entails determining needs, identifying vendors, requesting proposals, reviewing proposals, and selecting the software.

Now that Mete has established the foundation of the project plan, he will begin to put the plan into action.

 ### Project 1: Setting Deadlines and Establishing Multiple Pay Rates

Acting as Mete, you need to set a deadline for one of the tasks in the project. You then need to establish and apply multiple pay rates for a resource.

GET READY. Launch Microsoft Project if it is not already running.
 OPEN *RFP Bank Software Schedule* from the data files for this lesson.

1. In the Task Name column, click the name of Task 10, RFP Ready to release.
2. On the Task ribbon, click the Information button in the Properties group.
3. On the Advanced tab, in the dropdown date box next to Deadline, type or select 5/27/16.
4. Close the Task Information dialog box.
5. Scroll the Gantt bar chart to the right of Task 11 to view the deadline marker.
6. On the ribbon, click the View tab, and then click Resource Sheet.
7. In the Resource Name column, double-click the name of Resource 9, Marc J. Ingle.
   Because Marc J. Ingle's rate differs depending on whether he is doing document preparation or meeting facilitation, you need to enter a second rate for him.
8. In the Resource Information dialog box, click the Costs tab if not already selected.
9. Under Cost rate tables, click the B tab.
10. Select the default entry of $0.00/h in the field directly below the Standard Rate column heading, type 1200/w, and then [press Enter]. Click OK.
11. On the View ribbon, click the Task Usage button.
12. On the ribbon, click the Tables button and then select the Cost table.
13. Under Task 4, double-click on Marc J. Ingle to activate the Assignment Information dialog box.
14. Click the General tab, if it is not already selected.
15. In the Cost rate table box, key or select B, and then click OK.
16. SAVE the project plan as *RFP Bank Software Multiple Rates* in the solutions folder for this lesson as directed by your instructor.
    PAUSE. LEAVE Project and the project file open to use in the next exercise.

Project 2: Formatting and Printing the Project Plan

Acting as Mete, you need to change the appearance of some of your data before sharing it with stakeholders. You then need to prepare to print the project plan for distribution.

USE the project schedule from the previous exercise.

1. Save the schedule as **RFP Bank Software Formatted.**
2. Click the View tab, and then click Gantt Chart.
3. Click the Format tab, then click the check box next to Project Summary Task in the Show/Hide group.
4. Adjust your screen so that the Duration, Start and Finish columns are fully visible and expanded to show entire values.
5. Click the View tab, then click Other Views, and then select More Views.
6. Make sure that the Gantt Chart option is highlighted, and then click the Copy button.
7. In the Name field, key Custom Gantt Chart, and then click OK.
8. Make sure that the Custom Gantt Chart option is highlighted, and then click the Apply button.
9. Click the Format tab, and then select the check box next to Critical Tasks in the Bar Styles group.
10. SAVE the project schedule.
11. Click the File tab, then select Print.
12. On the Print Preview screen, click the Page Setup hyperlink.
13. Click the Header tab. Select the Center alignment tab if needed.
14. In the General box, click Company Name and then click the Add button.
15. Click the Legend tab, and then select the Left alignment tab.
16. In the Alignment box, position your cursor after "&[Date]" and then [press Enter].
17. Type Start Date: followed by a [Space]. In the General box, select Project Start Date from the dropdown list, and then click Add.
18. Click OK to close the Page Setup dialog box.
19. SAVE the project schedule.

   PAUSE. LEAVE Project and the project plan open to use in the next exercise.

Project 3: Tracking the Project Plan

Now that work is starting on your project, it is time to begin tracking progress. You need to save a baseline, track actual work, and enter completion percentages.

GET READY. SAVE the open project schedule as **RFP Bank Software Tracked.**

1. Click the Project tab.
2. In the Schedule group, click the Set Baseline button, then select Set Baseline.
3. Accept all the default options by clicking the OK button.
4. On the ribbon, click Update Project.
5. Make sure the Update work as complete through option and 0% – 100% complete are both selected. In the adjacent date box, type or select 5/15/16. Click OK.
6. Click the View tab, then click the Tables button, and then select the Work table.

7. Auto fit all columns and then drag your **center divider** to the right to reveal the %Work Complete column.

8. In the %Work Complete column for Task 6, type or select **100**, and then [press **Enter**].

9. If necessary, click the name of **Task 7, Draft RFP**. [Press **Ctrl+Shift+F5**] to scroll the Gantt Chart view to the Gantt Bar.

10. In the Actual cell for **Task 7**, type **88** and [press **Enter**].

11. In the Actual cell for **Task 8, Review RFP with management and commercial lending representatives**, type **48** and [press the **Tab** key].

12. In the Remaining cell for **Task 8**, type **0** and [press **Enter**].

13. **SAVE** and then **CLOSE** the project schedule.

   CLOSE Microsoft Project.

Advanced Project Schedule Tracking

LESSON SKILL MATRIX

SKILLS	TASKS
Recording Actual Start, Finish, and Duration Values of Tasks	Enter actual start date and duration for a task
Adjusting Remaining Work of Tasks	Adjust actual and remaining work for a task
Evaluating Performance with Earned Value Analysis	Set project status date and display the Earned Value table

You are a video project manager for Southridge Video, and one of your primary responsibilities recently has been to manage the new Don Funk Music Video project. In an earlier lesson, you learned about some of the basic project schedule tracking features in Microsoft Project. In this lesson, you will become familiar with some of the more advanced tracking functions that enable you to record progress details of your project.

KEY TERMS

actual cost of work performed (ACWP)

budget at completion (BAC)

budgeted cost of work performed (BCWP)

budgeted cost of work scheduled (BCWS)

Cost Performance Index (CPI)

cost variance (CV)

earned value (EV)

estimate at completion (EAC)

planned value (PV)

Schedule Performance Index (SPI)

schedule variance (SV)

variance at completion (VAC)

© njmcc/iStockphoto

SOFTWARE ORIENTATION

Microsoft Project's Earned Value Table

The Earned Value table displays several schedule indicator and cost indicator values that are useful in measuring the project's progress and forecasting its outcome through earned value analysis.

Figure 11-1

Earned Value table in the Task Sheet view

	Task Name	CPI	SPI	Planned Value - PV (BCWS)	Earned Value - EV (BCWP)	AC (ACWP)	SV	CV	EAC	BAC	VAC
0	**Don Funk Music Video**	0.89	1.03	$33,961.27	$35,042.14	$39,201.43	$1,080.88	($4,159.28)	$66,732.22	$59,651.64	($7,080.58)
1	**Pre-Production**	1.03	1.21	$18,999.64	$22,919.64	$22,223.48	$3,920.00	$696.16	$18,422.53	$18,999.64	$577.11
2	Pre-Production complete	0	0	$0.00	$0.00	$0.00	$0.00	$0.00	$0.00	$0.00	$0.00
3	Review screenplay	1	1	$4,590.00	$4,590.00	$4,590.00	$0.00	$0.00	$4,590.00	$4,590.00	$0.00
4	Develop scene blocking and schedule	1.02	1	$1,560.00	$1,560.00	$1,525.06	$0.00	$34.94	$1,525.06	$1,560.00	$34.94
5	Develop production layouts	1	1	$4,640.00	$4,640.00	$4,640.00	$0.00	$0.00	$4,640.00	$4,640.00	$0.00
6	Identify and reserve locations	1.11	1	$6,612.14	$6,612.14	$5,950.93	$0.00	$661.21	$5,950.93	$6,612.14	$661.21
7	Book musicians	1	1	$560.00	$560.00	$560.00	$0.00	$0.00	$560.00	$560.00	$0.00
8	Book dancers	1	1	$560.00	$560.00	$560.00	$0.00	$0.00	$560.00	$560.00	$0.00
9	Reserve audio recording equipment	1	1	$1,400.00	$1,400.00	$1,400.00	$0.00	$0.00	$1,400.00	$1,400.00	$0.00
10	Reserve video recording equipment	1	1	$1,400.00	$1,400.00	$1,400.00	$0.00	$0.00	$1,400.00	$1,400.00	$0.00
11	**Status Meeting**	1	1	$1,597.50	$1,597.50	$1,597.50	$0.00	$0.00	$1,597.50	$1,597.50	$0.00
27	Pre-Production complete	0	0	$0.00	$0.00	$0.00	$0.00	$0.00	$0.00	$0.00	$0.00
28	**Production**	0.71	0.81	$14,961.63	$12,122.50	$16,977.94	($2,839.13)	($4,855.44)	$32,911.89	$23,499.50	($9,412.39)
29	Production begins	0	0	$0.00	$0.00	$0.00	$0.00	$0.00	$0.00	$0.00	$0.00
30	**Scene 1**	0.78	1	$5,331.50	$5,331.50	$6,874.94	$0.00	($1,543.44)	$7,842.07	$6,081.50	($1,760.57)
31	Scene 1 begin	0	0	$0.00	$0.00	$0.00	$0.00	$0.00	$0.00	$0.00	$0.00
32	Scene 1 setup	1	1	$536.00	$536.00	$536.00	$0.00	$0.00	$536.00	$536.00	$0.00
33	Scene 1 rehearsal	1	1	$388.50	$388.50	$388.50	$0.00	$0.00	$888.50	$888.50	$0.00
34	Scene 1 vocal recording	0.88	1	$1,442.00	$1,442.00	$1,629.46	$0.00	($187.46)	$1,911.96	$1,692.00	($219.96)
35	Scene 1 video shoot	0.67	1	$2,717.00	$2,717.00	$4,072.98	$0.00	($1,355.98)	$4,072.98	$2,717.00	($1,355.98)
36	Scene 1 teardown	1	1	$248.00	$248.00	$248.00	$0.00	$0.00	$248.00	$248.00	$0.00
37	Scene 1 complete	0	0	$0.00	$0.00	$0.00	$0.00	$0.00	$0.00	$0.00	$0.00
38	**Scene 2**	0.66	1	$6,523.00	$6,523.00	$9,835.00	$0.00	($3,312.00)	$10,588.87	$7,023.00	($3,565.87)
39	Scene 2 begin	0	0	$0.00	$0.00	$0.00	$0.00	$0.00	$0.00	$0.00	$0.00
40	Scene 2 setup	1	1	$1,066.00	$1,066.00	$1,066.00	$0.00	$0.00	$1,066.00	$1,066.00	$0.00
41	Scene 2 rehearsal	0.43	1	$324.00	$324.00	$756.00	$0.00	($432.00)	$1,922.67	$824.00	($1,098.67)
42	Scene 2 vocal recording	0.33	1	$1,440.00	$1,440.00	$4,320.00	$0.00	($2,880.00)	$4,320.00	$1,440.00	($2,880.00)
43	Scene 2 video shoot	1	1	$3,445.00	$3,445.00	$3,445.00	$0.00	$0.00	$3,445.00	$3,445.00	$0.00
44	Scene 2 teardown	1	1	$248.00	$248.00	$248.00	$0.00	$0.00	$248.00	$248.00	$0.00
45	Scene 2 complete	0	0	$0.00	$0.00	$0.00	$0.00	$0.00	$0.00	$0.00	$0.00

The columns in the Earned Value table are:

1. *CPI – Cost Performance Index*, the ratio of budgeted to actual cost - calculated as EV divided by AC.

2. *SPI – Schedule Performance Index*, the ratio of performed to scheduled work - calculated as EV divided by PV.

3. *Planned Value-PV (or BCWS – budgeted cost of work scheduled)* – the value of the work scheduled to be completed as of the status date.

4. *Earned Value-EV (or BCWP – budgeted cost of work performed)* – the portion of the budgeted cost that should have been spent to complete each task's actual work performed up to the status date.

5. *AC – (ACWP) Actual Cost* – the actual cost incurred to complete each task's actual work up to the status date.

6. *SV – Schedule Variance*, the difference between the budgeted cost of work performed and the budgeted cost of work scheduled.

7. *CV – Cost Variance*, the difference between the budgeted and actual cost of work performed.

8. **EAC – Estimate at Completion**, the expected total cost of a task based on performance up to the status date.

9. **BAC – Budget at Completion**, the total planned cost.

10. **VAC – Variance at Completion**, the difference between the BAC (Budgeted at Completion) or baseline cost and EAC (Estimated at Completion).

■ Recording Actual Start, Finish, and Duration Values of Tasks

THE BOTTOM LINE

Once the details of the project schedule have been finalized and work has started, the project manager can begin to track progress on the project by recording actual start, finish, and duration values.

⊕ ENTER ACTUAL START DATE AND DURATION FOR A TASK

GET READY. Before you begin these steps, launch Microsoft Project.

1. OPEN the **Don Funk Music Video 11MA** project schedule from the data files for this lesson.

2. SAVE the file as **Don Funk Music Video 11A** in the solutions folder for this lesson as directed by your instructor.

3. Navigate to and select Task 7, **Book musicians**. On the Task ribbon, click the **Scroll to Task** button. This Task started one day ahead of schedule, so you need to record this.

4. On the ribbon, click the **down-arrow** next to the Mark on Track button and select **Update Tasks**. The Update Tasks dialog box appears.

5. Under the Actual label, in the Start box, type or select **March 25, 2016**.

6. In the Actual dur box, type or select **2w**, and then click **OK** to close the Update Tasks dialog box.

7. The Planning Wizard dialog box appears. Select **Continue. Allow the scheduling conflict.** Click **OK**. Microsoft Project records the actual start date and work for Task 7. Your screen should look similar to Figure 11-2.

Figure 11-2

Gantt Chart showing actual start and work for Task 7

Task 7 has a 2 week duration   Task 7 actual start date of March 25

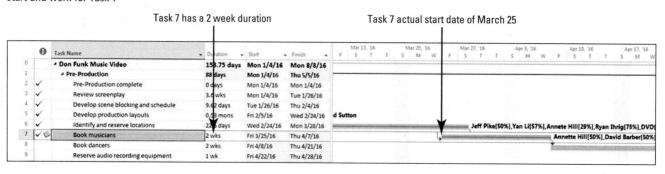

8. In the Task Name column, select the name of Task 8, **Book dancers**. You need to record that Task 8 started on time but took three days longer to complete.

9. On the ribbon, click the **down-arrow** next to the Mark on Track button and select **Update Tasks**. The Update Tasks dialog box reappears.

10. In the Actual dur box, key **13d**, and then click **OK**. The Planning Wizard dialog box appears again. Select **Continue. Allow the scheduling conflict.** Click **OK**.

11. Click the **Scroll to Task** button or scroll so that the Gantt bar for Task 8 is visible in the center of the Gantt Chart. Your screen should look similar to Figure 11-3.

Figure 11-3

Gantt Chart view showing updated progress for Task 8

Task 8 start date did not change, but the actual duration was 13 days...   ...which caused the finish date to be later than originally planned

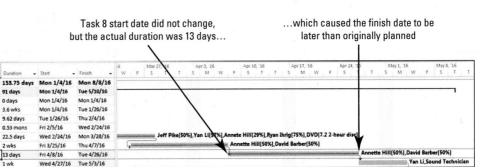

Microsoft Project records the actual duration of the task. Microsoft Project assumes that the task started as scheduled because you did not specify an actual start date. However, the actual duration that you entered causes Microsoft Project to calculate a finish date that is later than the originally scheduled finish date.

Next you will record that Task 9 was completed as scheduled and that task 10 took longer than scheduled to complete.

12. In the Task Name column, select the name of Task 9, **Reserve audio recording equipment**.

13. On the ribbon, click the **100% Complete** button in the schedule group. Microsoft Project updates Task 9 as 100% complete.

14. In the Task Name column, select the name of Task 10, **Reserve video recording equipment**. Click the **down-arrow** next to the Mark on Track button and select **Update Tasks**. The Update Tasks dialog box reappears.

15. In the Actual dur box, type or select **6d**, and then click **OK**. Microsoft Project records the actual duration of the task.

16. On the ribbon, click the **Scroll to Task** button. Microsoft Project scrolls the Gantt bar chart so that the bar for Task 10 is visible. Your screen should look similar to Figure 11-4.

Figure 11-4

Gantt Chart showing completion information for tasks 9 and 10

Task 9 is complete   Actual duration for task 10 was 6 days

Deadline Marker for Task 27 is on May 11

You can see that the Pre-Production phase of the Don Funk Music Video project has met its deadline of May 11, 2016.

17. **SAVE** the project schedule, and then **CLOSE** the file.

   PAUSE. LEAVE Project open to use in the next exercise.

In this exercise, you entered actual start dates and durations for several tasks. Remember, as you learned in Lesson 9, tracking actuals is essential to a well-managed project. As the project manager, you need to know how well the project team is performing and when to take corrective action. When you enter actual start, finish, or duration values, Microsoft Project updates the schedule and calculates the task's percentage of completion. When doing this, Microsoft Project uses the following rules:

- When you enter a task's actual start date, different from its planned start date, Microsoft Project recalculates the scheduled finish date.
- When you enter a task's actual finish date, Microsoft Project moves the scheduled finish date to match the actual finish dates and assigns a completion percentage of 100%.
- When you enter an actual duration for a task that is less than the scheduled duration, Microsoft Project subtracts the actual duration from the scheduled duration to determine the remaining duration.
- When you enter a task's actual duration that is equal to the scheduled duration, Microsoft Project sets the task to 100% complete.
- When you enter an actual duration for a task that is longer than the scheduled duration, Microsoft Project adjusts the scheduled duration to match the actual duration and sets the task to 100%.

Evaluating the status of a project is not always easy or straightforward. Keep in mind the following issues:

- For many tasks, it is difficult to evaluate a percentage of completion. For example, when is a design engineer 75% finished designing a new production process, or a computer engineer 50% finished coding a new software upgrade? Often, reporting work in progress is a best guess and therefore carries an inherent risk.
- The portion of a task's duration that has elapsed does not always equate to a percentage accomplished. For example, a front-loaded task might require a lot of effort initially, so that when 50% of its duration has elapsed, much more than 50% of its total work will have been completed.
- The resources assigned to a task might have different criteria for what determines the task's completion than does the project manager – or the resources assigned to successor tasks.

To avoid or minimize these and other problems that arise in project implementation, a good project manager needs to carry out good project planning and communication. Determining how you will track project progress is a decision made during planning, and this information will be clearly communicated to all team members. No matter how much planning is done, projects almost always have variance from the baseline.

■ Adjusting Remaining Work of Tasks

THE BOTTOM LINE

While tracking actual values, it is also possible to adjust the work or duration remaining on a task.

ADJUST ACTUAL AND REMAINING WORK FOR A TASK

GET READY. To continue with this lesson, you will use an updated version of the Don Funk Music Video project to simulate the passage of time since you completed the previous exercise.

1. OPEN the *Don Funk Music Video 11MB* project schedule from the data files for this lesson.

2. SAVE the file as *Don Funk Music Video 11B* in the solutions folder for this lesson as directed by your instructor.

3. Click on the View tab, and then click Task Usage. The Task Usage view appears. Your screen should look similar to Figure 11-5.

Figure 11-5

Task Usage View

Task Usage view shows the resources assigned to each task

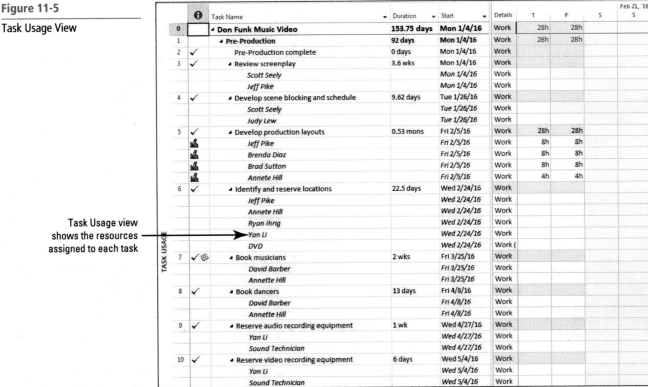

4. [Press the F5 key.] In the ID box, type 40, and then click OK. Microsoft Project scrolls the time-scaled portion of the view to display the scheduled work information for task 40.

5. On the ribbon, click the Tables button and then select the Work table. Microsoft Project displays the Work table in the Task Usage view.

6. Click and drag the vertical divider bar between the Work table and the Task Usage grid to the right until you can see all the columns in the Work table. Your screen should look similar to Figure 11-6.

> **TAKE NOTE** *
> The mouse pointer changes to a two-headed arrow (pointing left and right) when it is in the correct position to drag the vertical divider bar.

Figure 11-6

Work table in the Task
Usage view

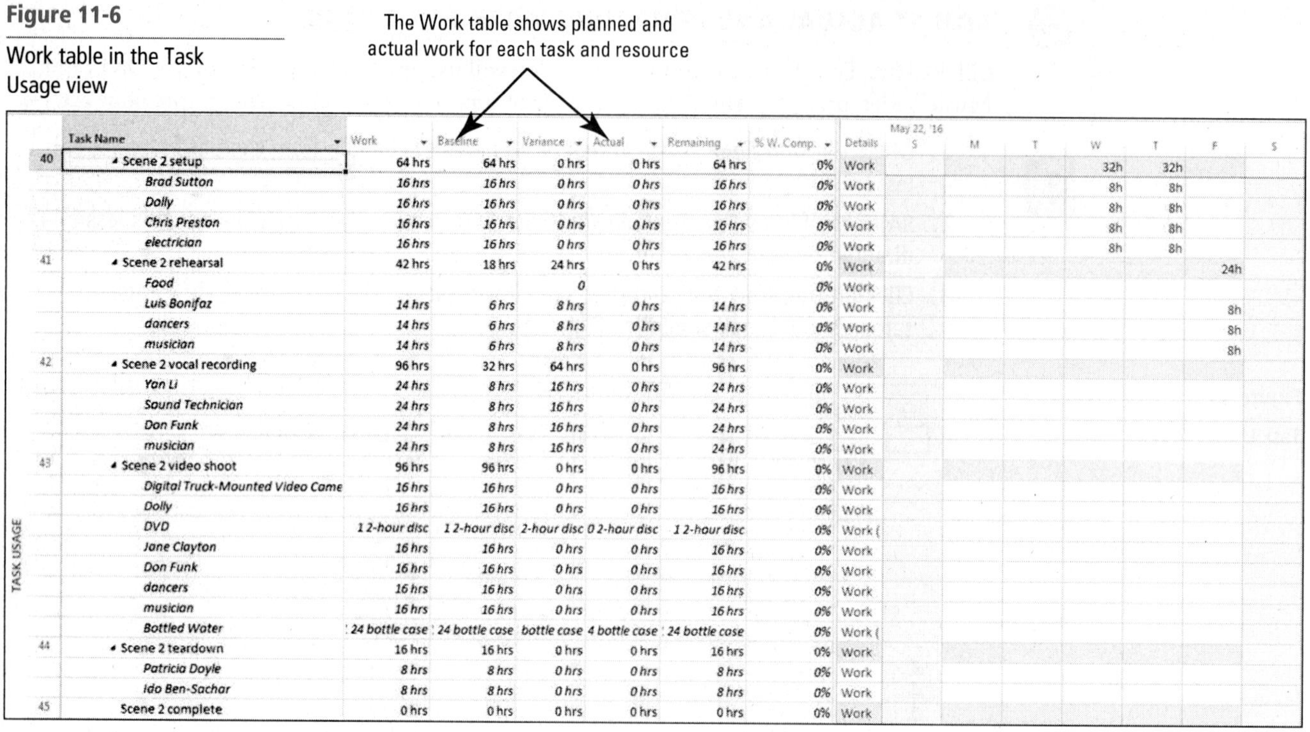

The Work table shows planned and
actual work for each task and resource

Task Name	Work	Baseline	Variance	Actual	Remaining	% W. Comp.	Details	May 22, '16 S	M	T	W	T	F	S
40 ◢ Scene 2 setup	64 hrs	64 hrs	0 hrs	0 hrs	64 hrs	0%	Work				32h	32h		
Brad Sutton	16 hrs	16 hrs	0 hrs	0 hrs	16 hrs	0%	Work				8h	8h		
Dolly	16 hrs	16 hrs	0 hrs	0 hrs	16 hrs	0%	Work				8h	8h		
Chris Preston	16 hrs	16 hrs	0 hrs	0 hrs	16 hrs	0%	Work				8h	8h		
electrician	16 hrs	16 hrs	0 hrs	0 hrs	16 hrs	0%	Work				8h	8h		
41 ◢ Scene 2 rehearsal	42 hrs	18 hrs	24 hrs	0 hrs	42 hrs	0%	Work						24h	
Food			0			0%	Work							
Luis Bonifaz	14 hrs	6 hrs	8 hrs	0 hrs	14 hrs	0%	Work						8h	
dancers	14 hrs	6 hrs	8 hrs	0 hrs	14 hrs	0%	Work						8h	
musician	14 hrs	6 hrs	8 hrs	0 hrs	14 hrs	0%	Work						8h	
42 ◢ Scene 2 vocal recording	96 hrs	32 hrs	64 hrs	0 hrs	96 hrs	0%	Work							
Yan Li	24 hrs	8 hrs	16 hrs	0 hrs	24 hrs	0%	Work							
Sound Technician	24 hrs	8 hrs	16 hrs	0 hrs	24 hrs	0%	Work							
Don Funk	24 hrs	8 hrs	16 hrs	0 hrs	24 hrs	0%	Work							
musician	24 hrs	8 hrs	16 hrs	0 hrs	24 hrs	0%	Work							
43 ◢ Scene 2 video shoot	96 hrs	96 hrs	0 hrs	0 hrs	96 hrs	0%	Work							
Digital Truck-Mounted Video Came	16 hrs	16 hrs	0 hrs	0 hrs	16 hrs	0%	Work							
Dolly	16 hrs	16 hrs	0 hrs	0 hrs	16 hrs	0%	Work							
DVD	1 2-hour disc	1 2-hour disc	2-hour disc 0	2-hour disc	1 2-hour disc	0%	Work (							
Jane Clayton	16 hrs	16 hrs	0 hrs	0 hrs	16 hrs	0%	Work							
Don Funk	16 hrs	16 hrs	0 hrs	0 hrs	16 hrs	0%	Work							
dancers	16 hrs	16 hrs	0 hrs	0 hrs	16 hrs	0%	Work							
musician	16 hrs	16 hrs	0 hrs	0 hrs	16 hrs	0%	Work							
Bottled Water	: 24 bottle case	24 bottle case	bottle case 4	bottle case	24 bottle case	0%	Work (							
44 ◢ Scene 2 teardown	16 hrs	16 hrs	0 hrs	0 hrs	16 hrs	0%	Work							
Patricia Doyle	8 hrs	8 hrs	0 hrs	0 hrs	8 hrs	0%	Work							
Ido Ben-Sachar	8 hrs	8 hrs	0 hrs	0 hrs	8 hrs	0%	Work							
45 Scene 2 complete	0 hrs	0 hrs	0 hrs	0 hrs	0 hrs	0%	Work							

7. In the Actual column for Task 40, type **20h**, and then [press **Tab**]. Change highlighting (the light blue shaded cells) shows that several things have occurred. First, because you entered the actual work at the task level, Microsoft Project distributed it equally among the assigned resources. Second, Microsoft Project recalculated the remaining work value. Your screen should look similar to Figure 11-7.

Figure 11-7

Work table showing the actual
work completed for Task 40

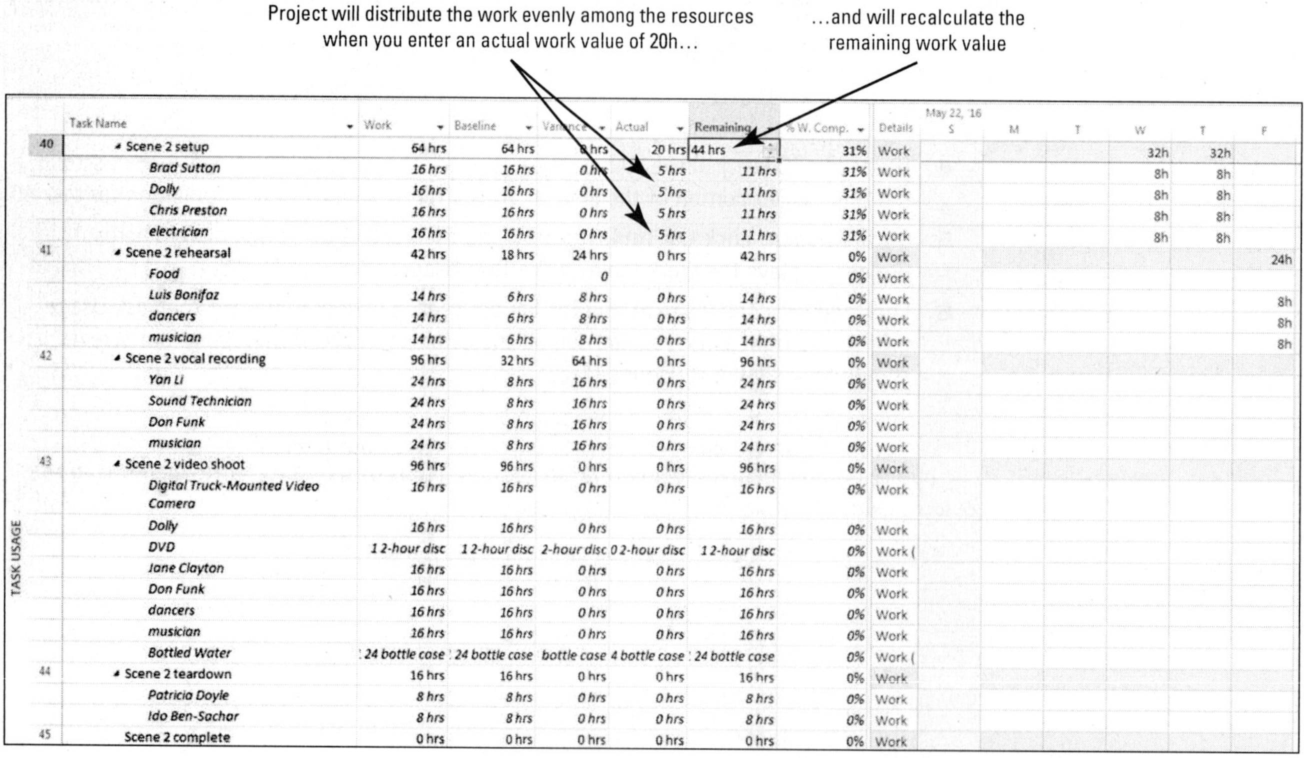

Project will distribute the work evenly among the resources
when you enter an actual work value of 20h...

...and will recalculate the
remaining work value

Task Name	Work	Baseline	Variance	Actual	Remaining	% W. Comp.	Details	May 22, '16 S	M	T	W	T	F
40 ◢ Scene 2 setup	64 hrs	64 hrs	0 hrs	20 hrs	44 hrs	31%	Work				32h	32h	
Brad Sutton	16 hrs	16 hrs	0 hrs	5 hrs	11 hrs	31%	Work				8h	8h	
Dolly	16 hrs	16 hrs	0 hrs	5 hrs	11 hrs	31%	Work				8h	8h	
Chris Preston	16 hrs	16 hrs	0 hrs	5 hrs	11 hrs	31%	Work				8h	8h	
electrician	16 hrs	16 hrs	0 hrs	5 hrs	11 hrs	31%	Work				8h	8h	
41 ◢ Scene 2 rehearsal	42 hrs	18 hrs	24 hrs	0 hrs	42 hrs	0%	Work						24h
Food			0			0%	Work						
Luis Bonifaz	14 hrs	6 hrs	8 hrs	0 hrs	14 hrs	0%	Work						8h
dancers	14 hrs	6 hrs	8 hrs	0 hrs	14 hrs	0%	Work						8h
musician	14 hrs	6 hrs	8 hrs	0 hrs	14 hrs	0%	Work						8h
42 ◢ Scene 2 vocal recording	96 hrs	32 hrs	64 hrs	0 hrs	96 hrs	0%	Work						
Yan Li	24 hrs	8 hrs	16 hrs	0 hrs	24 hrs	0%	Work						
Sound Technician	24 hrs	8 hrs	16 hrs	0 hrs	24 hrs	0%	Work						
Don Funk	24 hrs	8 hrs	16 hrs	0 hrs	24 hrs	0%	Work						
musician	24 hrs	8 hrs	16 hrs	0 hrs	24 hrs	0%	Work						
43 ◢ Scene 2 video shoot	96 hrs	96 hrs	0 hrs	0 hrs	96 hrs	0%	Work						
Digital Truck-Mounted Video Camera	16 hrs	16 hrs	0 hrs	0 hrs	16 hrs	0%	Work						
Dolly	16 hrs	16 hrs	0 hrs	0 hrs	16 hrs	0%	Work						
DVD	1 2-hour disc	1 2-hour disc	2-hour disc 0	2-hour disc	1 2-hour disc	0%	Work (						
Jane Clayton	16 hrs	16 hrs	0 hrs	0 hrs	16 hrs	0%	Work						
Don Funk	16 hrs	16 hrs	0 hrs	0 hrs	16 hrs	0%	Work						
dancers	16 hrs	16 hrs	0 hrs	0 hrs	16 hrs	0%	Work						
musician	16 hrs	16 hrs	0 hrs	0 hrs	16 hrs	0%	Work						
Bottled Water	: 24 bottle case	24 bottle case	bottle case 4	bottle case	24 bottle case	0%	Work (						
44 ◢ Scene 2 teardown	16 hrs	16 hrs	0 hrs	0 hrs	16 hrs	0%	Work						
Patricia Doyle	8 hrs	8 hrs	0 hrs	0 hrs	8 hrs	0%	Work						
Ido Ben-Sachar	8 hrs	8 hrs	0 hrs	0 hrs	8 hrs	0%	Work						
45 Scene 2 complete	0 hrs	0 hrs	0 hrs	0 hrs	0 hrs	0%	Work						

8. In the Remaining column for Task 40, type **54h** and [press **Enter**]. Notice that the new remaining work value was equally distributed among the assigned resources. Your screen should look similar to Figure 11-8.

Figure 11-8

Work table showing remaining work for Task 40

When you adjust the remaining work value, Project will redistribute the remaining work among the resources

	Task Name	Work	Baseline	Variance	Actual	Remaining	% W. Comp.	Details	May 22, '16 S	M	T	W	T	F
40	⊿ Scene 2 setup	74 hrs	64 hrs	10 hrs	20 hrs	54 hrs	27%	Work				32h	32h	10h
	Brad Sutton	18.5 hrs	16 hrs	2.5 hrs	5 hrs	13.5 hrs	27%	Work				8h	8h	2.5h
	Dolly	18.5 hrs	16 hrs	2.5 hrs	5 hrs	13.5 hrs	27%	Work				8h	8h	2.5h
	Chris Preston	18.5 hrs	16 hrs	2.5 hrs	5 hrs	13.5 hrs	27%	Work				8h	8h	2.5h
	electrician	18.5 hrs	16 hrs	2.5 hrs	5 hrs	13.5 hrs	27%	Work				8h	8h	2.5h
41	⊿ Scene 2 rehearsal	42 hrs	18 hrs	24 hrs	0 hrs	42 hrs	0%	Work						16.5h
	Food				0		0%	Work						
	Luis Bonifaz	14 hrs	6 hrs	8 hrs	0 hrs	14 hrs	0%	Work						5.5h
	dancers	14 hrs	6 hrs	8 hrs	0 hrs	14 hrs	0%	Work						5.5h
	musician	14 hrs	6 hrs	8 hrs	0 hrs	14 hrs	0%	Work						5.5h
42	⊿ Scene 2 vocal recording	96 hrs	32 hrs	64 hrs	0 hrs	96 hrs	0%	Work						
	Yan Li	24 hrs	8 hrs	16 hrs	0 hrs	24 hrs	0%	Work						
	Sound Technician	24 hrs	8 hrs	16 hrs	0 hrs	24 hrs	0%	Work						
	Don Funk	24 hrs	8 hrs	16 hrs	0 hrs	24 hrs	0%	Work						
	musician	24 hrs	8 hrs	16 hrs	0 hrs	24 hrs	0%	Work						
43	⊿ Scene 2 video shoot	96 hrs	96 hrs	0 hrs	0 hrs	96 hrs	0%	Work						
	Digital Truck-Mounted Video Camera	16 hrs	16 hrs	0 hrs	0 hrs	16 hrs	0%	Work						
	Dolly	16 hrs	16 hrs	0 hrs	0 hrs	16 hrs	0%	Work						
	DVD	1 2-hour disc	1 2-hour disc	2-hour disc	0 2-hour disc	1 2-hour disc	0%	Work (						
	Jane Clayton	16 hrs	16 hrs	0 hrs	0 hrs	16 hrs	0%	Work						
	Don Funk	16 hrs	16 hrs	0 hrs	0 hrs	16 hrs	0%	Work						
	dancers	16 hrs	16 hrs	0 hrs	0 hrs	16 hrs	0%	Work						
	musician	16 hrs	16 hrs	0 hrs	0 hrs	16 hrs	0%	Work						
	Bottled Water	24 bottle case	24 bottle case	bottle case	4 bottle case	24 bottle case	0%	Work (						
44	⊿ Scene 2 teardown	16 hrs	16 hrs	0 hrs	0 hrs	16 hrs	0%	Work						
	Patricia Doyle	8 hrs	8 hrs	0 hrs	0 hrs	8 hrs	0%	Work						
	Ido Ben-Sachar	8 hrs	8 hrs	0 hrs	0 hrs	8 hrs	0%	Work						
45	Scene 2 complete	0 hrs	0 hrs	0 hrs	0 hrs	0 hrs	0%	Work						

9. SAVE the project schedule.

PAUSE. LEAVE Project open to use in the next exercise.

In this exercise, you adjusted actual and remaining work for a task in the project schedule. In addition to adjusting work, as you track actuals you can also adjust duration and start and finish dates. Remember that only an incomplete task can have a remaining work or duration value. For example:

- A task that was scheduled for 40 hours is partially completed. The resources have performed 30 hours of work and expect to finish the entire task after working 6 more hours. As you learned in this lesson, you would enter 30 hours of actual work and 6 hours of remaining work using the Work table.
- A task that was scheduled for four days duration is partially complete. Two days have elapsed, and the resources working on the task estimate they will need three additional days to complete the task. You can enter the actual and remaining duration via the Update Tasks dialog box (on the Task ribbon, select the **down-arrow** next to Mark on Track, and then click **Update Tasks**).

It is important to remember that whenever you enter actual work values, Microsoft Project calculates actual cost values, by default, and you are not able to enter actual costs directly. If you want to enter actual cost values yourself, click the **File** tab, then select **Options**, then click the **Schedule** option. In the section under Calculation, set the option to **OFF**. In the section for *Calculation options for this* project, deselect the option that reads **Actual costs are always calculated by Project**.

Once you turn off automatic calculation, you can enter or import task-level or assignment-level actual costs in the Actual Cost field. This field is available in several locations, such as the Cost table. You can also enter actual cost values on a daily or any other interval in any usage view, such as the Task Usage view. Exercise caution, though, anytime you enter costs manually: entering actual costs for tasks or assignments prevents Microsoft Project from calculating costs based on resource rates and task progress.

■ Evaluating Performance with Earned Value Analysis

THE BOTTOM LINE

Earned value analysis is used to measure a project's progress in terms of both schedule and cost as well as to help predict its outcome. Earned value can be used on any project, in any industry, to objectively track project progress.

SET PROJECT STATUS DATE AND DISPLAY THE EARNED VALUE TABLE

USE the project schedule you created in the previous exercise.

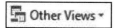

1. Click the **View** tab. In the Task Views group select **Other Views** then select **Task Sheet**.
2. Click the **Project** tab. Click the **calendar icon** in the Status date field.

3. In the Select date box, type or select **6/30/16**, and then click **OK**.
4. Click the **View** tab. Click the **Tables** button then select **More Tables**. The More Tables dialog box appears.
5. In the Tables list, select **Earned Value**, and then click **Apply**. Microsoft Project displays the Earned Value table in the Task Sheet view. If necessary, double-click between column headings to display all values. Your screen should look like Figure 11-9.

Figure 11-9

Earned Value table in the Task Sheet view

	Task Name	Planned Value - PV (BCWS)	Earned Value - EV (BCWP)	AC (ACWP)	SV	CV	EAC	BAC	VAC
0	Don Funk Music Video	$45,701.14	$25,183.56	$28,282.05	($20,517.58)	($3,098.49)	$66,991.10	$59,651.64	($7,339.46)
1	Pre-Production	$18,999.64	$21,322.14	$21,073.98	$2,322.50	$248.16	$18,778.50	$18,999.64	$221.14
2	Pre-Production complete	$0.00	$0.00	$0.00	$0.00	$0.00	$0.00	$0.00	$0.00
3	Review screenplay	$4,590.00	$4,590.00	$4,590.00	$0.00	$0.00	$4,590.00	$4,590.00	$0.00
4	Develop scene blocking and schedule	$1,560.00	$1,560.00	$1,525.06	$0.00	$34.94	$1,525.06	$1,560.00	$34.94
5	Develop production layouts	$4,640.00	$4,640.00	$4,640.00	$0.00	$0.00	$4,640.00	$4,640.00	$0.00
6	Identify and reserve locations	$6,612.14	$6,612.14	$5,950.93	$0.00	$661.21	$5,950.93	$6,612.14	$661.21
7	Book musicians	$560.00	$560.00	$560.00	$0.00	$0.00	$560.00	$560.00	$0.00
8	Book dancers	$560.00	$560.00	$728.00	$0.00	($168.00)	$728.00	$560.00	($168.00)
9	Reserve audio recording equipment	$1,400.00	$1,400.00	$1,400.00	$0.00	$0.00	$1,400.00	$1,400.00	$0.00
10	Reserve video recording equipment	$1,400.00	$1,400.00	$1,680.00	$0.00	($280.00)	$1,680.00	$1,400.00	($280.00)
11	Status Meeting	$1,597.50	$0.00	$0.00	($1,597.50)	$0.00	$1,597.50	$1,597.50	$0.00
27	Pre-Production complete	$0.00	$0.00	$0.00	$0.00	$0.00	$0.00	$0.00	$0.00
28	Production	$22,249.50	$3,861.42	$7,208.07	($18,388.08)	($3,346.65)	$43,866.80	$23,499.50	($20,367.30)
29	Production begins	$0.00	$0.00	$0.00	$0.00	$0.00	$0.00	$0.00	$0.00
30	Scene 1	$5,331.50	$3,573.37	$6,874.94	($1,758.13)	($3,301.57)	$11,700.49	$6,081.50	($5,618.99)
31	Scene 1 begin	$0.00	$0.00	$0.00	$0.00	$0.00	$0.00	$0.00	$0.00
32	Scene 1 setup	$536.00	$536.00	$536.00	$0.00	$0.00	$536.00	$536.00	$0.00
33	Scene 1 rehearsal	$388.50	$388.50	$388.50	$0.00	$0.00	$888.50	$888.50	$0.00
34	Scene 1 vocal recording	$1,442.00	$1,442.00	$1,629.46	$0.00	($187.46)	$1,911.96	$1,692.00	($219.96)
35	Scene 1 video shoot	$2,717.00	$958.87	$4,072.98	($1,758.13)	($3,114.11)	$11,541.02	$2,717.00	($8,824.02)
36	Scene 1 teardown	$248.00	$248.00	$248.00	$0.00	$0.00	$248.00	$248.00	$0.00
37	Scene 1 complete	$0.00	$0.00	$0.00	$0.00	$0.00	$0.00	$0.00	$0.00
38	Scene 2	$6,523.00	$288.04	$333.13	($6,234.96)	($45.08)	$8,122.27	$7,023.00	($1,099.27)
39	Scene 2 begin	$0.00	$0.00	$0.00	$0.00	$0.00	$0.00	$0.00	$0.00
40	Scene 2 setup	$1,066.00	$288.04	$333.13	($777.96)	($45.08)	$1,232.85	$1,066.00	($166.85)
41	Scene 2 rehearsal	$324.00	$0.00	$0.00	($324.00)	$0.00	$1,256.00	$824.00	($432.00)
42	Scene 2 vocal recording	$1,440.00	$0.00	$0.00	($1,440.00)	$0.00	$4,320.00	$1,440.00	($2,880.00)
43	Scene 2 video shoot	$3,445.00	$0.00	$0.00	($3,445.00)	$0.00	$3,445.00	$3,445.00	$0.00
44	Scene 2 teardown	$248.00	$0.00	$0.00	($248.00)	$0.00	$248.00	$248.00	$0.00
45	Scene 2 complete	$0.00	$0.00	$0.00	$0.00	$0.00	$0.00	$0.00	$0.00

Here you can see most of the earned value numbers detailed at the beginning of this lesson in the Software Orientation section.

 TAKE NOTE *

To see more information about any field, point to the column heading, and read the ToolTip that appears. Press the **F1** key for additional information.

6. Right-click the name of the Planned Value–PV column and select Insert Column.

7. Key **SPI** and [press **Enter**]. Microsoft Project displays the SPI column in the Earned Value table.

8. Right-click the name of the SPI column and select Insert Column.

9. Key **CPI** and [press **Enter**]. Microsoft Project displays the CPI column in the Earned Value table.

10. Auto fit the two columns you just added to the table. Your screen should look similar to Figure 11-10.

Figure 11-10

Earned Value table in the Task Sheet view with CPI and SPI columns added

	Task Name	CPI	SPI	Planned Value - PV (BCWS)	Earned Value - EV (BCWP)	AC (ACWP)	SV	CV	EAC	BAC	VAC
0	◢ **Don Funk Music Video**	0.89	0.55	$45,701.14	$25,183.56	$28,282.05	($20,517.58)	($3,098.49)	$66,991.10	$59,651.64	($7,339.46)
1	◢ **Pre-Production**	1.01	1.12	$18,999.64	$21,322.14	$21,073.98	$2,322.50	$248.16	$18,778.50	$18,999.64	$221.14
2	Pre-Production complete	0	0	$0.00	$0.00	$0.00	$0.00	$0.00	$0.00	$0.00	$0.00
3	Review screenplay	1	1	$4,590.00	$4,590.00	$4,590.00	$0.00	$0.00	$4,590.00	$4,590.00	$0.00
4	Develop scene blocking and schedule	1.02	1	$1,560.00	$1,560.00	$1,525.06	$0.00	$34.94	$1,525.06	$1,560.00	$34.94
5	Develop production layouts	1	1	$4,640.00	$4,640.00	$4,640.00	$0.00	$0.00	$4,640.00	$4,640.00	$0.00
6	Identify and reserve locations	1.11	1	$6,612.14	$6,612.14	$5,950.93	$0.00	$661.21	$5,950.93	$6,612.14	$661.21
7	Book musicians	1	1	$560.00	$560.00	$560.00	$0.00	$0.00	$560.00	$560.00	$0.00
8	Book dancers	0.77	1	$560.00	$560.00	$728.00	$0.00	($168.00)	$728.00	$560.00	($168.00)
9	Reserve audio recording equipment	1	1	$1,400.00	$1,400.00	$1,400.00	$0.00	$0.00	$1,400.00	$1,400.00	$0.00
10	Reserve video recording equipment	0.83	1	$1,400.00	$1,400.00	$1,680.00	$0.00	($280.00)	$1,680.00	$1,400.00	($280.00)
11	▷ **Status Meeting**	0	0	$1,597.50	$0.00	$0.00	($1,597.50)	$0.00	$1,597.50	$1,597.50	$0.00
27	Pre-Production complete	0	0	$0.00	$0.00	$0.00	$0.00	$0.00	$0.00	$0.00	$0.00
28	◢ **Production**	0.54	0.17	$22,249.50	$3,861.42	$7,208.07	($18,388.08)	($3,346.65)	$43,866.80	$23,499.50	($20,367.30)
29	Production begins	0	0	$0.00	$0.00	$0.00	$0.00	$0.00	$0.00	$0.00	$0.00
30	◢ **Scene 1**	0.52	0.67	$5,331.50	$3,573.37	$6,874.94	($1,758.13)	($3,301.57)	$11,700.49	$6,081.50	($5,618.99)
31	Scene 1 begin	0	0	$0.00	$0.00	$0.00	$0.00	$0.00	$0.00	$0.00	$0.00
32	Scene 1 setup	1	1	$536.00	$536.00	$536.00	$0.00	$0.00	$536.00	$536.00	$0.00
33	Scene 1 rehearsal	1	1	$388.50	$388.50	$388.50	$0.00	$0.00	$888.50	$888.50	$0.00
34	Scene 1 vocal recording	0.88	1	$1,442.00	$1,442.00	$1,629.46	$0.00	($187.46)	$1,911.96	$1,692.00	($219.96)
35	Scene 1 video shoot	0.24	0.35	$2,717.00	$958.87	$4,072.98	($1,758.13)	($3,114.11)	$11,541.02	$2,717.00	($8,824.02)
36	Scene 1 teardown	1	1	$248.00	$248.00	$248.00	$0.00	$0.00	$248.00	$248.00	$0.00
37	Scene 1 complete	0	0	$0.00	$0.00	$0.00	$0.00	$0.00	$0.00	$0.00	$0.00
38	◢ **Scene 2**	0.86	0.04	$6,523.00	$288.04	$333.13	($6,234.96)	($45.08)	$8,122.27	$7,023.00	($1,099.27)
39	Scene 2 begin	0	0	$0.00	$0.00	$0.00	$0.00	$0.00	$0.00	$0.00	$0.00
40	Scene 2 setup	0.86	0.27	$1,066.00	$288.04	$333.13	($777.96)	($45.08)	$1,232.85	$1,066.00	($166.85)
41	Scene 2 rehearsal	0	0	$324.00	$0.00	$0.00	($324.00)	$0.00	$1,256.00	$824.00	($432.00)
42	Scene 2 vocal recording	0	0	$1,440.00	$0.00	$0.00	($1,440.00)	$0.00	$4,320.00	$1,440.00	($2,880.00)
43	Scene 2 video shoot	0	0	$3,445.00	$0.00	$0.00	($3,445.00)	$0.00	$3,445.00	$3,445.00	$0.00
44	Scene 2 teardown	0	0	$248.00	$0.00	$0.00	($248.00)	$0.00	$248.00	$248.00	$0.00
45	Scene 2 complete	0	0	$0.00	$0.00	$0.00	$0.00	$0.00	$0.00	$0.00	$0.00

11. SAVE the project schedule.

PAUSE. LEAVE Project and your project schedule open so that you can refer to it as you are reading the exercise discussion later in the text.

In this exercise, you set the project status date, displayed the Earned Value table and added the Cost Performance Index (CPI) and the Schedule Performance Index (SPI) columns. The status date is the date you want Microsoft Project to use when calculating the earned value numbers.

Looking at task and resource variance throughout a project's duration is a key project management activity. Unfortunately, it does not give you the true picture of a project's long-term health. For example, a task might be over budget and ahead of schedule (possibly not good) or over budget and behind schedule (definitely not good). Looking at schedule and budget variance by themselves does not tell you very much about performance trends that may continue throughout the project.

Instead, earned value analysis gives you a more complete picture of overall project performance in relation to both time and cost. Earned value analysis is used to measure the project's progress and help forecast its outcome. It focuses on schedule and budget performance in relation to baseline plans. The key difference between earned value analysis and simpler budget/schedule analysis can be thought of in this way:

- "What are the current performance results we are getting?" is the question answered by simple variance analysis.
- "Are we getting our money's worth for the current performance results we are getting?" is the question answered by earned value analysis.

Although the difference is subtle, it is important. Earned value analysis allows you to look at project performance in a more detailed way. It allows you to identify two important things: the true cost of project results to date, and the performance trend that is likely to continue for the rest of the project.

Review the project schedule and steps you performed in this exercise. In order for Microsoft Project to calculate the earned value amounts for a project schedule, you must first do the following:

- Save a baseline so that Microsoft Project can calculate the budgeted cost of the work scheduled before you start tracing actual work. (The baseline was already saved when you opened the file for this lesson.)
- Record actual work on tasks or assignments. (You did this in previous exercises in this lesson.)
- Set the status date so that Microsoft Project can calculate actual project performance up to a certain point in time. If you do not specify a status date, Microsoft Project uses the current date.

Earned value analysis uses the following three key values to generate all other schedule indicator and cost indicator values:

- The planned value (PV) or budgeted cost of work scheduled (BCWS). This is the value of the work scheduled to be completed as of the status date. Microsoft Project calculates this value by adding up all the time-phased baseline values for tasks up to the status date.
- The actual cost (AC) or actual cost of work performed (ACWP) is the actual cost incurred to complete each task's actual work up to the status date.
- The earned value (EV) or budgeted cost of work performed (BCWP). This is the portion of the budgeted cost that should have been spent to complete each task's actual work performed up to the status date. This value is called earned value because it is literally the value earned by the work performed.

The earned value schedule and the cost variances are directly related. The earned value cost indicator fields are in one table. The earned value schedule indicators are in another table. A third table combines the key fields of both schedule and cost indicators.

Using the above key values, Microsoft Project can also calculate some other important indicators of project performance:

- The project's cost variance, or CV, is the difference between the earned value and the actual cost.
- The project's schedule variance, or SV, is the difference between the earned value and the planned value.

It might seem strange to think of being ahead of or behind schedule in terms of dollars. However, keep in mind that dollars buy work, and work drives tasks to be completed. You will find that viewing both cost and schedule variance in the same unit of measure makes it easier to compare the two, as well as other earned value numbers that are also measured in dollars.

Finally, there are two other earned value numbers that are very helpful indicators:

- The Cost Performance Index, or CPI, is the ratio of earned value to actual cost, or EV (BCWP) divided by AC (ACWP).
- The Schedule Performance Index, or SPI, is the ratio of earned value to planned value, or EV (BCWP) divided by PV (BCWS).

The CPI and SPI allow you to evaluate a project's performance and compare the performance of multiple projects in a consistent way. In the Don Funk Music Video, the CPI and SPI provide information about each task and phase in the project and about the project as a whole:

- The CPI for the Don Funk Music Video project (as of the status date) is .97. You can interpret this as every dollar's worth of work that has been paid for, 97 cents worth of work was actually accomplished.
- The SPI for the Don Funk Music Video project (as of the status date) is .98. This can be interpreted that for every dollar's worth of work that was planned to be accomplished, 98 cents worth of work was actually accomplished. You can also look at this as schedule efficiency, that is, you are progressing at 98% of your planned schedule.

Although the SPI and CPI are slightly different for the Don Funk Music Video project, keep in mind that these ratios can change as work is completed and other factors change.

Earned value analysis is one of the more complicated things you can do in Microsoft Project, but it provides very valuable project status information. This illustrates why it is a good idea to enter task and resource cost information into a project schedule any time you have it.

SKILL SUMMARY

In this lesson you learned:	Matrix Skill
To record actual start, finish, and duration values of tasks	Enter actual start date and duration for a task
To adjust remaining work of tasks	Adjust actual and remaining work for a task
To evaluate performance with earned value analysis	Set project status date and display the Earned Value table

■ Knowledge Assessment

Fill in the Blank

Complete the following sentences by writing the correct word or words in the blanks provided.

1. The _____ and _____ are measurements you can make and compare project-to-project cost and schedule performance.

2. One way of interpreting SPI is schedule _____.

3. _____ is the difference between the budgeted cost of work performed and the budgeted cost of work scheduled (SV).

4. The ratio of performed to scheduled work is the _____.

5. _____ is used to measure the project's progress by giving a more complete picture of overall project performance in relation to both time and cost.

6. You specify the _____ that you want Microsoft Project to use when calculating the earned value numbers.

7. The _____ is the actual cost incurred to complete each task's actual work up to the status date.

8. The difference between the budgeted and actual cost of work performed is the _____.

9. The ratio of budgeted to actual cost is the _____.

10. When you adjust the remaining work on a task, Microsoft Project _____ distributes the work.

Multiple Choice

Select the best response for the following statements.

1. The term that means the same as earned value (EV) is
    a. actual cost of work performed (ACWP).
    b. budgeted cost of work performed (BCWP).
    c. cost performance index (CPI).
    d. budgeted cost of work scheduled (BCWS).

2. Only a(n) _____ can have a remaining work or duration value.
    a. delayed task
    b. incomplete task
    c. complete task
    d. overbudget task

3. When you enter an actual duration of a task that is longer than the planned duration, Microsoft Project assumes which of the following?
    a. the task start date has changed
    b. the project is near done
    c. entering a larger number does nothing except update the duration
    d. the task is complete

4. The value of the work scheduled to be completed as of the status date is the
    a. SPI.
    b. EV.
    c. PV.
    d. CPI.

5. Which dialog box is used to record actual work done on a task?
    a. Update Tasks
    b. Project Information
    c. Task Drivers
    d. Task Information

6. By default, whenever you enter actual work values, Microsoft Project
    a. calculates actual cost values.
    b. determines estimated cost values.
    c. predicts the final project end date.
    d. all of the above.

7. The term that means the same as budgeted cost of work scheduled (BCWS) is
   a. planned value (PV).
   b. cost variance (CV).
   c. schedule variance (SV).
   d. earned value (EV).

8. Which of the following is NOT a rule used by Microsoft Project when updating the project schedule based on actual start, finish, or duration values you have entered?
   a. When you enter a task's actual start date, Microsoft Project calculates the scheduled finish date to match the actual start date and the task's planned duration.
   b. When you enter a task's actual duration that is equal to the scheduled duration, Microsoft Project sets the task to 100% complete.
   c. When you enter a task's actual finish date, Microsoft Project moves the scheduled finish date to match the actual finish date and assigns a completion percentage of 100%.
   d. When you enter an actual duration for a task that is longer than the scheduled duration, Microsoft Project subtracts the actual duration from the scheduled duration to determine the remaining duration.

9. Which of the following is NOT something that must be done in order for Microsoft Project to calculate earned value amounts for a project schedule?
   a. save a baseline plan
   b. finish at least 50% of the project schedule
   c. record actual work on tasks or assignments
   d. set a status date (or allow the default of the current date)

10. The portion of the budgeted cost that should have been spent to complete each task's actual work performed up to the status date is the
    a. CPI.
    b. PV.
    c. EV.
    d. SPI.

■ Competency Assessment

Project 11-1: Recording Actuals for Office Lunchroom Remodel

Work has finally started on the lunchroom remodel at your office. You need to update some of the task information to reflect actuals that have been provided to you: task 10 started one day early but took the scheduled amount of time, and task 11 started on time but took one day longer to complete.

GET READY. Launch Microsoft Project if it is not already running.

OPEN *Office Remodel 11-1* from the data files for this lesson.

1. Click the name of Task 10, **Re-run electrical in all stud walls.**
2. On the Task ribbon, click the **down-arrow** next to the Mark On Track button, then select **Update Tasks**.
3. Under the Actual label, in the Start box, type or select **10/26/15**.
4. In the Actual dur box, type or select **2d**, and then click **OK**.
5. Select the name of Task 11, **Re-run plumbing for sink and icemaker.**
6. Click the **down-arrow** next to the Mark On Track button, then select **Update Tasks**.
7. In the Actual dur box, type or select **3d**, and then click **OK**.

8. Select tasks 10 and 11. Click the 100% Complete button in the schedule group.
9. SAVE the project schedule as *Office Remodel Actuals*, and then close the file.
   PAUSE. LEAVE Project open to use in the next exercise.

Project 11-2: Adjust Work and Duration of HR Interview Schedule

The HR Interview project is nearly half complete. You now need to adjust the remaining work and duration of some of the tasks.

 OPEN *HR Interview Schedule 11-2* from the data files for this lesson.

1. On the View tab, click the Tables button, then select the Tracking table.
2. Select the Remaining duration cell for Task 11, Prepare interview questions.
3. Type 2.5d in the cell and [press Enter].
4. Type 100 in the % Comp. column.
5. On the ribbon, switch to the Task Usage view and display the Work table.
6. Click the name of Task 12, Conduct Interview(s), and then click the Scroll to Task button on the Task ribbon.
7. On the ribbon, mark this task as 100% complete.
8. Select the Remaining cell for Task 12, type 24 and [press Enter].
9. SAVE the project schedule as *HR Interview Adjusted*, and then CLOSE the file.
   PAUSE. LEAVE Project open to use in the next exercise.

■ Proficiency Assessment

Project 11-3: Adjust Remaining Work for the Office Lunchroom Remodel

You are about to begin the night work on the drywall installation portion of your office lunchroom remodel. You are told by the crew installing the drywall they can complete this in three days. This is great news since the deadline of completing the ceiling tile is in jeopardy.

 OPEN *Office Remodel 11-3* from the data files for this lesson.

1. Notice that on Task 14, there is a missed deadline icon in the indicators column.
2. On the View ribbon, select the Task Usage View.
3. Use the Tables button to display the Work table.
4. Select Task 12 and adjust the remaining work hours to 48.
5. [Press the F9 key] to manually recalculate the project.
6. Return to the Gantt Chart view; note the duration of Task 12 is now three days and the missing deadline icon indicator is now gone from Task 14.
7. Depending on the options selected at the time Microsoft Project 2013 was installed, you may have to press F9 to recalculate the schedule.
8. SAVE the project schedule as *Office Remodel Drywall Adjusted* and then CLOSE the file.
   PAUSE. LEAVE Project open to use in the next exercise.

Project 11-4: Don Funk Music Video Earned Value Analysis

More time has passed since you performed your previous earned value analysis on the Don Funk Music Video project, and additional tasks have been completed. You need to set a new status date and display the Earned Value Table.

 OPEN *Don Funk Music Video 11-4* from the data files for this lesson.

1. On the Project tab, set a status date of 5/30/16.
2. Change the view to the Task Sheet view.
3. Apply the Earned Value table from the More Tables dialog box.
4. Insert the SPI and CPI columns to the left of the Planned Value-PV column.
5. Auto fit all the columns.
6. Click the name of Task 63 and scroll your task list so that Task 63 is visible in the middle of your screen.
7. SAVE the project schedule as *Don Funk Earned Value* and then CLOSE the file.

   PAUSE. LEAVE Project open to use in the next exercise.

■ Mastery Assessment

Project 11-5: Rescheduled Work on Insurance Claim Process

On your Insurance Claim Process project, you have just been informed that there will be a delay in making repairs. Work has started but cannot continue because a part is backordered and will not arrive at the body shop until June 23, 2016.

 OPEN *Insurance Claim Process 11-5* from the data files for this lesson.

1. Update Task 18 to show that work is 50% complete.
2. Reschedule remaining work to start after 6/23/16.
3. SAVE the file as *Insurance Claim Process Reschedule*, and then CLOSE the file.

   PAUSE. LEAVE Project open to use in the next exercise.

Project 11-6: Adjusting Remaining Work and Duration on Don Funk Music Video Tasks

You now have more actuals to enter into the Don Funk Music Video project schedule. Update the work (as provided below) in the Work table of the Task Usage view.

 OPEN *Don Funk Music Video 11-6* from the data files for this lesson.

1. Mark Task 47 as complete.
2. For Task 48, Scene 3 setup, 34 hours of actual work have been completed and 0 hours of work are remaining.
3. For Task 49, Scene 3 rehearsal, 12 hours of actual work have been completed and 8 hours of work are remaining.
4. SAVE the project schedule as *Don Funk Adjusted*, and then CLOSE the file.

   CLOSE Project.

12 LESSON

Integrating Microsoft Project with Other Programs

LESSON SKILL MATRIX

SKILLS	TASKS
Using a GIF Image to Display Project Information	Using a GIF image to display project information
Using the Timeline View to Display Project Information	Using the timeline view to display project information
Saving Project Information in Other File Formats	Saving project information in other file formats

As a project manager for Southridge Video, communicating project information is a critical part of your role. You know that although printing project information is a common way to share details with shareholders, it has some limitations. Sometimes, project details are out of date by the time you print them. In addition, you must spend the time and financial resources to copy and distribute your information. On the other hand, publishing information online allows you provide updates in "real time" and more easily share details with a large audience of online viewers. In this lesson, you will learn various ways of getting information in and out of Microsoft Office Project by importing and exporting data between Microsoft Project and other applications.

KEY TERMS
Copy Picture
data map
export map
GIF
import map
OLE
Timeline view

© nyul/iStockphoto

■ **SOFTWARE ORIENTATION**

Microsoft Project's Copy Picture Dialog Box

The Copy Picture feature enables you to copy images and create snapshots of a view.

Figure 12-1

Copy Picture dialog box

Render the image for screen, printer or GIF file

Specifies the location of the GIF image file

Copy the image as shown on screen or for a specific date range

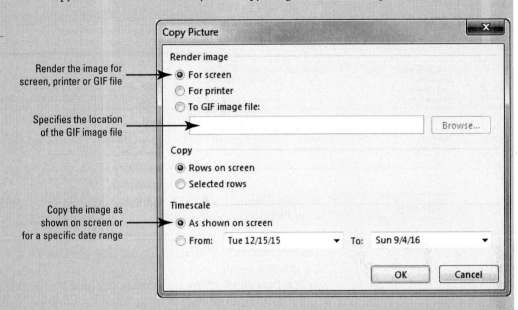

In the Copy Picture dialog box, you can render the image for screen, printer, or to a GIF file. You can also copy the entire view visible on the screen or just selected rows of a table, as well as a specified range of time.

■ Using a GIF Image to Display Project Information

THE BOTTOM LINE

It is often useful to copy project information from Microsoft Project into other programs and formats in order to communicate project details to stakeholders.

USE A GIF IMAGE TO DISPLAY PROJECT INFORMATION

GET READY. Before you begin these steps, launch Microsoft Project.

1. OPEN the **Don Funk Music Video 12M** project schedule from the data files for this lesson.
2. SAVE the file as **Don Funk Music Video 12** in the solutions folder for this lesson as directed by your instructor.
3. On the ribbon, click the View tab. Point to the Filter selection box, click the **down-arrow** and then select Summary Tasks. Microsoft Project filters the Gantt Chart to show only summary tasks.

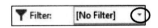

4. On the ribbon, in the Zoom group, click Entire Project. Your screen should look similar to Figure 12-2.

Entire Project

Figure 12-2

Gantt Chart view filtered for
summary tasks and entire
project duration visible

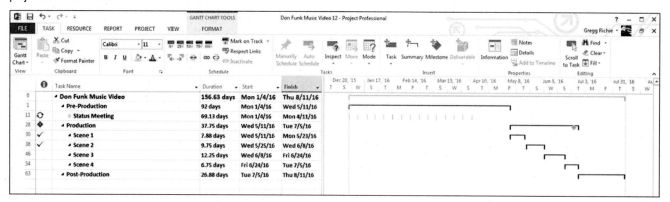

5. Click the **Task** tab, and then click the **down-arrow** next to the **Copy** button. Select the
Copy Picture button. The Copy Picture dialog box appears.

6. In the Copy Picture dialog box, under the *Render image* label, click **To GIF image file**.
The Microsoft Project default suggests that you save the file in the same location as
the practice file and with the same name, except with a GIF extension. (Save your file
as ***Don Funk Music Video 12 Image*** in the location specified by your instructor.) Your
screen should look similar to Figure 12-3.

Figure 12-3

Copy Picture dialog box with
file name for the image

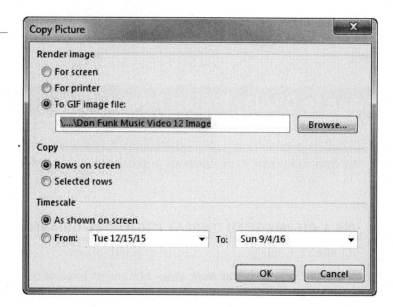

7. Click **OK** to close the Copy Picture dialog box. The GIF image is saved.

> **TAKE NOTE***
>
> When you take a snapshot of a view, the Copy Picture dialog box enables you to select how
> you want to render the image. The first two options, for screen and for printer, copy the
> image to the Windows clipboard. The To GIF image file option enables you to save the
> image as a GIF file.

8. Open Microsoft Word and begin with a blank document. Click the **Insert** tab and then
select **Picture(s)**.

9. Locate the GIF image named ***Don Funk Music Video 12 Image*** in the location where your instructor directed you to save it earlier. Select the GIF image, and then click Insert. Your screen should look similar to Figure 12-4.

Figure 12-4

Blank Word document with the GIF image inserted

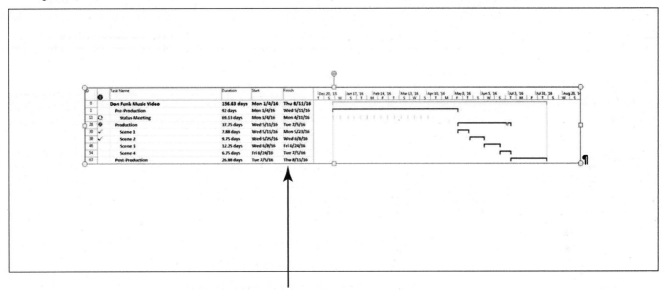

Gantt Chart view saved as a GIF file, which can be viewed in a
graphics program or inserted into another document as a picture

TROUBLESHOOTING   The Copy Picture feature is unavailable when a form view, such as the Task Form or Relationship Diagram view, is displayed.

10. CLOSE the program you used to display the GIF file without saving the changes. If the view does not automatically return to Microsoft Project, select **Don Funk Music Video 12** from the Project button at the bottom of your screen.

TAKE NOTE*   In addition to saving GIF images of views in Microsoft Project, you can also save Microsoft Project data as an XML file for publishing to the Web or to an intranet site.

11. SAVE the project schedule.

PAUSE. LEAVE Project open to use in the next exercise.

In this exercise, you made a copy of a view in Microsoft Project to display in another program. As you learned in previous lessons, communicating project details to resources, managers, and other stakeholders is a very important part of being a successful project manager. Making a copy of parts of your project to share with stakeholders is one way to effectively communicate your progress.

Microsoft Project supports the standard copy and paste functionality of most Microsoft Windows programs. As you saw in this exercise, it also has an additional feature, called ***Copy Picture,*** which enables you to take a snapshot of a view. With Copy Picture, you have several options when taking snapshots of the active view:

- You can copy the entire view that is visible on the screen, or just selected rows of a table in a view.

- You can copy a range of time that you specify or show on the screen.

With either of these options, you can copy onto the Windows Clipboard an image that is optimized for pasting into another program for onscreen viewing (such as in Microsoft PowerPoint) or for printing (such as Microsoft Word). As you did in this exercise, you can also save the image to a Graphics Interchange Format (*GIF*) file. Once you save the image to a GIF file, you can then use it in any program that supports the GIF format. You can also use it with HTML content on a Web page.

■ Using the Timeline View to Display Project Information

THE BOTTOM LINE

There are times when you may need to present high-level information from a project schedule in order to communicate an overview to stakeholders. While there are several methods and options available to transfer text and graphic images, Microsoft Project's new feature called the *Timeline View* can present high-level information clearly.

 USE THE TIMELINE VIEW TO DISPLAY PROJECT INFORMATION

USE the project schedule you created in the previous exercise.

Figure 12-5

Gantt Chart view with Timeline view above

1. Click the **View** tab. In the **Split View** group, select the **check box** next to Timeline. The Timeline view appears above the Gantt Chart view. Your screen should look like Figure 12-5.

The Timeline View appears above the Gantt Chart

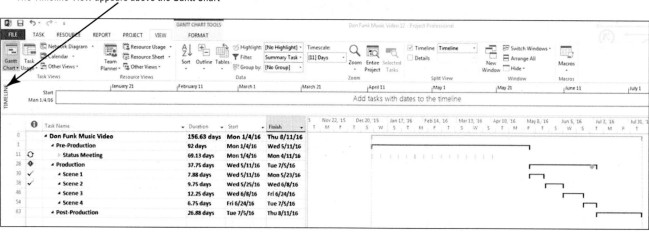

2. Select all **visible summary tasks**. Place your cursor on the selected cells and right-click. From the menu, select **Add to Timeline**. Note that the Status meetings were not added to the timeline.

3. You will be formatting the Timeline view area. Use your mouse to expand the timeline area in a similar way you move the vertical divider bar between the Gantt Chart and the table area. Your screen should look like Figure 12-6.

Figure 12-6

Expanded Timeline view area

As tasks are added to the timeline, they can be formatted to display under their respective summary tasks

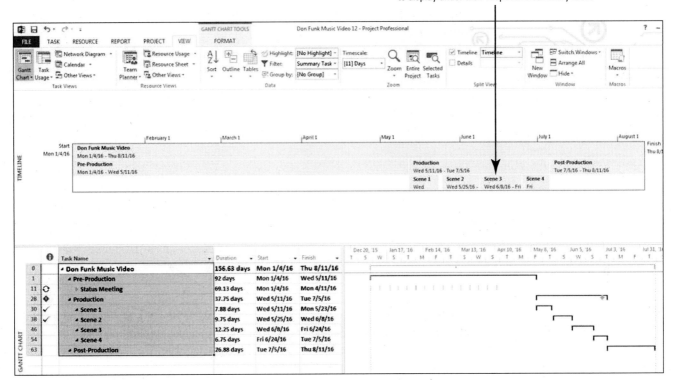

ANOTHER WAY   You can use the Existing Tasks button to add or remove tasks from the timeline.

4. Click in the Timeline view area to activate that window. Click the **Format** tab under the **Timeline Tools** tab.

5. Note that the dates listed for each of the Scene Summary tasks are not completely visible. On the ribbon, in the Show/Hide group, click the down-arrow for the **Text Lines:** box and select **2**.

6. On the ribbon, select the **Date Format** button. From the list, select the option that displays date in Month/Day format. Your screen should look like Figure 12-7.

Figure 12-7

Timeline view with reformatted dates

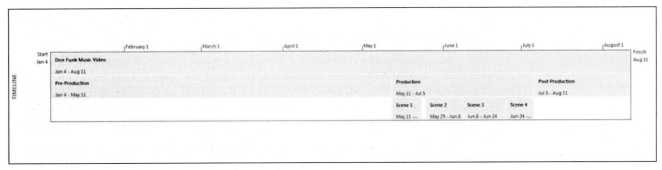

Display
as Callout

7. Depending on your screen resolution, Scenes 1 and 4 may still not show the starting and ending dates. On the Timeline, click the Scene 1 box. Then on the ribbon, in the Current Selection group, click Display as Callout.

8. Repeat step 7 for Scene 4. By default, Microsoft Project displays the tasks above the Timeline. Notice now the dates are visible.

9. Place your cursor on the Scene 1 task box above the Timeline and then drag it to below the timeline.

10. Repeat step 9 for Scene 4. Your screen should look similar to Figure 12-8.

Figure 12-8

Timeline view with Scenes
1 and 4 displayed as callouts

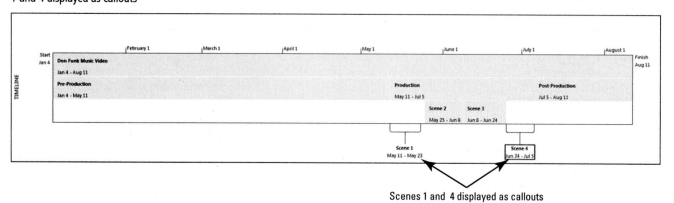

Scenes 1 and 4 displayed as callouts

Copy
Timeline▾

11. Now that you have the timeline formatted and displaying the information you want, you will copy it for presentation. On the ribbon, select the Copy Timeline button. From the list, select For Presentation.

12. Open Microsoft PowerPoint. Start with a new blank presentation. Right-click the first slide and select Layout. From the list, select Blank.

13. Insert the timeline view you just copied by [pressing Ctrl+V] or clicking the Paste button on the Home ribbon.

TAKE NOTE* You can also paste the image into an e-mail message or a variety of other types of documents.

14. CLOSE the PowerPoint document without saving the changes.

15. In Microsoft Project, click the View tab. On the ribbon, clear the check box for the Timeline view. Microsoft removes the split window with the Timeline area.

16. [Press the F3 key] to clear the Summary Tasks filter.

17. SAVE the project schedule.

PAUSE. LEAVE Project open to use in the next exercise.

In this exercise, you made a snapshot of a Timeline view and pasted the image into a blank PowerPoint presentation that you are preparing for Don Funk's agent. In general, you can copy and paste data to and from Microsoft Project using the various copy and paste commands in Microsoft Project (Copy, Copy Picture, Copy Cell, Paste, Paste Special, etc.). When you *copy data from* Microsoft Project, you can choose one of two options to achieve your desired results:

• You can copy text (such as task names or dates) from a table and paste it as text into the destination program. Using a Copy command enables you to edit data in the destination program.

- You can copy a graphic image of a view from Microsoft Project and paste it as a graphic image in the destination program (as you did in this exercise). You can create a graphic image of a view or part of a view using the Copy Picture command. Using the Copy Picture command results in an image that can only be edited with a graphics editing program (such as Microsoft Paint).

When you *paste data into* Microsoft Project from other programs, you also have two options to achieve your desired results:

- You can paste text (such as a task list) into a table in Microsoft Project. For example, you could paste a series of resource names that are organized in a vertical column from Microsoft Excel to the Resource Name column in Microsoft Project.
- You can paste a graphic image or an OLE object from another program into a graphical portion of a Gantt Chart view; to a task, resource, or assignment note; to a form view, such as the Task form view; or even to the header, footer, or legend of a view or report.

OLE is a protocol that allows you to transfer information, such as a chart or text (as an OLE object), to documents in different programs.

Be careful when pasting text as multiple columns. First, make sure that the order of the information in the source program matches the order of columns in the Microsoft Project table. (You can rearrange the order of the columns in the source program to match the order of the columns in Microsoft Project or vice versa.) Second, make sure that the columns in the source program support the same type of data as do the columns in Microsoft Project (text, currency, numbers, etc.).

Cross Ref

For more information about printing views and reports, go back to Lesson 9.

■ Saving Project Information In Other File Formats

THE BOTTOM LINE

You can import/export information from your project schedule from/to sources outside Microsoft Project. You can import/export in XML format, as a Microsoft Database file, or import/export directly from/to Excel. By using import/export maps to specify how the data will be used, Microsoft Project prepares the data for either importing or exporting.

 SAVE PROJECT INFORMATION IN OTHER FILE FORMATS

USE the project schedule you created in the previous exercise.

You have been asked to provide project cost information to the accounting department, which does not have or use Microsoft Project. You need to provide task level details on planned cost and actual costs for your project in Microsoft Excel format.

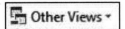

1. On the View ribbon, in the Task Views group, click the Other Views button, and then click More Views. The More Views dialog box appears.
2. In the dialog box, locate and select the Task Sheet view. Click the Apply button.
3. Click the Tables button and select the Cost table.

4. Click the File tab and select Save as. (Save your file in the location specified by your instructor.)
5. Click the down-arrow next to the Save as type: box and select Excel Workbook.

6. In the Filename: box, key **Music Video Task Costs**. Then click the **Save** button. The Export Wizard appears.

7. Click the **Next** button. The Export Wizard – Data page appears. Ensure **Selected Data** is selected.

8. Click the **Next** button. The Export Wizard – Map page appears. The Export Wizard uses maps to organize the way that data is structured when exporting from Microsoft Project.

9. Make sure that **New Map** is selected, and then click the **Next** button. The Export Wizard – Map Options page appears.

10. Select the **Tasks** check box. Make sure that the **Export includes headers** check box is also selected. (Headers means column headings, in this case.)

11. Click the **Next** button. The Export Wizard – Task Mapping page appears. This is where you select the table that will be used for the export and specify how you want to map the data from the source worksheet to the fields in Microsoft Project.

12. In the dialog box, select the **Base on Table** button. Microsoft Project displays a list of tables in the project file. Select the **Cost** table and click **OK**. Microsoft Project uses the column (field) names from the cost table, and then suggests the Microsoft Excel header row names in the preview area. Review the fields on this screen. Your screen should look similar to Figure 12-9.

Figure 12-9

Export Wizard – Task Mapping dialog showing preview of Excel data

Worksheet where information will be exported →

Mapping options to specify any specific field names →

Preview of how the information will be displayed in the Excel worksheet →

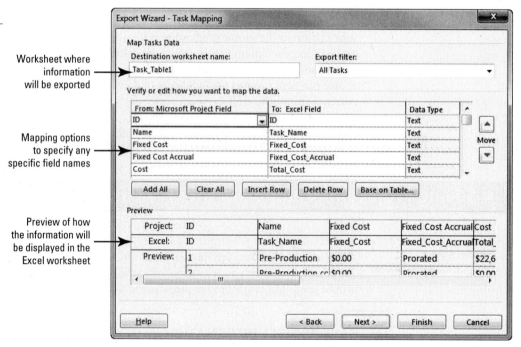

13. Click the **Next** button. The Import Wizard – End of Map Definition page appears. On this screen, you have the opportunity to save the settings for the new import map, if you desire. This is useful when you anticipate importing similar data into Microsoft Project in the future. For now, you will skip this step. Click the **Finish** button.

14. Locate the Excel Workbook file named **Music Video Task Costs** in the location where your instructor directed you to save it earlier, and open it.

15. In Microsoft Excel, auto fit the columns to display all the data. Note that the formatting is not in currency. Actually the numbers are stored as text. Using the features of Excel, convert columns C and E through I, currently stored as text, to a number. Then format the columns of Fixed Costs, Total Costs, Baseline, Variance, Actual and Remaining to the currency format. Format the column headers by changing them to a bold font. Your screen should look similar to Figure 12-10.

Figure 12-10

Excel spreadsheet after formatting the cost-related columns to currency

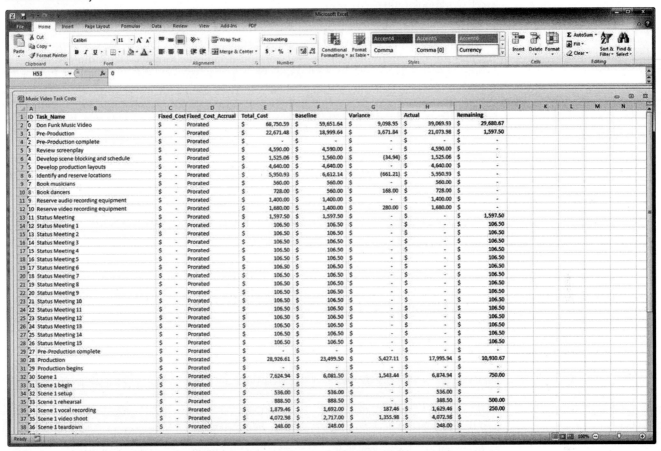

16. SAVE the Excel file in the solutions folder as directed by your instructor. CLOSE the Excel file.

17. SAVE the **Don Funk Music Video 12** project schedule, and then CLOSE this file.

    PAUSE. If you are continuing to the next lesson, keep Project open. If you are not continuing to additional lessons, CLOSE Project.

In this exercise, you saved information from the cost table in Microsoft Project into an Excel workbook and then set up an export map to control how the data is exported to Microsoft Excel. As you gain experience as a project manager, you may need to export data from a Microsoft Project schedule to a variety of sources. As you saw in this exercise, you exported an existing table to a spreadsheet. Microsoft Project uses export maps when saving data to other file formats. An *export map* specifies the exact data to export and how to structure it.

You could also import information such as resource costs from a database or a resource list from a document. Microsoft Project uses import maps when opening data from another file format in Microsoft Project. The *import map* specifies the exact data to import and how to structure it. In fact, the same maps are used for both opening and saving data, so they are often referred to as import/export maps, or *data maps*. Data maps allow you to specify how you want individual fields in the source program's file to correspond to individual fields in the destination program. Once you set up an import/export map, you can use it over and over again.

TROUBLESHOOTING

If you are working independently (outside of this lesson) and are trying to import an Excel file, but you are unable to view saved Microsoft Excel files from the Microsoft Project Open dialog box, you may need to save your files as Microsoft Excel 97-2003 files rather than Excel Workbook (2007–2013) files.

When importing information from other file formats, Microsoft Project has a security setting that may prevent you from opening legacy or non-default file formats. Depending on the default settings in your version of Microsoft Project, you may see a Microsoft Office Project dialog box with the following message when you try to open a file:

"You are trying to open a file saved in an older file format. Your settings do not allow you to open files saved in older file formats. To change your settings, navigate to the 'Security' tab in the Options dialog box."

In order to change your settings, click the **File** tab, then select **Options**. In the Options dialog box, click the **Trust Center** option. In the Microsoft Project Trust Center section, click the **Trust Center Settings** button. Click the **Legacy Formats** option, then select **Prompt when loading files with legacy or non default file format.** and click **OK**. Click **OK** to close the Options dialog box.

TROUBLESHOOTING

When creating a Microsoft Project file from a SharePoint list, your organization must use SharePoint 2013 or SharePoint Server 2013 to utilize this functionality. Also, the list must be a Task List rather than a simple List.

SKILL SUMMARY

IN THIS LESSON YOU LEARNED:	MATRIX SKILL
To use a GIF image to display project information	Use a GIF image to display project information
To use the Timeline view to display project information	Use the Timeline view to display project information
To save project information in other file formats	Save project information in other file formats

■ Knowledge Assessment

Matching

Match the term in column 1 to its description in column 2.

Column 1	Column 2
1. Copy Picture	**a.** a set of specifications for moving specific data to Microsoft Project fields
2. import map	**b.** a set of step-by-step prompts that walks you through opening a different file format in Microsoft Project
3. OLE	**c.** a set of specifications for moving specific data from Microsoft Project fields

4. export map

d. a function used to copy portions of a table rather than copying a graphic image

5. GIF

e. a feature that allows you to copy images and create snapshots of a view

6. Import Wizard

f. a protocol that enables you to transfer information to documents in different programs

7. Copy

g. also known as an import/export map

8. Copy Cell

h. a file type that enables you to publish Microsoft Project data to the Web or an intranet site

9. data map

i. Graphics Interchange Format, a file format that enables you to save an image for use in other programs

10. XML

j. a function that allows you to copy data from Microsoft Project and edit it in the destination program

True/False

Circle T if the statement is true or F if the statement is false.

T F **1.** When saving a snapshot as a GIF file, the default location and name recommended by Microsoft Project for saving is the same name and location as the file being copied, except with a .gif extension.

T F **2.** When moving data from another program into Microsoft Project, Microsoft Project is referred to as the source program.

T F **3.** It is possible to import data from many different sources for use in Microsoft Project.

T F **4.** The Timeline view can be printed directly to a printer.

T F **5.** Microsoft Project uses a GIF map to specify the exact data to export and how to structure it.

T F **6.** When you create a data map, it can only be used once.

T F **7.** When you copy the Timeline view, Microsoft Project allows the timeline to be saved in its original size only.

T F **8.** When importing or exporting data, Microsoft Project is always the destination program.

T F **9.** You can use the Paste function in Microsoft Project to paste a graphic image from another program into the graphical portion of a Gantt Chart view.

T F **10.** When you use the Copy Picture function in Microsoft Project, you can specify the range of time that you want to copy.

■ Competency Assessment

Project 12-1: Displaying Project Information

Several stakeholders of the Don Funk Music Video have asked for an update on the status and schedule for Scenes 3 and 4 of the music video. You need to take a snapshot of the current state of the project for these scenes so that you can send it to them for review. You have decided that the best way to accomplish this is to build a filter, then copy a picture of the Gantt view.

GET READY. Launch Microsoft Project if it is not already running.

OPEN the **Don Funk Music Video 12-1** project schedule from the data files for this lesson.

1. Ensure the AutoFilter is turned on. You can confirm this by the visible triangles in the column heading area. If it is not turned on, click the View tab and then select the down-arrow next to the Filter box. Select Display AutoFilter.

2. Select the AutoFilter down-arrow in the Task Name column heading. Select Filters then select Custom.

3. In the Custom AutoFilter dialog box, in the first row of boxes, select contains, then type Scene 3.

4. Select the OR option button.

5. In the second row, select contains and then type Scene 4. Click OK.

6. Click the Task tab, then click the down-arrow to the right of the Copy button and select the Copy Picture button.

7. In the Copy Picture dialog box, under the Render image label, click To GIF image file. Name the file **Don Funk GIF**, using the folder hierarchy as directed by your instructor. Click OK.

8. Locate the **Don Funk GIF** file in the location that you saved. Select the image file-name, and then click Open.

9. View the image in your default program for viewing the GIF files.

10. CLOSE the program you used to display the GIF file.

11. SAVE the project schedule as **Don Funk GIF** and then CLOSE the file.

    PAUSE. LEAVE Project open to use in the next exercise.

Project 12-2: HR Interview Critical Task Letter

Your manager is traveling on business but has asked for an update on the critical tasks of the HR Interview Schedule. You need to copy an image from your Project schedule and paste it into a memo to send to your manager.

OPEN the **HR Interview Schedule 12-2** project schedule from the data files for this lesson. START Microsoft Word or WordPad, and then locate and OPEN the document named **Memo to Manager 12-2** from the data files for this lesson.

1. Make sure Microsoft Project is in the active view. On the ribbon, click the Format tab. In the Bar Styles group, select the check box for Critical Tasks.

2. On the ribbon, click the View tab and then click the Filter box. Select Critical.

3. In the Zoom group, click Entire Project.

4. Click the Task tab, then click Copy, then select the Copy Picture button.

5. Under the Render image label, select For screen, if necessary, and then click OK.

6. Switch the view to Microsoft Word or WordPad.

7. In Memo to Manager 12-2, highlight the phrase "INSERT IMAGE HERE"

8. PASTE the snapshot into Memo to Manager 12-2. If you are using WordPad, you may need resize the image (by dragging the handles on the image sides and/or corners) so that it will fit within the memo area.

9. SAVE the document as **Memo to Manager**. CLOSE the document.

10. SAVE the project schedule as **HR Interview Critical**, and then CLOSE the file.

    PAUSE. LEAVE Project open to use in the next exercise.

■ Proficiency Assessment

Project 12-3: Preparing an Actual Cost Report

You have been asked to prepare a schedule of costs for your project. You have worked with several co-workers in accounting to get a general idea of how detailed the information needs to be, and the accounting department has requested that this information be provided to them in Microsoft Excel. Now you need to export this information from Microsoft Project.

GET READY. Launch Microsoft Project if it is not already running.

OPEN the *Don Funk Music Video 12-3* project schedule from the data files for this lesson.

1. Activate the Task Sheet view and display the Cost table.
2. Hide the Fixed Cost and Fixed Cost Accrual columns and display the Project Summary Task.
3. Save the filename as *Don Funk Video Costs to Date.* Save the file as an Excel Workbook in the same location as the data files for this lesson.
4. Using the Export Wizard, select the following:

   Data: Selected Data

   Map: New map

   Map Options: Tasks, Export includes headers

   Task Mapping: Base the export on the Cost Table
5. Finish the Export Wizard. If you receive a Microsoft Office Project message regarding older file formats, click Yes.
6. Open Microsoft Excel and verify that the information was exported in the proper format. Format the Excel file as needed.
7. SAVE and CLOSE the Excel file.
8. SAVE the new project schedule as *Don Funk Actual Costs* and leave the file OPEN for the next exercise.

   PAUSE. LEAVE Project open to use in the next exercise.

Project 12-4: Internship Report

An intern who has been working with you on the Don Funk Music Video is writing a report to turn in to the Internship office at her university. She has asked if you could provide a snapshot of Scenes 1 and 2 of the project schedule to use as an illustration in her report.

USE the project schedule you created in the previous exercise.

1. Display the Gantt Chart view.
2. Use the AutoFilter to filter out everything but Scene 1 and Scene 2.
3. Zoom the view to show Scene 1 and Scene 2 tasks.
4. Click on the name of Task 30, Scene 1. Scroll the view so that Task 29 is the first task below the Task Name column heading. Scroll the bar chart to this task.
5. Click and drag your cursor to select Tasks 30 through 45.
6. Copy the picture using these options:

   For screen
   Selected rows
   As shown on screen
7. Switch your view to Microsoft Word or WordPad.
8. PASTE the image into the open blank document.
9. SAVE the document as *Don Funk Scene 1-2*, and then CLOSE Word or WordPad.

10. **SAVE** the updated project file as *Don Funk Filtered Scenes 1-2* then **CLOSE** the file.
    PAUSE. LEAVE Project open to use in the next exercise.

■ Mastery Assessment

Project 12-5: Building a Resource List

You are assembling a resource list for several upcoming projects at Southridge Video. Because there are several people who will use this resource list for different purposes, you want to build this list in an Excel file for ease of use by everyone.

GET READY. START Microsoft Excel and **OPEN** a new workbook, if necessary.

1. Enter the following data into the Microsoft Excel worksheet, using column names. You may use the column names provided, or substitute a column name that you think

Name	Initials	Rate
Mary Baker	MB	18.50/hr
Ryan Calafato	RC	20.00/hr
John Frum	JF	1000/wk
Arlene Huff	AH	2.5.00/hr
Linda Martin	LM	2000/wk
Merav Netz	MN	18.50/hr
John Peoples	JP	20.00/hr
Ivo Salmre	IS	1500/wk
Tony Wang	TW	19.00/hr

   more closely corresponds with the column names in Microsoft Project.
2. Name the worksheet *Resources* (on the tab at the lower left corner of the workbook).
3. **SAVE** the file as *General Resources List*. If you are using Excel 2013, set the file type as Microsoft Excel 97-2003 Workbook.
4. **CLOSE** the file, and then **CLOSE** Microsoft Excel.
   PAUSE. Continue to the next exercise.

Project 12-6: General Resource Project Schedule

Now that you have developed and distributed a general resource list, you would like to import it into Microsoft Project so that you can begin to use it on your own projects.

START Microsoft Project if it is not already running.
1. Locate and open the *General Resources List* Microsoft Excel workbook you created in the previous exercise.
2. Using the Import Wizard, create a new map, as a new project, to map resource information.
3. Map the data using the sheet named *Resources*, and then verify or edit the mapping that Microsoft Project suggests.
4. Finish the mapping without saving the map.
5. In the new project schedule that is generated, change the view to the Resource Sheet.
6. **SAVE** the project schedule as *Imported General Resources List*, and then **CLOSE** the file.
   CLOSE Project.

Project Schedule Optimization

LESSON SKILL MATRIX

SKILLS	TASKS
Making Time and Date Adjustments	Adjust fiscal year settings within Microsoft Project
Viewing the Project's Critical Path	View the project's critical path
Delaying the Start of Assignments	Delay the start of a resource assignment
Applying Contours to Assignments	Apply a contour to a resource assignment
	Edit a task assignment manually
Optimizing the Project Schedule	Identify the project finish date and total cost
	Compress the project schedule to pull in the project finish date

You are a video project manager for Southridge Video, and one of your primary responsibilities recently has been to manage the new Don Funk Music Video project. Your project is underway and is slightly behind schedule. Recently, you have been focusing on using some of the more advanced features of Microsoft Project to save a baseline, commence and track project work. In this lesson, you will perform additional fine-tuning activities on your project schedule by focusing on assignment adjustments, critical paths, and the project's finish date.

KEY TERMS
contour
crashing
fast-tracking
optimizing
predefined contour

© bjones27/iStockphoto

■ SOFTWARE ORIENTATION

Microsoft Project's Schedule Options

The Calendar Options, located in the Schedule section of the Project Options dialog box, are used to provide basic time values, such as the hours per day or week, fiscal year settings, and the first day of the week.

Figure 13-1

Calendar Options in the Schedule section of the Project Options dialog box

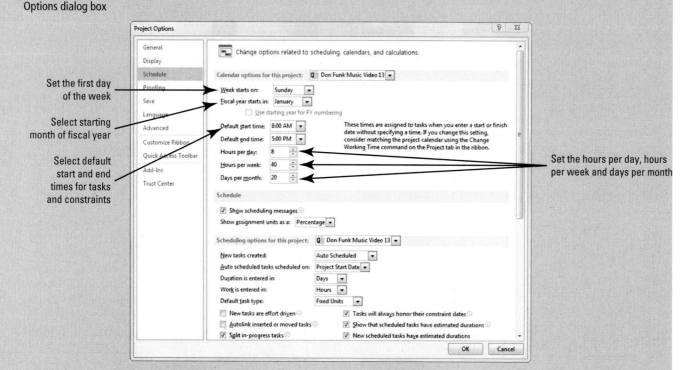

Keep in mind that the Calendar tab has nothing to do with Microsoft Project's base, project, resource, or task calendars. The settings on the Calendar tab affect only the time conversions for task durations that you enter into Microsoft Project, not when work can or should be scheduled.

■ Making Time and Date Adjustments

THE BOTTOM LINE

As part of its project management capabilities, Microsoft Project has a scheduling engine that works with time. Because time is always part of the "project equation," it is critical that the project manager understand the array of time and date settings used by Microsoft Project.

 ⊕ ADJUST FISCAL YEAR SETTINGS WITHIN MICROSOFT PROJECT

GET READY. Before you begin these steps, launch Microsoft Project.

1. **OPEN** the *Don Funk Music Video 13M* project schedule from the data files for this lesson.
2. **SAVE** the file as *Don Funk Music Video 13* in the solutions folder for this lesson as directed by your instructor.

3. On the Gantt Chart, drag the **divider** bar (between the table portion and the graph portion of the Gantt Chart) to the right until the Start and Finish columns are visible.

4. On the ribbon, click the **File** tab and then select **Options**. In the Project Options dialog box, select **Schedule**.

5. In the Calendar Options area, click the **Fiscal year starts in:** box, select **July**, and then click **OK** to close the Options dialog box.

6. [Press the **F5** key.] In the **ID** box, type **60** and click **OK**. Your screen should look similar to Figure 13-2.

Figure 13-2

Gantt Chart View showing the fiscal year timescale

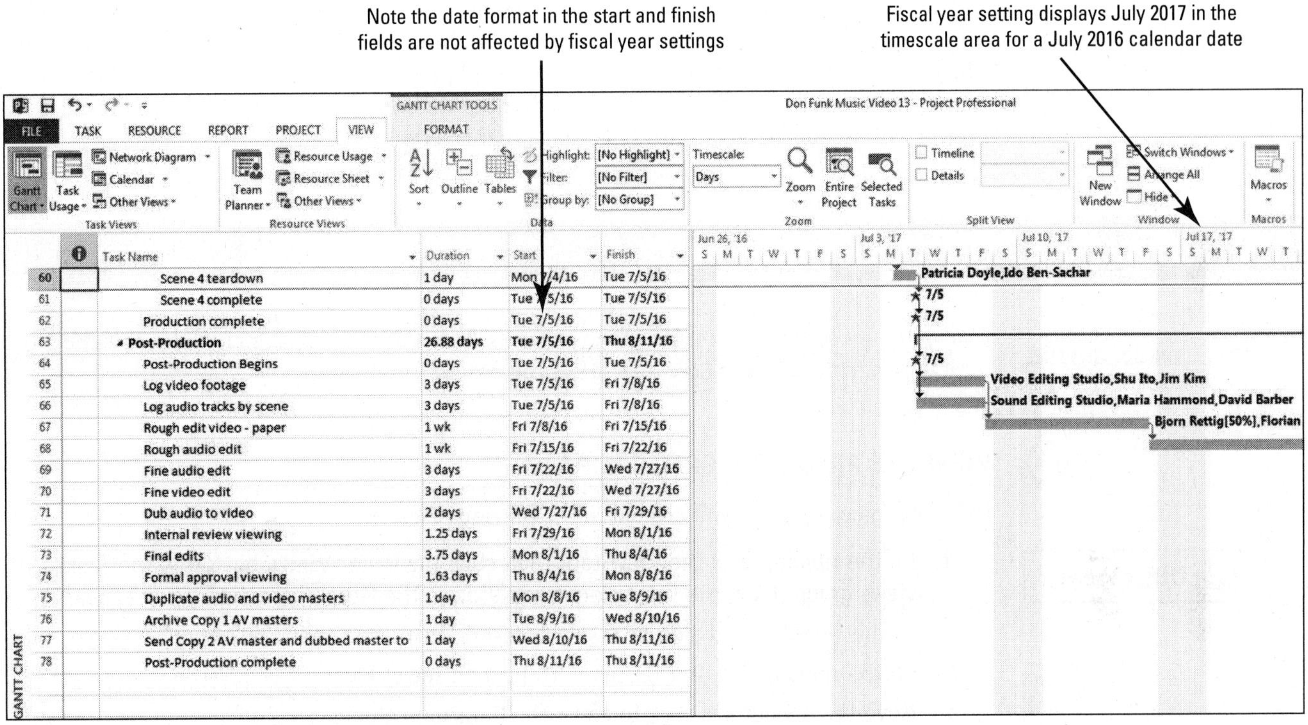

Note the date format in the start and finish fields are not affected by fiscal year settings

Fiscal year setting displays July 2017 in the timescale area for a July 2016 calendar date

When you select the starting month of the fiscal year, Microsoft Project reformats the dates on the Gantt Chart timescale to use the fiscal year, not the calendar year. The months of July–December 2016 now show a 2017 year to reflect that the 2017 fiscal year runs from July 1, 2016, through June 30, 2017.

7. Click the **Undo** button twice to restore the dates to the calendar year format.

8. Drag the **divider** back to the right edge of the Duration column.

9. **SAVE** the project schedule.

PAUSE. LEAVE Project open to use in the next exercise.

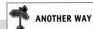

ANOTHER WAY

You can restore the calendar year format by returning to the Calendar tab of the Options dialog box and selecting January in the Fiscal year starts in: box.

In this exercise, you changed the timescale view to accommodate a fiscal year – any 12 consecutive month period defined for accounting purposes – rather than a calendar year – a 12 month period from January to December. Using a fiscal year timescale is most appropriate if there are stakeholders who are accustomed to analyzing information in a fiscal year format. Otherwise, use the calendar year format.

There are many other options for controlling time in Microsoft Project through the Calendar options of the Project Options dialog box. You use the Calendar options to define basic time values, such as how many hours a day or a week should equal, or how many days should equal one month. You can also control other time settings, such as which day is the first day of the week (this varies from country to country).

The Calendar options can be confusing, however, because it has nothing to do with Microsoft Project's base, project, resource, or task calendars. (You control these calendars through the Change Working time dialog box on the Project tab.) The Calendar settings affect only the time conversions for task durations that you enter into Microsoft Project, such as how many hours equal one day – not when work can be scheduled. For example, if your project is planned for 10 hours a day, 5 days per week, set the hours per day to 10 and the hours per week to 50.

The Default Start Time and Default End Time settings on the Calendar tab can also be confusing. These settings are not related to working time values for calendars. Rather, the Default Start Time and Default End Time settings have a very specific purpose. These settings supply the default start and end time for task constraints or for actual start and finish dates in which you enter a date but do not include a time. For example, if you enter a Must Start On constraint value of January 14, 2016, for a task but do not specify a start time, Microsoft Project will use the Default Start Time value that is set on the Calendar tab.

■ Viewing the Project's Critical Path

  THE BOTTOM LINE One of the most important parts of the project schedule is the project's critical path. The critical path is the series of tasks that affect the project's end date.

→ VIEW THE PROJECT'S CRITICAL PATH

USE the project schedule you created in the previous exercise.

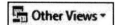

1. On the ribbon, click the **View** tab, then click the **Other Views** button in the Task views group. From the list, select **More Views**. The More Views dialog box appears.

2. In the More Views dialog box, select **Detail Gantt**, and then click **Apply**.

3. On the ribbon, click the **Tables** button, then select **Entry**.

4. Move the divider bar back to cover the Duration column.

5. [Press the F5 key.] In the ID box, type **54**, and then click **OK**. Microsoft Project displays the Scene 4 summary task at the top of your screen; this is a convenient location to view both noncritical and critical tasks.

6. On the ribbon, click the **Format** tab. Click the **Slippage** button. Select any baseline that does not have a date. Microsoft Project removes the slippage lines from in front of the tasks. Your screen should look similar to Figure 13-3.

Figure 13-3

Detail Gantt view showing critical tasks, non-critical task and slack (float)

Non-Critical tasks (blue)   Critical tasks (red)   Slack (Float)

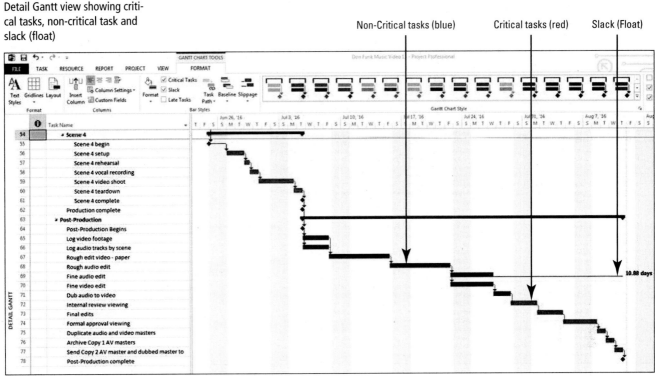

In the Detail Gantt view, noncritical tasks appear in blue and critical tasks are in red. In this view, you can also see some tasks that have slack (float). A thin teal line represents the total slack for a given task. Why does the critical path seem to stop in the middle of the project? The answer lies in the total slack.

7. On the ribbon, click the **View** tab, click the **Tables** button, and then click **Schedule**. The Schedule table appears in the Detail Gantt view.

8. Drag the **divider** bar to the right until all columns in the Schedule table are visible, then auto fit all the columns until you see all information easily.

9. [Press the **F5** key.] In the ID box, type **69** and click **OK**. Your screen should look similar to Figure 13-4.

Figure 13-4

Schedule table showing free float and total float for each task

Slack values for each task

#	Task Name	Start	Finish	Late Start	Late Finish	Free Slack	Total Slack
51	Scene 3 video shoot	Tue 6/21/16	Fri 6/24/16	Fri 6/17/16	Wed 6/22/16	0 days	-1.25 days
52	Scene 3 teardown	Fri 6/24/16	Fri 6/24/16	Wed 6/22/16	Thu 6/23/16	0 days	-1.75 days
53	Scene 3 complete	Fri 6/24/16	Fri 6/24/16	Thu 6/23/16	Fri 6/24/16	0 days	-1.75 days
54	◢ Scene 4	Fri 6/24/16	Tue 7/5/16	Thu 6/23/16	Fri 7/1/16	0 days	-1.75 days
55	Scene 4 begin	Fri 6/24/16	Fri 6/24/16	Thu 6/23/16	Thu 6/23/16	0 days	-1.75 days
56	Scene 4 setup	Mon 6/27/16	Tue 6/28/16	Thu 6/23/16	Mon 6/27/16	0 days	-1.75 days
57	Scene 4 rehearsal	Wed 6/29/16	Wed 6/29/16	Mon 6/27/16	Mon 6/27/16	0 hrs	-14 hrs
58	Scene 4 vocal recording	Wed 6/29/16	Thu 6/30/16	Tue 6/28/16	Tue 6/28/16	0 days	-1.75 days
59	Scene 4 video shoot	Thu 6/30/16	Mon 7/4/16	Wed 6/29/16	Thu 6/30/16	0 days	-1.75 days
60	Scene 4 teardown	Mon 7/4/16	Tue 7/5/16	Fri 7/1/16	Fri 7/1/16	0 days	-1.75 days
61	Scene 4 complete	Tue 7/5/16	Tue 7/5/16	Fri 7/1/16	Fri 7/1/16	0 days	-1.75 days
62	Production complete	Tue 7/5/16	Tue 7/5/16	Fri 7/1/16	Fri 7/1/16	0 days	-1.75 days
63	◢ Post-Production	Tue 7/5/16	Thu 8/11/16	Wed 7/6/16	Thu 8/11/16	0 days	0 days
64	Post-Production Begins	Tue 7/5/16	Tue 7/5/16	Wed 7/6/16	Wed 7/6/16	0 days	0.25 days
65	Log video footage	Tue 7/5/16	Fri 7/8/16	Wed 7/6/16	Fri 7/8/16	0 days	0.25 days
66	Log audio tracks by scene	Tue 7/5/16	Fri 7/8/16	Wed 7/6/16	Fri 7/8/16	0 days	0.25 days
67	Rough edit video - paper	Fri 7/8/16	Fri 7/15/16	Mon 7/11/16	Fri 7/15/16	0 wks	0.05 wks
68	Rough audio edit	Fri 7/15/16	Fri 7/22/16	Mon 7/18/16	Fri 7/22/16	0 wks	0.05 wks
69	Fine audio edit	Fri 7/22/16	Wed 7/27/16		Thu 8/11/16	10.88 days	10.88 days
70	Fine video edit	Fri 7/22/16	Wed 7/27/16	Mon 7/25/16	Wed 7/27/16	0 days	0.25 days
71	Dub audio to video	Wed 7/27/16	Fri 7/29/16	Thu 7/28/16	Fri 7/29/16	0 days	0.25 days
72	Internal review viewing	Fri 7/29/16	Mon 8/1/16	Mon 8/1/16	Mon 8/1/16	0 days	0.25 days
73	Final edits	Mon 8/1/16	Thu 8/4/16	Mon 8/1/16	Thu 8/4/16	0 days	0 days
74	Formal approval viewing	Thu 8/4/16	Mon 8/8/16	Thu 8/4/16	Mon 8/8/16	0 days	0 days
75	Duplicate audio and video masters	Mon 8/8/16	Tue 8/9/16	Mon 8/8/16	Tue 8/9/16	0 days	0 days
76	Archive Copy 1 AV masters	Tue 8/9/16	Wed 8/10/16	Tue 8/9/16	Wed 8/10/16	0 days	0 days
77	Send Copy 2 AV master and dubbed master to	Wed 8/10/16	Thu 8/11/16	Wed 8/10/16	Thu 8/11/16	0 days	0 days
78	Post-Production complete	Thu 8/11/16	Thu 8/11/16	Thu 8/11/16	Thu 8/11/16	0 days	0 days

Review the free slack and total slack for each task. Recall from Lesson 4 that *free slack* is the amount of time the finish date of a task can be delayed before the start of any successor task is affected. *Total slack* is the amount of time the finish date on a task can be delayed before the completion of the project will be delayed. A task may have total slack, free slack, or both. Slack can be a positive value, negative value or a value of zero.

Selected Tasks

10. Drag the **divider** bar back to the left to show just the Task Name column. Select **tasks 54** through **78**.

11. On the ribbon, in the Zoom group, click **Selected Tasks**.

12. On the ribbon, click the **File** tab and then click **Options**. Select **Advanced**, and then scroll to the bottom of the window until you reach the Calculation options for this project: section.

13. Select the **Calculate multiple critical paths** check box near the bottom of this dialog box, and then click **OK**. Microsoft Project reformats the tasks in the remaining scenes and the Production phase to show a clearer picture of the critical path. Your screen should look similar to Figure 13-5.

Figure 13-5

Detail Gantt with multiple
critical path option on

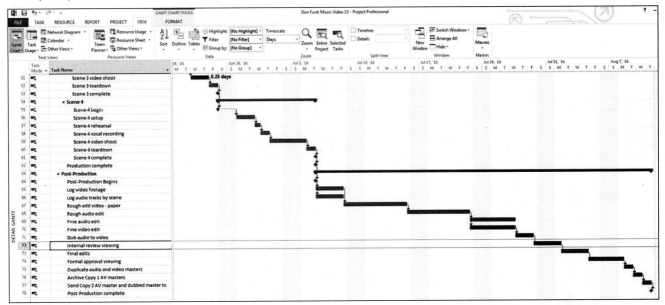

14. On the Quick Access Toolbar, click the **Undo** button. Microsoft Project reverts to the single critical path for the project.

15. On the ribbon, click the **View** tab if necessary, then click the **Tables** button, and then click **Entry**.

16. Drag the vertical divider bar to the right of the Duration column.

17. **SAVE** the project schedule.

PAUSE. LEAVE Project open to use in the next exercise.

In this exercise, you reviewed the critical path of your project schedule and the free and total slack for some of the tasks. As discussed in several previous lessons, one of the most important factors that should be monitored in any project schedule is the project's critical path. Keep in mind that "critical" does not refer to the importance of these tasks in relation to the overall project, but rather to how their scheduling will affect the project's finish date. As a project manager, it is very important for you to understand how changes in schedule, resource assignments, constraints, etc., will affect this key series of tasks. After a task on the critical path is complete, it is no longer critical, because it can no longer affect the project finish date. During the life of the project, it is normal that the critical path will occasionally change.

■ Delaying the Start of Assignments

THE BOTTOM LINE

If more than one resource is assigned to a task, you may not want all the resources to start working on the task at the same time. You can delay the start of work for one or more resources assigned to a task.

DELAY THE START OF A RESOURCE ASSIGNMENT

USE the project schedule you created in the previous exercise.

1. On the ribbon, click the **View** tab, and then click **Task Usage**. The Task Usage view appears.
2. [Press the **F5** key.] Type **75** in the ID box, and then click **OK**. Microsoft Project displays the "Duplicate audio and video masters" task. Your screen should look similar to Figure 13-6.

Figure 13-6

Task usage view at Task 75

You want to delay the start of Luis Bonifaz's work on this task until August 10, 2016

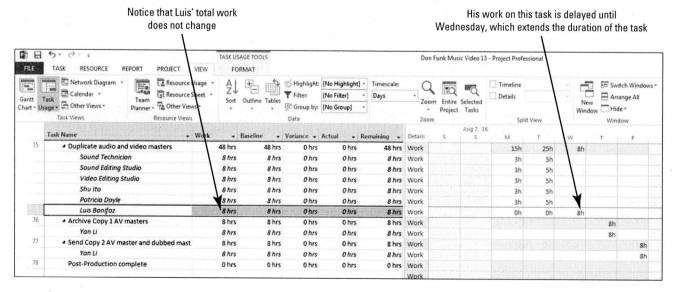

Luis Bonifaz will inspect the final copies of the masters, so you want to delay his work on this task until Wednesday, August 10, 2016.

3. In the Task Name column, double-click the name of the resource **Luis Bonifaz**. The Assignment Information dialog box appears. You can also click on the name of the resource, then click Resource tab and select the Information button.
4. Click the **General** tab if it not already selected.
5. In the Start box, type or select **8/10/16**, and then click **OK** to close the **Assignment Information** dialog box. Microsoft Project adjusts Luis Bonifaz's assignment on this task so that he works eight hours on Wednesday. The other resources assigned to this task are not affected. Your screen should look similar to Figure 13-7.

Figure 13-7

Task Usage view showing the delay in Luis Bonifaz's work

Notice that Luis' total work does not change

His work on this task is delayed until Wednesday, which extends the duration of the task

6. **SAVE** the project schedule.

PAUSE. LEAVE Project open to use in the next exercise.

In this exercise, you delayed the start of work for a resource assigned to a task. You can delay the start of work for any number of resources assigned to a task. However, if you need to delay the start of work for all resources on a particular task, it is better to just reschedule the start date of the task (rather than adjusting each resource's assignment).

■ Applying Contours to Assignments

THE BOTTOM LINE   You can control the amount of time a resource works on a task by applying a work contour. A contour describes the way the resource's work is distributed over time.

Applying a Contour to a Resource Assignment

To optimize your project schedule, you can apply a predefined contour to a task's assignments.

➔ APPLY A CONTOUR TO A RESOURCE ASSIGNMENT

USE the project schedule you created in the previous exercise.

1. [Press the **F5** key.] Type **70** in the ID box, and then click **OK**. Microsoft Project scrolls to Task 70.

2. On the ribbon, click the **Tables** button, select the **Entry** table and then bring the center divider to the left so the duration column is the last one visible. Your screen should look similar to Figure 13-8.

Figure 13-8

Timescaled data for Task 70

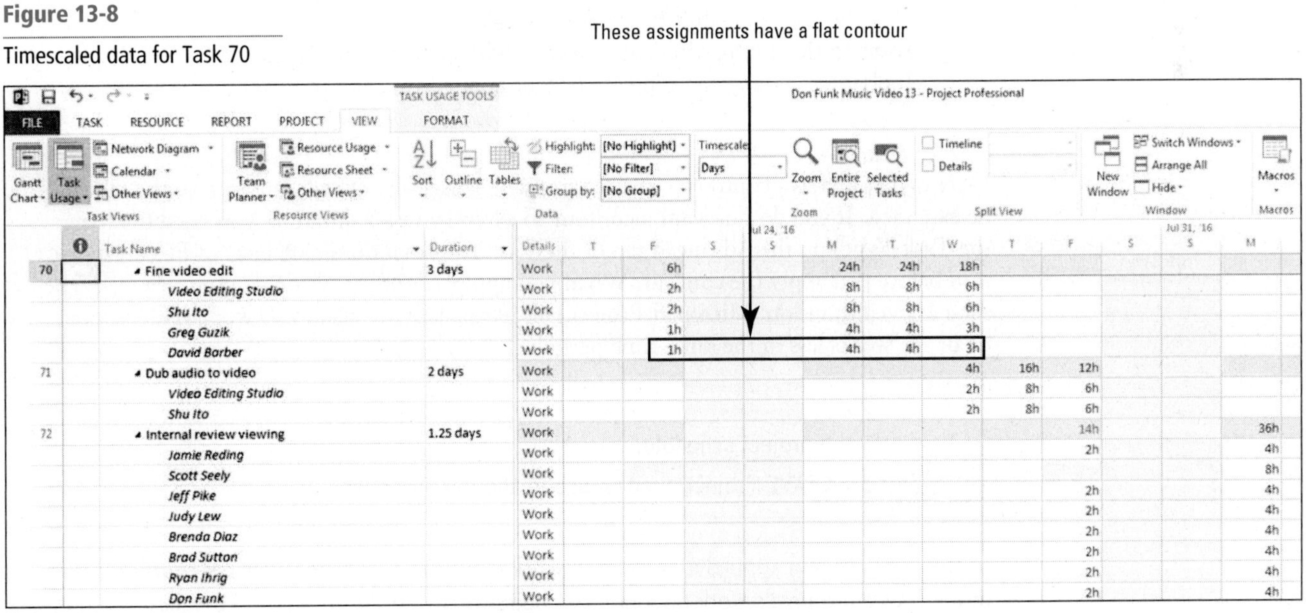

These assignments have a flat contour

This task has four resources assigned to it. The time-scaled data illustrates that two of the four resources are scheduled to work on this task for two hours the first day, eight hours the next two days, and six hours the last day. The last two resources, Greg Guzik and David Barber, are only working on this project half-time. All these assignments have a flat contour – Microsoft Project schedules their work based on a regular rate of eight hours per day. (The resources only work a portion on the first day because they are scheduled on another task.) This is the default work contour type that Microsoft Project uses when scheduling work.

You want to change Greg Guzik's assignment on this task so that he starts with a brief daily assignment and increases his work time as the task progresses. He will still be working on the task after the other resources have finished their assignments.

2. In the Task Name column under Task 70, double-click the **row heading cell of Greg Guzik**. The Assignment Information dialog box appears.

3. Click the **General** tab, if it not already selected.

4. In the Work contour box, select **Back Loaded**, and then click **OK** to close the Assignment Information dialog box. Microsoft Project applies the contour to Greg Guzik's assignment and reschedules his work on the task. Scroll your screen so that you can see all of Greg's planned work on this task. Your screen should look similar to Figure 13-9.

Figure 13-9

Task Usage view with a back-loaded contour on Greg Guzik's assignment

Indicator for a back-loaded contour

This assignment is now back-loaded. Note the work increases each day

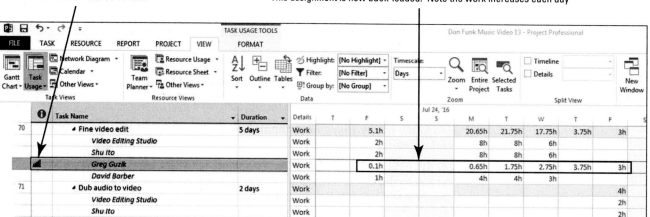

5. Point to the contour indicator in the Indicators column. Microsoft Project displays a ToolTip describing the type of contour applied to this assignment.

TROUBLESHOOTING Note that applying a contour to this assignment caused the overall duration of the task to be extended. If you do not want a contour to extend a task's duration, you need to change the Task Type (on the Advanced tab of the Task Information dialog box) to Fixed Duration before you apply the contour. When you apply a contour after changing to a task type such as fixed duration, Microsoft Project will recalculate the resource's work value so that he or she works less in the same time period.

6. **SAVE** the project schedule.

PAUSE. LEAVE Project open to use in the next exercise.

In this exercise, you applied a predefined work contour to an assignment. A *contour* determines how a resource's work on a task is scheduled over time. In general, *predefined contours* describe how work is distributed over time in terms of graphical patterns. Some options are Bell, Front Loaded, Back Loaded, Double Peak, and Turtle. Predefined contours work best for assignments where you can estimate a probable pattern of effort. For instance, if a task might require significant ramp-up time, a back loaded contour might be beneficial, since the resource will be most productive toward the end of the assignment.

Keep in mind that because Greg Guzik's assignment to this task finishes later than the other resource assignments, Greg Guzik sets the finish date of the task. In this situation it would said that Greg Guzik is the "driving resource" of this task because his assignment determines, or drives, the finish date of the task.

Manually Editing a Task Assignment

It is also possible to manually edit the assignment values for a resource assigned to a task rather than applying a contour. Since the reality is that a project manager does not plan Greg Guzik's work for 6 minutes (or 0.1h) on 7/22/16, a manual editing of the assignment is necessary.

→ EDIT A TASK ASSIGNMENT MANUALLY

USE the project schedule you created in the previous exercise.

1. In the time-scaled grid area, click the cell at the intersection of Greg Guzik and 7/22/16.

   After conferring with Greg, you want to change this assignment to make it more realistic. Greg states that he can work for an hour on the first two days, 3 hours on the next two days and 4 hours on the fifth day to complete his work. Note that you are not changing Greg's total assigned work on this task, which is 12 hours.

2. Type the following hours in the corresponding cells:

   7/22/16 - 1

   7/25/16 - 1

   7/26/16 - 3

   7/27/16 - 3

   7/28/16 - 4

   7/29/16 - 0

3. Point to the contour indicator in the Indicators column. Microsoft Project displays a different ToolTip on this assignment. Notice now that Greg's assignment is a bit more realistic. Your screen should look similar to Figure 13-10.

Figure 13-10

Task Usage view with edited work assignments for Greg Guzik

Indicator for an edited assignment

The edited assignments are now more realistic

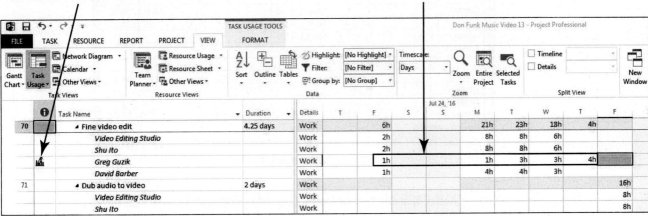

4. SAVE the project schedule.

   PAUSE. LEAVE Project open to use in the next exercise.

In this exercise, you manually edited the assignment for a resource by directly changing the assignment values in the time-scaled grid of the Task Usage view. You may have noticed that when you deleted the last contoured work day, by entering zero work hours, the tasks after task 70 shifted back to reflect the shortened duration of task 70.

You can use either predefined contours or make manual edits to a resource's work assignments. How you contour or edit an assignment depends on what you need to accomplish.

■ Optimizing the Project Schedule

↓
THE BOTTOM LINE

As the work continues on your project, you will be tracking actuals and updating your project schedule. An important part of project management is verifying that the project has been optimized. This might mean reducing cost, duration, scope, or any combination of these aspects.

Identifying the Project Finish Date and Total Cost

In order to optimize a project schedule, you must first identify and understand the project's duration, finish date, and total cost.

→ IDENTIFY THE PROJECT FINISH DATE AND TOTAL COST

USE the project schedule you created in the previous exercise.

Gantt
Chart ▾

Project
Information

1. On the ribbon, in the Task Views group, click the **Gantt Chart** button.
2. On the ribbon, click the **Project** tab, and then click the **Project Information** button. Click the **Statistics** button. The Project Statistics dialog box appears. Your screen should look similar to Figure 13-11.

Figure 13-11

Project Statistics box

Baseline Project Cost   Current Project Cost

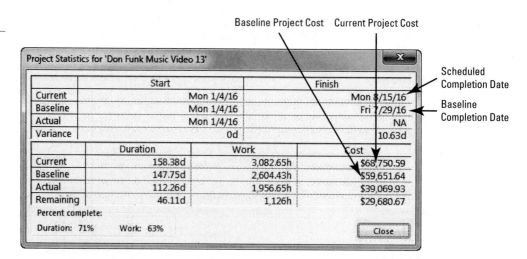

Scheduled Completion Date

Baseline Completion Date

Project Statistics for 'Don Funk Music Video 13'

	Start	Finish
Current	Mon 1/4/16	Mon 8/15/16
Baseline	Mon 1/4/16	Fri 7/29/16
Actual	Mon 1/4/16	NA
Variance	0d	10.63d

	Duration	Work	Cost
Current	158.38d	3,082.65h	$68,750.59
Baseline	147.75d	2,604.43h	$59,651.64
Actual	112.26d	1,956.65h	$39,069.93
Remaining	46.11d	1,126h	$29,680.67

Percent complete:

Duration: 71%   Work: 63%

Close

Notice that the Current Finish Date is 8/15/16. This is later than the Baseline Finish Date of 7/29/16. You have a positive duration variance of 10.63 days, which means you are scheduled to finish more than 10 working days later than planned. This box also provides the current cost: just over $68,750. This value is the sum of all actual costs to date and the remaining planned task and resource costs in the project. These include actual and planned fixed costs, per-use costs, and the costs of resource assignments.

3. Click **Close** to close the **Project Statistics** dialog box.

4. SAVE the project schedule.

PAUSE. LEAVE Project open to use in the next exercise.

In this exercise, you reviewed project details such as the duration, finish date, and total costs. It is helpful to review this information so that you understand the nature of your project and how it can best be optimized. Optimizing is adjusting the aspects of the project schedule, such as cost, duration, and scope (or any combination of these), to achieve a desired project schedule result. A desired result may be a target finish date, duration, or overall cost.

Now let's look forward to the next exercise. Assume that you have shared the project details from above with the project sponsor. The sponsor expected that the project would be slightly over budget, but they did not expect that it would be a week or more beyond the agreed finish date. The current projected budget overrun is acceptable, and can even increase slightly, if the project manager can get the project completed by 8/8/16.

Compressing the Project Schedule

Now that you have reviewed the project details, you will focus on pulling in the project finish date.

 COMPRESS THE PROJECT SCHEDULE TO PULL IN THE PROJECT FINISH DATE

USE the project schedule you created in the previous exercise.

1. [Press the F5 key.] In the ID box, type 54 and click OK. Since you need to pull in the project finish date, your focus will be on the critical tasks.

2. Scroll through and review the task list. Note that only tasks 69 and 73 are non-critical. Shortening the duration of non-critical tasks will have no effect on the project finish date. To shorten the project finish date, you must work with the critical tasks.

3. If necessary, scroll the Gantt Chart view to the right so that you can see the entire Gantt bar for task 70. Your screen should look similar to Figure 13-12.

Figure 13-12

Gantt Chart displaying Critical Task 70

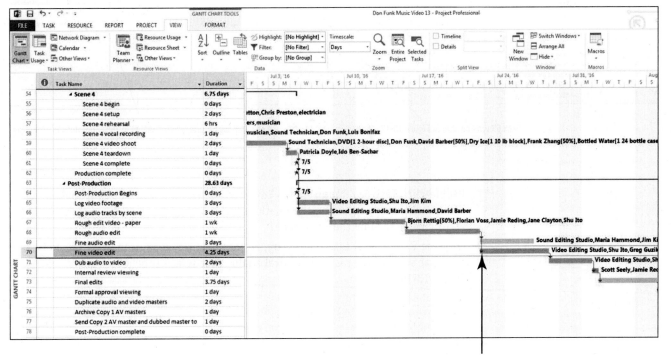

Task 70 has a back-loaded contour, which increased its duration

Recall that in an earlier exercise, you applied a back loaded contour to Greg Guzik's assignment to this task, lengthening its duration. To leave this assignment contour in place but start subsequent tasks earlier, you will add lead time to Task 71, Task 70's successor task.

4. In the Task Name column, double-click the name of Task 71, **Dub audio to video**. The Task Information dialog box appears.

5. Click the **Predecessors** tab.

6. In the Lag field for the predecessor Task 70, type **−25%** and [press **Enter**]. Click **OK** to close the **Task Information** dialog box.

Applying a lead time to the task relationship between tasks 70 and 71 causes Task 71 and all successor tasks to start earlier. Entering this lead causes the successor Task 71 to begin when 75% duration of the predecessor Task 70 has elapsed. Also note that some of the tasks that were critical before you added the lead are no longer critical. This is temporary. Your screen should look similar to Figure 13-13.

Figure 13-13

Gantt Chart view showing a lead has been applied between tasks 70 and 71

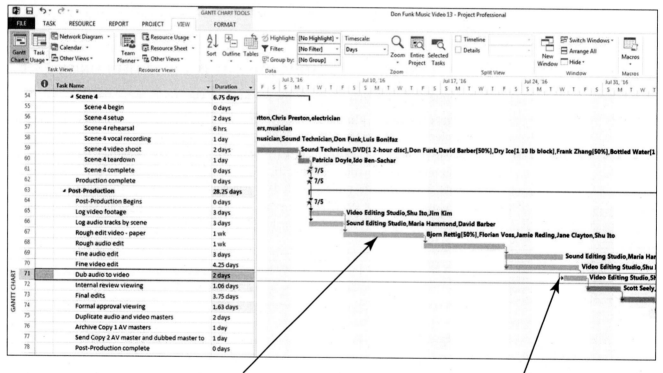

Task 67 was critical in Figure 13-12 – now it is not

Task 71 now begins when Task 70 is 75% complete is complete

7. Double-click Task 68, **Rough Audio Edit**. You realize that you can gain some additional time by adjusting the relationship of tasks 67 and 68 since these can be performed at roughly the same time.

8. Click the **Predecessor** tab if necessary. In the **Lag** field, type **−2d**. Click **OK**. Notice now that some of the tasks are critical again. Your screen should look similar to Figure 13-14.

Figure 13-14

Gantt Chart with 2 days lead
between tasks 67 and 68

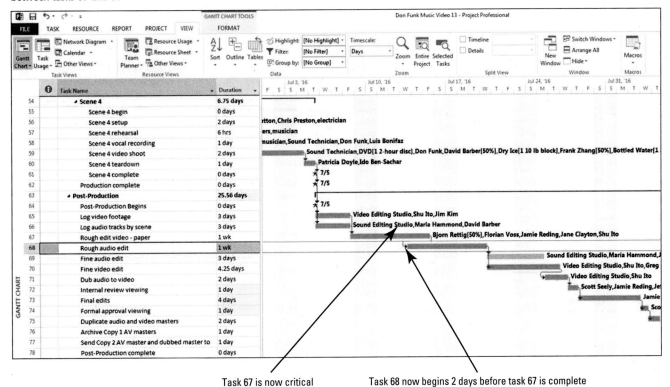

Task 67 is now critical   Task 68 now begins 2 days before task 67 is complete

This process is called fast-tracking, which is defined as doing tasks in parallel that were originally planned to be done in series. You can review the Gantt Chart view (or display the Project Information dialog box) to see that the final task of the project now ends on 8/10/16. This is still about 8 working days later than your desired finish date. To compress the project duration further, you will apply overtime work to some assignments.

9. On the View ribbon, click the Task Usage button. The Task Usage view appears. Click the Tables button, then select the Usage table.

10. Right-click the Work column heading. On the quick menu that appears, select Insert Column.

11. Type Over, and then select Overtime Work from the list. Microsoft Project inserts the Overtime Work column between the Task Name and Work columns. Drag the divider bar between the table and chart portions of the Gantt Chart to the right until the Duration column is visible. The specific task for which you wish to apply overtime is task 67.

12. [Press the F5 key.] In the ID box, type 67 and click OK. Microsoft Project scrolls the Task Usage view to display the assignments of Task 67. Your screen should look similar to Figure 13-15.

Figure 13-15

Task Usage view with Task 67 and the work data displayed

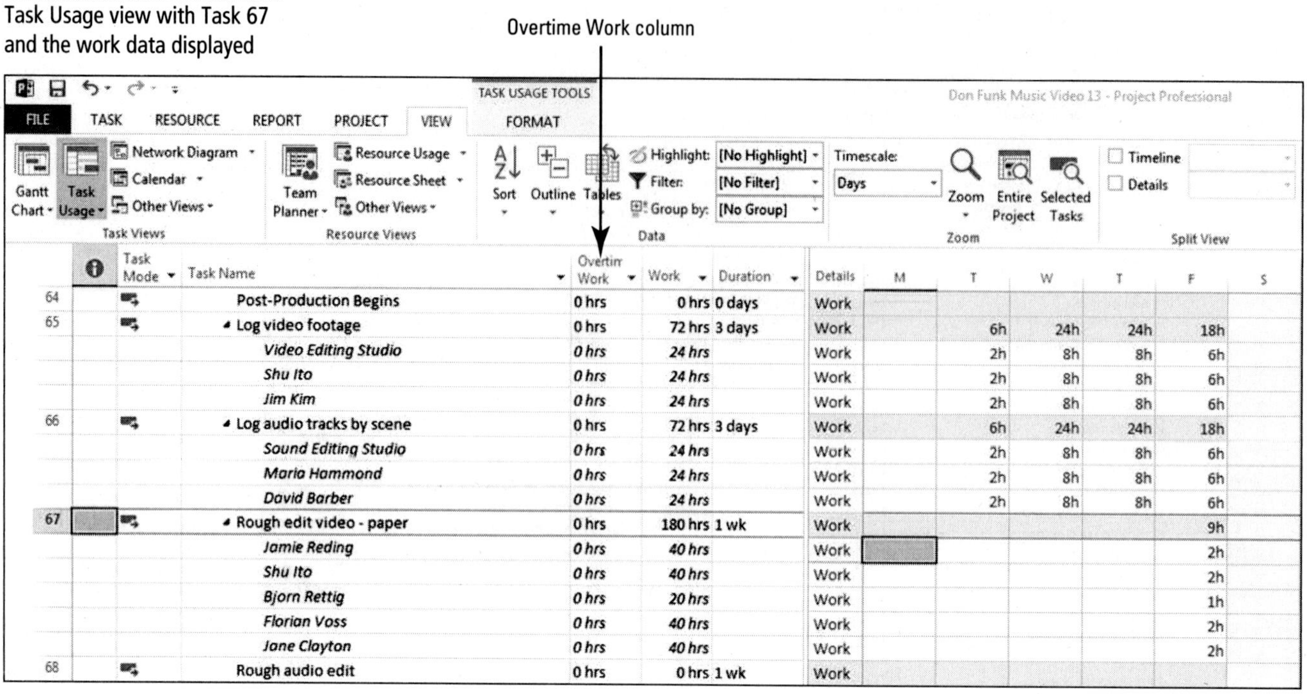
Overtime Work column
TASK USAGE TOOLS
Don Funk Music Video 13 - Project Professional
FILE TASK RESOURCE REPORT PROJECT VIEW FORMAT
Gantt Chart
Task Usage
Network Diagram
Calendar
Other Views
Task Views
Team Planner
Resource Usage
Resource Sheet
Other Views
Resource Views
Sort
Outline
Tables
Highlight: [No Highlight]
Filter: [No Filter]
Group by: [No Group]
Data
Timescale:
Days
Zoom
Entire Project
Selected Tasks
Zoom
Timeline
Details
Split View
Task Mode
Task Name
Overtime Work
Work
Duration
Details
M T W T F S
64 Post-Production Begins 0 hrs 0 hrs 0 days Work
65 Log video footage 0 hrs 72 hrs 3 days Work 6h 24h 24h 18h
Video Editing Studio 0 hrs 24 hrs Work 2h 8h 8h 6h
Shu Ito 0 hrs 24 hrs Work 2h 8h 8h 6h
Jim Kim 0 hrs 24 hrs Work 2h 8h 8h 6h
66 Log audio tracks by scene 0 hrs 72 hrs 3 days Work 6h 24h 24h 18h
Sound Editing Studio 0 hrs 24 hrs Work 2h 8h 8h 6h
Maria Hammond 0 hrs 24 hrs Work 2h 8h 8h 6h
David Barber 0 hrs 24 hrs Work 2h 8h 8h 6h
67 Rough edit video - paper 0 hrs 180 hrs 1 wk Work 9h
Jamie Reding 0 hrs 40 hrs Work 2h
Shu Ito 0 hrs 40 hrs Work 2h
Bjorn Rettig 0 hrs 20 hrs Work 1h
Florian Voss 0 hrs 40 hrs Work 2h
Jane Clayton 0 hrs 40 hrs Work 2h
68 Rough audio edit 0 hrs 0 hrs 1 wk Work

Currently, four of the resources are assigned 40 hours of regular work to this task. Bjorn Rettig is assigned 20 hours of work because his Max Units value is 50%. To shorten the task's duration without changing the total work in the task (for each assignment except Bjorn Rettig), you will record that 10 of the 40 hours of work is overtime work. You will record 5 hours of overtime work for Bjorn Rettig.

TAKE NOTE* Entering overtime work for an assignment does not add work to the assignment. Rather, it indicates how much of the work assigned is overtime. Adding overtime work reduces the overall duration of the assignment.

13. Click the **Overtime Work cell** for Jamie Reding, the first resource assigned to Task 67.
14. Type **10** and [press **Enter**].
15. Repeat steps 13 and 14 for Shu Ito, Florian Voss, and Jane Clayton.
16. Repeat steps 13 and 14 for Bjorn Rettig, except type **5** in the Overtime Work cell. Your screen should look similar to Figure 13-16.

Figure 13-16

Task Usage view showing the change in task duration with overtime work added

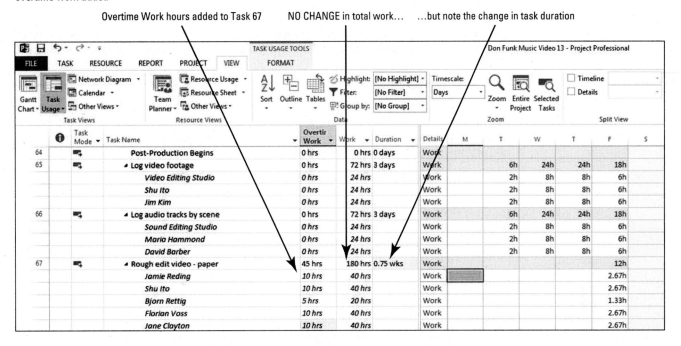

Overtime Work hours added to Task 67   NO CHANGE in total work...   ...but note the change in task duration

17. On the ribbon, click the **Project** tab, then click **Project Information**, and then select the **Statistics** button. Note the new projected finish date of 8/9/16. Remember the sponsor asked the scheduled be compressed to complete the project no later than 8/8/16 – you are almost there.

18. **Close** the Project Statistics dialog box. Now click the **Task** tab, and then click the **Gantt Chart** button.

19. [Press the **F5** key.] Type **69** in the ID box, and then click **OK**. Notice now how Task 69 is no longer critical.

20. Look at Task 76 and its relationship with Task 75. After speaking with your team, you realize that Task 76 can be started one-half day after Task 75 starts. Double-click **Task 76**.

21. On the Predecessors tab, type **−1.5d** in the Lag column, and then click **OK**.

22. On the Project ribbon, click **Project Information**. Click the **Statistics** button. The Project Statistics dialog box appears. Note that the new finish date is 8/5/16. **CLOSE** the **Project Information** dialog box. The finish date is now before the newly mandated finish date of 8/8/16, which is acceptable to the sponsor. You will stop your project optimization work here.

23. **SAVE** the project schedule, and then **CLOSE** the file.

    PAUSE. If you are continuing to the next lesson, keep Project open. If you are not continuing to additional lessons, **CLOSE** Project.

In this exercise, you compressed a project schedule by applying lead time to some tasks and allowing overtime for another task. *Optimizing* a project schedule and responding to variance are issues that Microsoft Project cannot automate. As a project manager, you must know the nature of your projects and how they should be optimized. As you saw in this exercise, you might need to make trade-offs, such as cutting scope, adding resources, allowing overtime, or adding lead time.

Although you stopped your optimization work when you achieved your desired finish date, keep in mind that once actual work starts, variance will almost certainly appear and the critical path and project finish date are likely to change. For this reason, properly identifying and responding to variance is a key project management skill.

In previous lessons, only a single critical path per project has been emphasized: the critical path that determines the project finish date. However, as you saw in this exercise, Microsoft Project can identify a critical path within any chain of linked tasks. This is especially useful when the project is divided into distinct phases. Usually, the critical path within a phase will have a much more distinct line of tasks in it.

Most projects have a specific due date by which they need to be completed. If you want to shorten the duration of the project to make the end date occur sooner, you must shorten the critical path (in project management jargon, this is called "schedule compression"). In reality, compressing the schedule happens in various ways, but these can be classified into two categories:

- *Fast-Tracking* – Performing two or more project tasks in parallel that would otherwise be done in series, or one right after the other. By overlapping the tasks, more work gets completed in a shorter amount of time.
- *Crashing* – Adding more resources to the critical path tasks. This could take the form of working extra shifts, working overtime, adding more work resources to a task, or outsourcing (paying to have some work done outside the organization).

Prior to starting actual work on the project, it is critical that the project manager closely manage both the critical path and the float (called "slack" in Microsoft Project). This involves:

- Knowing the tasks that are on the critical path and being able to evaluate the risk-to-project success if any of the tasks are not completed as scheduled. Any delays in completing tasks on the critical path delay the completion date of the project.

- Knowing where the slack is in the project. On a complex project, the critical path may change frequently. Tasks with very little free slack might become critical as the project begins and the actuals start to vary from the schedule. In addition, tasks that had no free slack initially (and therefore were on the critical path) might get free slack as other tasks move onto the critical path.

SKILL SUMMARY

In this lesson you learned:	Matrix Skill
To make time and date adjustments	Adjust fiscal year settings within Microsoft Project
To view the project's critical path	View the project's critical path
To delay the start of assignments	Delay the start of a resource assignment
To apply a contour to assignments	Apply a contour to a resource assignment
	Edit a task assignment manually
To optimize the project schedule	Identify the project finish date and total cost
	Compress the project schedule to pull in the project finish date

■ Knowledge Assessment

Fill in the Blank

Complete the following sentences by writing the correct word or words in the blanks provided.

1. A(n) _____ determines how a resource's work on a task is scheduled over time.

2. The _____ section of the Options dialog box provides an option to change the view to fiscal year rather than calendar year.

3. The _____ is the series of tasks which will extend the project's end date if they are delayed.

4. Adjusting the aspects of the project schedule, such as cost, duration, and scope, to achieve a desired project schedule result is known as _____.

5. For a task on the critical path, critical refers to how its scheduling will affect the project's _____.

6. _____ is the amount of time that the finish date of a task can be delayed before the start of a successor task must be rescheduled.

7. A(n) _____ contour describes how work is distributed over time in terms of graphical patterns.

8. It is important to optimize your project schedule prior to saving a(n) _____.

9. Decreasing the project's duration is known as _____.

10. The amount of time the finish date on a task can be delayed before the completion of the project will be delayed is known as _____.

Multiple Choice

Select the best response for the following statements.

1. Using a fiscal year view is most appropriate when
   a. you want to view the costs for individual tasks.
   b. you need to pull in the project end date.
   c. there are stakeholders who are accustomed to analyzing data in this format.
   d. you need to combine projects with other project managers.

2. Predefined contours work best when you can estimate
   a. the finish date of the task.
   b. a probable pattern of effort.
   c. the over-allocation of a resource.
   d. none of the above.

3. A task may have
   a. total slack.
   b. free slack.
   c. partial slack.
   d. both A and B above.

4. A task that has free slack before a project begins
   a. might become critical as the project gets underway and actuals are entered.
   b. will always have free slack.
   c. cannot ever affect the critical path.
   d. should be optimized as soon as possible.

5. You cannot use the Calendar options to
   a. define how many hours are in a day.
   b. identify which is the first day of the week.
   c. set up the base calendar.
   d. define how many days should equal one month.

6. If a resource's assignment determines the finish date of a task, it is said that the resource is the
   a. driving resource.
   b. critical resource.
   c. final resource.
   d. end resource.

7. Which of the following is not a predefined contour?
   a. Bell
   b. Half Pike
   c. Front Loaded
   d. Turtle

8. You can view the costs of a project in the
   a. Project Information dialog box.
   b. Project Cost dialog box.
   c. Project Statistics dialog box.
   d. Detailed Gantt Chart view.

9. Once work has commenced on a project,
   a. the critical path cannot change.
   b. variance can no longer appear.
   c. the finish date is likely to change.
   d. a task cannot move from noncritical to critical.

10. The Default Start Time and Default End Time settings on the Calendar options
    a. are not related to the working time values for calendars.
    b. supply the default start and end time for task constraints.
    c. supply the default start and end time for actual start and finish dates in which you enter a date but do not include a time.
    d. all of the above.

■ Competency Assessment

Project 13-1: Fiscal Year View for Office Remodel

The Facility Management department would like to see the project schedule for your lunchroom office remodel in a fiscal year view. For your company, the fiscal year begins on October 1.

GET READY. Launch Microsoft Project if it is not already running.

 OPEN *Office Remodel 13-1* from the data files for this lesson.

1. On the Gantt Chart, drag the **vertical divider** bar to the right to expose the Start and Finish columns.
2. On the ribbon, click the **File** tab, and then select **Options**.
3. Click the **Schedule** section.
4. In the Fiscal year starts in: box, select **October**, and then click **OK** to close the Options dialog box.

5. SAVE the project schedule as *Office Remodel Fiscal Year* and then CLOSE the file.

PAUSE. LEAVE Project open to use in the next exercise.

Project 13-2: Compressing the HR Interview Project Schedule

After a team meeting regarding the HR Interview project schedule, it is decided that you need to wrap up your interviewing process before the middle of April. April 15 is your target date. Make lead time and overtime adjustments to your project schedule to bring in the finish date.

OPEN *HR Interview Schedule 13-2* from the data files for this lesson.

1. On the ribbon, click the View tab, and then in the task views group click the Other Views button. From the list, select More Views.
2. In the More Views dialog box, select Detail Gantt, and then click Apply.
3. [Press the F5 key.] Type 30 in the ID box, and then click OK. Note the finish date of task 30.
4. [Press the F5 key.] Type 5, and then click OK.
5. Double-click the name of task 5.
6. In the Task Information dialog box, click the Predecessors tab, if necessary.
7. In the Lag field for the predecessor Task 5, type −50% and press Enter. Click OK.
8. On the ribbon, click the Task Usage button.
9. Right-click the Work column heading and select Insert Column from the dropdown list.
10. Type Overtime, and then select the Overtime Work field name.
11. Scroll down in the task list until you reach Task 11.
12. Under Task 11, click the Overtime Work cell for Keith Harris.
13. Type 8 and [press Enter].
14. Repeat steps 12 and 13 for Mu Zheng and Megan Sherman.
15. On the ribbon, click the Other Views button in the Task Views group, and then click More Views. In the More Views dialog box, select Detail Gantt, and then click Apply.
16. [Press the F5 key.] Type 30 in the ID box, and then click OK. Point your cursor to the Interview Process Complete Milestone and note the new finish date.
17. SAVE the project schedule as *HR Interview Compressed* and then CLOSE the file.

PAUSE. LEAVE Project open to use in the next exercise.

■ Proficiency Assessment

Project 13-3: Office Remodel Cost and Finish Date

Before you begin to optimize your Office Remodel project schedule, you need to identify the project finish date and total cost.

OPEN *Office Remodel 13-3* from the data files for this lesson.

1. Activate the More Views dialog box, and then apply the Detail Gantt view.
2. Activate the Project Information dialog box.
3. In a separate Word document, document the Finish date of the project.
4. Activate the Project Statistics dialog box.
5. Continuing in the same Word document, document the current cost of the project.
6. CLOSE the Project Statistics dialog box.

7. SAVE the project schedule as *Office Remodel Finish-Cost*. SAVE the Word document as *Office Remodel Finish-Cost*. CLOSE both files.

PAUSE. LEAVE Project open to use in the next exercise.

Project 13-4: Don Funk Resource Assignment Contour

You are working on the Don Funk Music Video and want to apply a predefined contour for Annette Hill's assignment to Task 7, Book musicians. Because of other commitments, she will work more hours on the front end of this task.

 OPEN *Don Funk Music Video 13-4* from the data files for this lesson.

1. Activate the Task Usage view.
2. Scroll to Task 7.
3. Select the name Annette Hill.
4. Activate the General tab of the Assignment Information dialog box.
5. Apply a front loaded contour to this resource for this assignment.
6. Scroll the screen so that you can see Annette's later assignments on this task.
7. SAVE the project schedule as *Don Funk Contour* and then CLOSE the file.

PAUSE. LEAVE Project open to use in the next exercise.

■ Mastery Assessment

Project 13-5: Employee Orientation Assignment Delay

During your employee orientation, you will be presenting an overview of the profit sharing plan at your company. Kevin McDowell will talk to the new hires after Sidney Higa has finished. You need to delay the start of Kevin's assignment until after Sidney Higa has finished her assignment.

 OPEN *Employee Orientation 13-5* from the data files for this lesson.

1. Switch to the Task Usage view.
2. For Task 19, Overview of profit sharing plan, delay Kevin McDowell's 0.5h assignment from 10:45 AM until 11:30 AM.
3. SAVE the project schedule as *Employee Orientation Manual Edit* and then CLOSE the file.

PAUSE. LEAVE Project open to use in the next exercise.

Project 13-6: Insurance Claim Process Delayed Start

On your Insurance Claim Process project schedule, you need to edit Chris Gray's assignment on task 18, Repair performed, so that he does not start work until after the other resource assigned to the task.

 OPEN *Insurance Claim Process 13-6* from the data files for this lesson.

1. Activate the Task Usage view.
2. Using the Assignment Information dialog box, edit Chris Gray's assignment on task 18 so that the start of his work on this task is delayed until Wednesday, June 15, 2016.
3. SAVE the project schedule as *Insurance Claim Delayed Start*, and then CLOSE the file.

CLOSE Project.

Advanced Project Schedule Formatting

LESSON SKILL MATRIX

SKILLS	TASKS
Customizing the Calendar View	Format bar styles for tasks in the Calendar view
Using Task IDs and WBS Codes	Work with Unique ID and WBS codes
Formatting the Network Diagram	Format items in the Network Diagram view

You are a video project manager for Southridge Video, and one of your primary responsibilities recently has been to manage the new Don Funk Music Video project. In an earlier lesson, you learned about some of the basic formatting features in Microsoft Project 2013 that allow you to change the way your data appears. In this lesson, you will learn about some of the more powerful formatting and reporting features that enable you to organize and analyze data using additional tools, such as a spreadsheet application.

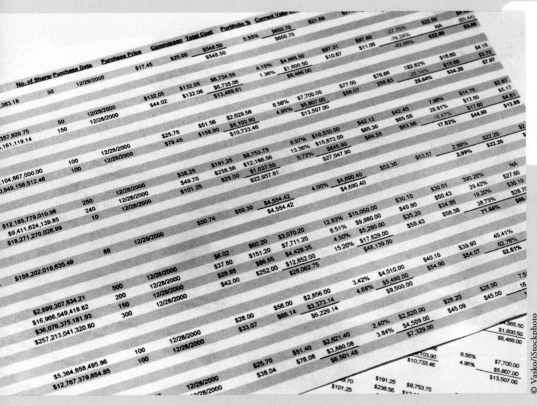

© Vasko/iStockphoto

KEY TERMS
mask
Network Diagram
node
outline number
Unique ID
work breakdown
structure (WBS)

SOFTWARE ORIENTATION

WBS Codes and Unique IDs in the Task Sheet View

Unique IDs are unique identifiers that track the order in which you enter tasks and resources. WBS codes are numeric representations of the outline hierarchy of a project.

Figure 14-1

WBS Codes and Unique IDs in the Task Sheet view

Unique ID is the entry order of tasks and resources

WBS column represents the hierarchal outline of the tasks

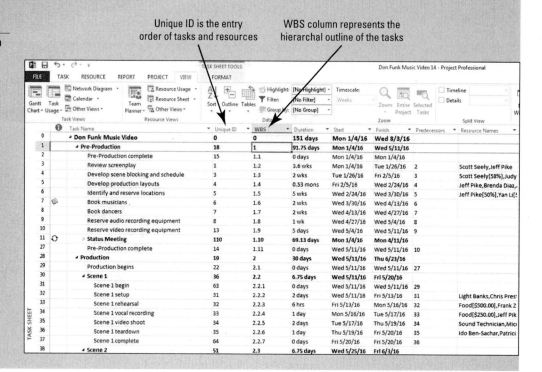

■ Customizing the Calendar View

THE BOTTOM LINE

The Calendar view is one of the simplest views available in Microsoft Project 2013. It can be customized in several different ways.

➔ FORMAT BAR STYLES FOR TASKS IN THE CALENDAR VIEW

GET READY. Before you begin these steps, launch Microsoft Project.

1. **OPEN** the *Don Funk Music Video 14M* project schedule from the data files for this lesson.
2. **SAVE** the file as *Don Funk Music Video 14* in the solutions folder for this lesson as directed by your instructor.
3. On the ribbon, click the **View** tab, and then click the **Calendar** button. The Calendar view appears. Your screen should look similar to Figure 14-2.

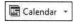
Calendar

Figure 14-2

Calendar view

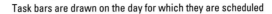
Task bars are drawn on the day for which they are scheduled

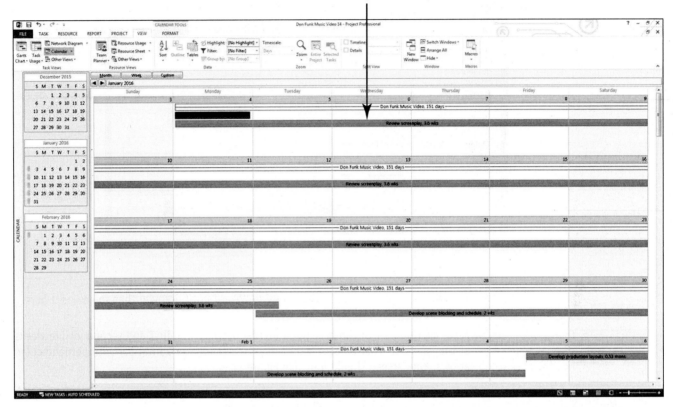

The Calendar view displays approximately four weeks at a time (depending on your screen resolution) and looks similar to a month-at-a-glance calendar. Task bars are drawn on the days for which tasks are scheduled.

Bar Styles

4. On the ribbon, under Calendar Tools, click the **Format** tab, and then click **Bar Styles**. The Bar Styles dialog box appears.

5. In the Task type box, click **Summary**.

6. In the Bar type box, click **Line**. Summary tasks will be shown with a line.

7. In the Task type box, click **Critical**.

8. In the Pattern box, click the second option, the **solid bar**.

9. In the Color box, click **Red**. Critical tasks will be shown with a solid red bar.

10. Make sure that the check boxes for Shadow, Bar rounding, and Wrap text in bars are selected. Your screen should look similar to Figure 14-3.

Figure 14-3

Bar Styles dialog box with selected formatting of critical tasks

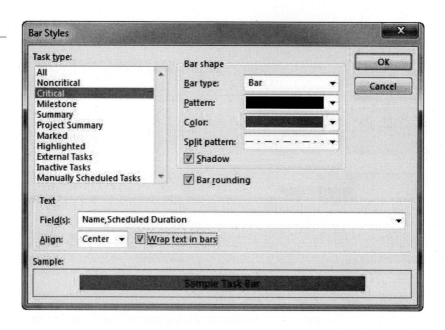

11. Click OK to close the Bar Styles dialog box.

12. You will see a message from the Planning Wizard notifying you that some Gantt bars may be different heights. Click OK.

13. Move your pointer to the horizontal divider between the first and second visible weeks of the calendar. Your pointer will change to a small, horizontal bar with perpendicular arrows. Your screen should look like Figure 14-4.

Figure 14-4

Calendar view with pointer positioned on the horizontal dividing bar

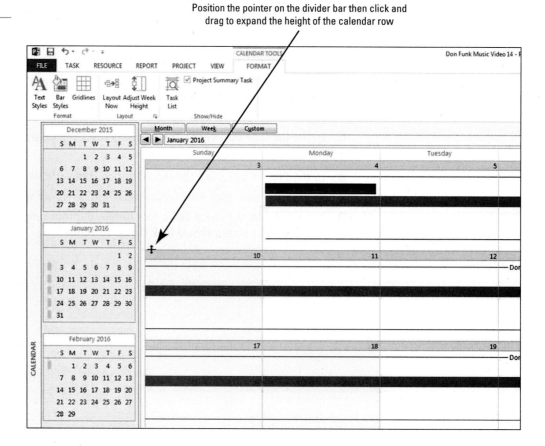

14. Click and hold to drag the line downward to the approximate horizontal center of the screen to show only two weeks at a time.

15. [Press the F5 key.] In the Date box (not the ID box), type or select 06/12/16, and then click OK. The Calendar view now displays a section of the project where critical, noncritical and summary tasks are located using the revised formatting. Also note the dark gray tasks are the milestones. Your screen should look similar to Figure 14-5.

Figure 14-5

Calendar view showing reformatting of critical tasks

Summary tasks shown as a line   Milestone tasks shown in dark gray

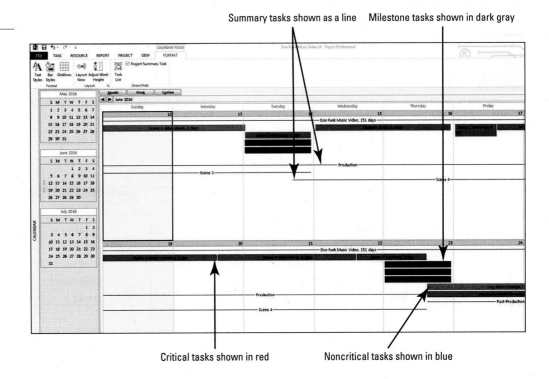

Critical tasks shown in red   Noncritical tasks shown in blue

16. SAVE the project schedule.

PAUSE. LEAVE Project open to use in the next exercise.

In this exercise, you reformatted two of the bar styles in the Calendar view. The Calendar view is one of the simplest views available in Microsoft Project, and it offers several formatting options. This view is often used for reporting schedule information with resources or other stakeholders who prefer a more traditional monthly or weekly view rather than a detailed view such as the Gantt Chart. As you may recall from an earlier lesson, reports are the primary way project managers communicate with the project stakeholders.

■ Using Task IDS and WBS Codes

THE BOTTOM LINE

Microsoft Project organizes and tracks the tasks entered into a project schedule using several unique identifiers: Task IDs, Unique IDs, and Work Breakdown Structure (WBS) codes. You can structure the Task Sheet view so that columns for these identifiers are displayed.

⊕ WORK WITH UNIQUE ID AND WBS CODES

USE the project schedule you created in the previous exercise.

Other Views ▾

1. On the ribbon, click the View tab. Then in the Task Views Group, click the Other Views button, and then click More Views.

2. In the More Views dialog box, select **Task Sheet**, and then click the **Apply** button. The project appears in the Task Sheet view.

3. Right-click the **Duration** column heading. On the menu, click **Insert Column**.

4. From your keyboard, type **un**. Three fields appear at the top of the column. Your screen should look similar to Figure 14-6.

Figure 14-6

Column field list narrowed to all fields that start with the letters UN

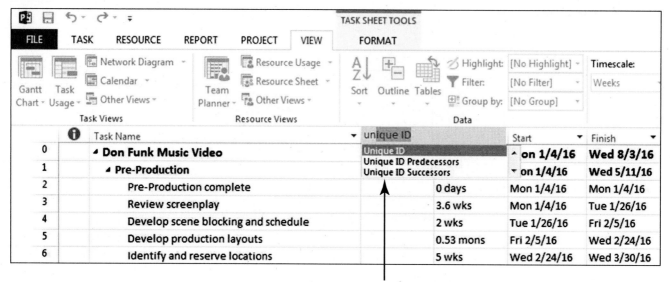

As you key in names of fields, the list is reduced to match

5. In the list that remains, click **Unique ID**. Microsoft Project inserts the Unique ID column to the left of the Task Name column.

The Unique ID column indicates the order in which the tasks were entered into the project. Cutting and pasting a task causes its Unique ID value to change. You can see that the tasks in this project were entered in a different order than they are currently displayed.

ANOTHER WAY You can also insert a column by clicking the Format tab and selecting the Insert Column button.

6. Right-click the **Duration** column heading again. On the menu, click **Insert Column**.

7. From your keyboard, type **WBS**. Three fields appear at the top of the column.

8. In the list that remains, click **WBS**. Microsoft Project inserts the WBS column to the left of the Task Name column. WBS codes represent the hierarchy of summary and subtasks in the project.

TAKE NOTE* If you ever want to reorder tasks to reflect the order in which they were entered, you can sort the Task Sheet by Unique ID.

The WBS numbering system is standard in project management. You can see that in the WBS structure, the top-level summary tasks are sequentially numbered with a single digit, the second-level summary or subtasks add a period and a second digit to the first digit, and so on.

9. Place your cursor on the right dividing line between the WBS column heading and the Duration column heading, then double-click to auto-fit the column. Repeat the same procedure for the Unique ID column. Your screen should look similar to Figure 14-7.

Figure 14-7

Task Sheet view with the inserted WBS and Unique ID fields

Notice that the Unique ID Column and the ID Column are different

	❶	Task Name	Unique ID	WBS	Duration	Start	Finish	Predecessors	
0		**Don Funk Music Video**	0	0	**151 days**	**Mon 1/4/16**	**Wed 8/3/16**		
1		⊿ **Pre-Production**	18	1	**91.75 days**	Mon 1/4/16	Wed 5/11/16		← First level of WBS
2		Pre-Production complete	15	1.1	0 days	Mon 1/4/16	Mon 1/4/16		
3		Review screenplay	1	1.2	3.6 wks	Mon 1/4/16	Tue 1/26/16	2	
4		Develop scene blocking and schedule	3	1.3	2 wks	Tue 1/26/16	Fri 2/5/16	3	
5		Develop production layouts	4	1.4	0.53 mons	Fri 2/5/16	Wed 2/24/16	4	
6		Identify and reserve locations	5	1.5	5 wks	Wed 2/24/16	Wed 3/30/16	5	
7	📝	Book musicians	6	1.6	2 wks	Wed 3/30/16	Wed 4/13/16	6	
8		Book dancers	7	1.7	2 wks	Wed 4/13/16	Wed 4/27/16	7	
9		Reserve audio recording equipment	8	1.8	1 wk	Wed 4/27/16	Wed 5/4/16	8	← Second level of WBS
10		Reserve video recording equipment	13	1.9	5 days	Wed 5/4/16	Wed 5/11/16	9	
11	🔄	▷ **Status Meeting**	110	1.10	69.13 days	Mon 1/4/16	Mon 4/11/16		
27		Pre-Production complete	14	1.11	0 days	Wed 5/11/16	Wed 5/11/16	10	
28		⊿ **Production**	19	2	**30 days**	Wed 5/11/16	Thu 6/23/16		
29		Production begins	22	2.1	0 days	Wed 5/11/16	Wed 5/11/16	27	
30		⊿ **Scene 1**	36	2.2	6.75 days	Wed 5/11/16	Fri 5/20/16		
31		Scene 1 begin	63	2.2.1	0 days	Wed 5/11/16	Wed 5/11/16	29	
32		Scene 1 setup	31	2.2.2	2 days	Wed 5/11/16	Fri 5/13/16	31	
33		Scene 1 rehearsal	32	2.2.3	6 hrs	Fri 5/13/16	Mon 5/16/16	32	
34		Scene 1 vocal recording	33	2.2.4	1 day	Mon 5/16/16	Tue 5/17/16	33	
35		Scene 1 video shoot	34	2.2.5	2 days	Tue 5/17/16	Thu 5/19/16	34	
36		Scene 1 teardown	35	2.2.6	1 day	Thu 5/19/16	Fri 5/20/16	35	← Third level of WBS
37		Scene 1 complete	64	2.2.7	0 days	Fri 5/20/16	Fri 5/20/16	36	
38		⊿ **Scene 2**	51	2.3	6.75 days	Wed 5/25/16	Fri 6/3/16		
39	🖼	Scene 2 begin	65	2.3.1	0 days	Wed 5/25/16	Wed 5/25/16	37	
40		Scene 2 setup	52	2.3.2	2 days	Wed 5/25/16	Thu 5/26/16	39	
41		Scene 2 rehearsal	53	2.3.3	6 hrs	Fri 5/27/16	Fri 5/27/16	40	
42		Scene 2 vocal recording	54	2.3.4	1 day	Fri 5/27/16	Tue 5/31/16	41	
43		Scene 2 video shoot	55	2.3.5	2 days	Tue 5/31/16	Thu 6/2/16	42	
44		Scene 2 teardown	56	2.3.6	1 day	Thu 6/2/16	Fri 6/3/16	43	
45		Scene 2 complete	66	2.3.7	0 days	Fri 6/3/16	Fri 6/3/16	44	

10. In the Task ID column (the left-most column), select 7 and 8. This selects the entire rows for the tasks "Book musicians" and "Book dancers."

11. On the ribbon, click the Task tab. In the Schedule group, click the Indent button. Microsoft Project makes tasks 7 and 8 subtasks of Task 6. Your screen should look similar to Figure 14-8.

Figure 14-8

Task Sheet view showing the reordering of tasks 7 and 8

The WBS codes now show tasks 7 and 8 at the third level of the WBS

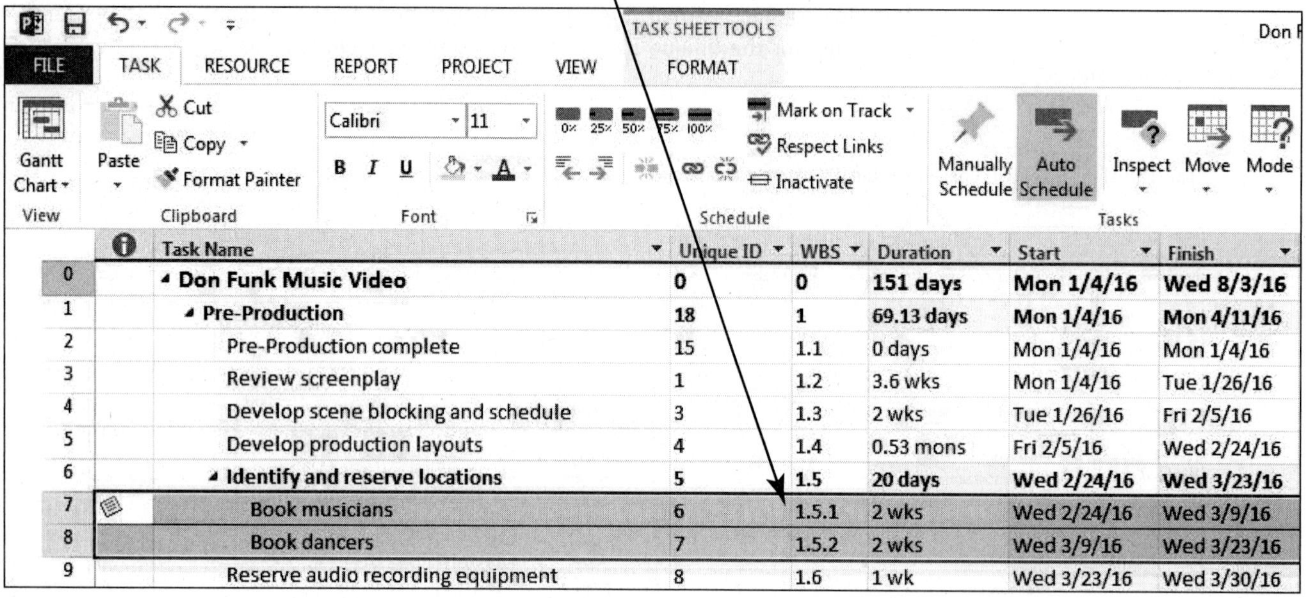

TASK SHEET TOOLS
FILE
TASK
RESOURCE
REPORT
PROJECT
VIEW
FORMAT
Cut
Copy
Format Painter
Gantt Chart
Paste
Calibri
11
Mark on Track
Respect Links
Inactivate
Manually Schedule
Auto Schedule
Inspect
Move
Mode
View
Clipboard
Font
Schedule
Tasks
Task Name
Unique ID
WBS
Duration
Start
Finish
0 Don Funk Music Video 0 0 151 days Mon 1/4/16 Wed 8/3/16
1 Pre-Production 18 1 69.13 days Mon 1/4/16 Mon 4/11/16
2 Pre-Production complete 15 1.1 0 days Mon 1/4/16 Mon 1/4/16
3 Review screenplay 1 1.2 3.6 wks Mon 1/4/16 Tue 1/26/16
4 Develop scene blocking and schedule 3 1.3 2 wks Tue 1/26/16 Fri 2/5/16
5 Develop production layouts 4 1.4 0.53 mons Fri 2/5/16 Wed 2/24/16
6 Identify and reserve locations 5 1.5 20 days Wed 2/24/16 Wed 3/23/16
7 Book musicians 6 1.5.1 2 wks Wed 2/24/16 Wed 3/9/16
8 Book dancers 7 1.5.2 2 wks Wed 3/9/16 Wed 3/23/16
9 Reserve audio recording equipment 8 1.6 1 wk Wed 3/23/16 Wed 3/30/16

Note that the Task and Unique ID values for these tasks are not affected, but the WBS codes were changed. The WBS codes for tasks 7 and 8 now list them at the third level of the project hierarchy. In addition, the other tasks in the 1.x branch of the WBS are renumbered. For example, "Reserve audio recording equipment" is renumbered from 1.8 to 1.6.

Cut

12. Click any cell in the table area to deselect tasks **7** and **8**. Now select the entire row of task 7, **Book Musicians**, by clicking the **Task ID**. On the ribbon, click **Cut**. Microsoft Project cuts the selected task to the Windows Clipboard. Your screen should look similar to Figure 14-9.

Figure 14-9

Task Sheet view showing renumbering of tasks after Task 7 is removed

Note that the Unique ID field does NOT renumber other tasks when a task is removed

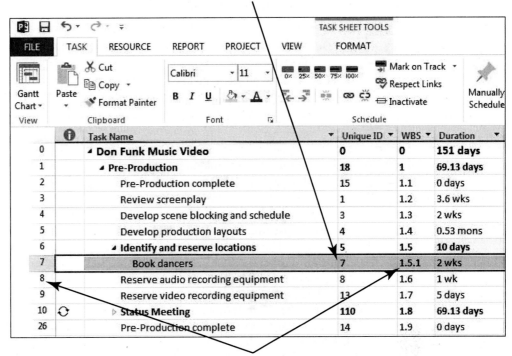

Note how the ID column and WBS Column numbering changes when Task 7 is removed

Note that the Task IDs are renumbered, the Unique IDs are unchanged, and only the WBS codes in the Pre-Production phase are renumbered. The WBS codes in the other phases of the project are unaffected because that part of the project hierarchy did not change.

Paste

13. Select Task 4. On the ribbon, click the Paste button. Click OK if a warning message is displayed. Microsoft Project pastes the task you previously cut back into the task list. Your screen should look similar to Figure 14-10.

Figure 14-10

Task Sheet view with the Book Musicians task inserted

Unique ID field brings up the next sequential number to show the order it was added to the project file

Note the renumbering of the WBS field for other tasks in the Pre-Production Phase

Note again, the Task IDs and the WBS codes in the Pre-Production phase are renumbered. The Unique ID for the pasted task is then updated with the next sequential number to specify when it was added to the project.

14. On the quick access toolbar, click the Undo button thrice. The task list is restored to its original order.

15. SAVE the project schedule.

PAUSE. LEAVE Project open to use in the next exercise.

TAKE NOTE*   If you want to preserve Unique ID values when you rearrange tasks, drag and drop tasks rather than cutting and pasting them.

In this exercise, you added Unique ID and WBS code columns to the Task Sheet view and then explored how these identifiers change when you move, delete, or add tasks. Each task in a Microsoft Project schedule has a unique identifier, called the Task ID. Microsoft Project assigns sequential ID numbers to each task that you enter. When you insert, move, or delete a task, Microsoft Project updates the ID numbers so that the numbers always reflect the current task order. The Task ID column appears (by default) on the left side of most task tables in Microsoft Project. Note that resources have Resource IDs assigned to them, and that they behave like a Task ID.

Microsoft Project also tracks the order in which you enter tasks and resources. The **Unique ID** task and resource fields store this entry order. If tasks or resources are reorganized, and you later need to see their original entry order, you can view this in the Unique ID field.

Although these identifiers uniquely identify each task, they do not give you any information about the task's place in the hierarchy of the project structure. For example, you can't tell if a task is a summary or a subtask by simply looking at a Task ID. A better way to show the hierarchy of a project structure is to display the **outline numbers** or **work breakdown structure (WBS)** codes of tasks – the numeric representations of the outline hierarchy of a project. You can change WBS codes to include any combination of letters and numbers that you desire, but outline numbers are numeric only and are generated by Microsoft Project. When working with these codes, the **mask**, or appearance, defines the format of the code – the order and number of alphabetic, numeric, and alphanumeric strings in a code and the separators between them. Initially, outline numbers and WBS codes of tasks are identical. Microsoft Project also stores the Predecessor and Successor values for tasks' Unique IDs and WBS codes. Because the WBS codes indicate the place of every task in the project hierarchy, it is common to use WBS codes instead of Task ID or names when referencing tasks between team members on a project.

If you are working on a complex project, the WBS or standard outline options available in Microsoft Project may not be sufficient for your report or analysis requirements. If this occurs, you can investigate Microsoft Project's capabilities to handle custom outline numbers to identify a hierarchy within a project schedule. For example, you can define a custom outline number that links different outline levels of a project's structure with different levels of the organization's structure. (The top level might be a regional division, the second level a business unit, and the third level a local team.) You could also use custom outline numbers to associate different outline levels of a project's WBS with internal cost centers or job tracking codes.

After you have applied a custom outline number to your project schedule, you can then group, sort, and filter tasks and resources by their outline numbers. You can apply up to ten levels of a custom outline number for tasks and ten for resources in a single Microsoft Project file.

■ Formatting the Network Diagram

↓
THE BOTTOM LINE   In traditional project management, a Network Diagram is a standard way for representing project activities and their relationships in a flowchart format.

In this lesson, you apply and format the Network Diagram. The ***Network Diagram*** is a standard way of representing the logical order of project activities and their relationships. Tasks are represented as boxes, or ***nodes***, and the link lines represent the relationships between the nodes. The Network Diagram is not a time-scaled view like the Gantt Chart. Rather, it shows project activities in a flowchart format so that you can focus on the relationships between activities rather than on their durations.

→ FORMAT ITEMS IN THE NETWORK DIAGRAM VIEW

USE the project schedule you created in the previous exercise.

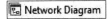

1. On the ribbon, click the View tab, and then click Network Diagram. The Network Diagram view appears. Your screen should look similar to Figure 14-11.

Figure 14-11

Network Diagram view

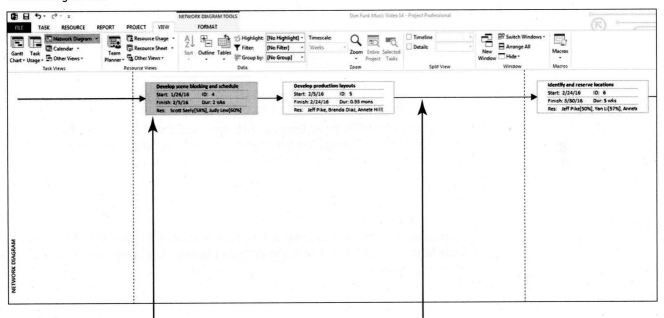

Each task is represented as a node   Lines between the nodes represent the task relationships

The focus of the Network Diagram is task relationships and sequencing (rather than durations). Each task is represented as a box, or node, containing several pieces of information about the task. The relationships between tasks are represented as lines and arrows. You will note that not much information is visible. You can zoom in and out by using the zoom slider at the lower right corner of the screen.

Box
Styles

2. On the ribbon, click the **Format** tab, and then click **Box Styles**. The Box Styles dialog box appears. Your screen should look similar to Figure 14-12.

Figure 14-12

Network Diagram's Box Styles dialog box

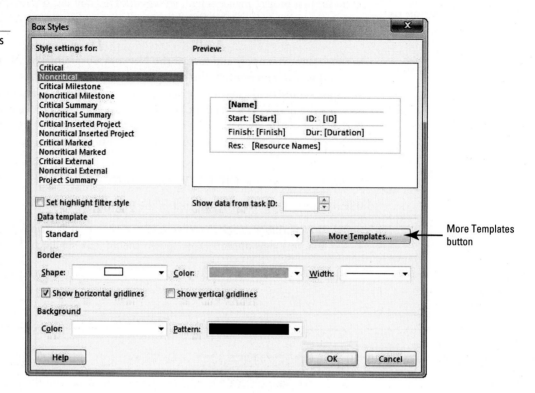

3. Click **More Templates**. The Data Templates dialog box appears.

4. In the Templates in "Network Diagram" list, make sure that **Standard** is selected, and then click the **Copy** button. The Data Template Definition dialog box appears. You will add the WBS code value to the lower right corner of the node.

5. In the Template name box, type **Standard + WBS**.

6. Below Choose cell(s), click the **empty cell** below Duration and to the right of Resource Names.

7. In the dropdown list that becomes active, type or select **WBS**. This will add the WBS code to the standard box style in the Network Diagram. Your screen should look similar to Figure 14-13.

Figure 14-13

Data Template Definition box customized with WBS field

New template name

Add the WBS field here

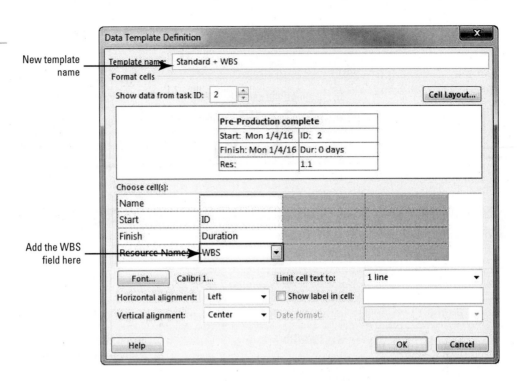

8. Click **OK** to close the Data Template Definition box. Click **Close** to close the Data Templates dialog box.

9. In the Box Styles dialog box, under Style settings for, select both **Critical** and **Noncritical**.

10. In the Data template box, click **Standard + WBS**, and then click **OK** to close the Box Styles dialog box. Microsoft Project applies the revised box style to the critical and noncritical task nodes in the Network Diagram. Your screen should look similar to Figure 14-14.

Figure 14-14

Network Diagram with revised box style applied to both critical and noncritical tasks

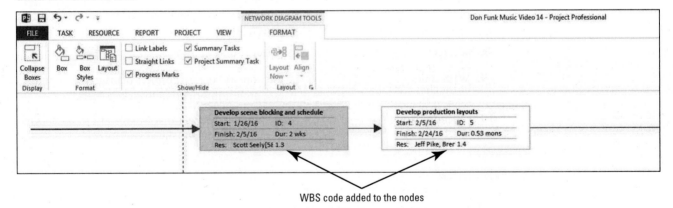

WBS code added to the nodes

Microsoft Project adds the WBS code to the nodes for critical and noncritical tasks. Scroll left and right to review some of the other nodes in the Network Diagram. As you can see, the node representing other types of tasks, such as summary tasks, are not affected. If you want to apply the new template to other task types, you would do so in the Box Styles dialog box.

11. **SAVE** the project schedule.

PAUSE. LEAVE Project open to use in the next exercise.

SKILL SUMMARY

In this lesson you learned:	Matrix Skill
To customize the calendar view	Format bar styles for tasks in the Calendar view
To use Task IDs and WBS codes	Work with Unique ID and WBS codes
To format the Network Diagram	Format items in the Network Diagram view

■ Knowledge Assessment

Matching

Match the term in column 1 to its description in column 2.

Column 1	Column 2
1. Task ID	**a.** a numeric-only representation of the outline hierarchy of a project, generated by Microsoft Project
2. nodes	**b.** defines the format of the outline and WBS codes
3. Unique ID	**c.** the view that looks similar to a "month-at-a-glance"
4. Network Diagram	**d.** a representation of the outline hierarchy of a project, which you can change to include any combination of letters and numbers
5. link lines	**e.** a unique identifier that tracks the order in which you enter tasks and resources
6. outline numbers	**f.** represent the relationships between tasks on a Network Diagram
7. mask	**g.** a standard way of representing project activities in a flowchart format
8. reports	**h.** the boxes used to represent tasks in a Network Diagram
9. WBS codes	**i.** the primary way that project managers communicate project information to stakeholders
10. Calendar	**j.** the unique identifier that Microsoft Project assigns to each task sequentially as you enter it

True/False

Circle T if the statement is true or F if the statement is false.

T F 1. The Network Diagram is drawn against a timeline.

T F 2. You can apply up to ten levels of a custom outline number for tasks in a single Microsoft Project file.

T F 3. You can apply any combination of letters and numbers to a WBS mask.

T F 4. WBS codes can include letters and numbers.

T F 5. The Network Diagram view is one of the simplest views available in Microsoft Project.

T | F   **6.** If you want to reorder tasks by the order in which they were entered, you can sort by the Task ID.

T | F   **7.** In the WBS structure, top-level summary tasks are sequentially numbered with a single digit.

T | F   **8.** The Network Diagram focuses on task durations.

T | F   **9.** By default, the Calendar view displays two weeks at a time.

T | F   **10.** The Unique ID shows a task's place in the hierarchy of the project schedule.

■ Competency Assessment

Project 14-1: WBS Codes for New Employee Orientation

You and your team are reviewing the project schedule for your company's new employee orientation. You agree that it would be easier to refer to tasks by their WBS codes, so you need to change the view of your schedule to reflect this. You also need to make changes in the hierarchy for a few of the tasks.

GET READY. Launch Microsoft Project if it is not already running.

OPEN *Employee Orientation Schedule 14-1* from the data files for this lesson.

1. On the ribbon, click View, then in the Task Views group click Other Views, and then click More Views.

2. In the More Views dialog box, select Task Sheet, and then click Apply.

3. Right-click the Task Name column heading. On the menu that appears, click Insert Column.

4. From your keyboard, type WBS, then select WBS from the field list.

5. In the Task ID column, click and drag to select tasks 22 and 23.

6. On the ribbon, click the Task tab. In the Schedule group, click the Indent button.

7. SAVE the project schedule as *Employee Orientation WBS* and then CLOSE the file.

   PAUSE. LEAVE Project open to use in the next exercise.

Project 14-2: Don Funk Enhanced Network Diagram

One of the finance managers on the Don Funk Music Video has asked you to include some financial data on the network diagram. You will modify your existing network diagram box template to include this data.

OPEN *Don Funk Music Video 14-2* from the data files for this lesson.

1. On the ribbon, click the View tab, and then click the Network Diagram button.

2. On the ribbon, click the Format tab, and then click Box Styles.

3. In the Box Styles dialog box, select More Templates.

4. Ensure the Standard template is selected the click the Copy button.

5. In the Data Template Definition box, give the new template the name of Standard + Costs.

6. In the Choose Cell(s) section, click once the Resource Names cell. Change this cell to Cost.

7. Click once the blank cell to the right of the newly created Cost cell. Using the submenu arrow that appears at the right, select or type Actual Cost. Check the check box next to Show label in cell. Click OK.

8. Click Close to CLOSE the Data Templates dialog box.

9. In the Box Styles dialog box, select **Critical** and **Noncritical**. Select the newly created **Standard + Costs** template in the Data Template box. Click **OK**.

10. **SAVE** the project schedule as ***Don Funk Enhanced Network Diagram*** and then **CLOSE** the file.

   PAUSE. LEAVE Project open to use in the next exercise.

■ Proficiency Assessment

Project 14-3: Calendar View for Insurance Claim Process

You would like to hand out a monthly view of the insurance claim process so that agents and adjustors can keep a quick reference of this process at their fingertips. You need to change the view of your project schedule to a calendar view as well as change the bar style formatting for a couple of task types.

 OPEN *Insurance Claim Processing 14-3* from the data files for this lesson.

1. Change to the Calendar view from the View ribbon.
2. Activate the **Bar Styles** dialog box on the Format ribbon.
3. Select **Critical** in the Task type box. Change the pattern to the **last** bar (checkered) in the dropdown list and change the color to **Red**.
4. Select **Project Summary** in the Task type box. Change the bar type to **None**.
5. Select **Milestone** in the Task type box. Change the color to **Green** and the pattern to the **horizontal** bars in the dropdown list
6. **CLOSE** the **Bar Styles** dialog box.
8. Double-click the **divider** bar between the calendar rows (weeks) to expand the row height.
9. **SAVE** the project schedule as ***Insurance Claim Calendar View*** and then **CLOSE** the file.

   PAUSE. LEAVE Project open to use in the next exercise.

Project 14-4: New Employee Orientation Network Diagram

Because the timeline for your New Employee Orientation is so short, you would like to focus on the relationships between tasks rather than their durations. You want to change the view to the Network Diagram and reformat some of the elements of the Network Diagram.

 OPEN *Employee Orientation Schedule 14-4* from the data files for this lesson.

1. Activate the **Network Diagram** from the View ribbon.
2. Activate the **Box Styles** dialog box from the Format ribbon.
3. Select **Critical Summary** from the Style settings for box if it is not already selected. Set the Data template for these boxes to **WBS**.
4. Select **Noncritical Summary** from the Style settings for box. Set the Data template for these boxes to **WBS**.
5. **CLOSE** the **Box Styles** dialog box.
6. **SAVE** the project schedule as ***Employee Orientation Network Diagram***, and then **CLOSE** the file.

   PAUSE. LEAVE Project open to use in the next exercise.

■ Mastery Assessment

Project 14-5: HR Interview Visual Critical Tasks

The HR Group Manager has requested a report for weekly resource work assignments on this project but would like to see it in calendar form. You need to create this report.

OPEN *HR Interview Schedule 14-5* from the data files for this lesson.

1. Activate the Calendar view.
2. Activate the Bar Styles dialog box.
3. Include the fields of Name and Resource Names and ensure the text is wrapped.
4. Look through the report and manually move (vertically) any tasks or milestones that are overlapping each other.
5. SAVE the project schedule as *HR Interview Weekly Work Calendar Report* and then CLOSE the file.

   PAUSE. LEAVE Project open to use in the next exercise.

Project 14-6: Insurance Claim Processing WBS Codes

You want to add the Unique ID and WBS columns to your Insurance Claim Processing project schedule. You would also like to explore how several changes to your project schedule will affect the Unique ID and WBS codes.

OPEN *Insurance Claim Processing 14-6* from the data files for this lesson.

1. Insert the Unique ID and WBS columns to the left of the Task Name column.
2. Save the project schedule as *Insurance Claim WBS*.
3. In a separate Word document, explain how the Unique ID and WBS codes are affected for each of the following independent situations (*Hint:* After documenting the changes for a given situation, click the Undo button.)

   • Tasks 7 and 8 are indented under Task 3.
   • Task 25 is indented under Task 22.
   • Task 11 is cut and then inserted below Task 7. (*Hint:* Describe each part of this step separately.)

4. SAVE the Word document as *Insurance Claim WBS*.
5. CLOSE both files.

   CLOSE Project.

15 LESSON

Managing Multiple Projects

LESSON SKILL MATRIX

SKILLS	TASKS
Managing Consolidated Projects	Create a consolidated project schedule
Creating Task Relationships Between Projects	Link tasks from two different project schedules

As a project manager for Southridge video, you are responsible for managing several other projects in addition to the Don Funk Music Video. Now that progress is occurring on some of your projects, you would like to find an easier way to work with multiple project files. In this lesson, you will learn to use some of the features that Microsoft Project provides to enable you to consolidate multiple project files and create links between projects.

KEY TERMS
consolidated project
external task
ghost task
inserted project
master project
subproject

© strategicimpulse/iStockphoto

■ SOFTWARE ORIENTATION

Consolidated Project Gantt Chart View

The Gantt Chart view of a consolidated project allows you to see multiple projects collected in one project schedule so you can filter, sort, and group the data as well as see task relationships between projects.

Figure 15-1

Gantt Chart view of a consolidated project file

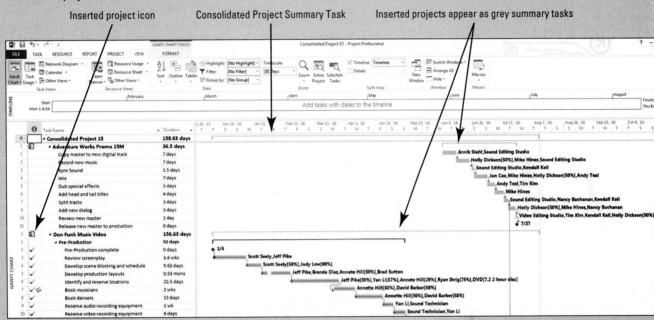

In the Gantt Chart view of a consolidated project, the inserted projects appear as summary tasks with gray Gantt bars and an inserted project icon appears in the Indicators column.

■ Managing Consolidated Projects

THE BOTTOM LINE

In Microsoft Project 2013, a consolidated project enables a project manager to link and manage multiple projects within one master project file. This method allows the project manager to see the effects of one project on another single project or many other projects in the same file.

⊙ CREATE A CONSOLIDATED PROJECT SCHEDULE

GET READY. Before you begin these steps, launch Microsoft Project.

1. OPEN the *Don Funk Music Video 15M* and *Adventure Works Promo 15M* project schedules from the data files for this lesson.

2. SAVE the files, respectively, as *Don Funk Music Video 15* and *Adventure Works Promo 15* in the solutions folder for this lesson as directed by your instructor. Make sure the *Don Funk Music Video 15* project schedule is in the active window.

New
Window

3. On the ribbon, click the **View** tab, and then click **New Window**. The New Window dialog box appears.

4. In the Projects list, select the names of both open projects either by holding down the **Ctrl** key while clicking or clicking and dragging to select both names. After you have selected both project schedules, click the **OK** button. Microsoft Project opens both files in a new window with the Timeline view at the top.

Entire
Project

5. On the ribbon, click **Entire Project** in the Zoom group. Microsoft Project adjusts the timescale in the Gantt Chart so that the full duration of both projects is visible. Make sure that the Name, Duration, Start, and Finish columns are visible on your screen. If necessary, double-click the right edge of any columns that display pound signs (###). Your screen should look similar to Figure 15-2.

Figure 15-2

Gantt Chart view with both
inserted projects

Inserted project icon

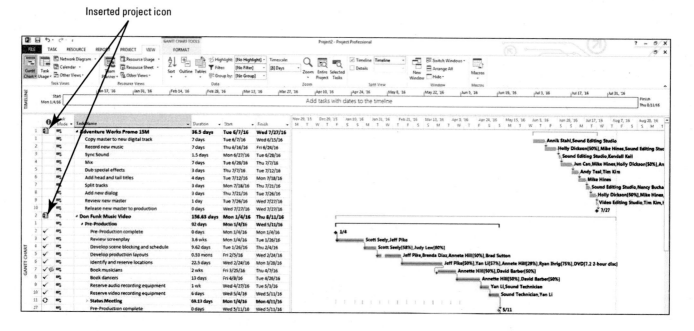

TAKE NOTE* When you point to the Inserted Project icon in the Indicators column, Microsoft Project displays the full path to the inserted project file.

6. Right-click the **Task Mode** column and select **Hide Column**.

7. **SAVE** the consolidated project schedule as ***Consolidated Project 15***. When you are prompted to save changes to the inserted projects, click the **Yes to All** button.

☐ Project Summary Task

8. On the ribbon, click the **Format** tab. In the Show/Hide group, click the check box to activate the **Project Summary Task**. Microsoft Project displays the Consolidated Project 15 summary task at the top of your Task Name column as task 0 (zero). Your screen should look similar to Figure 15-3.

Figure 15-3

Gantt Chart with Consolidated
Project summary task

Consolidated Project
Summary Task →

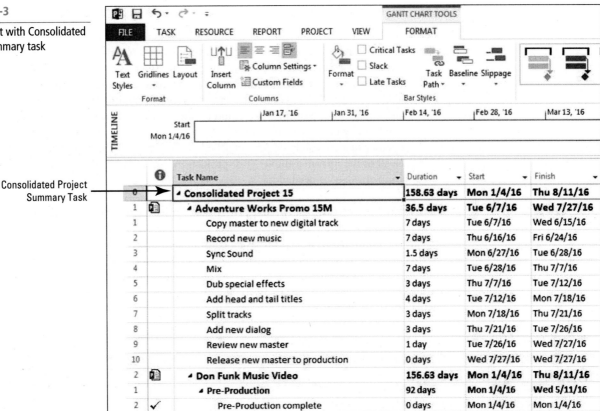

The values of the consolidated project summary task, such as duration and work, represent the rolled-up (or combined) values of both inserted projects. As Southridge Video acquires contracts for more projects, inserting them into the consolidated project schedule in this way provides a single location in which to view all the activities of the company.

TAKE NOTE * If you want to add more project schedules to a consolidated project, click the Project tab and then select Subproject from the Insert command group.

> **9.** SAVE the consolidated project schedule as well as the individual project schedules.
>
> PAUSE. LEAVE Project open to use in the next exercise.

In real life, it is rare that a project manager would manage only a single, small project from beginning to end. Usually, there are several complex projects that involve several people working on different tasks at different times and locations and often for different supervisors.

As you saw in this exercise, Microsoft Project enables you to combine two (or more) projects to form a consolidated project. A ***consolidated project*** is a Microsoft Project file that contains more than one Microsoft Project file, called inserted projects. An ***inserted project*** is the Microsoft Project file that is inserted into another Microsoft Project file. Consolidated projects are also known as ***master projects***, and inserted projects are also known as ***subprojects***. The inserted projects do not really reside within the consolidated project. They are linked to it in such a way that they can be viewed and edited from the consolidated project. If an inserted project is edited outside the consolidated project, the updated information appears in the consolidated project the next time it is opened. When you save a consolidated project, any changes you have made to inserted projects are saved in the source file as well.

Using a consolidated project gives you the capability to do such things as:

- see all of your organization's project schedules in a single view.
- "roll up" project information to higher management levels. For example, one group's project may be an inserted project for the department's consolidated project, which then may be an inserted project for the company's consolidated project.
- divide your project schedule into separate project schedules to match the nature of your project. For example, you could divide your project schedule into separate schedules by phase, component, or location. You can then group the information back together in a consolidated project schedule for a view of the complete project.
- see all of the information for your projects in one location, so you can filter, sort, and group the data as needed.

Consolidated projects use the standard Microsoft Project outlining features. For a consolidated project, the Gantt bar for an inserted project is gray and an inserted project icon appears in the Indicators column. Also, when you save a consolidated project, any changes you have made to inserted projects are saved in the source file as well. Theoretically, it is possible to add an unlimited number of project schedules to a consolidated project file. However, as a practical matter, and depending on the size of the files, you will notice performance issues such as slow calculation times as you add more inserted projects.

■ Creating Task Relationships Between Projects

 THE BOTTOM LINE Sometimes, tasks in one project may need to be linked to tasks in other projects. Microsoft Project allows you to show these task relationships by linking tasks between projects.

 LINK TASKS FROM TWO DIFFERENT PROJECT SCHEDULES

USE the project schedules you created in the previous exercise.

1. On the ribbon, click the **View** tab. In the Window group, click the **Switch Windows** button. Click **Adventure Works Promo 15**. The Adventure Works Promo 15 project schedule is now visible in the active window.

2. In the Task Name column, click the name of Task 7, **Split tracks**.

3. [Press **Ctrl+Shift+F5**]. To the right of the task's Gantt bar, note that one of the resources assigned to this task is Video Editing Studio. You want to use this sound editing studio for work on the Don Funk Music Video 15 project after this task is completed, so you need to link Task 7 to a task in the Don Funk Music Video 15.

4. On the ribbon, click the **Switch Windows** button, and then click *Don Funk Music Video 15*.

5. [Press the **F5** key.] In the ID box, type **69**, and then click **OK**. Notice the Sound Editing Studio is a resource on this task.

6. On the ribbon, click the **Switch Windows** button, and then click **Consolidated Project 15**.

7. In the task name column, in the Adventure Works Promo 15 project, click the name of Task 7, **Split tracks**.

8. Scroll down in the task name column to the Don Funk Music Video 15 project and locate Task 69, **Fine audio edit**. Hold down the **Ctrl** key and select Task 69.

9. On the ribbon, click the **Task** tab. In the Schedule group, click the **Link the Selected Tasks** button.

ANOTHER WAY When viewing a consolidated project, you can quickly create cross-project links by pressing the F2 key.

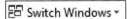 Switch Windows ▾

10. On the ribbon, click the **View** tab. In the Window group, click the **Switch Windows** button. Click **Adventure Works Promo 15**. The Adventure Works Promo 15 project schedule is now visible in the active window.

Microsoft Project inserted a ghost task named Fine audio edit into the project. The ghost task represents task 69 from the ***Don Funk Music Video 15*** project. Because task 9 is a successor task with no other links to this project, it has no effect on other tasks here. Your screen should look similar to Figure 15-4.

Figure 15-4

Gantt Chart view with ghost task from Don Funk Video

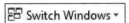

	❶	Task Mode	Task Name	Duration	Start	Finish
1			Copy master to new digital track	7 days	Tue 6/7/16	Wed 6/15/16
2			Record new music	7 days	Thu 6/16/16	Fri 6/24/16
3			Sync Sound	1.5 days	Mon 6/27/16	Tue 6/28/16
4			Mix	7 days	Tue 6/28/16	Thu 7/7/16
5			Dub special effects	3 days	Thu 7/7/16	Tue 7/12/16
6			Add head and tail titles	4 days	Tue 7/12/16	Mon 7/18/16
7			Split tracks	3 days	Mon 7/18/16	Thu 7/21/16
8			Fine audio edit	3 days	Fri 7/22/16	Wed 7/27/16
9			Add new dialo	3 days	Thu 7/21/16	Tue 7/26/16
10			Review new master	1 day	Tue 7/26/16	Wed 7/27/16
11			Release new master to production	0 days	Wed 7/27/16	Wed 7/27/16

Ghost tasks appear in grey on the task list

Ghost task (external task)

Now you will switch views to look at the ghost task in the ***Don Funk Music Video 15*** project schedule.

TAKE NOTE If you point to the Gantt bar for the ghost task, Microsoft Project will display a Screen-Tip that contains details about the ghost task, including the full path to the external project where the ghost task (the external predecessor) resides.

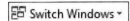 Switch Windows ▾

11. On the ribbon, click the **Switch Windows** button, and then click **Don Funk Music Video 15**. You can see that the ghost Task 69, Split tracks, is a predecessor for Task 70, Fine audio edit. The link between these two project schedules will remain until you break it. If this task is delayed it could affect Task 70. When you delete a task in the source schedule or the ghost task in the destination schedule, Microsoft Project also deletes the corresponding task or ghost task in the other schedule.

12. On the ribbon, click the **Switch Windows** button, and then click **Consolidated Project 15**. You can see the link between the task Review new master (Task 7) in the first inserted project and the task Fine audio edit (Task 70) in the second inserted project. The cross-project link does not appear as a ghost task because you are looking at the consolidated project file. Your screen should look similar to Figures 15-5 and 15-6 (note that you may need to scroll your screen to see the entire link).

Figure 15-5

Consolidated project files
displaying the link between
Adventure Works Task 7 . . .

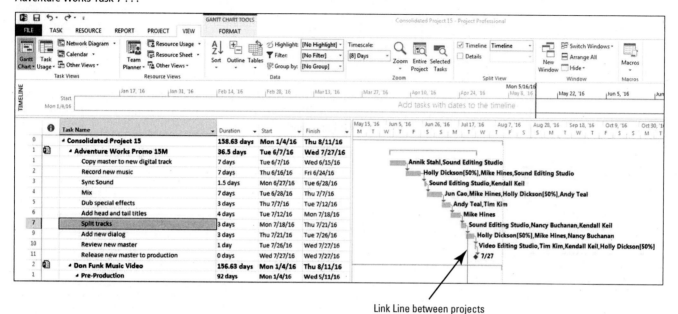

Link Line between projects

Figure 15-6

. . . and Don Funk Task 70

Link Line between projects

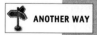

ANOTHER WAY
You can also view the links between projects by selecting the Links Between Projects button, located on the Project Ribbon. This will only display links when you have the source file in the active window.

TAKE NOTE
If you do not want to see cross-project links, click the **File** tab, and then click **Options**. Under the Advanced options, in the Cross project linking options section, clear the **Show external successors** or **Show external predecessors** check box.

TAKE NOTE

Whenever you open a project schedule with cross-project links, Microsoft Project will prompt you to update these cross-project links. You can suppress this prompt if you prefer not to be reminded. You can also tell Microsoft Project to automatically accept updated data from the linked project file. To do this, click the **File** tab, and then click **Options**. Under the Advanced options, in the Cross project linking options section, select the options you want.

13. SAVE the all of the project schedules, and then CLOSE all files.

PAUSE. If you are continuing to the next lesson, keep Project open. If you are not continuing to additional lessons, CLOSE Project.

In this exercise, you linked a task in one project to a task in another project to show a relationship between the two tasks and projects. Most projects are like this – they do not exist in a vacuum. There are various reasons you might need to create links between projects. Some of the more common reasons are:

- The completion of a task in one project might have an effect on a task in another project. For example, one project manager may need to complete a geological study before a second project manager can begin to construct a building. These two tasks may be managed in separate project files (perhaps because they are being completed by different departments of the same company, or even two different companies), but they still have a logical relationship on each other.
- A person or piece of equipment may be assigned to a task in one project, and you need to delay the start of a task in another project until that resource completes the first task. The only commonality between the two tasks is that the same resource is required for both.

Task relationships between project files are similar to the task links (relationships) between tasks within a project file, except that external predecessor and successor tasks have gray task names and Gantt bars. By definition, these are called *external tasks* and are sometimes referred to as *ghost tasks* because they are not linked to tasks within the project file, only to tasks in other project files.

SKILL SUMMARY

IN THIS LESSON YOU LEARNED:	MATRIX SKILL
To manage consolidated projects	Create a consolidated project schedule
To create a task relationship between projects	Link tasks from two different project schedules

■ Knowledge Assessment

Fill in the Blank

Complete the following sentences by writing the correct word or words in the blanks provided.

1. For a consolidated project, the Gantt bar is _____ in color, by default.

2. A(n) _____ _____ is the Microsoft Project file that is put into another Microsoft Project file.

3. If you point to the Gantt bar for a ghost task, Microsoft Project displays a(n) _____ _____ that contains the details about the ghost task.

4. Another name for an inserted project is a(n) _____.

5. To initially select the projects that you want to combine into a consolidated project, use the _____ dialog box.

6. Another name for a ghost task is a(n) _____ task.

7. The values of a consolidated project, such as duration and work, represent the rolled-up _____ _____ values of the inserted projects.

8. Another name for a consolidated project is a(n) _____ project file.

9. You can create a(n) _____ between projects if the completion of a task in one project has an effect on a task in another project.

10. A(n) _____ _____ is not linked to a task within the consolidated project file, only to tasks in another project file.

Multiple Choice

Select the best response for the following statements.

1. How many project schedules can you add to a consolidated project file?
   a. two
   b. three
   c. ten
   d. unlimited

2. By default, when you save a consolidated project,
   a. only the consolidated project is saved.
   b. only changes to the inserted project source files are saved.
   c. changes to both the consolidated project and the inserted project source files are saved.
   d. the consolidated project is saved within the first inserted project.

3. When you insert a project in a consolidated project, an inserted project icon appears
   a. in the Task Information dialog box.
   b. in the Indicators column.
   c. in the Task Name column.
   d. in the Project Information dialog box.

4. In a consolidated project, inserted projects
   a. do not actually reside within the consolidated project.
   b. can only be edited outside the consolidated project.
   c. reside within the consolidated project.
   d. none of the above

5. What is a reason to use a consolidated project schedule?
   a. to see all of your company's project schedules in a single view
   b. to see all of your projects' information in a single view, so you can filter, group, and sort data
   c. to "roll up" project information to higher levels of management
   d. all of the above

6. A cross project link may be required when:
   a. a single resource is shared between two projects.
   b. the completion of one project task affects the task of another project.
   c. neither A or B.
   d. both A and B.

7. The external predecessor and successor tasks in the task relationships between project files are sometimes called
   a. inserted tasks.
   b. phantom tasks.
   c. ghost tasks.
   d. subtasks.

8. To add schedules to a consolidated project,
   a. on the Project ribbon, click Move Project.
   b. on the View ribbon, click Add Project.
   c. on the File ribbon, click New.
   d. on the Project ribbon, click Subproject.

9. Another name for a consolidated project is a(n)
   a. inserted project.
   b. subproject.
   c. master project.
   d. summary project.

10. When you create a task dependency between projects, what format do you key in the ID column of the Predecessors tab of the Task Information dialog box?
    a. File Name\Task ID
    b. File Name, Task ID
    c. File Name/Task ID
    d. File Name – Task ID

■ Competency Assessment

Project 15-1: Southridge Video Consolidated Project Schedule

The director of Southridge Video would like to see a consolidated project schedule for all of the projects on which Southridge Video is currently working, both internal and external. You are beginning to assemble the consolidated schedule.

GET READY. Launch Microsoft Project if it is not already running.

OPEN the *Don Funk Music Video 15-1* and *Gregory Weber Biography 15-1* project schedules from the data files for this lesson. **SAVE** the files as *Don Funk Consolidated* and *Gregory Weber Consolidated*, respectively.

1. On the ribbon, click the **View** tab, and then click **New Window**.

2. In the Projects list, select the names of both open projects. After you have selected both project schedules, click the **OK** button.

3. Right-click the **Task Mode** column and select **Hide Column**.

4. On the ribbon, click **Entire Project** in the Zoom group.

5. **SAVE** the consolidated project schedule as *Southridge Video Consolidated*. When you are prompted to save changes to the inserted projects, click the **Yes to All** button.

6. On the ribbon, click the **Format** tab. In the Show/Hide group, click the check box to activate the **Project Summary Task**.

7. **SAVE** the consolidated project schedule, as well as the individual project schedules. **DO NOT** close the files.

   LEAVE Project and the three files open to use in the next exercise.

Project 15-2: Don Funk – Gregory Weber Dependency

Now that you have created a consolidated file for the Don Funk and Gregory Weber projects, you need to link the inserted schedules to show a dependency between them. Due to resource constraints, one of the tasks (task 3) in the Gregory Weber project cannot begin until another task (task 62) in the Don Funk project is complete.

USE the project schedules you created in the previous exercise.

1. On the ribbon, click **Switch Windows**, and then click *Southridge Video Consolidated*.

2. In the Task Name column, click the name of Task 62, **Production Complete** in the *Don Funk Consolidated* schedule.

3. Scroll up in the file and locate Task 3, **Review Screenplay**, in the *Gregory Weber Consolidated* schedule.

4. Press and hold the **Ctrl** key while selecting Task 3.

5. On the ribbon, click the **Task** tab. In the Schedule group, click the **Link the Selected Tasks** button.

6. **SAVE** the consolidated file as *Southridge Video Consolidated 2*. When you are prompted to save changes to the inserted projects, click the **Yes to All** button. **CLOSE** all files.

   LEAVE Project open to use in the next exercise.

■ Proficiency Assessment

Project 15-3: Gregory Weber Biography Inserted Project

You are the project manager on a new project for Southridge Video, a biography of Gregory Weber. An interview with Gregory Weber is a part of the production phase of the overall project. Make the Gregory Weber Interview an inserted project of the Gregory Weber Biography project schedule, inserted below the Production phase.

OPEN *Gregory Weber Biography 15-3* from the data files for this lesson.

1. Click on the name of Task 11, **Post-Production**.
2. On the ribbon, click the **Project** tab, and then click **Subproject**.
3. Using the Insert Project dialog box, find and select the *Gregory Weber Interview 15-3* file, and then click **Insert**.
4. On the ribbon, click the **Task** tab, and then click **Indent** button (right facing green arrow).
5. Click the **expand** button next to the inserted project task name of Gregory Weber Interview. (If necessary, identify the location of the file.)
6. **SAVE** the project schedule as *Gregory Weber Biography Consolidated*. If you are prompted to save changes to the inserted project, click the **Yes to All** button. **CLOSE** the file.

   PAUSE. Leave Project open to use in the next exercise.

Project 15-4: Southridge Video Consolidated Dependencies

You need to create a consolidated project schedule for Southridge Video, and then you need to create a dependency between the inserted projects.

OPEN *Don Funk Music Video 15-4* and *Gregory Weber Interview 15-4* from the data files for this lesson.

SAVE the files as *Don Funk Dependency* and *Gregory Weber Dependency*.

1. On the ribbon, click the **View** tab, and then click **New Window**.
2. In the Projects list, select the names of both open projects. After you have selected both project schedules, click the **OK** button.
3. **SAVE** the consolidated project schedule as *Southridge Video Dependency*. When you are prompted to save changes to the inserted projects, click the **Yes to All** button.
4. Make sure the consolidated project schedule is visible in the active window.
5. Click the name of Don Funk Music Video **Task 73**.
6. Hold down the **Ctrl** key and click on the name of Task 5, **Set up for interview**.
7. [Press **Ctrl+F2** key] to link the tasks.
8. Click the name of **Task 73** of the *Don Funk Dependency* inserted project, and then scroll the Gantt Chart so the Gantt bar for this task is visible.
9. **SAVE** all project schedules and then **CLOSE** all files.

   PAUSE. LEAVE Project open to use in the next exercise.

■ Mastery Assessment

Project 15-5: Triple Consolidated Project

In addition to two Human Resource-based projects you manage, you have also just been asked to oversee the remodel of the lunchroom at your office. You have decided to put all three projects in a consolidated project so that you can see all of your responsibilities in one place.

OPEN *HR Interview Schedule 15-5*, *Office Remodel 15-5*, and *Employee Orientation 15-5* from the data files for this lesson.

SAVE the files as *HR Interview 3Consolidated*, *Office Remodel 3Consolidated* and *New Employee 3Consolidated*.

1. Insert all three project schedules into a new project schedule.

2. **SAVE** the new project schedule as *Triple Consolidated*. If you are prompted to save changes to the inserted projects, click the **Yes to All** button.

3. Hide the **Task Mode** column and **auto fit** all the columns.

4. Activate the summary task for this project schedule.

5. Zoom the Gantt Chart to show the entire project.

6. **SAVE** all the project schedules.

LEAVE Project and the project schedules open to use in the next exercise.

Project 15-6: Establishing Dependencies in Triple Consolidated Schedule

Now that you have created a consolidated schedule for the projects for which you are responsible, you also need to establish some task links across inserted projects.

USE the *Triple Consolidated*, *HR Interview 3Consolidated*, and *New Employee 3Consolidated* project schedules you created in the previous exercise.

1. Link Task 30 of *HR Interview 3Consolidated* with Task 3 of *New Employee 3Consolidated* by making Task 30 a predecessor of Task 3. (*Hint:* Make sure that New Employee 3Consolidated is in the active window, and use the Predecessors tab of the Task Information dialog box to make Task 30 of *HR Interview 3Consolidated* a predecessor of New Employee Consolidated.)

2. Change the active window to Triple Consolidated, and review the link you just created.

3. **SAVE** the project schedule as *Triple Consolidated Dependency*. When you are prompted to save changes to the inserted projects, click the **Yes to All** button.

4. **CLOSE** all open files.

CLOSE Project.

Working with Resource Pools

LESSON SKILL MATRIX

SKILLS	TASKS
Developing a Resource Pool	Develop a resource pool
Viewing Assignment Details in a Resource Pool	View assignment details in the resource pool
Revising Assignments in a Sharer File	Revise assignments in a sharer file
Updating Resource Information in a Resource Pool	Update working time for a resource in a resource pool
Updating Working Time for All Projects in a Resource Pool	Update working time for all sharer files via the resource pool
Adding New Project Schedules to a Resource Pool	Add new files to the resource pool
Revising a Sharer File and Updating a Resource Pool	Revise a sharer file and manually update the resource pool

You are a video project manager for Southridge Video, and one of your primary responsibilities recently has been to manage the new Don Funk Music Video project. However, you also have several other projects that you manage. These projects often share resources and are worked on simultaneously. Microsoft Project has several features that facilitate working with multiple project schedules. In this lesson, you will learn how to work with a resource pool as well as review consolidated projects and how they relate to resource pools.

KEY TERMS

line manager
program office
resource manager
resource pool
sharer files

© sturti/iStockphoto

307

■ SOFTWARE ORIENTATION

Microsoft Project's Share Resources Dialog Box

In Microsoft Project, you can use the Share Resources dialog box to create a resource pool.

Figure 16-1

Share Resources dialog box

When using a resource pool, this file will become a sharer plan

Select resources from the sharer plan or the resource pool

If conflicts exist between the sharer plan and the resource pool, you can chose which one takes precedence

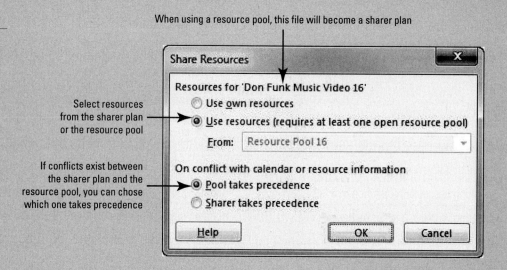

The Share Resources dialog box enables you to select the options you want when creating a resource pool, including the project schedule or resource pool to which you want to add your file as a sharer file and whether you want the resource pool or sharer file to take precedence in case of conflict.

■ Developing a Resource Pool

THE BOTTOM LINE

A resource pool can help a project manager see the extent to which resources are utilized across multiple and simultaneous projects.

In this exercise, you create a resource pool across two individual project schedules. A *resource pool* is a project file from which other project schedules gather their resource information, and it contains only resource information. As a project manager works to manage multiple projects, work resources are often assigned to more than one project at a time. It can be difficult to manage the resources' time among multiple projects, especially if different project managers are involved for each different project. For example, a technical editor might have task assignments on three different productions. In each project, the editor might be fully allocated or even under allocated, but when you add together all of the tasks from the three projects, you might find out that the editor is actually over allocated.

A resource pool can help you monitor how resources are utilized across multiple projects. It contains information about all resources' task assignments from all the project schedules linked to the resource pool. If you change resource information – such as cost rates, maximum units, and nonworking time – in the resource pool, all linked project schedules will use the updated information. The project schedules that are linked to the resource pool are called *sharer files*.

If you only manage one project and your resources are not used in other projects, then using a resource pool will provide no additional benefit to you. However, if your organization must manage multiple projects at the same time, setting up a resource pool allows you to do such things as:

- Enter resource information one time, but use it in multiple project schedules.
- View resources' assignment details from multiple projects in a single place.
- View assignment costs per resource across multiple projects.
- Identify resources that are over allocated across multiple projects, even if they are fully- or under allocated in individual projects.
- Enter resource information, such as nonworking time, in any of the individual schedules or in the resource pool so that it is available in the other sharer files.

A resource pool is particularly beneficial when you are working with other Microsoft Project users across a network. The resource pool can be stored in a central location – such as a network server – and the individual owners of the sharer files share the network resource pool.

In this exercise, the resource pool contains the resource information from both sharer files. Microsoft Project consolidates the information from sharer files based on the name of the resource. Annete Hill, for example, is listed only once in the resource pool, no matter how many sharer files list her as a resource. Keep in mind, however, that Microsoft Project can't match variations of a resource's name – say, Annete Hill from one sharer file and Annete L. Hill from another. It is good to develop a convention for naming a resource and stick with it.

Any Microsoft Project schedule, with or without tasks, can serve as a resource pool. It is considered a best practice, though, to specify a file that does not contain tasks as the resource pool. This is because any project with tasks will come to an end at some point, and you might not want assignments for those tasks (along with their costs and other details) to be included indefinitely in the resource pool. In addition, a dedicated resource pool file without tasks allows people such as line managers or resource managers to maintain some information about their resources in the resource pool. A *line manager* is a manager of a group of resources and is also sometimes called a functional manager. A *resource manager* oversees resource usage in project activities specifically to manage the time and cost of resources. These people might not have a role in project management and therefore would not need to deal with task-specific details in the resource pool.

⊕ DEVELOP A RESOURCE POOL

GET READY. Before you begin these steps, launch Microsoft Project.

1. OPEN the **Don Funk Music Video 16M** project schedule from the data files for this lesson.
2. SAVE the file as **Don Funk Music Video 16** in the solutions folder for this lesson as directed by your instructor.

3. OPEN the **Adventure Works Promo 16M** project schedule from the data files for this lesson.
4. SAVE the file as **Adventure Works Promo 16** in the solutions folder for this lesson as directed by your instructor.
5. On the ribbon, click the File tab, and then click New. Double-click Blank Project. A blank project opens.
6. On the ribbon, click the File tab, and then click Save As.
7. Locate your solution folder as directed by your instructor. The Save As dialog box appears. In the File name box, type **Resource Pool 16**, and then click Save.

TAKE NOTE＊   Although you can choose any name you want for a resource pool, it is a best-practice to indicate that it is a resource pool as part of the file name.

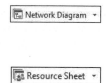
Network Diagram

Resource Sheet

8. On the ribbon, click the **View** tab, then in the Window group, click **Arrange All**. Microsoft Project arranges the three project schedule windows within the Microsoft Project window. (It is not necessary to arrange the project windows this way to create a resource pool, but it is helpful for viewing purposes in this lesson.)

9. On the View ribbon, click **Resource Sheet**. Your screen should look similar to Figure 16-2.

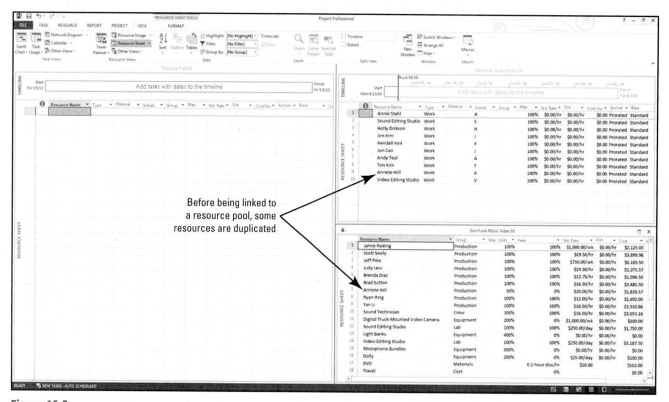

Figure 16-2

Resource Sheet views of all three project files

Notice that in the resource lists for the two project schedules, a few of the resources appear in both lists. These include Annete Hill, Sound Editing Studio, and Video Editing Studio. None of these resources are over allocated in either project.

10. Click the **title bar** of the Don Funk Music Video 16 window.

Resource Pool

11. On the ribbon, click the **Resource** tab, then select the **Resource Pool** button. From the drop down list, click **Share Resources**. The Share Resources dialog box appears.

12. Under Resources for 'Don Funk Music Video 16,' click **Use resources**. In the From: list, select **Resource Pool 16** from the dropdown list if it is not already selected. Your screen should look similar to Figure 16-3.

Figure 16-3

Share Resources dialog box

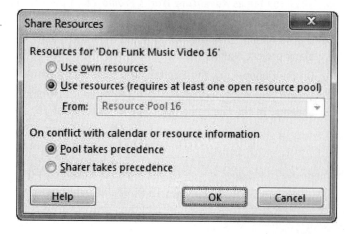

13. Click **OK** to close the Share Resources dialog box. The resource information from the Don Funk Music Video 16 project schedule appears in the Resource Pool 16 file.

14. Click the **title bar** of the Adventure Works Promo 16 window.

15. On the ribbon, click the **Resources** tab, then select the **Resource Pool** button. From the drop down list, click **Share Resources**. The Share Resources dialog box appears.

16. Under Resources for 'Adventure Works Promo 16,' click **Use resources**. In the From: list, make sure that **Resource Pool 16** is selected.

17. Under the On conflict with calendar or resource information label, make sure that **Pool takes precedence** is selected. Selecting this option causes Microsoft Project to use resource information (such as cost rates) in the resource pool rather than in the sharer file should it find any differences between the two project schedules.

18. Click **OK** to close the Share Resources dialog box. The resource information from the Adventure Works Promo 16 project schedule appears in the resource pool. Your screen should look similar to Figure 16-4.

Figure 16-4

Resource Pool 16 with resources shared

After sharer plans have been linked to the resource pool, duplicated resources are combined into one

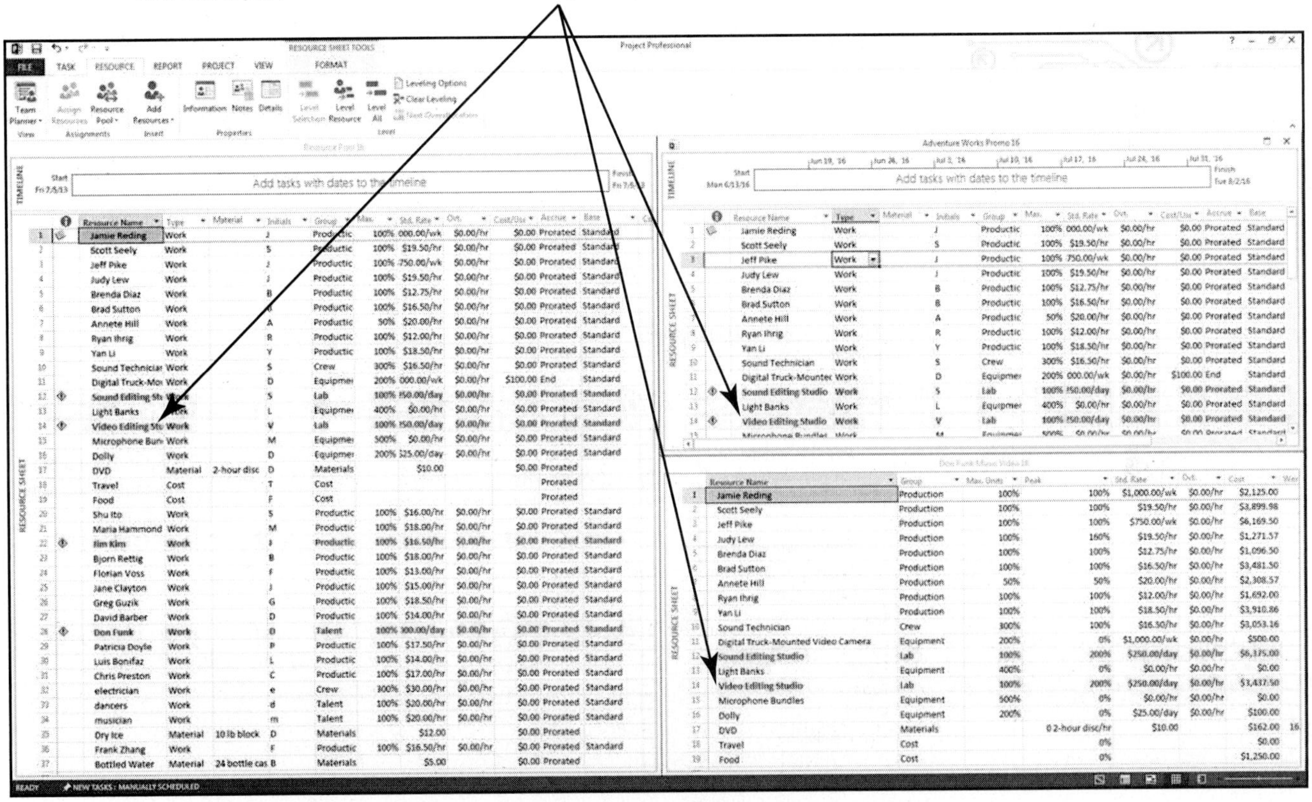

TAKE NOTE

If you decide at some point in the future that you do not want to use a resource pool with a project schedule, you can break the link. On the ribbon, click the **Resources** tab, then click the **Resource Pool** button. From the dropdown list, click **Share Resources**. In the **Share Resources** dialog box, under Resources for '<current project name>' click **Use own resources**.

19. SAVE each project schedule by clicking the **title bar** of each file, then clicking the File tab, and then clicking Save.

   PAUSE. LEAVE Project open to use in the next exercise.

■ Viewing Assignment Details in a Resource Pool

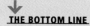

THE BOTTOM LINE   By viewing project assignments in a resource pool, you can see, in a combined format, how all the resources for the sharer projects are allocated.

 VIEW ASSIGNMENT DETAILS IN THE RESOURCE POOL

USE the project schedules you created in the previous exercise.

1. Double-click the **title bar** of the Resource Pool 16 window. The resource pool window maximizes to fill the active window. In the resource pool, you can view all resources from the two sharer files.

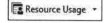

2. On the ribbon, click the **View** tab, and then click **Resource Usage**. The Resource Usage view appears.

3. Auto fit the Resource name column and then scroll to select the name of Resource 14, **Video Editing Studio**. Click the **expand** button next to Video Editing Studio's name to expand the assignment list. Your screen should look similar to Figure 16-5.

Figure 16-5

Resource Usage view with all of the Video Editing Studio assignments showing

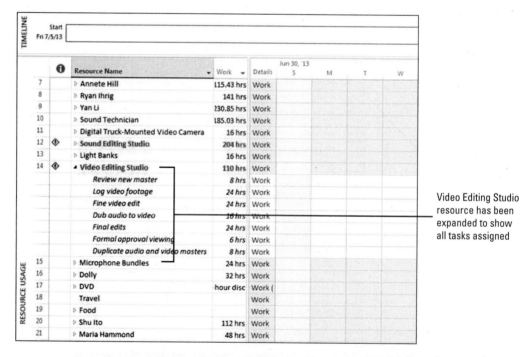

Video Editing Studio resource has been expanded to show all tasks assigned

4. [Press **Ctrl+Shift+F5**.] The timescale details on the right side of the active window scroll horizontally to show the Video Editing Studio's earliest assignments.

5. Scroll the timescale details to the right until you can see the assignments for the Video Editing Studio during the weeks of July 31, 2016 and August 7, 2016.

Cross Ref   For a review of resolving problems with resource allocation, see Lesson 6.

6. On the View ribbon, click the **Details** check box. The Resource Usage/Resource Form combination view is activated.

Figure 16-6

Combination view comprised of the Resource Usage view (top) and the Resource Form (bottom) for Video Editing Studio

7. In the Resource Form portion of the view, manually expand the **Project** column to see the entire project name in the list. (Auto fit does not function in this view.) Your screen should look similar to Figure 16-6. Your projects may be listed in a different order in the Resource Form window depending on which one you opened first.

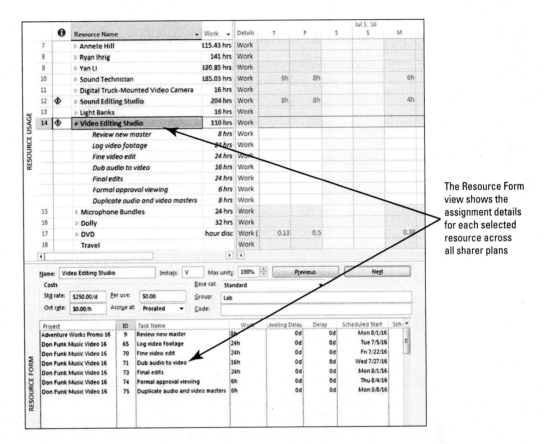

The Resource Form view shows the assignment details for each selected resource across all sharer plans

In this view, you can see all of the resources in the resource pool and their assignments (in the upper pane), as well as the additional details for the resources (in the lower pane) for all sharer files. Note, for example, that Task 75, Duplicate audio and video masters, to which the Video Editing Studio is assigned, is from the Don Funk Music Video project, and the Review new master, Task 9, is from the Adventure Works Promo project. While the Video Editing Studio was not over allocated in either project, it is actually over allocated when you look at its assignments across projects in this way.

Take a minute to select different resource names in the Resource Usage view to see their assignment details in the Resource Form.

8. On the ribbon, clear the **Details** check box.

9. **SAVE** the project schedule.

PAUSE. LEAVE Project open to use in the next exercise.

☐ Details

In this lesson, you changed the view of the resource pool to better view and analyze the information it contains. One of the most important benefits of using a resource pool is that it enables you to see how resources are allocated across projects. You can pinpoint resources that are over allocated across the multiple projects to which they are assigned.

■ Revising Assignments in a Sharer File

 THE BOTTOM LINE When you make changes to resource assignments in a sharer file, these changes will be reflected in the resource pool as well.

 REVISE ASSIGNMENTS IN A SHARER FILE

USE the project schedules you used in the previous exercise. Make sure that ***Resource Pool 16*** is the project schedule in the active window.

1. In the Resource Usage view, scroll until you see Resource 48, **Arlene Huff**, in the Resource Name column, and then click her name.

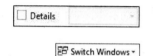

2. On the ribbon, click the **Details** check box. In the lower window, you can see that Arlene Huff has no task assignments in either sharer file.

3. On the ribbon, click the **Switch Windows** button, and then click **Don Funk Music Video 16**. The Don Funk Music Video 16 project is in the active window.

4. On the ribbon, click the **Gantt Chart** button. The Gantt Chart appears.

5. [Press the **F5** key.] In the ID box, type **68**, and then click **OK**. The Gantt Chart view scrolls to Task 68.

6. Click on the name of Task 68, **Rough audio edit**.

7. On the ribbon, click the **Resource** tab, then click the **Assign Resources** button. The Assign Resources dialog box appears.

8. In the Resource Name column in the Assign Resources dialog box, select **Arlene Huff**, and then click **Assign**.

9. Click **CLOSE** to close the Assign Resources dialog box.

10. On the ribbon, click the **View** tab, then click the **Switch Windows** button.

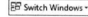

11. From the list, click **Resource Pool 16** to switch back to the resource pool. Arlene Huff's new task assignment appears in the resource pool. You may need to scroll the upper window (the Resource Usage view) to see Arlene Huff's name. Your screen should look similar to Figure 16-7.

Figure 16-7

Resource Pool 16 with Arlene Huff assigned to Task 68 in the Don Funk project

Arlene Huff has been assigned to the *Rough Audio Edit* task from the Don Funk Music Video 16 project

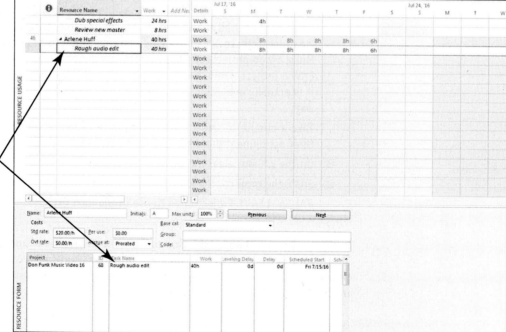

12. SAVE each project schedule. (You can either use the task bar at the bottom of your screen to bring each schedule to the active window to save it, or you can click Switch Windows on the ribbon and then select each schedule.)

13. After saving the project schedules, make sure that *Resource Pool 16* is in the active window.

   PAUSE. LEAVE Project open to use in the next exercise.

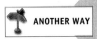

ANOTHER WAY You can also use the Go To dialog box (the F5 key) and enter Arlene's resource ID number to move the view to Arlene Huff's name.

In this exercise, you made a resource assignment from the resource pool into a sharer file and then viewed the change posted to the resource pool. Recall that an assignment is the matching of a resource to a task. The resource's assignment details originate in a sharer file, and Microsoft Project updates the resource pool with assignment details as you make them in the sharer file.

■ Updating Resource Information in a Resource Pool

THE BOTTOM LINE When a resource's information is updated in a resource pool, it is also updated in all of the sharer files linked to that resource pool.

 UPDATE WORKING TIME FOR A RESOURCE IN A RESOURCE POOL

USE the project schedules you used in the previous exercise.

You have just been told that Jim Kim is not available to work on July 25–26, 2016, because he will be attending a training program.

1. In the Resource Name column, scroll to select resource name 22, **Jim Kim**.

2. Click the **expand** button next to Jim Kim's name to display all of his assignments below his name. If necessary, scroll the Resource Usage view vertically so that all of Jim Kim's assignments are visible. Note that Jim is assigned 24 hours of work on the task of Fine audio edit for the Don Funk Music Video 16 project during the week of July 24th.

3. Double-click **Jim Kim's** name. The Resource Information dialog box appears. Click the **General** tab, if necessary.

4. Click the **Change Working Time** button. The Change Working Time dialog box appears.

5. Drag the **vertical scroll** bar or click the **up** and **down arrows** next to the calendar until July 2016 appears.

6. Select the dates **July 25** and **26**.

7. On the Exceptions tab below the calendar, under the Name column heading, click the first **empty cell**. Type **Training Class** and [press **Enter**]. Microsoft Project fills the Start and Finish cells with 7/25/2016 and 7/26/2016, respectively, and sets these dates to nonworking time. Your screen should look like Figure 16-8.

Figure 16-8

Change Working Time dialog
box for Jim Kim

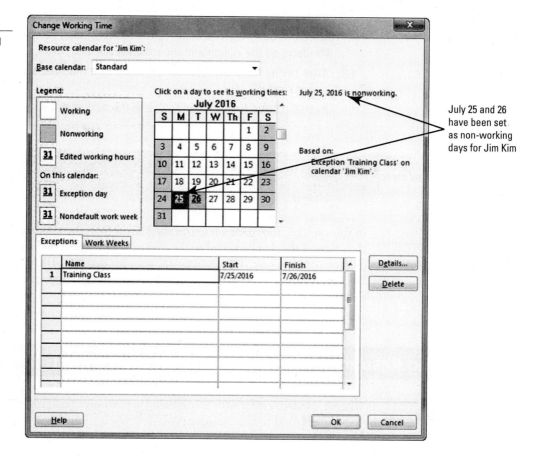

8. Click **OK** to close the Change Working Time dialog box. Click **OK** again to close the
Resource Information dialog box. Scroll the screen so that July 25 and 26 are visible.
Notice that Jim Kim now has no work scheduled for July 25 and July 26, 2016
(previously he had). Your screen should look similar to Figure 16-9.

Figure 16-9

Resource Usage view showing
the nonworking days for Jim Kim

	ⓘ	Resource Name	Work	Add New	Details	F	S	S	M	T	W	T	F
16		▷ Dolly	32 hrs		Work								
17		▷ DVD	·hour disc		Work (								
18		Travel			Work								
19		▷ Food			Work								
20		▷ Shu Ito	112 hrs		Work	2h			8h	8h	8h	8h	6h
21		▷ Maria Hammond	48 hrs		Work	2h			8h	8h	6h		
22		▲ Jim Kim	54 hrs		Work	2h				8h	8h	6h	
		Fine audio edit	24 hrs		Work	2h				8h	8h	6h	
		Scene 1 rehearsal	6 hrs		Work								
		Log video footage	24 hrs		Work								
23		▷ Bjorn Rettig	20 hrs		Work								
24		▷ Florian Voss	56 hrs		Work								
25		▷ Jane Clayton	77 hrs		Work								
26		▷ Greg Guzik	48 hrs		Work	2h			8h	8h	6h		
27		▷ David Barber	148 hrs		Work	1h			4h	4h	3h		
28	◈	▷ Don Funk	133.03 hrs		Work								2h
29		▷ Patricia Doyle	40 hrs		Work								
30		▷ Luis Bonifaz	30 hrs		Work								
31		▷ Chris Preston	95 hrs		Work								

Since July 25 and 26 are nonworking days for Jim Kim, no work is scheduled

TROUBLESHOOTING Anytime you make changes in a resource pool, make sure you have it open as read-write (as it is in this lesson). When you create a resource pool, it is automatically created as read-write. When you open any resource pool, if Microsoft Project asks whether you want to open it as read-only or read-write, select read-write.

9. On the ribbon, click the Switch Windows button, and then click Adventure Works Promo 16.

10. In the Resource Name column, select the resource name of Jim Kim (resource 22).

11. Double-click Jim Kim's name. In the Resource Information dialog box that appears, click the Change Working Time button. The Change Working Time dialog box appears.

12. Drag the vertical scroll bar or click the up and down arrows next to the calendar until July 2016 appears. Click the date July 25, and then click July 26. The notes next to the calendar indicate that both of these days are nonworking.

13. Click Cancel to close the Change Working Time dialog box. Click Cancel again to close the Resource Information dialog box.

14. SAVE all of the project schedules.

PAUSE. LEAVE Project open to use in the next exercise.

In this exercise, you updated a resource's calendar in the resource pool and then verified that this change was reflected in the sharer file. This is another key benefit of using resource pools – you have a central location to enter resource details, such as working time and cost rates, and any updates you make to the resource pool are made available in all of the sharer files. This is particularly useful in organizations with large numbers of resources working on multiple projects. In larger organizations, employees such as line managers, resource managers, or even staff in a program office may be responsible for keeping general resource information updates. A *program office* is a group that oversees a collection of projects (such as producing doors and producing engines), each of which is part of a complete deliverable (such as an automobile) and the organization's strategic objectives. Depending on the organization, a program office may also be called a project management office or a PMO.

■ Updating Working Time for All Projects in a Resource Pool

THE BOTTOM LINE   Any working time change that you make in the resource pool will update to all sharer files.

UPDATE WORKING TIME FOR ALL SHARER FILES VIA THE RESOURCE POOL

USE the project schedules you used in the previous exercise.

The entire company (Southridge Video) will be attending a company picnic on July 15, 2011, and you want this to be a nonworking day for all sharer projects.

 1. On the View ribbon, click the Switch Windows button, and then click Resource Pool 16.

2. On the ribbon, click the Project tab, then click the Change Working Time button. The Change Working Time dialog box appears.

 3. In the For calendar box, select Standard (Project Calendar) from the dropdown list.

4. Drag the vertical scroll bar or click the up and down arrows next to the calendar until July 2016 appears. Click the date July 15.

5. On the Exceptions tab below the calendar, under the Name column heading, click the first **empty cell**. Type **Company Picnic** and [press **Enter**]. Microsoft Project fills the Start and Finish cells with 7/15/2016 and sets the time to nonworking. Your screen should look similar to Figure 16-10.

Figure 16-10

Change Working Time dialog box for the Project Calendar

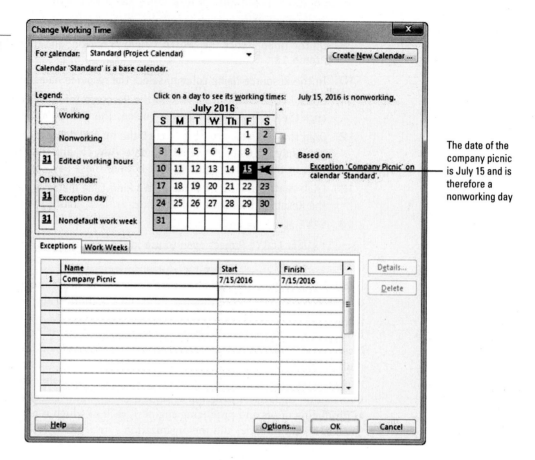

6. Click **OK** to close the Change Working Time dialog box.

7. On the ribbon, click the **View** tab, then click the **Switch Windows** button, and then click **Don Funk Music Video 16**.

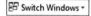

8. On the ribbon, click the **Project** tab, then click the **Change Working Time** button. The Change Working Time dialog box appears.

9. Make sure that **Standard (Project Calendar)** is selected in the For calendar box, and then drag the **vertical scroll** bar or click the **up** and **down arrows** next to the calendar until July 2016 appears. Notice that July 15, 2016, is flagged as a nonworking day and the details are shown on the Exceptions tab below the calendar.

10. Click **Cancel** to close the Change Working Time dialog box.

   If you desire, you can switch the view to the Adventure Works Promo 16 project and use the same steps to verify that July 15, 2016, is also a nonworking day for that project.

11. **SAVE** all project schedules and then **CLOSE** all files.

   PAUSE. LEAVE Project open to use in the next exercise.

In this exercise, you made a change to the base calendar for the resource pool, and then verified this change in one of the sharer files. This is another key advantage of using a resource pool. By changing the base calendar for the resource pool, the change is updated for ALL sharer files that use that calendar.

TROUBLE**SHOOTING** By default, all sharer files share the same base calendars, and any changes you make in a base calendar in one sharer file are reflected in all other sharer files using that base calendar through the resource pool. If you have a certain sharer file for which you want to use different base calendar working times, you must change the base calendar that sharer file uses. This different base calendar will still be available for use in all other sharer files through the resource pool, but will only apply to those sharer files in which you select it as the base calendar.

■ Adding New Project Schedules to a Resource Pool

↓
THE BOTTOM LINE Project schedules can be made into sharer files for a resource pool at any time. For this reason, it is a good idea to make all project schedules into sharer files (once you have set up a resource pool).

→ ADD NEW FILES TO THE RESOURCE POOL

GET READY. To add new files to the resource pool, do the following:

1. OPEN *Resource Pool 16* from the solution files for this lesson. When prompted, click the **second option** to open the file as read-write, and then click OK.

TAKE NOTE* The default option is for Microsoft Project to open resource pools as read-only. You might want to choose this option if you and other Microsoft Project users are sharing a resource pool across a network. However, if you store the resource pool locally, you should open it as read-write.

2. On the ribbon, click the View tab, and then click **Resource Sheet**. The Resource Sheet View appears.

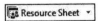

3. On the View ribbon, clear the **check box** for Details in the Split View group.
4. On the ribbon, click the File tab, then select New. Double-click **Blank Project**. A blank project opens.
5. On the ribbon, click the File tab, and then click Save As.
6. Locate your solution folder as directed by your instructor. The Save As dialog box appears. In the File name box, key **Graphic Design Project 16**, and then click Save.

7. On the ribbon, click the Resource tab, then click the **Assign Resources** button. The Assign Resources dialog box appears.

   The Assign Resources box is currently empty because you have not yet entered any resource information into this project schedule.

8. On the ribbon, click the **Resource Pool** button, and then click **Share Resources**. The Share Resources dialog box appears.
9. Under Resources for 'Graphic Design Project 16,' select **Use Resources**.
10. In the From list, make sure that **Resource Pool 16** is selected in the dropdown list. Your screen should look similar to Figure 16-11.

Figure 16-11

Share Resource dialog box

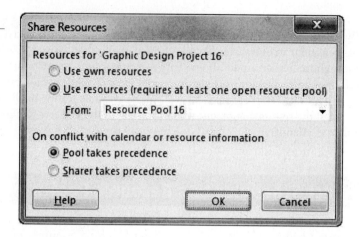

11. Click **OK** to close the Share Resources dialog box. In the Assign Resources dialog box, you can now see all of the resources from the resource pool. These resources are now ready for assignment to tasks in this project. Your screen should look similar to Figure 16-12.

Figure 16-12

Assign Resources dialog box for Graphic Design Project 16

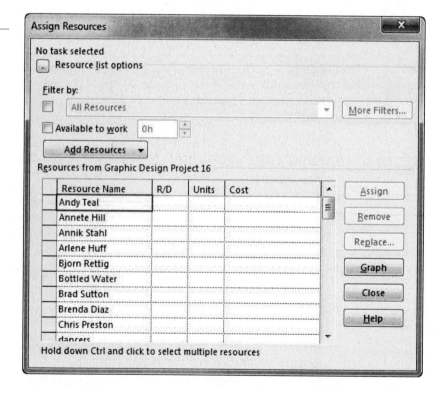

12. Click **Close** to close the Assign Resources dialog box.
13. **SAVE** the project schedules, and then **CLOSE** the files.

     PAUSE. LEAVE Project open to use in the next exercise.

In this exercise, you created a project schedule and made it a sharer file for the resource pool. You can do this at any time: when initially entering the project schedule's tasks, after you have assigned resources to tasks, or even after work has begun. Once you have set up a resource pool, you might find it helpful to make sharer files of projects in progress and of all new projects. This is a good way to become accustomed to relying on the resource pool for resource information.

■ Revising a Sharer File and Updating a Resource Pool

↓
THE BOTTOM LINE
Sometimes, you may have the resource pool open as read-only. In this case, you would have to manually update resource information to the resource pool.

REVISE A SHARER FILE AND MANUALLY UPDATE THE RESOURCE POOL

GET READY. To revise a sharer file and manually update the resource pool, do the following:

1. OPEN *Adventure Works Promo 16* from your solution files for this lesson (this is a project schedule you used in a previous exercise, but we want to open it now as read-only). Select the **Open resource pool to see assignments across all sharer files** option, and then click **OK**.

Gantt
Chart ▾

2. On the ribbon, click the **View** tab, and then click **Gantt Chart**.

3. In the Task Name column, click on the name of Task 6, **Add head and tail titles**. [Press **Ctrl+Shift+F5**] to bring the data into view.

Assign
Resources

4. On the ribbon, click the **Resource** tab, and then click the **Assign Resources** button. The Assign Resources dialog box appears.

5. In the Resource Name column in the Assign Resources dialog box, select the name of **Frank Zhang**, and then click the **Assign** button.

6. In the Task Name column, click the name of Task 9, **Review new master**.

7. In the Resource Name column in the Assign Resources dialog box, scroll to locate and select **Holly Dickson**, and then click the **Remove** button.

   You have made two assignment changes in the sharer file. Because the resource pool is open as read-only, these changes were not automatically saved in the resource pool. You need to manually update the resource pool.

8. On the ribbon, click the **Resource Pool** button, and then click **Update Resource Pool**. Microsoft Project updates the assignment information in the resource pool file with the new details from the sharer file. If anyone opens or refreshes the resource pool from now on, the updated assignment information will be available.

TAKE NOTE *
Keep in mind that only assignment information is saved to the resource pool from the sharer file. Any changes you make to resource details, such as cost rates or Max. units, in the sharer file are not saved in the resource pool when you update. If you want to change resource details, you must open the resource pool as read-write. Once it is open as read-write, you can change resource details in either the resource pool or the sharer file, and Microsoft Project will update the other file.

9. In the Task Name column, click on the name of task 3, **Sync Sound**.

10. In the Assign Resources dialog box, scroll to locate and select **Arlene Huff**, and then click the **Assign** button.

11. Click the **Close** button to close the Assign Resources dialog box. Your screen should look similar to Figure 16-13.

Figure 16-13

Adventure Works Promo
schedule with revised resources

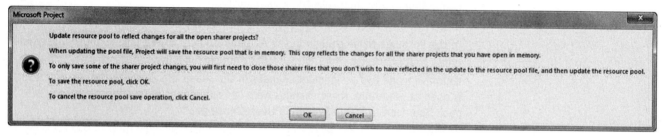

Frank Zhang added to task 6

Holly Dickson removed from task 9

12. On the ribbon, click the **File** tab, and then click **Close**. When prompted to save changes, click **Yes**. Microsoft Project determines that because the resource pool was opened as read-only, the assignment changes you just made in the sharer file have not been updated in the resource pool file. A dialog box appears, and you are offered a choice as to whether or not you want to update the resource pool. Your screen should look similar to Figure 16-14.

Figure 16-14

Dialog box asking to save the
resource pool information

> **Microsoft Project**
>
> Update resource pool to reflect changes for all the open sharer projects?
>
> When updating the pool file, Project will save the resource pool that is in memory. This copy reflects the changes for all the sharer projects that you have open in memory.
>
> To only save some of the sharer project changes, you will first need to close those sharer files that you don't wish to have reflected in the update to the resource pool file, and then update the resource pool.
>
> To save the resource pool, click OK.
>
> To cancel the resource pool save operation, click Cancel.
>
> [OK]　[Cancel]

13. After you review the options in the dialog box, click **OK**. Microsoft Project updates the assignment information with the new details from the sharer file. The resource pool remains open as read-only.

14. On the ribbon, click the **File** tab, and then click **Close**. Since the resource pool was opened as read-only, Microsoft Project closes it without prompting you to save changes.

PAUSE. If you are continuing to the next lesson, keep Project open. If you are not continuing to additional lessons, **CLOSE** Project.

In this exercise, you made changes to a sharer file and updated a resource pool that had been opened as read-only (as if you were on a network, rather than working with local files). This is an important concept because if you are sharing a resource pool with other Microsoft Project users across a network, whoever has the resource pool open as read-write prevents others from updating resource information. For this reason, it is a good idea to open the resource pool as read-only and to use the Update Resource Pool command only when you need to update the resource pool with assignment information. Once this is done, anyone else who opens the resource pool will see the latest assignment information.

SKILL SUMMARY

In this lesson you learned:	Matrix Skill
To develop a resource pool	Develop a resource pool
To view assignment details in a resource pool	View assignment details in the resource pool
To revise assignments in a sharer file	Revise assignments in a sharer file
To update resource information in a resource pool	Update working time for a resource in a resource pool
To update working time for all projects in a resource pool	Update working time for all sharer files via the resource pool
To add new project schedules to a resource pool	Add new files to the resource pool
To revise a sharer file and update a resource pool	Revise a sharer file and manually update the resource pool

■ Knowledge Assessment

Matching

Match the term in column 1 to its description in column 2.

Column 1	Column 2
1. line manager	**a.** project schedules that are linked to the resource pool
2. resource pool	**b.** a group that oversees a collection of projects, each of which may be part of a complete deliverable
3. assignment	**c.** the work assigned to a resource is more than can be done within the normal work capacity of the resource
4. program office	**d.** a manager of a group of resources
5. underallocated	**e.** dialog box that enables you to specify how resources will be used across project schedules
6. resource manager	**f.** a project file from which other project schedules gather their resource information
7. split view	**g.** the matching of a resource to a task
8. Share Resources	**h.** the active view is composed of two views which divide the screen horizontally
9. overallocated	**i.** the work assigned to a resource is less than the resource's maximum capacity
10. sharer file	**j.** a manager who oversees resource usage in project activities to manage the time and cost of resources

True/False

Circle T if the statement is true or F if the statement is false.

T | F **1.** You can link a maximum of three sharer files to a resource pool.

T | F **2.** Any Microsoft Project schedule can serve as a resource pool.

T | F **3.** If you decide that you do not want to use a resource pool with a project schedule, it is possible to break the link between the resource pool and sharer file.

T | F **4.** If you have a resource pool open as read-only and make changes to a sharer file, only assignment information is saved to the resource pool from the sharer file.

T | F **5.** Microsoft Project does not update the resource pool with assignment details as you make them in the sharer file.

T | F **6.** When you save a resource pool, you must use 'resource pool' as part of the filename.

T | F **7.** A project schedule can be made into a sharer file for a resource pool only before work has started.

T | F **8.** For a resource pool on a network, multiple users can simultaneously have the resource pool open as read-write.

T | F **9.** If you change resource information, such as costs rate, in the resource pool, all linked projects will use the updated information.

T | F **10.** By default, all sharer files use the same base calendar.

■ Competency Assessment

Project 16-1: Adding a Sharer File to the Southridge Video Resource Pool

You have created a resource pool for two of the Southridge Video projects on which you are working. You have been assigned to work on another project and want to add this sharer file to the resource pool.

GET READY. Launch Microsoft Project if it is not already running.

OPEN *Southridge Video Resource Pool 16-1* from the data files for this lesson. When prompted, click the second option to open the file as read-write, and then click OK.
OPEN *Gregory Weber Biography 16-1* from the data files for this lesson.

SAVE the files as *Southridge Video Resource Pool* and *Gregory Weber Biography*.

1. On the View ribbon, click Switch Windows, and then click Gregory Weber Biography.
2. On the ribbon, click Resource Sheet.
3. On the ribbon, click the Resource tab, then click the Resource Pool button, and then click Share Resources.
4. Under Resources for 'Gregory Weber Biography,' select the Use resources option.
5. In the From list, make sure that Southridge Video Resource Pool is selected from the dropdown list, and then click OK.
6. SAVE the project schedules.
7. CLOSE the *Gregory Weber Biography* project schedule. Leave the *Southridge Video Resource Pool* project schedule open.

   PAUSE. LEAVE Project open to use in the next exercise.

Project 16-2: Updating Working Time in the Southridge Video Resource Pool

Arlene Huff has just informed you that she is unable to work on July 20, 2016, because of a personal commitment. You need to update her resource information to reflect this date as nonworking time.

SAVE the open *Southridge Video Resource Pool* as *Southridge Video Resource Pool 2*.

1. On the ribbon, click the View tab, and then click Resource Usage.
2. In the Resource Name column, double-click the name Arlene Huff.
3. In the Resource Information dialog box, click the Change Working Time button.
4. Drag the vertical scroll bar or click the up and down arrows next to the calendar until July 2016 appears.
5. Select the date July 20.
6. On the Exceptions tab below the calendar, under the Name column heading, click the first empty cell. Type Vacation Day and [press Enter].
7. Click OK in the Change Working Time dialog box.
8. Click OK in the Resource Information Dialog box.
9. SAVE the project schedule, and then CLOSE the file.

   PAUSE. LEAVE Project open to use in the next exercise.

■ Proficiency Assessment

Project 16-3: Revising the Employee Orientation Sharer File and Updating the HR Resource Pool.

You need to make several changes to the Employee Orientation Schedule, but want to open the HR Resource Pool as read-only so that others can still read the file while you are using it. You will then need to update the resource pool with your changes.

(To set up this exercise, you will first need to build a resource pool from the Employee Orientation Schedule and HR Interview Schedule projects. After creating and saving the resource pool and sharer files, you will reopen the necessary files for this exercise.)

OPEN *Employee Orientation Schedule 16-3* and *HR Interview Schedule 16-3* from the data files for this lesson.

SAVE the project schedules as *Employee Orientation Schedule 3* and *HR Interview Schedule 3*.

1. OPEN a new, blank project schedule.
2. SAVE the new file as *HR Resource Pool 3*.
3. Change the view to the Resource Sheet for all files.
4. Arrange all three open files in the active window.
5. Use the Share Resources dialog box to add the resources from *HR Interview Schedule 3* to *HR Resource Pool 3*.
6. Use the Share Resources dialog box to add the resources from *Employee Orientation Schedule 3* to *HR Resource Pool 3*.
7. SAVE all three open files, and then CLOSE the files.
8. OPEN *Employee Orientation Schedule 3* from your solution file location. When prompted, select the option to open the resource pool.
9. Make sure that the *Employee Orientation Schedule 3* project fills the active window. Change the view to the Gantt Chart.

10. Select the name of Task 11, **Tour Customer Service Center**.

11. Activate the Assign Resources dialog box.

12. Assign Jason Watters to this task.

13. Select the name of Task 10, **Measuring for uniforms**.

14. Assign Britta Simon to this task.

15. CLOSE the Assign Resources dialog box.

16. Activate the Resource Pool options on the Resource tab, and then update the resource pool.

17. CLOSE *Employee Orientation Schedule 3*. When you are prompted to save, click Yes. In the dialog box that appears, click OK.

18. CLOSE *HR Resource Pool 3*.

PAUSE. LEAVE Project open to use in the next exercise.

Project 16-4: Updating Working Time for All Projects in Southridge Video Resource Pool

You need to make a change to working time for all employees of Southridge Video to reflect two days that everyone will be spending at the National Videographer's Conference. You need to reflect this as nonworking time in all sharer files.

 OPEN *Southridge Video Resource Pool 16-4* from the data files for this lesson. When prompted, click the second option to open the file as read-write, and then click OK. OPEN *Don Funk Music Video 16-4* and *Adventure Works Promo 16-4* from the data files for this lesson.

SAVE the files as *Don Funk Music Video 4*, *Adventure Works Promo 4*, and *Southridge Video Resource Pool 4*.

1. Expand Southridge Video Resource Pool 4 to fill the active window, if it is not already expanded.

2. Activate the Change Working Time dialog box from the Project tab.

3. Select the Standard (Project Calendar) as the calendar to which you want to apply your change.

4. Select the dates of July 27-28, 2016.

5. Add the National Videographers' Conference to the Exceptions tab.

6. Close the Change Working Time dialog box.

7. Verify the working time change in the two sharer files.

8. SAVE all open project schedules, and then CLOSE the files.

PAUSE. LEAVE Project open to use in the next exercise.

■ Mastery Assessment

Project 16-5: Creating a Human Resources Schedule Resource Pool

You have several human resources project schedules that are active in your department. You need to create a resource pool and link these schedules to it.

 OPEN *Employee Orientation Schedule 16-5* and *HR Interview Schedule 16-5* from the data files for this lesson.

SAVE the files as *Employee Orientation Schedule 5* and *HR Interview Schedule 5*.

1. Open a new file and save it as *HR Resource Pool 5*.

2. Link the Employee Orientation Schedule 5 to the resource pool using the Share Resources dialog box.

3. Link the HR Interview Schedule 5 project to the resource pool using the Share Resources dialog box. Make sure that the pool takes precedence.

4. SAVE all three project schedules.

   PAUSE. LEAVE Project and all three schedules open to use in the next exercise.

Project 16-6: Updating Assignments in a Sharer File to the HR Resource Pool

You now need to make several updates to the sharer schedules linked to the HR Resource Pool.

USE the open schedules from the previous exercise.

1. In the *HR Interview Schedule 5* project schedule, for Task 9, replace Keith Harris with Garth Fort using the Assign Resources dialog box.

2. In the *HR Interview Schedule 5* project schedule, for Task 20, remove Keith Harris' assignment to this task using the Assign Resources dialog box.

3. In the *Employee Orientation Schedule 5* project schedule, for Task 12, assign Karen Berg to this task using the Assign Resources dialog box.

4. SAVE all of the project schedules, and then CLOSE the files.

   CLOSE Project.

Customizing Microsoft Project

LESSON SKILL MATRIX

SKILLS	TASKS
Defining General Preferences	Specify the default path for use in the Open and Save As dialog boxes
Working with Templates	Create a new template based on a current project schedule
Working with the Organizer	Copy a custom view from one project schedule to another using the organizer

Now that you have worked with project schedules extensively, it is time to learn about some of the ways you can customize Microsoft Project to fit your own preferences. Some of the customization options you see in Microsoft Project are similar to those you see in other Microsoft Office programs, such as Microsoft Word or Microsoft Excel. In this lesson, you will learn how to customize some general settings, create your own templates, and use the Organizer.

KEY TERMS
global template
Organizer
template

© Pinopic/iStockphoto

SOFTWARE ORIENTATION

Microsoft Project's Organizer Dialog Box

In Microsoft Project, the Organizer is the feature that enables you to share elements between Microsoft Project files.

Figure 17-1

The Organizer dialog box

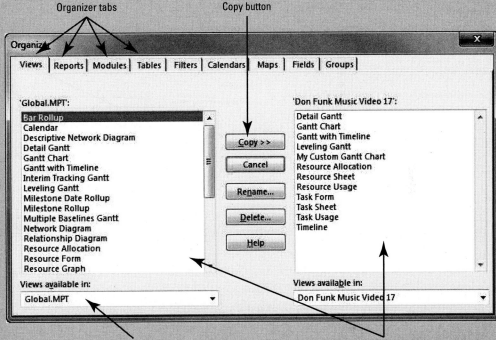

Global.mpt is the default file in the left Views available in: box   Lists of available elements for the selected tab

The Organizer dialog box enables you to copy views, tables, filters, and other items between the Global.mpt template and other Microsoft Project files or between two different Microsoft Project files.

■ Defining General Preferences

THE BOTTOM LINE

You are able to make choices that will customize Microsoft Project. These choices enable you to specify personal preferences regarding how Microsoft Project will operate.

⊙ SPECIFY THE DEFAULT PATH FOR USE IN THE OPEN AND SAVE AS DIALOG BOXES

GET READY. Before you begin these steps, launch Microsoft Project.

1. OPEN the **Don Funk Music Video 17M** project schedule from the data files for this lesson.
2. SAVE the file as **Don Funk Music Video 17** in the solutions folder for this lesson as directed by your instructor.
3. On the ribbon, click the File tab, and then click Options. The Options dialog box appears.

4. In the Project Options dialog box, click **Save**. Your screen should look similar to Figure 17-2.

Figure 17-2

Project Options dialog box under the Save section

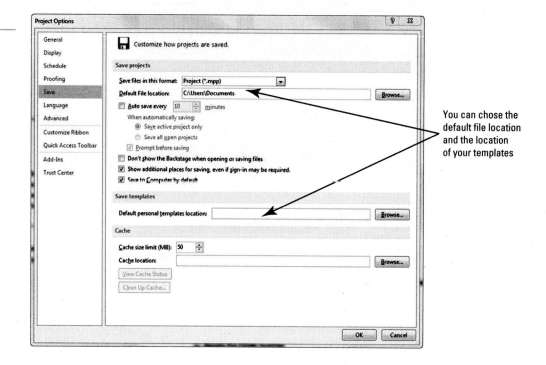

You can chose the default file location and the location of your templates

5. In the Save Projects section, ensure **Project.mpp** is selected in the Save Files in this format box.

6. To the right of the Default File Locations box, click the **Browse** button. The Modify Location dialog box appears.

7. Select your desired folder location as directed by your instructor, and then click **OK**. If you are not changing your file location, click **Cancel**.

8. **CLOSE** the **Options** dialog box.

9. To verify that the new location you have selected is now the default folder location, you can view the Open dialog box.

10. [Press **Ctrl+F12**]. The Open dialog box appears, using the path specified.

11. Click **Cancel** to close the **Open** dialog box.

12. **SAVE** the project schedule.

PAUSE. LEAVE Project open to use in the next exercise.

TAKE NOTE[*]

Specifying the folder you want to open by default in the Open and Save As dialog boxes can be very helpful if you usually keep all of your Microsoft Project files in one location.

In this exercise, you specified the folder that you wanted to open as the default in the Open and Save As dialog boxes. This can be quite helpful if you tend to keep most or all of your Microsoft Project files in one location. Like many other Microsoft Office applications, you have the capability within Microsoft Project to make choices about how you work with this application. By selecting these preferences, the person working with Microsoft Project (such as the project manager or the organization) can personalize the software to fit their needs.

■ Working with Templates

THE BOTTOM LINE

A template provides the basic structure of a new project schedule. It may include information such as resources, tasks, assignments, views, tables, and more.

CREATE A NEW TEMPLATE BASED ON A CURRENT PROJECT SCHEDULE

USE the project schedule you created in the previous exercise.

1. On the ribbon, click the File tab, and then click Save As.

2. Locate the file where the Lesson 17 solutions folder is located or any other location as directed by your instructor. The Save As dialog box appears.

3. In the File name box, key Music Video Template.

4. In the Save as type box, select Project Template.mpt.

5. Click the Save button. The Save As Template dialog box appears.

   The **Don Funk Music Video 17** file contains both baseline and actual values, and you do not want to include these with the template.

6. Select the Values of all baselines, Actual Values, and Fixed Costs check boxes. You are indicating that these items should be removed from your template. Your screen should look like Figure 17-3.

Figure 17-3

Save As Template dialog box

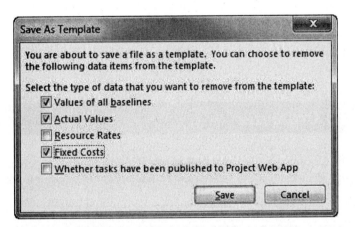

7. Click the Save button. Microsoft Project creates a new template based on the **Don Funk Music Video 17** file.

   Based on the options you selected in the Save As Template dialog box, Microsoft Project removes the data you chose not to include with the template. However, the task list, relationships, resources, and assignments are conserved as entered in the original **Don Funk Music Video 17** file. If Southridge Video has a similar project in the future, you could start with this template and modify it to fit the new project.

 TAKE NOTE*

When you first save a template from a current Microsoft project file, you are working in the template (note the .mpt file extension in the title bar). Any changes you make before saving and closing this file will remain in the template.

TROUBLESHOOTING

When you create a new project file based on a template, you may need to adjust more than the project start date to preserve the task relationships and schedule logic. For example, if the template contains hard constraints with dates prior to the current date, Microsoft Project may not be able to properly schedule tasks.

8. Make sure that the *Music Video Template* file is in the active window. On the ribbon, click File, and then click Close. If prompted to save changes to the *Music Video Template*, click Yes. Microsoft Project returns to the Backstage area.

9. On the navigation bar, click Open. In the Recent Project section, click Don Funk Music Video 17. Microsoft Project reopens the *Don Funk Music Video 17* file, just as you left it.

10. SAVE the project schedule.

    PAUSE. LEAVE Project open to use in the next exercise.

In this exercise, you saved your current project schedule as a template. A *template* is a Microsoft Project file format that greatly reduces the amount of set up time associated with new projects. It lets you begin a new project with most of the basic information, such as Project Phases, WBS, tasks, task links, resources, assignments custom views, tables, filters, etc. You use the template as the basis for the new project schedule.

As you saw in this exercise, you can save any Microsoft Project file, at any time, as a template to use in the future. When saving a template from a current file, you usually exclude baseline and actual values, as these would not be useful as part of a template. You can also exclude things such as resource cost rates and fixed costs, if there is a need to protect this information as confidential.

■ Working with the Organizer

THE BOTTOM LINE
The Organizer is a feature in Microsoft Project that enables you to reset custom elements or to copy elements (such as views, reports, tables, etc.) from one project schedule to another.

 COPY A CUSTOM ITEM FROM ONE PROJECT SCHEDULE TO ANOTHER USING THE ORGANIZER

USE the *Don Funk Music Video 17* project schedule you opened in the previous exercise.

1. OPEN the *Adventure Works Promo 17M* project schedule from the data files for this lesson.

2. SAVE the file as *Adventure Works Promo 17* in the solutions folder for this lesson as directed by your instructor.

3. On the ribbon, click the View tab. In the Window group, click the Switch Windows button, and then click Don Funk Music Video 17. The Don Funk Music Video 17 project schedule is brought into the active window.

4. Click the Project tab, then select Project Information.

5. In the Calendar box, click the down-arrow to activate the sub-menu. Your screen should look similar to Figure 17-4.

Figure 17-4

Project Information dialog box
for Don Funk Music Video 17
showing the custom calendar

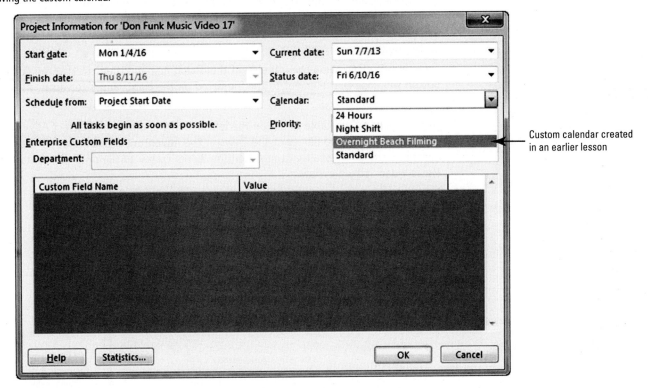

Custom calendar created in an earlier lesson

Notice that this file has the "Overnight Beach Filming" custom calendar you created in an earlier lesson. You'd like to copy this custom calendar to the Adventure Works Promo 17 project schedule using the Organizer.

6. Close the Project Information dialog box by selecting **Cancel**.

7. On the ribbon, click the **File** tab, and then click **Organizer**. The Organizer dialog box appears. Your screen should look similar to Figure 17-5.

Figure 17-5

Organizer dialog box

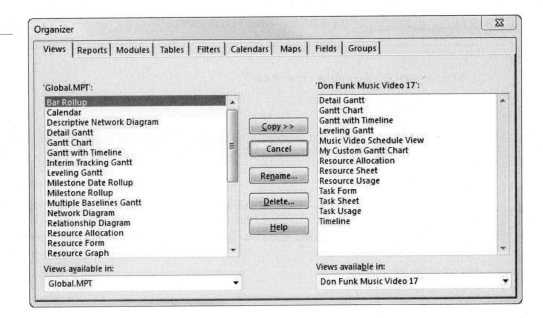

8. Click several of the tabs in the dialog box to get an overview of the available options.

   Notice that each tab of the Organizer dialog box is structured in the same way: elements such as views and tables appear on the left and right sides of the dialog box. The element on the left are from one file, and the elements on the right are from another file. By default, the elements from the Global.mpt file appear on the left side of the dialog box, and the corresponding elements from the active project file appear on the right.

   Selecting an element on the left side of the dialog box and then clicking the Copy button will copy that element to the file listed on the right, and vice versa.

9. Click the Calendars tab.

10. In the Calendars available in list on the left side of the dialog box, select **Adventure Works Promo 17**. The names of the views in the Adventure Works Promo 17 file appear on the left. Note that the Adventure Works Promo 17 file does not contain the Music Video Schedule View.

11. In the list of calendars to the right of the dialog box, click **Overnight Beach Filming**. Your screen should look similar to Figure 17-6.

TAKE NOTE*

The global template is a Microsoft Project template named Global. mpt. This is the base template used each time you open a blank Microsoft project File.

Figure 17-6

Calendars tab selected showing available calendars in both projects

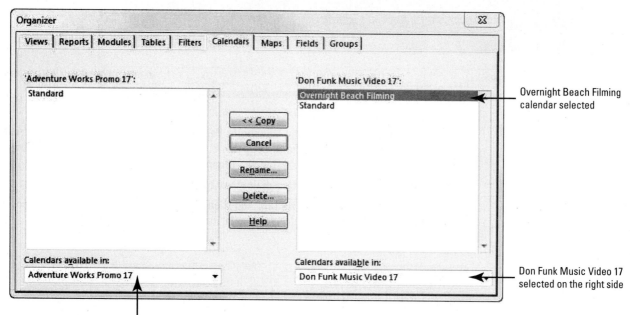

Adventure Works Promo 17 selected on the left side

TAKE NOTE*   Notice that the two arrow symbols (>>) beside the Copy button switch direction (<<) when you select an element on the right side of the dialog box.

12. Click the <<Copy button. Microsoft Project copies the Music Video Schedule View from the Don Funk Music Video 17 project schedule to the Adventure Works Promo 17 project schedule. Your screen should look similar to Figure 17-7.

Figure 17-7

Organizer dialog box with
Overnight Beach Filming
calendar in both project files

Overnight Beach Filming calendar now in both files

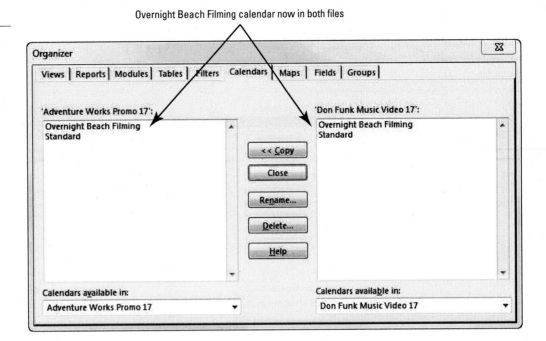

13. Select the Overnight Beach Filming Calendar for Adventure Works Promo 17 (to the left of the dialog box.)

    Because this filming will not actually occur on a beach in this project, you want to change the name to simply "Overnight Filming." This will communicate clearly to anyone else that this calendar is for overnight filming, regardless of location.

14. Click the Rename button. In the Rename dialog box that appears, remove the word "Beach" from the Calendar name. Your screen should look similar to Figure 17-8.

Figure 17-8

Rename dialog box with
Overnight Filming calendar
name

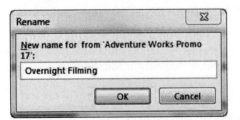

15. Click OK to close the Rename dialog box. Your screen should look similar to Figure 17-9.

Figure 17-9

Organizer dialog box with Overnight Filming calendar name only for Adventure Works file

Custom calendar name only changed in Adventure Works Promo file

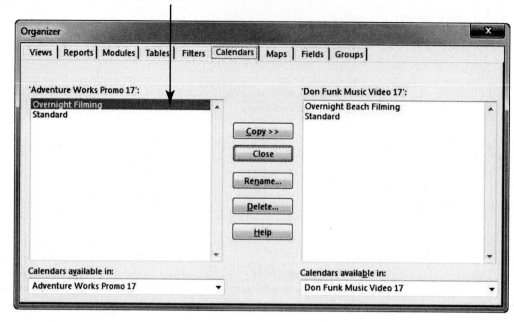

16. Click the Close button to close the Organizer.

17. SAVE and CLOSE both project schedules.

    PAUSE. LEAVE Project open to use in the next exercise.

In this exercise, you used the Organizer to share a calendar between two Microsoft Project files and you modified the name of the calendar to communicate its clear purpose. The *Organizer* is a feature you use to organize elements between Microsoft Project files so that they can be shared, edited, and reset. The names of the tabs in the Organizer dialog box indicate the elements you can copy between project schedules.

One feature of Microsoft Project that you can work with via the organizer is the global template, a Microsoft Project template named Global.mpt. The *global template* provides the default views, tables, and other elements in Microsoft Project, including:

- Calendars
- Filters
- Forms
- Groups
- Import/export maps
- Ribbons
- Reports
- Tables
- Modules (macros)
- Views

At first, the specific definitions of all views, tables, and other elements are contained in the global template. The first time you display a view, table, or similar element in a Microsoft Project file, it is copied from the global template to that file. From then on, the element resides in the Microsoft Project file. If you customize that element in the Microsoft Project file (for example, you change the columns displayed in a table), the changes apply only to the Microsoft Project file, not to the global template. By default, when you create a custom element, it is copied to the Global.mpt file.

However, you have the option not to save all custom items in the Global.mpt file (File tab, options, Advanced, Display). While saving a copy of custom items may sound like a good idea, using this feature can make searching for custom items difficult in your Global.mpt file. One way to quickly discern between a default element and a custom element from a list of items is to use all caps when creating the custom item name. For example, the custom calendar we shared in this exercise would have been created with the name OVERNIGHT BEACH FILMING.

It is possible to use Microsoft Project extensively and never need to use the global template. If you do need to work with the global template, however, there are two primary actions you can accomplish with it:

- Create a customized element, such as a custom table, and make it available in all project schedules with which you work by copying the custom view into the global template.
- Replace a customized element, such as a custom table in a project schedule, by copying the original, unmodified element from the global template to the project schedule in which you've customized the same element.

Take note that customized data maps, modules, and toolbars are not normally stored in individual Microsoft Project files, unlike other elements with which you work via the Organizer. Instead, these elements are stored in the global template and are available for the global template for all Microsoft Project schedules with which you work. If you want to share a data map or module with another Microsoft Project user, you need to copy it from the global template to a Microsoft Project schedule and then send the project schedule to the other user.

When using the Organizer, if you attempt to copy a view, table, or other element from a project schedule to the global template, Microsoft Project alerts you if you will overwrite that same element in the global template. If you choose to overwrite it, that customized element (such as the Overnight Beach Filming calendar in this exercise) will be available in all new project schedules and any other project schedules that do not already contain that element. If instead you choose to rename the customized element, it becomes available in all project schedules, but does not affect the existing elements already stored in the global template. You cannot share or copy any Visual Report templates with the Organizer.

SKILL SUMMARY

In this lesson you learned:	Matrix Skill
To define general preferences	Specify the default path for use in the Open and Save As dialog boxes
To work with templates	Create a new template based on a current project schedule
To work with the organizer	Copy a custom view from one project schedule to another using the organizer

Knowledge Assessment

Fill in the Blank

Complete the following sentences by writing the correct word or words in the blanks provided.

1. The file name of the global template is _____.

2. Creating a(n) _____ is a process that lets you use an existing project schedule as the basis for a new project schedule.

3. The _____ allows you to share elements between Microsoft Project files.

4. A template is saved to be used in the _____.

5. The names of the _____ in the Organizer dialog box indicate the elements you can copy between project schedules.

6. The _____ _____ provides the default views, tables, and other elements in Microsoft Project.

7. Actual data and _____ data should be removed from a file when creating a template.

8. The _____ section in the Options dialog box enables you to specify where you want your files to be saved.

9. The _____ button on the Organizer allows you to change the name of elements in the Organizer tabs.

10. When working in a newly created template, the _____ file extension will be displayed on the title bar.

True/False

Circle T if the statement is true or F if the statement is false.

T | F **1.** Your Microsoft Project files must always be stored in the default file folder.

T | F **2.** When you create a template, you can choose not to include information such as baseline and actual values.

T | F **3.** The two primary actions you can accomplish with a global template are to create a customized element and to replace a customized element.

T | F **4.** You can share custom views, fields, reports and other custom information with any other Microsoft Project file.

T | F **5.** You can save a Microsoft Project file as a template only if a baseline has not yet been saved.

T | F **6.** You must save templates in the default folder.

T | F **7.** The global.mpt file contains all the views, tables, and other elements that have been added.

T | F **8.** Templates can include information such as task and resource lists, assignments, customized views, tables, filters, and macros.

T | F **9.** It is not possible to overwrite elements in the global template.

T | F **10.** The Organizer enables you to reset custom elements in a project schedule.

■ Competency Assessment

Project 17-1: Copy the Critical Tasks report to the Office Remodel Project Schedule

You want to copy the Critical Tasks report from the global template for use in the Office Remodel project schedule. Use the Organizer to do this.

GET READY. Launch Microsoft Project if it is not already running.

OPEN *Office Remodel 17-1* from the data files for this lesson.
SAVE the file as *Office Remodel Critical Tasks Report*.

1. On the ribbon, click **File**, and then click **Organizer**.
2. Click the **Reports** tab, if it is not already selected.

3. Make sure that in the *Reports available in* box to the left of the dialog box, Global.mpt is selected. Make sure that in the *Reports available in* box on the right side of the dialog box, Office Remodel Critical Tasks Report is selected.

4. In the list of reports to the left of the dialog box, click Critical Tasks.

5. Click the Copy>> button.

6. Click Close.

7. SAVE the project schedule, and then CLOSE the file.

   PAUSE. LEAVE Project open to use in the next exercise.

Project 17-2: HR Interview Template

Because your department is currently in a hiring mode, you want to save the HR Interview project schedule as a template so that it can be used by anyone in your department to develop an interview schedule. You do not want to save baselines, cost rates, and fixed cost data in the template.

 OPEN *HR Interview 17-2* from the data files for this lesson.

1. On the ribbon, click File, and then click Save As.

2. Locate and select your Lesson 17 solution folder (or as otherwise directed by your instructor).

3. In the File name box, key *HR Interview Template*.

4. In the Save as type box, select Template.

5. Click the Save button.

6. In the Save As Template dialog box, select the Values of all baselines, Actual Values, and Fixed Costs check boxes.

7. Click Save.

8. CLOSE the file.

   PAUSE. LEAVE Project open to use in the next exercise.

■ Proficiency Assessment

Project 17-3: Copying a Custom Filter

Your Adventure Works Promo project will use the same custom filter as the Unfinished Shoots filter you used in the Don Funk Music Video project. Use the Organizer to copy the filter to the Adventure Works project file.

 OPEN *Don Funk Music Video 17-3* and *Adventure Works Promo 17-3* from the data files for this lesson.

1. Activate the Organizer from the File tab.

2. Place the Don Funk Music Video file in the left portion and the Adventure Works Promo in the right portion of the Organizer.

3. Switch to the Filters tab.

4. Copy the Unfinished Shoots filter from Don Funk to Adventure Works.

5. CLOSE the Organizer.

6. CLOSE the Don Funk Music Video file.

7. Activate the Filter dropdown list from the View tab in the Adventure Works Promo project. Verify the Unfinished Shoots filter is there.

8. SAVE the file as *Adventure Works Shoots Filter*, and then CLOSE the file.

   PAUSE. LEAVE Project open to use in the next exercise.

Project 17-4: Restoring a Customized Table to the Default Settings

While you were working with the Litware project schedule, you accidentally customized the default Usage table rather than making a copy of the default table and then customizing the copy. You want to restore the customized Usage table by replacing it with the default "factory settings" Usage table from the Global.mpt file.

OPEN *Litware 17-4* from the data files for this lesson.

1. Change the view to the Task Usage view.
2. Activate the Organizer dialog box.
3. Activate the Tables tab.
4. Make sure that the Global.mpt table list is to the left of the dialog box and that the Litware 17-4 table list is on the right side of the dialog box.
5. Copy the Usage table from the Global.mpt list to the Litware 17-4 list.
6. Select Yes when you are alerted that you are about to replace the Usage table and then close the Organizer.
7. Activate the new Usage table from the Tables list on the View menu.
8. SAVE the file as *Litware New Usage*.

PAUSE. LEAVE Project open to use in the next exercise.

■ Mastery Assessment

Project 17-5: Copying a Custom Table Using the Organizer

You have several custom views, tables and reports already defined in the HR Interview project schedule. You want to copy the Interview Schedule Table from the HR Interview schedule to the Gregory Weber Biography schedule.

OPEN *Gregory Weber Biography 17-5* and *HR Interview Schedule 17-5* from the data files for this lesson.

1. Use the Organizer to copy the Interview Schedule Table from the HR Interview Schedule 17-5 project schedule to the Gregory Weber Biography 17-5 project schedule.
2. SAVE the project schedules as *HR Interview Custom Table and Gregory Weber Custom Table*, and then CLOSE the files.

PAUSE. LEAVE Project open to use in the next exercise.

Project 17-6: Defining General Preferences

You want to set some more preferences for how Microsoft Project looks and works for you. In a separate Word or WordPad document, explain the steps you would follow to set the following preferences. Use any Microsoft Project file with which you are familiar to explore these options. DO NOT make the actual changes in the file; just explain in a separate document how you would set these preferences.

1. Use the Options dialog box to:
   • Set the number of Undo levels to 25.
   • Have Microsoft Project prompt you for project information for new projects.
   • Have Microsoft Project automatically save your active project every 10 minutes, prompting you before saving.
2. SAVE the Word document as *Defining General Preferences*.

CLOSE Project.

■ Circling Back

Mete Goktepe is a project management specialist at Woodgrove Bank. He is managing a project schedule for a Request for Proposal (RFP) process to evaluate and select new commercial lending software. This process entails determining needs, identifying vendors, requesting proposals, reviewing proposals, and selecting the software.

Now that Mete has established the foundation of the project schedule, he will begin using some of the more advanced features of Microsoft Project to fine-tune the tasks and resources and to format the project schedule.

→ Project 1: Sharing, and Importing Data into, the Project Schedule

Next, you need to prepare some of your data to share with your stakeholders. Finally, you will import some additional tasks to add to your project schedule.

GET READY. OPEN *RFP Bank Software Schedule 3* from the data files for this lesson.

SAVE the file as *RFP Bank Software Imported* in the solution folder for this lesson as directed by your instructor.

1. Click the View tab, then click the down-arrow under the Gantt Chart button, and then select the Built-In Gantt Chart.
2. Adjust the table and bar chart so that only the Task Name and Duration columns are visible in the table.
3. On the ribbon, click the View tab, and then click Entire Project in the Zoom group.
4. Click the Task tab, then click the Copy button in the Clipboard group, and then select Copy Picture.
5. In the Copy Picture dialog box, select For printer and then click OK.
6. Launch either Microsoft Word or WordPad.
7. PASTE the snapshot into a new blank document to send to your stakeholders. You will finish the memo to the stakeholders later.
8. SAVE the document as *RFP Bank Software Memo*, and then CLOSE the document.
9. SAVE the project schedule.
10. [Press Ctrl+F12] to launch the Open dialog box.
11. Click the File type selection button, located to the right of the File Name box, and select Excel Workbook from the list.
12. Locate the RFP Additional Tasks Microsoft Excel workbook in the data files for this exercise. Double-click the RFP Additional Tasks file.
13. In the Import Wizard, select the following options:

    Map: New map

    Import Mode: Append the data to the active project

    Map Options: Tasks, including headers
14. On the Task Mapping page of the Import Wizard, select Sheet 1 from the Source worksheet name list.
15. Click Finish.
16. SAVE the project schedule.

    PAUSE. LEAVE Project and the project schedule open to use in the next exercise.

Project 2: Contours, WBS Codes, Updating Progress

Next, you want to apply a work contour to one of Kevin Kennedy's assignments. You will then add Unique ID and WBS columns to help you track and analyze your project data. Finally, you will update progress information.

GET READY. SAVE the open project schedule as *RFP Bank Software Contoured* in the solution folder for this lesson as directed by your instructor.

1. On the ribbon, click the View tab, then click the Task Usage button.
2. On the ribbon, click the Tables button and ensure the Usage table is selected.
3. [Press F5] to activate the Go To dialog box. Type 13 in the ID box, and then click OK.
4. In the Task Name column under Task 13, right-click on the resource name of Kevin Kennedy.
5. From the shortcut menu, click Information. Click the General tab, if it is not already selected.
6. In the Work contour box, select Front Loaded, and then click OK.
7. Click in the timephased field that intersects Kevin Kennedy's assignment on Task 13 and June 6, 2016, type 2.5 and [press Tab].
8. In the timephased field for June 7, 2016, type 1.86 and [press Tab].
9. In the timephased field for June 8, 2016, type 0 and [press Enter].
10. On the ribbon, click the Gantt Chart button. Click the Other Views button in the Task Views group, and then click More Views. In the More Views dialog box, select Task Sheet, and then click Apply.
11. Right-click the Task Name column heading. On the shortcut menu bar, click Insert Column. Type UNI and [press Enter].
12. Right-click the Task Name column heading. On the shortcut menu bar, click Insert Column. Type WBS and [press Enter].
13. Auto fit each of the columns you just inserted.
14. On the ribbon, click the Tables button, and then select the Tracking table. Auto fit each of the columns.
15. Click on the Act. Start field of Task 9, type 5/27/16 and [press Tab].
16. Click the Task tab, and then click the 100% Complete button in the Schedule group.
17. Click on the name of Task 13. In the Act. Dur. cell, type or select 8d, and then [press Tab].
18. Select the name of Task 14. Click the 50% Complete button on the ribbon.
19. Click in the Rem. Dur. cell for Task 14, type 2h and [press Enter].
20. SAVE the project schedule.

   PAUSE. LEAVE Project and the project schedule open to use in the next exercise.

 Project 3: Creating a Resource Pool and Copying a View from Another File

You have decided to create a resource pool using another project from within the bank as an additional sharer file. While you have the additional sharer file open, you will copy a view from the file using the Organizer and you will apply this view to your project.

GET READY. SAVE the open project schedule as *RFP Bank Software Organizer* in the solution folder for this lesson as directed by your instructor.

 OPEN the *Check Processing Rework* project schedule from the data files for this lesson.

SAVE the newly opened file as *Check Processing Rework Pool* in the solution folder for this lesson as directed by your instructor.

1. Make sure that the RFP Bank Software Organizer file is in the active window.
2. On the ribbon, click the View tab, and then click Resource Sheet.
3. Click the File tab, and then select New.
4. Double-click Blank Project.
5. On the ribbon, click the File tab, and then click Save As. Locate the solution folder for this lesson as directed by your instructor. In the File name box, key Bank Resource Pool, and then click Save.
6. On the ribbon, click the View tab, and then click Resource Sheet.
7. On the ribbon, in the Window group, click Arrange All.
8. Click the title bar of the RFP Bank Software Organizer window.
9. On the ribbon, click the Resource tab, then click Resource Pool, and then click Share Resources.
10. In the Share Resources dialog box, under Resources for 'RFP Bank Software Organizer,' click Use resources. In the From list, select Bank Resource Pool, if it is not already selected. Click OK.
11. Click the title bar of the Check Processing Rework Pool window.
12. On the ribbon, click the Resource tab, then click Resource Pool, and then click Share Resources.
13. In the Share Resources dialog box, under Resources for 'Check Processing Rework Pool,' click Use resources. In the From list, select Bank Resource Pool, if it is not already selected. Under the On conflict with calendar or resource information label, make sure that Pool takes precedence is selected. Click OK.
14. SAVE the Bank Resource Pool project schedule.
15. Double-click the title bar of the RFP Bank Software Organizer project schedule to expand the window to fill the active window.
16. On the ribbon, click the File tab, and then click Organizer.
17. Click the Views tab if it is not already selected.
18. In the Views available in list on the left side of the dialog box, select Check Processing Rework Pool. In the Views available in list to the right of the dialog box, select RFP Bank Software Organizer, if it is not already selected.
19. In the list of views to the left of the dialog box, click My Custom Gantt Chart.
20. Click the Copy>> button, and then close the Organizer.
21. On the ribbon, click the View tab, then click the Other Views button in the Task Views group and then select More Views. In the More views dialog box, click My Custom Gantt Chart.
22. Select Task 16 and [press Ctrl+Shift+F5] to see the new formatting.
23. SAVE and then CLOSE the *RFP Bank Software Organizer* file.
    SAVE and then CLOSE the *Check Processing Rework Pool* file.
    SAVE and then CLOSE the *Bank Resource Pool* file.
    CLOSE Project.

Glossary

A

Actions tag an indicator that signals the user of a change, additional information, formatting options, etc.

actuals actual project performance data, such as actual work values on tasks actual resource costs, and actual durations.

actual cost the cost that has been incurred so far.

actual cost of work performed (ACWP) the actual cost incurred to complete each task's actual work up to the status date.

allocation the portion of a resource's capacity devoted to work on a specific task.

assignment the matching of a specific resource to a particular task, to either perform work or as a material or cost.

AutoFilter a quick way to view only the task or resource information that meets the criteria you choose.

availability determines when and how much of a resource's time can be assigned to work on tasks.

B

base calendar specifies default working and nonworking times for a project, a task, or specified resources. Microsoft Project provides three base calendars: Standard, 24-Hours, and Night Shift, and each can be customized.

baseline a snap-shot of the scope, schedule and budget of a project, such as the planned start and finish dates (schedule), planned costs (budget) and the tasks (scope) after tasks/subtasks have been entered and resources assigned.

baseline cost the total planned cost of the project when the baseline was saved, and used to measure performance.

bottom-up planning develops a project schedule by beginning with the lowest level tasks/work packages and then organizing them into phases or summary tasks. This approach works from specific to general.

budget at completion (BAC) the total planned cost.

budgeted cost of work performed (BCWP) *(or EV – earned value)* – the portion of the budgeted cost that should have been spent to complete each task's actual work performed up to the status date: calculated as EV = % complete * BAC.

budgeted cost of work scheduled (BCWS) *(or PV-planned value)* – the value of the work scheduled to be completed as of the status date: the authorized budget assigned to scheduled work.

C

calendar a scheduling tool that determines the standard working time and nonworking time (such as evening or holidays) for the project, resources, and tasks.

chart view presents information graphically, such as the Gantt Chart.

consolidated project *(or master project)* a Microsoft Project file that contains more than one Microsoft Project file.

constraint a limit which controls the start or finish date or the extent to which the task can be adjusted.

contour determines how a resource's work on a task is scheduled over time using preset shapes or patterns.

Copy Picture enables you to take a snapshot of a view/display screen.

cost how much money will be needed to pay for the resources on a project.

Cost Performance Index (CPI) the ratio of earned value to actual cost: calculated as CPI = EV/AC.

cost rate tables are one of five resource pay rates stored under the Costs tab of the Resource Information dialog box.

cost resource financial obligations to your project.

cost variance (CV) the difference between earned value and actual costs of work performed: calculated as CV = EV−AC.

cost % complete percent complete based on the approved budget: calculated as Percent Complete = EV/BAC * 100.

crashing adding more resources to critical path tasks.

critical path a series of tasks that directly affect the finish date of the project.

current cost the sum of the actual and remaining cost values.

custom field a user-defined field.

D

dashboard a generic term used to mean an easy to read, single page interface that senior management can access to obtain a convenient, high-level view of current project status.

data map a tool that allows you to specify how you want individual fields in the source program's file to correspond to individual fields in the destination program's file.

deadline a date value constraint indicating the latest date the task can be completed.

deliverable a tangible/intangible product available at completion of a project or task.

dependency a relationship that exists between two elements.

diagram view presents information in a diagram format, such as the Network Diagram.

duration the amount of working time required to complete a task.

duration formula similar to the work formula but in the context of duration, used in effort-driven scheduling. The formula is Duration = Work / Units.

E

earned value (EV) *(or BCWP – budgeted cost of work performed)* – the portion of the budgeted cost that should have been spent to complete each task's actual work performed up to the status date: calculated as EV = % complete * BAC.

effort-driven scheduling a scheduling method in which the duration of a task increases or decreases as you remove resources from or assign resources to a task; here, the amount of work needed to complete a task does not change.

elapsed duration the total length of working and nonworking time expected to complete a task.

estimate at completion (EAC) the expected total cost of a task based on performance up to the status date: calculated as EAC = AC + ETC.

export map specifies data fields in the order of their export to another file type.

external task *(or ghost task)* task that is not linked to tasks within the active project file, but that is linked to tasks in other project files and may have an effect on the active project file.

F

fast-tracking performing two or more project tasks in parallel that would otherwise be performed sequentially.

filter a tool that enables you to view only that task or resource information that meets your chosen criteria.

fixed consumption rate a resource consumption rate in which an absolute quantity of the resources will be used, regardless of task duration.

fixed duration a type of task in which the duration value is fixed.

fixed units a type of task where the units value does not change.

fixed work a type of task in which the work value is held constant.

flexible constraint gives Project the ability to change start and finish dates (this is the default type).

float *(or slack)* is the amount of time a task can be delayed without causing a delay to another task or the overall project.

forms view presents detailed information in a structured format about one task or resource at a time, such as the Task Form.

free slack *(or free float)* the amount of time a task can be delayed before it will delay another task or the project end date.

free float *(or free slack)* is the amount of time a task can be delayed before it will delay another task or the project end date.

fully allocated the condition of a resource when the total work of its task assignments is exactly equal to that resource's work capacity.

G

Gantt Chart view default view of task data in a project schedule and the visual representation of that task data.

ghost task *(or external task)* task that is not linked to tasks within the project file, only to tasks in other project files.

GIF Graphics Interchange Format.

global template provides the default views, tables, and other elements in Microsoft Project.

group a way to reorder task or resource information in a table and to display summary values according to various criteria you can choose.

I

import map specifies the data filed to import and their order in the new file type.

inflexible constraint forces a task to begin or end on a specific date, and should be used only when necessary.

inserted project *(or subproject)* a Microsoft Project file that is inserted into another Microsoft Project file.

L

line manager a first-level manager of a group of resources.

link a dependency between tasks.

M

manually scheduled tasks that must be manually scheduled, calculated, and set by the operator.

mask appearance that defines the format of the code – the order and number of alphabetic, numeric, and alphanumeric strings in a code and the separators between them.

master project a Microsoft Project file that contains inserted project files to allow them to be managed as a whole.

material resources consumable items used up as the tasks in a project are completed.

maximum units the maximum capacity of a resource to accomplish tasks. The default value for maximum units is 100%.

milestone represents a major event or a significant point in a project.

N

negative float *(or negative slack)* the amount of time that tasks overlap due to a conflict between task relationships and constraints.

negative slack *(or negative float)* the amount of time that tasks overlap due to a conflict between task relationships and constraints.

Network Diagram a visual representation of the logical order of project activities and their relationships.

node representations of tasks as boxes containing basic task information.

noncritical tasks tasks whose finish date does not impact the scheduled project end date.

note supplemental text that you can attach to a task, resource, or assignment.

O

OLE (object linking and embedding) – prod: please bold this a protocol that allows you to transfer information, such as a chart or text to documents in other applications.

optimizing adjusting the aspects of the project schedule, such as cost, duration, and scope to achieve a desired project schedule result.

Organizer a feature used to organize elements between Microsoft Project files so that they can be shared, edited, and reused.

outline number *(or WBS-work breakdown structure)* the hierarchical decomposition of the work to complete the project.

over-allocated the work assigned to a resource is more than the resource's maximum capacity.

P

phases groups of closely related tasks that comprise specific sections of your project.

physical % complete percent complete based on physical assessment and entered into Project.

planning developing and communicating the details of a project before actual work begins.

planned value (PV) *(or BCWS – budgeted cost of work scheduled)* – the value of the work scheduled for an activity or for a WBS component to be completed as of the status date.

predecessor a task whose start or end date determines the start or finish of another task or tasks.

predefined contours describe how work is distributed over time in terms of graphical patterns.

program office a group that oversees a collection of similar projects.

progress bar in the Gantt Chart view, the progress bar shows how much of each task has been completed.

project calendar the base calendar that defines the default normal working and nonworking times.

project schedule a project model depicting desired work, desired deliverables, and desired costs associated with the project.

R

recurring task a task that is repeated at specified intervals, such as daily, weekly, or monthly.

remaining cost the difference between the current cost and actual cost.

report anything the project manager uses to transmit information about the project.

resources the people, equipment, materials, and money used to complete the tasks in a project.

resource calendar defines working and nonworking times for an individual work resource.

resource leveling the process of realigning a resource's work on a task or a project to resolve over-allocations.

resource manager oversees resource usage in project activities specifically to manage the time and cost of resources.

resource pool a project file of resources that can be shared among multiple projects.

ribbon Microsoft Project's user interface.

risk an uncertain event or condition that, if it occurs, will have an impact on your project, either positively or negatively.

S

schedule performance index (SPI) the ratio of performed to scheduled work: calculated as SPI = EV/PV.

schedule variance (SV) the difference between the earned value of work performed and the planned value of work scheduled: calculated as SV = EV/PV.

schedule % complete percent complete based on planned duration.

semi-flexible constraint gives Project the ability to change task start and finish dates (but not duration) within one date boundary.

sequence the chronological order in which tasks must occur.

sharer files project schedules that are linked to the resource pool.

sheets view presents information in rows and columns, such as the Task Sheet or the Resource Sheet.

slack *(or float)* the amount of time a task can be delayed without causing a delay to another task or to the project end date.

sort a way to order task or resource information based on criteria you specify.

split an interruption in a task, represented in by a dotted line between the two segments of the Gantt bar representing the task.

sponsor the individual or organization that provides financial support and ultimate decision making.

stakeholders the people or organizations that are actively involved or affected by project activities.

status date the date up to or through which all progress information is collected and reported for a project.

subproject the Microsoft Project file that is inserted into another Microsoft Project file, or that represents a major phase of an overall project file.

successor a task whose start or finish is driven by another task's start or finish date.

summary task made up of and summarizes all of the tasks within its hierarchical structure, which could also include other summary tasks, detail tasks, or subtasks that it encompasses.

T

tasks represent the individual work activities that must be completed to accomplish a project's final goal, or deliverable.

task calendar the base calendar created for individual tasks to manage the scheduling of these tasks differently from the project calendar – used for ensuring the integrity of leveling.

Task ID a unique number that is assigned to each task in the project that appears on the left side of the task's row.

task priority a numeric ranking between 0 and 1000 indicating a task's priority.

task type specifies which value in the formula remains fixed if one of the other two values changes.

template a predefined file used to standardize project data completion. A template can be blank with the default characteristics set, or could contain project, task, and resource information.

Timeline view transfers text and graphic images and presents high-level information in relation to the project timeline.

timephased fields task, resource, and assignment values distributed over a duration of time.

top-down planning develops a project schedule by identifying the highest level phases or summary tasks before breaking them into lower level components or subtasks. This approach works from general to specific.

total float *(or total slack)* is the amount of time a task can be delayed without delaying the project end date.

total slack *(or total float)* is the amount of time a task can be delayed without delaying the project end date.

tracking all of the collecting, entering, and analyzing of actual project performance data, such as actual work values on tasks actual resource costs, and actual durations.

U

under-allocated the work assigned to a resource is less than the resource's maximum capacity.

Unique ID unique identifiers that track the order in which you enter tasks and resources.

unit the measurement of the capacity of a resource to work when you assign that resource to a task.

usage view presents task or resource information on the left side and time-phased information on the right, such as the Resource Usage or Task Usage views.

V

variable consumption rate means that the amount of the material resource consumed is dependent upon the duration of the task.

variance difference between the baseline start, finish, and cost estimate and the actual start, finish, and costs incurred.

variance at completion (VAC) the difference between the BAC (Budgeted At Completion) or baseline cost and EAC (Estimated At Completion): calculated as VAC = BAC−EAC.

view a window through which you can see various elements of your project schedule.

visual report a specific type of report that uses the tools of Microsoft Excel or Microsoft Visio to represent the data in your project file.

W

work the total amount of effort expended to complete a task.

work breakdown structure (WBS) *(or outline number)* the hierarchical decomposition of the work to complete the project: can be customized.

work formula Work = Duration × Units.

work periods work values recorded by day, week, or other time interval.

work resources the people and equipment that do work to accomplish project tasks.

work % complete percent complete based on the planned amount of work.

Index

A

AC (actual cost), 190, 234
Actions tag
    to change in project schedule, 66–68
    defined, 66
Actual cost (AC), 190, 234
Actual cost of work performed (ACWP), 190, 234
Actual(s)
    defined, 186
    duration, 226–232
    finish date, 226–228
    start date, 226–228
    work, 228–232
ACWP (actual cost of work performed), 190, 234
Allocation
    under allocated resources, 96
    defined, 93
    fully allocated resources, 96
    over allocated resources, 96 (*See also* Over allocated resources)
    reviewing, 93–96
Annual Report Preparation template, 4
Assignment database, 6, 7
Assignment(s), 59–75
    applying contours to, 263–266
    applying different cost rates to, 126–127
    defined, 61
    manual editing, 265–266
    material resources, 69–70
    multiple pay rates for resource, 125–126
    multiple resources, simultaneously, 62–63
    to recurring task, 88
    revising in sharer files, 314–315
    start of, delaying, 261–263
    viewing details in resource pools, 312–313
    work resources, 61–68
Assign Resources dialog box, 122, 320
AutoFilters, 151–153, 154
Automatically scheduled tasks
    manually scheduled tasks *vs.*, 111
Automatic scheduling mode
    Manually Scheduled mode *vs.*, 21–22
Availability, resources
    defined, 40
    resolving over allocations manually, 129–132
    specifying, 127–129

B

BAC (budget at completion), 226
Backstage Area, 6
Bar styles, tasks
    formatting, in Calendar view, 278–281
Bar Styles dialog box, 162–165
Base calendar, 16, 52, 318, 319

B (continued)

Baseline cost, 190
Baseline(s)
    defined, 183
    establishing, 183–187
    field types, 186
    multiple, 184
BCWP (budgeted cost of work performed), 225, 234
BCWS (budgeted cost of work scheduled), 225, 234
Bill of Material (BOM), 44
Bottom-up planning, 25
Box Styles dialog box, Network Diagram, 288
Budget analysis *vs.* earned value analysis, 234
Budget at completion (BAC), 226
Budgeted cost of work performed (BCWP), 225, 234
Budgeted cost of work scheduled (BCWS), 225, 234

C

Calendar
    base, 52, 318, 319
    defined, 16
    options for, 18, 256
    project, defining, 14–16
    resource, 49
    task (*See* Task calendar)
    types of, 16 (*See also* specific types)
Calendar Options, 256
Calendar tab, 256
Calendar view, 9–10
    customizing, 278–281
Change Working Time dialog box, 15, 77, 316, 318
Charts, 165. *See also* Gantt Chart view
Combination view, 165
Completion percentage, for task, 188–189
    types, 189
Compression, project schedule, 267–272
Consolidated projects
    defined, 297
    Gantt Chart view, 295
    managing, 295–298
Constraints, 89–92
    defined, 89
    finish time, 90
    flexible, 89
    inflexible, 89
    managing, 102–105
    semi-flexible, 89
    start time, 90
Consumption rates
    fixed, 123
    material resource, entering, 122–123
    variable, 122–123
Contour(s)
    applying to assignments, 263–266

Contour(s) (*Continued*)
  defined, 264
  predefined, 264
Copy Picture dialog box, 241, 242
Copy Picture feature, 243
Cost % Complete, 189
Cost performance index (CPI), 225, 235
Cost rates, 126–127. *See also* Pay rate, resources
Cost rate table, 124–125
Cost resources, 45–46
Cost(s), 173
  actual, 190, 225
  baseline, 190
  current, 190
  defined, 40
  fixed, 46
  per-use, 123–124
  remaining, 190
Cost variance (CV), 225, 234
CPI (cost performance index), 225, 235
Crashing, 272
Create New Base Calendar dialog box, 77
Critical path, 272
  defined, 92
  reviewing, 92–93
  viewing, 258–261
Cross-project links, 298–301
Current cost, 190
Custom AutoFilter dialog box, 153
Custom fields, 171–173
  categories, 173
  creating, 171–172
  defined, 172
Custom Fields dialog box, 172
Custom filter, 153
  creating, 154–155
Customiziation, 328–343
  defining general preferences, 329–330
  with Organizer, 332–337
  report, 203–205
  templates, working with, 330–332
Custom tables, creating, 174–175
Custom views
  copying from one schedule to another, 332–337
  creating, 176–177
CV (cost variance), 225, 234

D

Dashboard, defined, 203
Data
  copying, 246–247
  filtering, 151–155
  grouping, 148–151
  pasting, 247
  sorting, 143–147
Databases, 6–7. *See also* specific databases
  default views and, 9–11
Data handling, 7–9
Data maps, 249
Data Template Definition box, 289
Date(s), 173

adjustment, 256–258
deadline, 105–106
end, 13
finish, 13
start, 12–13
status, 188, 233
Deadline(s)
  defined, 105
  setting, 106
Default views, and databases, 9–11
Deliverables, 16
Dependency(ies)
  defined, 26
  managing, 102–105
  types of, 26–27 (*See also* specific types)
Diagrams, 165. *See also* Network Diagram
Discretionary dependencies, 27
Documentation, tasks, 29–30
Duration formula, 65
Duration(s), 173
  adjusting, 228–232
  defined, 18
  elapsed, 20
  fixed, 81–84
  project schedule, reviewing, 31–32
  recording actuals, 226–228
  tasks, 18–21

E

EAC (estimate at completion), 226
Earned value (EV), 225, 234
Earned value analysis, 232–235
  budget/schedule analysis *vs.*, 234
Earned Value table, 225–226, 232–233
Effort-driven scheduling, 65, 68
Effort-driven tasks, 65
Elapsed duration, 20
End date, 13
Equipment resources, 42–43
  adjusting working times, 49–52
  cost information for, 46–49
Estimate at completion (EAC), 226
EV (earned value), 225
Exporting information, 247–250
Export map, 249
Export Wizard—Task Mapping dialog box, 248
External dependencies, 27
External tasks, 301

F

Fast-tracking, 272
FF (finish-to-finish) relationships, 27
Field(s)
  baseline types, 186
  timephased, 185
File formats
  GIF, 241–244
  for saving project information, 247–250
Filter Definition dialog box, 155
Filters, 151–155

AutoFilters, 151–153, 154
  creating and applying, 151–153
  custom/predefined, 153, 154–155
  defined, 153
Finish date, 13, 173
  in optimizing project schedule, 266–267
  recording actual, 226–228
Finish time, constraint, 90
Finish-to-finish (FF) relationships, 27
Finish-to-start (FS) relationships, 27
Fiscal year settings, adjusting, 257 258
Fixed consumption rate, 123
Fixed costs, cost resources vs., 46
Fixed duration, 81–84
Fixed units, 81–84
Fixed work, 81–84
Flag, as custom field category, 173
Flexible constraint, 89
Float. See Slack
Formatting, project schedule, 161–181, 277–293
  Bar Styles dialog box, 162–165
  creating and editing tables, 173–176
  custom fields, creating, 173–176
  custom views, creating, 176–177
  Gantt Chart view, 163–168
  task relationships between projects, 298–301
  text appearance in view, modification, 168–171
  using Network Diagram, 287–289
Forms, 165
Formula dialog box, 206
Free slack/float, 92, 93, 260
FS (finish-to-start) relationships, 27
Fully allocated resources, 96

G

Gantt, Henry L., 165
Gantt Chart Styles, 165–168
Gantt Chart view, 2–3, 295
  customizing and printing, 211–215
  format ribbon for, 162
  formatting, 163–168
  modification (using Bar Styles dialog box), 163–165
  modification (using Gantt Chart Styles), 165–168
  parts of, 163
  progress bar in, 188
Generic resource, 40
Ghost tasks, 301
GIF (Graphics Interchange Format), 241–244
Global template, 334, 336
Graphic image, copying, 247
Graphics Interchange Format (GIF), 241–244
Group, defined, 151
Group Definition dialog box, 149
Grouping, data, 148–151
Group resources, 40–41

I

Importing information, 247–250
Import map, 249
Individual people resources, 38–40, 61–62

Inflexible constraint, 89
Inserted project, 297

L

Line manager, 309
Link(s)
  cross-project, 298–301
  milestones, 28–29
  between tasks, 26–29

M

Mandatory dependencies, 27
Manual editing, assignments, 265–266
Manually resource pool updation, 321–322
Manually Scheduled mode, 12, 19
  vs. Automatic scheduling mode, 21–22
Manually scheduled tasks, 108–111
  vs. automatically scheduled tasks, 111
Mask, 286
Master projects, 297
Material resources, 44–45
  assignment to tasks, 69–70
  consumption rate, 122–123
  per-use cost for, 123–124
Maximum units, resources, 40
Microsoft Excel
  importing/exporting from/to, 247–250
Milestone(s)
  creating, 22–23
  defined, 22
  linking, 28–29
Multiple Level Undo function, 147
Multiple projects, managing
  consolidated projects, 295–298
  Gantt Chart view, 295
  with resource pools, 308

N

Named single view, 165
Negative slack, 91, 105
Network Diagram, 10, 287–289
  Box Styles dialog box, 288
Nodes, 287
Noncritical tasks, 93
Non-working times, 49–50, 110
Note(s)
  resource, 53
  tasks, 30
Numbering system, WBS, 283

O

OLE protocol, 247
Open dialog box, specifying default path for, 329–330
Optimization, project schedule, 255–276
  assignments, delaying start of, 261–263
  Calendar Options, 256
  compressing project schedule, 267–272
  contours, applying to assignments, 263–266
  critical path, viewing, 258–261

Optimization, project schedule (*Continued*)
    defined, 271
    finish date and total cost, identifying, 266–267
    time and date adjustments, 256–258
Organizer, 329, 332–337
Outline code, 173
Outline numbers, 286
Over allocated resources, 80, 96
    leveling, 134–137
    manual resolution of, 129–132
Overbudget tasks/resources
    identifying, 190–193

P

Page Setup dialog box, 202, 213
Pay rate, resources, 46–49, 124–126
People resources, 38–41, 38–42
    adjusting working times, 49–52
    group, 40–41
    individuals, 38–40, 61–62
Performance evaluation, 232–235
Per-use cost, material resource, 123–124
Phases
    defined, 23
    organizing tasks into, 23–25
Physical % Complete, 189
Planned value (PV), 225, 234
Planning
    bottom-up, 25
    defined, 186
    top-down, 25
Planning Wizard dialog box, 103
Predecessor tasks, 26
Predefined contours, 264
Predefined filter. *See* Custom filter
Preferences, defining, 329–330
Printing
    reports, 203–205
    views, 211–215
Program office, 317
Progress bar, 188
Project baseline. *See* Baseline(s)
Project calendar, 16
    changes to, 50
    defining, 14–16
Project information. *See also* specific types of information
    displaying (with GIF), 241–243
    displaying (with Timeline View), 244–247
    saving, in other file formats, 247–250
Project Information dialog box, 31
Project Options dialog box, 256, 330
Project Overview Dashboard, 200
    print preview of, 202, 203
    report, printing, 201–203
Project reports. *See* Report(s)
Project schedule, 76–100
    Action tag to change in, 66–68
    adding new project to resource pools, 319–320
    applying task calendar to individual tasks, 78–80
    compressing, 267–272
    consolidated, 295–298

copying custom views from, 332–337
creating, 11–14
cross-project links, 298–301
current, creating new template based on, 331–332
defined, 3, 5
duration, reviewing, 31–32
formatting (*See* Formatting, project schedule)
new blank, opening, 11–12
optimization (*See* Optimization, project schedule)
project's critical path, 92–93
recurring tasks, establishing, 86–88
resource allocations, 93–96
reviewing, 234
saving, 13–14
splitting task, 84–86
start date, 12–13
task constraints, 89–92
task types, changing, 80
tracking (*See* Tracking, project schedule)
Project Statistics dialog box, 32
Project status
    evaluating, 228
    reporting, 205–207
Project variance, reporting, 205–207
PV (planned value), 225, 234

R

Recurring task
    assigning resources to, 88
    defined, 86
    establishing, 86–88
    schedule, 87
Recurring Task Information dialog box, 87
Remainning cost, 190
Rename dialog box, 335
Renumbering, resources, 144, 147
Reordering, tasks, 282
Report Ribbon, 200
Report(s), 199–223
    customizing, 203–205
    defined, 203
    printing, 203–205
    Project Overview Dashboard, 201–203
    project's status, 205–207
    Report Ribbon, 200
    Visual Reports, 207–211
Rescheduling
    start date, 263
    uncompleted work, 193–195
Resource allocation. *See* Allocation
Resource calendar, 16, 49
    changes to, 50
Resource database, 6, 7
Resource Information dialog box, 124
Resource leveling
    defined, 108
    limitations, 137
    over allocated resources, 134–137
    tasks split by, 86
Resource Leveling dialog box, 133–134
Resource manager, 309

Resource pools, 307–327
  adding new project schedules to, 319–320
  defined, 308
  developing, 308–311
  manually updating, 321–322
  opening, 319
  revise assignments in sharer file, 314–315
  Share Resources dialog box, 308
  update working time for sharer files via, 317–319
  updating resource information in, 315–317
  viewing assignment details in, 312–313
Resource(s). *See also* specific resources
  allocation (*See* Allocation)
  applying different cost rates to, 126–127
  assignments (*See* Assignment(s))
  availability of, 127–129
  costs, 45–46, 70–71
  crashing, 272
  equipment, 42–43
  fully allocated, 96
  generic, 40
  information, updating in resource pool, 315–317
  material, 44–45, 69–70
  maximum units, 40
  multiple pay rates for, 124–126
  notes, 53
  over allocated (*See* Over allocated resources)
  overbudget, 190–193
  pay rate, establishing, 46–49
  people, 38–41
  per-use cost for, 123–124
  pools (*See* Resource pools)
  renumbering, 144, 147
  Unassigned, 95
  underallocated, 96
  work (*See* Work resources)
  working times, adjusting, 49–52
  work schedules for, 50–52
Resource Sheet view, 38
Resource Usage view, 10–11
Restore Down/Maximize button, 5
Ribbon, 2
  dynamic view of, 5–6
  at full resolution, 6
Risk, defined, 21
Roll-ups, 151

S
Save As dialog box, specifying default path for, 329–330
Save As Template dialog box, 331
Schedule
  effort-driven, 65, 68
  manual tasks, 108–111
  problems, tracking, 193–195
  project (*See* Project schedule)
  recurring task, 87
  tasks, effects of constraints and relationships on, 103–105
  work, 50–52
Schedule analysis *vs.* earned value analysis, 234
Schedule % Complete, 189
Schedule formatting. *See* Formatting, project schedule

Schedule performance index (SPI), 225, 235
Schedule variance (SV), 193–195, 225, 234
Scheduling Options dialog box, 104
Semi-flexible constraint, 89
Sequence, tasks, 26
SF (start-to-finish) relationships, 27
SharePoint, 250
Share Resources dialog box, 308, 310, 320
Sharer file
  base calendars for, 318, 319
  defined, 308
  revising, 321–322
  revising assignments in, 314–315
  updating working time for, 317–319
Sheets, 165
Slack, 272
  free, 92, 93, 260
  negative, 91, 105
  total, 93, 260
  value, 260
Sort dialog box, 143
  with multiple sort criteria, 146
Sorting, 143–147
  defined, 147
  nested levels of criteria, 144
SPI (schedule performance index), 225, 235
Split
  defined, 84
  task, 84–86
Sponsor, project, 186
SS (start-to-start) relationships, 27
Stakeholders, 205
Start date, 12–13, 173
  delaying, 261–263
  recording actual, 226–228
  rescheduling, 263
Starting Microsoft Project, 3
Start screen, 2
Start time, constraint, 90
Start-to-finish (SF) relationships, 27
Start-to-start (SS) relationships, 27
Status, project
  evaluating, 228
  reporting, 205–207
Status date, 188, 233
Subprojects, 297
Successor tasks, 26
Summary task, 84
  creating, 24–25
  deadline date and, 106
  defined, 23
SV (schedule variance), 193–195, 225

T
Table Definition dialog box, 174, 175
Table(s)
  cost rate, 124–125
  creating and editing, 173–176
  Earned Value, 225–226, 232–233
  Variance Table, 183, 185
Task calendar, 16

Task calendar (*Continued*)
   applying to individual tasks, 78–80
   defined, 78
Task database, 6, 7
Task IDs, 18, 147, 281–286
Task Information dialog box, 83–84
   General tab of, 102
Task Inspector pane, 92
Task priority
   defined, 107
   establishing, 107–108
   and resource leveling, 108
Task(s)
   applying task calendar to, 78–80
   assignment, manually editing, 265–266
   automatically scheduled, 111
   bar styles, formatting, in Calendar view, 278–281
   completion percentage, 188–189
   constraints (*See* Constraints)
   cost resources assignment to, 70–71
   cross-project links, 298–301
   defined, 16
   documenting, 29–30
   duration, 18–21
   effort-driven, 65
   entering, 16–18
   fast-tracking, 272
   linking, 26–29
   manually scheduled, 108–111
   material resources assignment to, 69–70
   noncritical, 93
   notes, 30
   organizing into phases, 23–25
   overbudget, 190–193
   predecessor, 26
   priorities (*See* Task priority)
   recurring, 86–88
   relationships, managing, 102–105
   remaining work, adjusting, 228–232
   reordering, 282
   scheduling, effects of constraints and relationships on, 103–105
   sequence of, 26
   setting deadline dates, 105–106
   splitting, 84–86
   successor, 26
   summary, 23–25, 84
   work resources assignment to, 61–68
Task Sheet view, 278
Task type
   changing, 80–84
   defined, 80
Task Usage view, 8, 81
Template(s)
   Annual Report Preparation, 4
   defined, 3, 332
   global, 334, 336
   new, creation of, 331–332
   opening, 4–5
   working with, 330–332
Text, 173
   appearance in view, modification, 168–171
   copying, 246
   custom fields, 171–173
   single piece of, modifying appearance of, 170–171
Text Styles dialog box, 169
Time adjustments, 256–258
Timeline View, 244–247
Timephased fields, 185
Time problems, tracking, 193–195
Top-down planning, 25
Total cost, identification, 266–267
Total slack/float, 93, 260
Tracking, project schedule, 182–198, 224–239
   actual durations, recording, 226–232
   adjusting remaining work of tasks, 228–232
   defined, 186
   earned value analysis of performance, 232–235
   Earned Value table, 225–226
   levels of, 186–187
   overbudget tasks and resources, 190–193
   project baseline, establishing, 183–187
   as scheduled, 187–188
   task completion percentage, 188–189
   time and schedule problems, 193–195
   Variance Table, 183

U

Unassigned resources, 95
Uncompleted work, rescheduling, 193–195
Under allocated resources, 96
Unique IDs, 278, 281–286
   values, preserving, 286
Unit(s)
   defined, 63
   fixed, 81–84
Usage view, 165. *See also* Resource Usage view; Task Usage view

V

VAC (variance at completion), 226
Variable consumption rates, 122–123
   defined, 123
Variance
   cost, 225, 234
   project, reporting, 205–207
   schedule, 193–195, 225, 234
Variance at completion (VAC), 226
Variance Table, 183, 185
View Definition dialog box, 176
View(s)
   Calendar, 9–10, 278–281
   categories, 165
   custom, creating, 176–177
   customizing and printing, 211–215
   defined, 165
   formats, 165
   Gantt Chart, 2–3
   Network Diagram, 10, 287–289
   Resource Usage, 10–11
   Task Sheet, 278
   Task Usage, 8, 81
   text appearance in, modification, 168–171

Visual report, defined, 211
Visual Reports, 207–211

W
WBS (work breakdown structure), 23–24
    codes, 278, 281–286
    numbering system, 283
Work
    defined, 65
    fixed, 81–84
    remaining, adjusting, 228–232
    uncompleted, rescheduling, 193–195
Work breakdown structure (WBS), 23–24
    codes, 278, 281–286

    numbering system, 283
Work % Complete, 189
Work formula, 65
    task types and, 81–83
Working times
    adjusting, 49–52
    updating in resource pools, 315–319
Work resources, 40. *See also* Equipment resources; People resources
    assignment to tasks, 61–68
Work schedules, 50–52

X
XML format, 247